CONFLICT, AROUSAL, AND CURIOSITY

McGRAW-HILL SERIES IN PSYCHOLOGY

HARRY F. HARLOW, *Consulting Editor*

CONFLICT, AROUSAL, AND CURIOSITY

D. E. Berlyne

ASSOCIATE PROFESSOR OF PSYCHOLOGY
BOSTON UNIVERSITY

McGRAW-HILL BOOK COMPANY, INC.

New York   Toronto   London

1960

CONFLICT, AROUSAL, AND CURIOSITY

04875
II

In the same manner, we must condemn those who employ that curiosity and love of knowledge which nature has implanted in the human soul upon low and worthless objects, while they neglect such as are excellent and useful. Our senses, indeed, by an effect almost mechanical, are passive to the impression of outside objects, whether agreeable or offensive; but the mind, possessed of a self-directing power, may turn its attention to whatever it thinks proper. It should, therefore, be employed in the most useful pursuits, not barely in contemplation but in such contemplation as may nourish its faculties.

(Plutarch, *Life of Pericles*)

Curiosity is, in great and generous minds, the first passion and the last.
(Samuel Johnson, *The Rambler*, no. 150)

I loathe that low vice, curiosity.

(Byron, *Don Juan*)

Prétendre qu'il ne faut pas changer de vins est une hérésie; la langue se sature; et après le troisième verre le meilleur vin n'éveille plus qu'une sensation obtuse.
(J.-A. Brillat-Savarin, *Physiologie du goût*)

N'est-ce pas un premier élément de complexité ordonnée, c'est-à-dire de beauté, quand en entendant une rime, c'est-à-dire quelque chose qui est à la fois pareille et autre que la rime précédente, qui est motivée par elle, mais y introduit la variation d'une idée nouvelle, on sent deux systèmes qui se superposent, l'un de pensée, l'autre de métrique?
(Marcel Proust, *Le Côté de Guermantes*) *

The philosophic brain responds to an inconsistency or a gap in its knowledge, just as the musical brain responds to a discord in what it hears.
(William James, *Principles of Psychology*)

Prudens interrogatio quasi dimidium scientiae. (Judicious questioning is virtually the half of knowledge.)
(*Anonymous motto*)

PREFACE

The topics that are to be treated in this book were unduly neglected by psychology for many years but are now beginning to come to the fore. My own researches into attention and exploratory behavior began in 1947, and at about the same time several other psychologists became independently impressed with the importance of these matters and started to study them experimentally. It is interesting that those were also the years when information theory was making its appearance and when the reticular formation of the brain stem was first attracting the notice of neurophysiologists. What came out of these two developments is, as we shall see, of the utmost relevance to our inquiry.

During the last ten years, the tempo of research into exploratory behavior and related phenomena has been steadily quickening. This research has gone on in a number of countries, but mostly in those where English or Russian is spoken. The book is prompted by the feeling that it is now time to pause and take stock: to review relevant data contributed by several different specialties, to consider what conclusions, whether firm or tentative, are justified at the present juncture, and to clarify what remains to be done. The primary aim of the book is, in fact, to raise problems. The process of raising problems is often hard to separate from the process of suggesting solutions to problems. I should not like to guess how long my own attempts at theory will survive the cumulative erosion of future research, although I have endeavored to keep them in line with available data. They will, however, amply serve their purpose if the problems they bring into view are recognized as ripe for an all-out onslaught on the part of experimenters and theoreticians alike. These problems are worth intensive and methodical study, not because they form a picturesque backwater that psychologists may enjoy taking a look at when not otherwise occupied, but because, until we are less ignorant about them, our knowledge of general psychological principles must be sadly deficient, even in the areas that have received most study.

The book is intended as a contribution to behavior theory, i.e., to psychology conceived as a branch of science with the circumscribed objective of explaining and predicting behavior. But interest in attention and exploratory behavior and in other topics indissociably bound up with them, such as art, humor and thinking, has by no means been confined to professional psychologists. I have had to assume the kind of previous knowledge that is contained in introductory textbooks on psychology. Nevertheless, I have tried to supply enough explanation for the nonpsychologist not to feel lost. This has obliged me, here and there, to give information that will seem trite to the specialist.

The book has two features that would have surprised me when I first set out to plan it. One is that it ends up sketching a highly modified form of drive-reduction theory. Drive-reduction theory has appeared more and more to be full of shortcomings, even for the phenomena that it was originally designed to handle. Facts about exploratory behavior, etc., are often summoned to administer the *coup de grâce*. It would be ironical if, after all, the study of curiosity provided this type of theory with its firmest stronghold, and if the study of the role of curiosity in learning as a whole served to buttress its claim to far-ranging jurisdiction. There can, however, be little doubt that more satisfactory formulations will come to light before long and replace it.

The second surprising feature is the prominence of neurophysiology. Up to about ten years ago, behavior theorists tended largely to keep aloof from neurophysiological data, and "neurologizing" became a term of abuse. It was felt that the psychologist had his own distinct work to do without following the physiologist like a jackal, and what was then known about the nervous system seemed too flimsy to be of much use. Recently things have changed. Momentous discoveries about the nervous system are now coming in at a rate that leaves the psychologist with hardly enough time to catch his breath, let alone digest them unhurriedly as they demand. In the areas with which this book is concerned, it would be too much to say that a clear neurophysiological picture is already taking shape. But there is certainly a mass of closely relevant data that nobody interested in our topics can afford to overlook. Moreover, the techniques for testing hypotheses about the physiological processes underlying attention and exploration are readily available. Theoretical assumptions like those presented can, if one insists, be shorn of their physiological content and treated as pure "molar behavior theory." But to construct such theory without taking advantage of the guidance that neurophysiology is now in a position to offer would be improvident in the extreme.

There remains the pleasant task of acknowledging indebtedness to persons and organizations who have helped in the work of which the book is an outgrowth. I have been fortunate enough to spend three years, relieved of teaching duties, at places with unique facilities for reading, thinking, experimenting, and, above all, talking to colleagues with similar interests. These opportunities, to all of which the book owes an immense debt, were provided by the English Speaking Union-Yale University Fellowship at Yale University in 1951–1952, a fellowship at the Center for Advanced Study in the Behavioral Sciences in 1956–1957, and an appointment as Membre-Résident of the Centre International d'Epistémologie Génétique in 1958–1959. Experimental and other research within the purview of the book was carried out at Cambridge University, the University of St. Andrews, the University of Vermont, Brooklyn College, the University of Aberdeen, and the University of California. The help received from the head or chairman of the psychology department, colleagues, and students at each of these institutions is gratefully recalled. My thanks are also due to the Carnegie Trust for the Universities of Scotland, which financed some early experiments on exploration in the rat, and to the behavioral sciences division of the Ford Foundation, whose grant-in-aid supported various expenses incurred in the writing of the book and some of the research reported in it.

Those whose ideas, conveyed through conversation or through correspondence, are inevitably woven into the texture of the book are too numerous to list, but discussions with Mlle. M. Bonvallet, Dr. M. Jouvet, Dr. R. D. Luce, Dr. B. F. Ritchie, and Dr. I. R. Savage were particularly valuable. Finally, I must address a special word of thanks to Dr. H. F. Harlow and Dr. C. T. Morgan, who read carefully through an early draft and whose critical comments prompted important changes, and to Mr. R. Walley, who helped with the compilation of the bibliography and supplied the frontispiece.

I should like to express my thanks to the following persons and organizations who kindly gave permission for the use of quotations or figures from their publications or of data transmitted through personal communication: Dr. J. E. Desmedt; Dr. Harry F. Harlow; Dr. Woodburn Heron; Dr. A. Hugelin; Dr. K. Lorenz; Dr. H. W. Magoun; Dr. Gardner Murphy; Dr. Arlo K. Myers; Dr. W. C. Obrist; Dr. Charles E. Osgood; Prof. J. Piaget; Dr. Roy Schafer; Dr. E. N. Sokolov; Dr. T. E. Starzl; Dr. O. W. Taylor; Dr. Jack Vernon; the American Psychological Association; the British Psychological Society; La Fondation Singer-Polignac; International Universities Press, Inc., New York; Librairie Gallimard, Paris; Masson & Cie., Paris; Moscow University Press, Moscow; W. W. Norton & Company, Inc., New York; Oxford University Press, London; Charles C Thomas, Publisher, Springfield, Illinois; and The Williams & Wilkins Company, Baltimore.

D. E. Berlyne

CONTENTS

ous Forms of Arousal Potential—Intraindividual and Interindividual Differences—Exploration, Arousal, Perceptual Curiosity, and Learning in General.

CONFLICT, AROUSAL, AND CURIOSITY

Chapter 1

STIMULUS SELECTION AND CONFLICT

It has, in some ways, been a misfortune for psychology that human beings are so obliging and compliant. An experimenter has only to ask them to look at this or that, and they look. He instructs them to think out the answer to a question, and they make some sort of effort to do so. The desire not to offend and the fear of appearing foolish will usually be sufficiently motivating, although some more palpable inducement, such as monetary reward, may be used to supplement them.

Principles that these methods have brought to light in laboratories must obviously be applicable to spontaneous perceptual and intellectual activities in the outside world as well, since the subject does not hang up his nervous system on entering a laboratory and put on one of quite a different design. Nevertheless, the ease with which artificial and extraneous motivations can be induced in human beings has prevented us from studying the motivational factors that take control when these are lacking. Human beings are prone to look at and look for, ask about and think about things, even when nobody tells them to do so. They indulge in these activities even when there is nobody at hand to please or impress except themselves and when there are no obvious and tangible purposes that could be served. Such activities seem, in fact, often to be pursued "for their own sake." And we are very much in the dark about the conditions that instigate and guide them in such circumstances.

Courtesy on the part of subjects does not present quite the same problems to the animal psychologist. But even he is wont to study animals when they are faced with some urgent and specific need, such as to avoid or escape from pain, to secure food, to find and avail themselves of an opportunity to mate. Until recently, rather little has been done to find out how animals behave, whether in the wild or in captivity, when they have nothing particular to do.

This book is going to be concerned with the *motivation of perceptual and intellectual activities*. It is, however, singularly difficult

1

to decide which factors are motivational and which are not. As research and theoretical analysis have progressed, the problems that have been recognized as motivational have become harder and harder to separate from other psychological problems. When definitions of "motivation" and other terms associated with it have been offered, they have usually been so closely bound up with one particular theoretical system or another as to be largely meaningless and useless to anybody who does not subscribe to that system. Nevertheless, there are a number of problems that are generally included among the problems of motivation, and, whether one uses that word or not, they are ones that psychology must take up.

1. *Internal Predisposing Factors.* The need for motivational concepts in psychological theory became generally recognized once Watson's (1919) hope that "given the stimulus, psychology can predict what the response will be; or, on the other hand, given the response, it can specify the nature of the effective stimulus" was seen to be unrealizable as long as "stimulus" meant external stimulus. Watson himself was fully aware of this limitation, but it took some time for behavior theory to make adequate provision for the fact that responses depend jointly on external stimuli and on factors within the organism. These internal factors determine when a particular sequence of behavior will start and when it will end. They must also determine the course of the sequence in conjunction with external cues; virtually every external stimulus situation is capable of evoking any of a large number of responses at different times, and the internal state of the organism must decide which of them will actually occur.

Among the internal factors that predispose an organism for a certain line of action are the various motivational states—"drives," "appetites," "desires," and "wishes"—that are aroused by deprivations or by disturbances from without. They account for the fact that organisms will sometimes eagerly plunge into activities that at other times leave them indifferent and for their remaining restlessly mobile until certain "goals" or "purposes" are fulfilled.

There is, of course, a huge variety of internal factors that can influence the mode of reaction to an external event, and it is by no means easy to delimit motivational states among them. To some extent, it is a matter of how long the factor is active. Motivational states are generally at work for a matter of minutes or hours, thus exerting their directing influence over a whole succession of responses. In this respect they differ from thoughts, which are transitory and control a few responses at a time, and also from habits, which affect behavior over a large part of a lifetime.

Sometimes, clinical psychologists and other specialists in individual differences picture motives as enduring tendencies to seek certain ends, lifelong characteristics that distinguish one personality from another. But these factors are best described as motivational *dispositions* and are to be distinguished from motivational *states*.

2. *The Nature of Reward (Reinforcement)*. One fact that psychological experiments have established beyond any doubt is that certain responses are strengthened, i.e., they become more likely to recur, if they are closely followed by certain consequences, known as *rewards* or *reinforcing conditions*. Whether all responses can be strengthened in this way, or, in other words, whether all learning is affected by reward, is still a matter of some controversy. The latest evidence seems to suggest not. But a large part of behavior is clearly the result of such instrumental conditioning.

Much of what is commonly called motivation theory might with advantage be called reinforcement theory or reward theory instead. But unfortunately the term "reinforcement theory" has already been reserved for quite a different meaning, namely, the sort of theory of learning that attaches importance to reward. It is natural to inquire, once the importance of rewards has been made clear, why certain agents are rewarding and others not. Other ways of framing the same question are: "What do all rewards have in common?" and "How can one predict whether something will act as a reward before trying it out?" It is a question that some psychologists have preferred to leave alone, either because they are not interested or because they think it is impossible to answer for the time being. But others have accepted the question as a legitimate and challenging one.

It is important to note that, although rewards have usually been studied as factors affecting learned behavior, promoting its acquisition and staving off its extinction, they may have a bearing on unlearned behavior as well. Unlearned responses are apt to weaken and disappear through adaptation or habituation if they are repeatedly elicited, but their accompaniment by certain environmental events seems to preserve them. For example, defensive reactions to danger signals will often cease with repeated elicitation, but only if more immediate indexes of danger no longer follow the signals.

3. *Biological Utility*. On the whole, agents that act as rewards tend to be ones that remove threats to survival, and the internal states that predispose an animal to seek them tend, on the whole, to occur at times when the physiological need for them is acute. But the association between motivational states and rewards on the one hand and biological utility on the other is far from complete. Human beings, in particular, have plenty of wants that are not merely unnecessary for survival but even inimical to it. Nevertheless the motivational aspects

3

of a piece of behavior are usually discussed in conjunction with the biological functions that it may perform.

Some of these points will be considered in greater detail in Chapter 7, when the concept of drive, the most widely used motivational concept, will be examined.

LUDIC BEHAVIOR

Perceptual and intellectual activities have many indispensable contributions to make to the preservation of life and limb and the gratification of deep-seated biological needs such as hunger and sexual appetite. They can help in the guidance of more or less any response that acts on the outside environment, and they can thus be influenced by any of the more familiar and obvious sources of motivation.

The cases that raise the most acute motivational problems, however, and therefore the ones that will be most instructive to study from our present point of view, are those in which perceptual and intellectual activities are engaged in for their own sake and not simply as aids to the handling of practical problems. In these cases, none of the more conspicuous kinds of motivation and reward may be in evidence, suggesting that perceptual and intellectual activities can draw on special sources of motivation that are peculiar to themselves. The result is what we normally classify as play or, to use a more technical and comprehensive term, "ludic behavior" (Latin *ludare*, to play).

When Darwin's theory of evolution first began slowly permeating psychology, which took a few decades after the publication of *The Origin of Species* in 1859, it dawned on psychologists that behavior depends on bodily structures that have emerged from the evolutionary process. These bodily structures have become established because their possession favors survival to the age of procreation and prolificity once that age is reached.

It was therefore only natural that psychologists, once they had taken the lessons of evolutionary theory to heart, should concentrate on those forms of behavior that are of unmistakable relevance to the survival of the individual and the species, such as those bound up with eating, drinking, mating, rearing of young, sleeping, fighting, fleeing from enemies, and escaping from noxious agents. And it is not surprising that the intensive study of these should have deflected attention from other forms of behavior, which occupy animals whenever they enjoy respite from urgent threats and which are not so manifestly essential to adaptation. The higher mammals, at least, when temporarily freed from tasks connected with survival, will usually spend no more time on rest and inactivity than the minimum required for recuperation. In human beings, ludic behavior includes everything that is classified as recreation, entertainment, or "idle curiosity," as well as art, philosophy, and pure (as distinct from applied) science. To gauge the strength of the motivations to which these activities respond, one has only to think of the immense industries that have grown up to cater to them and consider the economic resources that are devoted to them by advanced societies, i.e., those that have self-preservative necessities most firmly under control.

Ludic behavior consists in large measure of what we are calling perceptual and intellectual activities—seeking out particular kinds of external stimulation, imagery, and thought. They also include other elements, such as motor activity and emotional arousal, but these are apparently, at least in some cases, cultivated for the sake of the stimulation that results from them.

Hypotheses about the function of ludic behavior have been embarrassingly plentiful. There are those who regard it as a collection of remedies for current difficulties—a safety valve for surplus energy, an alternative outlet for motives whose direct expression is blocked, or a means of distraction from other, more distressing matters. According to other hypotheses, ludic behavior improves the organism's capacity to cope with future contingencies: it keeps the body's equipment in trim by providing exercise, it gives parts of that equipment a rest by bringing other parts into play, or it furnishes skills or knowledge that may prove serviceable on later occasions. Still other hypotheses see in it an assortment of by-products, which may be useless in themselves, of processes that serve the needs of adaptation: it consists of an aimless freewheeling of mechanisms that participate in more earnest operations or of remnants of earlier behavior patterns that have now been superseded.

There have been few if any efforts to work out and test the implications of these hypotheses. Ludic behavior forms such a motley assortment that it is highly unlikely that all of it has just one function. We can, in fact, hardly expect to make much progress toward explaining it as long as we are so unsure about the ways in which the odds and ends that we place in that category are actually related to one another. So far, it is mainly our ignorance that binds them all together; ludic behavior can best be defined as any behavior that does not have a biological function that we can clearly recognize.

Most of the attempts that have been made to express the distinction between ludic and nonludic behavior have begged questions. The motives associated with nonludic behavior have been referred to by terms like "physiological needs" or "homeostatic drives." But ludic behavior must depend just as much as any other behavior on physiological processes. As far as we know, it may have its contribution to make to biological adaptation and, in particular, to the state of bodily equilibrium and well-being that so-called homeostatic processes serve to maintain. It may well affect prospects of survival. After all, as every zoo director knows to his cost, animals will often not live long in captivity; they may well refuse to feed or to reproduce. And how long human beings survive after retirement is frequently thought to be influenced by whether they can keep themselves occupied and find interests.

In what follows, we do not hope to dispose of all the problems of ludic behavior. But we shall be specially concerned with the nature and conditions of "disinterested" perceptual and intellectual activity. It is true that the responses that constitute such activity, like the responses that constitute play, may at other times help to defend the organism against threats to self-preservation. The very enigmas posed by activities that are eagerly indulged in when there is no clear biological need for them make it vitally important to study them. If there are hidden motivational factors capable of keeping organisms perceptually and intellectually active in the absence of the more obvious sources of motivation, these hidden factors may well be at work and collaborating with more familiar motives whenever looking and thinking assist in the solution of practical problems.

So far, we have been using the phrase "perceptual and intellectual activities" rather freely without explanation. The time has now come to characterize the processes that we intend to place under this heading. At first glance, there are two properties that they all seem to have in common: they can be described as devices for *stimulus selection*, and they can be regarded as ways of *reducing or avoiding psychological conflict*. We had best take up these two points in turn.

STIMULUS SELECTION

So far, psychology, and especially behavior theory, has concentrated on problems of *response selection*. The question that researches have usually been designed to answer is "What response will this animal make to this stimulus?" It is a reasonable question with which to begin the quest for the laws governing behavior and one that can be answered with the artificially simple experimental situations on which a science must depend in its early stages. Most of the standard experimental situations used by psychologists are designed to study the effects of one stimulus factor at a time; the stimulus of interest is made to predominate in determining behavior, and the influence of

6

other background stimuli is reduced to a minimum. This is accomplished in various ways. The range of background stimuli is kept down by restricting the subject's stimulus field. Rats are confined to narrow maze alleys or to soundproof Skinner boxes. Human subjects are placed in small rooms or cubicles, sometimes in darkness. Such background stimuli as are left are made as drab and uniform as they can be. Distracting sounds and lights are excluded. Pretraining trials are given to habituate rats to the apparatus, i.e., to remove any control the background may originally have over behavior, and human subjects are told that they must pay attention. As a result of these and similar expedients, what the subject does reflects the effect on his behavior of the sight of a choice point, the sight of a bar projecting from the wall of a Skinner box, the sound of a buzzer, a visual figure painted on a card, a question asked by the experimenter or printed on a sheet of paper, the flash of a light, or the sight of a mechanical device that is to be manipulated. The experimenter may vary these factors between groups of subjects or between different phases of the experiment undergone by the same subjects, or he may vary other factors and keep these constant. But the effects of background stimuli can be discounted or marked up to experimental error.

As soon as the experimental situation is made more complex by introducing several conspicuous stimuli at once or as soon as animals are studied in surroundings resembling their natural environments, in which their receptors are inundated with an endless variety of stimuli coming from all directions, a new question arises: "To which stimulus will this animal respond?"

It may be felt that this is a bad way to formulate the question. For one thing, many psychological problems can be put either way. Suppose we have a rat at the choice point of a Y-shaped maze. We want to know which of the two branching alleys he will enter. We can ask, equally well, which response—going right or going left—he will make to the sight of the choice point, or to which stimulus—the sight of the right-hand alley or the sight of the left-hand alley—he will respond by approaching. We can ask how a voter will respond to the sight of a ballot slip or, alternatively, to which candidate's name he will respond by marking a cross against it.

Which is the more profitable way to frame the question depends on the subject's relevant previous behavior. If he has an innate tendency to react to a complex of stimuli in a particular way, or if he has learned to perform a particular response in the presence of the whole complex, we had best talk about the selection of a response to the situation. If, on the other hand, the subject has innate or learned responses to separate elements of the complex and has rarely or never been

7

exposed to the whole complex together, we can treat the problem more appropriately as one of stimulus selection.

In the kind of experiment usually performed with the Y maze, a rat has been exposed to the sight of both alleys at the choice point on every trial, and he has occasionally gone up the one alley and occasionally up the other. The problem thus calls for a response-selection interpretation. If, as sometimes happens, the animal has been given a series of forced trials, i.e., trials in which only one alley or the other is accessible and the second alley is blocked off, and he is being confronted with the sight of both together for the first time, it would be better to ask which alley will prevail as a stimulus object. The voter has probably met each of the candidate's names, and acquired an attitude to each of them, separately. But it may so happen that he has seen a poster listing the candidates and showing a cross against one of the names, and that this poster has taught him what to do in the polling booth.

A further objection might come from psychologists who have taken the lessons of the Gestalt school to heart. They might remind us that the pattern consisting of stimulus A and stimulus B presented simultaneously forms a new stimulus that is distinct from either stimulus A or stimulus B presented alone. It is, therefore, a matter of which response the subject will make to the new stimulus as a whole, and it is wrong to ask which component of the pattern will determine the response. There is undoubtedly a great deal of justice in this complaint. Subjects faced with a pattern of successive or simultaneous stimuli will often perform some response that is quite different from any that one of the stimuli would elicit if it were alone. This is a phenomenon that even associationistically inclined learning theorists have long recognized and called "patterning" (Hull 1943) or "configural conditioning" (Razran 1939a). The sight of a speed-limit sign combined with the sight of a policeman may cause a motorist to apply the foot brake when neither of those stimuli separately would do so.

Nevertheless, the response evoked by a combination of stimuli is often more or less identical with what would have occurred if one element of the combination were present alone. In fact, this state of affairs may well be commoner than patterning, which has been given prominence in psychological literature because of the problems it raises. A rat at a choice point may turn his head from side to side, which he would not do if only one path were available. On the other hand, he may immediately run down the left-hand alley, which is precisely what he would have done if that had been the only one open. The chairman of a meeting, seeing several members raising their hands, may say, "I am sorry that there will not be enough

8

time for all those who wish to speak to do so." He would not have said this if only one hand had been up. Alternately, he may look at Mr. X and call on him to speak, which is how he would have reacted if Mr. X's hand had been the only one raised.

There could, in fact, be no regularity in behavior, and no psychology to record it, if behavior were not dominated by a small part of the stimulus situation but depended equally on everything in the environment. No complete environment is ever duplicated and, in any case, it would be impossible to catalogue it. It is therefore necessary and, as it turns out, feasible to make inferences about behavior in the face of a complex pattern of stimuli from a knowledge of how the organism behaves in the face of part of the pattern. The problem is to determine which part of the pattern will be the one to concentrate on.

The problems of stimulus selection are mostly ones that are just beginning to be taken seriously by behavior theory. There are good reasons why they had to be neglected in favor of problems of response selection for a long time, but a concerted attack on them will be necessary before behavior theory is equipped for complex and realistic forms of behavior, especially in human beings. In the guise of questions about awareness, some of the aspects of stimulus selection figured prominently in the writings of the early, introspective experimental psychologists, but they were shelved when the behaviorist revolution took place, largely because the principal preoccupations of the psychologists of that period masked them. Some aspects of stimulus selection have continued to interest the psychology of perception, which has been dealing with questions of prime importance for behavior theory but has often been carried on in a language that harks back to the days when psychologists were mainly occupied with conscious experience and consequently does not always dovetail neatly into the terminology favored by behavior theorists. During the last ten years, however, efforts to merge the study of perceptual phenomena with behavior theory have been rapidly increasing and some topics, like exploration and curiosity, that psychologists have never really done much about are being eagerly taken up.

CONFLICT

When the introduction of a certain stimulus into a randomly selected stimulus situation increases the probability that a certain response will occur, we can speak of the stimulus as *associated* with the response. The response will not always be performed when that stimulus is present, as the influence of the stimulus may be counter-

9

acted by some other factor. The conflict situations that we are going to discuss are illustrations of this. But, to use statistical language, there will be a significant correlation or contingency coefficient between the occurrence of the stimulus and the performance of the response. The word "association" is actually used by statisticians in the sense we are giving to it, although the usage of the word in psychology has a long and different history.

When a stimulus, external or internal, that is associated with a certain response occurs, we shall say that the response is *aroused*, whether or not it is actually performed. If a stimulus or a set of stimuli associated with a certain response is present, and the response is performed, we shall say that the stimulus or set of stimuli has *evoked* the response. And when two or more incompatible responses are aroused simultaneously in an organism, we shall say that the organism is in *conflict*. A conflict can, of course, arise in a variety of ways. For example, there may occur a stimulus associated with each of the incompatible responses, or there may occur one stimulus associated with all of them. The stimuli that exert discordant influences may be internal stimuli, connected with opposing motives or drives.

This use of the word "conflict" may seem questionable. For one thing, the word suggests something wild and dramatic. Its popularization in psychoanalytic writings has made the connotation of a violent clash between motivational or emotional forces cling to it and made it hard to dissociate from other distinctive features of Freudian theory. But the kinds of psychological conflict that Freud wrote about are only some of many kinds that can occur. And the effects of conflict so graphically described by Freud and his followers are only some of the ways in which conflict can influence behavior. Conflict of other, and often milder, varieties is an inseparable accompaniment of the existence of all higher animals, because of the endless diversity of the stimuli that act on them and of the responses that they have the ability to perform.

The word "conflict" is also used in social psychology and sociology to denote quite a different phenomenon, namely, conflict between individuals or groups, and that is another reason for misgivings about it. Hull always used the word "competition" for intraindividual conflict, while Pavlov used the word "collision" (*stolknovenie*). But it is probably too late now to replace the word "conflict" in the vocabulary of psychology, and certainly hopeless to dispense with the notion that it represents.

There are several ways or senses in which responses may be incompatible with one another.

1. *Innate Antagonism.* Two responses might be impossible to carry

10

out at the same time because of the way the organism is constructed. It is obvious that no organism, no matter how it were designed, could move backward and forward or raise and lower the same limb at once. But quite apart from these physical impossibilities, the nervous system is so arranged that certain pairs of responses, which could otherwise take place together to the detriment of the organism's adaptation, will be mutually exclusive. Sherrington (1906) found several examples of such "antagonisms" between reflexes in the course of his classical work on spinal reflexes, just as he found other pairs of reflexes to be "allied" or mutually facilitatory. Thus, when the muscles which bend a limb are contracted, the muscles whose con- tractions would straighten the same limb are kept inactive by "re- ciprocal innervation." When one limb is brought up to scratch a spot on the skin, the corresponding limb on the opposite side is prevented from bending, by a similar inhibitory mechanism, and thus made to support the body's weight.

There is evidence from the literature on conditioned responses (Konorski 1948) of antagonism between such major classes of activity as feeding and defense. The formation of a conditioned salivary response to a painful stimulus or to any extremely intense stimulus is slow and difficult, apparently because such stimuli elicit strong innate defensive reactions which conflict with alimentary activity. It has been shown (Lissák 1955) that the stimulation of certain areas of the hypothalamus will facilitate alimentary, and inhibit defensive, conditioned responses, while there are other areas whose stimulation has the opposite effects.

Innate antagonism evidently exists between perceptual responses also. It is possible to see Fig. 1-1a either as a windmill, in which case lines 1 and 2 are grouped together to form a sail, or as a Maltese cross, in which case lines 2 and 3 are grouped together to form an arm. But it is not possible for a grouping of 1 and 2, excluding 3, and of 2 and 3, excluding 1, to occur at the same time. The way the nervous system is made similarly enables us to perceive Fig. 1-1b in either of two ways but not in both ways at once.

2. *Learned Antagonism.* Responses that are initially quite capable of simultaneous performance may become incompatible through learn- ing. This could happen either through *mutual conditioned inhibition* or through *patterned fear conditioning* (see N. E. Miller 1944).

The familiar principle of conditioned inhibition tells us that when- ever a response is repeatedly reinforced in the absence of a certain stimulus and repeatedly not reinforced in its presence, the stimulus acquires the power to inhibit the response. Let us suppose, then, that two responses, R_1 and R_2, are regularly reinforced if performed

11

separately but not if performed together. We can then expect the proprioceptive and other stimuli that result from the arousal of R_1 to exert conditioned inhibitory influence on R_2 and vice versa.

The second case—that of patterned fear conditioning—would be realized if the combined performance of the two responses were habitually followed by punishment, but the performance of either alone were not. The response-produced stimuli from both would then come to evoke conditioned fear, whereas the response-produced stimuli from either response alone would not. This is an instance of patterning, the familiar phenomenon in experiments on learning in which a discrimination is built up between a combination of stimuli and the components of the combination, so that the combination evokes a response which is not evoked by any of the components presented in isolation. Cessation or avoidance of the punished combination of responses would be reinforced by fear reduction.

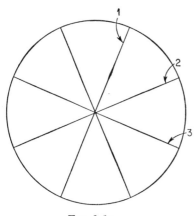

FIG. 1-1a.

Social psychology provides plenty of examples of both cases. Asking a favor of somebody in authority while adopting a threatening posture is rarely rewarded, and so it rarely happens. Children in our culture are taught not to speak and chew food at the same time and not to frown while shaking hands. Simultaneous performance is in such cases punished by representatives of society. In other cases, a pattern of simultaneous responses may have punishing consequences through leading the organism into maladaptive behavior, as when a child kicks a ball away while stooping to pick it up.

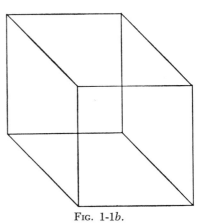

FIG. 1-1b.

The learning that creates antagonisms between responses can, like all learning, be incomplete. The responses may actually be performed simultaneously but with the strength of one or all of them reduced. In the patterned-fear-condition-

12

ing case, the responses may even be performed at full strength, but with a state of discomfort or drive ensuing from their contiguity.

3. *Occlusion*. The third reason for incompatibility between responses is that an organism can do only a limited number of things at once, even of things no two of which are mutually exclusive. No more than a few stimuli or aspects of stimuli can be reacted to, and no more than a few stimuli or aspects of stimuli can be remembered or represented by traces for future action. This is in spite of the fact that the body has such a huge range of effectors, all of which could physically be activated at once, and the fact that the external and internal surfaces of the body contain myriads of receptors, all of which not only can but mostly do receive stimulation and excite sensory neurons all the time. The bottleneck must clearly lie in the capacity of the brain to make use of incoming nerve processes and initiate outgoing ones.

There is a legend that Julius Caesar could read, talk, write, and think about different topics at once. This is not the place to examine the historical evidence for this legend, but we can safely assume that if Julius Caesar was capable of this feat, few other human beings have been able to emulate it. Broadbent (1952*b*) did an experiment on speaking and listening simultaneously. The subjects in his experimental group were asked a series of questions about some visual figures displayed in front of them. The next question was heard while they were uttering the answer to the last question, and this overlapping reduced the percentage of correct answers to 70 per cent, whereas a control group who had no overlapping gave answers of which 98 per cent were correct. The reciprocal interference between speaking and listening occurred even though the two activities employ quite distinct end organs and peripheral nerves.

A further illustration is provided by Mowbray's experiment (1952), comparing simultaneous with successive presentation of distinct information to the eye and the ear. The material consisted of sequences of letters of the alphabet and of numbers, presented in the normal order with some elements missing. Subjects were required to write down the missing elements. The simultaneous use of vision and hearing produced significantly more errors of omission than the successive use. Yet, the two sensory channels are quite separate and noninteracting until the brain is reached. The capacity of the brain, therefore, must be setting limits to the efficiency with which information from two simultaneously active sources is utilized.

But what exactly do we mean when we say that an organism can handle only a limited number of stimuli or responses or stimulus-response bonds in so much time? How can these be counted or

13

measured? A large body of recent researches (Broadbent 1958) indicates that the most suitable unit with which to measure them is the *bit* of information, introduced by information theory (Shannon and Weaver 1949), and that how many of them an organism can cope with depends on their *information content*. The measurement of information and the bearing of information theory on the questions that are of interest to us will be taken up in more detail in Chapter 2.

Meanwhile, we need only mention that it is possible to estimate how much information resides in the stimuli that an organism is receiving and how much of that information is preserved in the responses to which the stimuli give rise. According to computations of this sort (Luce 1956), the human ear alone appears capable of receiving 10,000 or more bits per second, while the eye, even with color differences disregarded, can receive over 4 million bits per second. But the human being passes on no more than about fifty bits per second in responding to stimuli. This means that well over 99 per cent of the information contained in the stimuli exciting human sense organs is not utilized and has no influence on behavior. It has been argued that, in any case, the number of cells in the nervous system is not nearly sufficient to transmit all the information reaching the receptors.

That the limitation is one of information-transmitting capacity rather than anything else is shown by the fact that two or even more tasks can often be performed at once, provided that the information-transmission requirements of all of them together is not too high. This will be the case, for example, when all the tasks except one call for well-practiced, mechanical sequences of actions in response to familiar sequences of stimuli. Stimuli that form a familiar, frequently repeated sequence will be highly probable and foreseeable, which, as we shall see, means that their information content will be small.

The Biological Significance of Conflict

All these forms of conflict are consequences of the high pitch of coordination achieved by the higher animals. The lowest invertebrates have an extremely limited repertoire of behavior; feeding and reproduction, for them, are not subject to much variation or amenable to much planning, and, apart from these two activities, behavior is mainly a matter of moving in this general direction or that. Their sensory capacities are restricted to detecting gross differences of intensity between one sector of the stimulus field and another or between the stimulus field as a whole from one moment to the next. There is thus little scope for mutual interference and obstruction among processes that are launched simultaneously, although this can occasionally happen. If edible objects touch opposite points on the rim of a jellyfish's umbrella at once, the manubrium (snout), which normally bends over toward a stimulated point, may miss both. An excited starfish may tear out its own tube feet with its pedicellaria (nippers).

With the advance of evolution, the range of possible responses continually widens. The elaboration of musculature permits movement to be aimed at innumerable precise targets and the body to assume many postures. The possibilities are augmented beyond measure by the manipulatory capacities of primates and by the endless variety of verbal utterances, emotional attitudes, and memory images open to the human being. At the same time, the range of simultaneously acting factors that can initiate responses grows commensurately with the development of specialized sense organs and with the expanding control over behavior acquired by habits, memories, and thoughts.

Concomitantly with these changes, the nervous system becomes capable of handling and utilizing more and more information. The rate with which information is coming in from increasingly refined sensory apparatus is, however, rising at a much faster rate, so that there is more and more room for occlusion.

With anything approaching the human level of organization, therefore, every waking moment must bring along a torrent of events which are all potentially capable of instigating behavior processes. To some extent, the effects of these events will converge, but their demands on the organism's equipment and ultimately on its musculature must be mostly irreconcilable and therefore mutually impeding.

It is thus necessary to have arrangements like those that produce innate and learned antagonisms if a process that is once under way is not to be constantly tugged from its course by the claims of rival processes. These arrangements will work well as long as one process is strong enough to dominate the others. But there will be dangers inherent in them whenever incompatible response tendencies of comparable strength are present. In physics, equal and opposite forces produce states of immobility and equilibrium. In biology and psychology, immobility in the face of conflict is sometimes advantageous. It might prevent unduly precipitate action and postpone a decision until more information is forthcoming. It might prevent an animal from making itself conspicuous to an enemy.

If continued beyond a few minutes, however, immobility can be one of the gravest threats to survival that can face an animal. This will be especially true in the situations that generate severe conflicts, since these will usually be ones involving urgent biological needs or imminent dangers. It is thus desirable for the organism to be so constructed

15

that it does not yield to conflict with paralysis, at least not for long, but actively strives to overcome the conflict. In most situations of biological need, an animal is generally better off doing something than doing nothing, since remaining active holds out the best hopes of discovering a means of relief.

In some circumstances, e.g., when there are a number of equally effective ways of compassing the same end, a device for selecting one of the competing courses of action at random will suffice. It is evident that such devices exist. A hungry animal midway between two rations of food soon makes for one or the other (Miller 1944). A human being, told that he must press a key either forward or backward when a red and a green light appear together, will sometimes do the one and sometimes the other, but he will in any case select one of the responses within a second or so (Berlyne 1957b). Yet it is noteworthy how often people faced with a choice between mutually exclusive but equally acceptable actions will prefer to let fortuitous external stimuli settle the issue by resorting to something like divination or coin tossing.

Keeping active and making random choices will not, however, suffice for all conditions. The order of precedence among competing responses must be governed by rules that maximize biological advantage. Moreover, the choice among alternative processes should preferably occur as early as possible in the chain of events between stimulus and response, both because the earlier the choice, the less the possibility of disruption, and because limited information-processing capacity will supervene quite early and compel some rejection of proposals for action.

The means that higher animals have for handling conflict work remarkably well in normal conditions, well enough for psychologists to have unduly neglected their study. But they will, of course, sometimes fail, especially in the face of unusual and exceptionally severe forms of conflict. Sometimes, an organism is reduced to long-lasting and perilous immobility. At other times, the product of the conflict is an unsatisfactory compromise between the competing responses, which fulfills the aims of none of them. Then there are all the unfortunate disruptive by-products, many of them outlasting the conflict that gave rise to them, that we find in emotional disturbance and psychological ill-health.

In conclusion, we must recall that not all conflicts are amenable to resolution by stimulus selection. Conflicts between incompatible responses that are associated with the same stimulus (e.g., conflicts between habits) and conflicts between responses that are aroused primarily by internal stimuli (e.g., emotional or motivational conflicts) require other measures to alleviate them. Sometimes, as in the Freud-

16

ian mechanism of denial, stimulus selection may help to remove behavior from the control of the external confederates of troublesome internal factors, but this is likely to prove a temporary palliative.

When, however, conflict occurs because incoming information is excessive or deficient or discrepant, stimulus-selection processes form the principal means of defense. Such conflicts are rarely among the most explosive and spectacular ones that can rack an organism. But they are among the most ubiquitous and recurrent.

Chapter 2

NOVELTY, UNCERTAINTY, CONFLICT, COMPLEXITY

In the next four chapters, we are going to examine such data as we have on the factors that govern the various forms of stimulus selection. We shall be finding, again and again, that the chances of a particular stimulus pattern in the contest for control over behavior depend, among other properties, on how novel the pattern is, to what extent it arouses or relieves uncertainty, to what extent it arouses or relieves conflict, and how complex it is. All these properties figure in other areas of psychology, but they come into their own and force themselves on our notice with especial importunity when we approach the problems of stimulus selection.

All of them are eminently quantitative properties. They can plainly exist in varying degrees, and so ways of measuring them will eventually have to be devised. Yet their measurement presents difficulties. They are all interrelated, and, although our present knowledge does not allow us to characterize their interrelations with adequate precision and confidence, the links between them must be uncovered if their importance for the nervous system is to be understood. There can be little doubt that the four concepts—novelty, uncertainty, conflict, and complexity—are among our most valuable tools for research into stimulus selection. We must, therefore, attempt to find some tolerably stable meanings that can be attached to them and to look at some of the most manifest ways in which they are connected with one another.

NOVELTY

Novelty seems to be the most straightforward and the least technical concept of the four. The word "new" is used commonly in everyday speech, and most people seem to understand it without much difficulty. But when we ask what exactly it means to say that a stimulus pattern is novel and how novel it is, we face a whole succession of snares and dilemmas.

18

Short-term, Long-term, and Complete Novelty

To begin with, there are several quite distinct senses in which something can be new. It can be new with respect to an organism's *total* experience or new with respect merely to its *recent* experience; it may never have been encountered before, or it may not have been encountered within the last few minutes. We shall call the former case *complete* novelty and the latter *short-term* novelty. There will also be intermediate cases of *long-term* novelty when something has not been encountered for a period of days. The difference between a stimulus pattern with short-term novelty and one without must depend on short-lived traces, such as outlast stimulation for a brief period. But completely novel patterns can contrast with others only if those which have occurred before effect permanent changes, of a sort that can be called *learning*.

Absolute and Relative Novelty

Another distinction that calls for consideration is that between *absolute* and *relative* novelty. An absolutely novel stimulus would be one with some quality that had never been perceived before, while a relatively novel stimulus or stimulus pattern would possess familiar elements or qualities in a combination or arrangement that had not been met with in the past.

This dichotomy itself raises problems immediately. Any new experience, even if it does not seem to be a combination of familiar experiences, must have some definite degree of resemblance to experiences that have occurred before. It will inevitably be possible to insert it into an ordering of familiar stimuli or to assign to it values along dimensions that are used to classify them. The new stimulus can be related to well-known stimuli by expressing the differences between it and them quantitatively. A man taller than any seen before clearly differs only in degree from other men. A hue or an odor may be qualitatively different from any others that have been met. But it will be possible to allot the hue a location in the spectrum and to locate the odor in any of the multidimensional schemes for classifying odors that have been proposed.

These facts might be of minor importance for psychology if it were merely a matter of classification by an external observer. But what is important is that the nervous system relates any novel incoming stimulus to stimulus categories that it already recognizes; a new stimulus will evoke responses corresponding to familiar stimuli by generalization, and it will evoke them with strengths corresponding to its resemblance to the stimuli with which the responses were originally asso-

19

ciated. For any adult human being, or even any adult dog, cat, or rat, a new stimulus must be similar to, and relatable to, a host of familiar and frequently experienced entities. However bizarre a nonsense figure may be that is shown to a human adult, it must consist of lines, angles, and curves such as he has seen on countless occasions. Experiments like those of Bartlett (1932) show that human subjects invariably react to unfamiliar, meaningless material by observing that it is like something with which they are acquainted, while noting in what ways it differs. When we come to new ideas or facts, which are expressed in familiar words arranged according to familiar grammatical forms, the point is too plain to be worth laboring.

The Problem of Novelty

These considerations lead us to what is really the crucial puzzle about novelty. If all novel stimuli (in whatever sense of the word "novel") have certain effects on the organism that stimuli lacking in novelty do not have, they must have some property in common to produce this effect. But what do all novel stimuli have in common except the purely negative property of not having occurred earlier? One would suppose that if they have positive effects on the organism —and the following chapters will contain evidence suggesting strongly that they do—a positive effect must be produced by something positive. Most classes of stimuli that share a common effect on behavior do so because they share definite physicochemical properties that cause them to activate particular receptors in particular ways and ultimately to activate particular units of the nervous system. But novel stimuli cannot be distinguished by physicochemical properties; stimuli with identical physicochemical properties will later be familiar.

There would appear to be two possible solutions to the problem of novelty. They are not necessarily mutually exclusive alternatives. It seems, on the contrary, that both have some validity. The first hypothesis (which we may call the *habituation hypothesis*) is that novel stimuli owe their collective properties to the fact that *they have not yet had a chance to lose effects that all stimuli originally possess.* It is obvious that all stimuli are novel at some time, and so all stimuli must at some time have the effects peculiar to novelty. But having once occurred, and especially having occurred repeatedly, they must lose these effects. This might be the result of some process resembling the habituation of an unlearned response. Unlearned responses, if repeatedly evoked, often undergo both temporary and chronic declines in strength (Peckham and Peckham 1887), and such temporary and chronic habituation processes could rob stimulus patterns of the effects

20

peculiar to short-term novelty and to complete or long-term novelty respectively.

The second hypothesis is that novel stimuli are alike in *inducing conflict*. There are various reasons for the feeling that the habituation hypothesis by itself is not enough. From what we know of stimulus generalization, we can assume that any new pattern of stimulation that impinges on a sophisticated adult mammal will be sufficiently similar to several familiar stimulus patterns to evoke responses appropriate to all of them and that many of these responses will be incompatible. Furthermore, many responses of adult mammals will have figured in previous discrimination learning; they will have been reinforced only in the presence of stimuli with certain characteristics. This implies that the organism will have learned to perform them only in the presence of members of the appropriate stimulus class and that they will be inhibited in the presence of stimuli that fall clearly into other classes. A novel stimulus is likely to fall midway between two classes that have figured in a piece of discrimination learning, so that it will arouse both generalized excitation and generalized inhibition of the response, which again means conflict.

Many writers (e.g., Berlyne 1950a, McDougall 1908, Piaget 1936) have pointed out that some of the effects proper to novel stimuli, including their ability to influence stimulus selection, are apparently not at their strongest with maximum novelty. They seem rather to be most strongly elicited by an intermediate degree of novelty, with a stimulus that is rather like something well known but just distinct enough from it to be "interesting." We are indifferent to things that are either too remote from our experience or too familiar. A relatively slight variation in a familiar pattern has a unique piquancy. A side show at a fairground that has a two-headed lady on display may very well attract more customers than one offering a collection of geological specimens. Yet the geological specimens may be quite different from anything that most visitors will ever have seen, whereas all of them will have seen plenty of ladies' heads, and two heads on one lady are not so unlike two heads on two ladies.

Human beings will, in fact, often attribute the special interest of an experience not to its novelty in general but to its novelty in comparison with a particular set of previous experiences. The two-headed lady, for example, attracts their patronage not merely because she is a different phenomenon from any they have previously encountered but because she differs from the *ladies* they have encountered in the past. If a stimulus pattern owes its status as something novel to comparison with a specific class of familiar patterns, then the presumption is that the

21

reactions it arouses include some of those associated with the familiar patterns as well as other reactions with which these are incompatible.

Degree of Novelty

When we face the problem of measuring degree of novelty, as we shall have to sooner or later if future developments confirm its importance as a psychological variable, the desirability of exploring its relations with conflict obtrudes itself still more ineluctably.

How novel a particular pattern is will presumably be inversely related to (1) how *often* patterns that are similar enough to be relevant have been experienced before, (2) how *recently* they have been experienced, and (3) how *similar* they have been.

But what do we mean by "similar enough to be relevant," and how is similarity to be measured? The best answers to these questions seem to be that a pattern is relevant if some response associated with it is detectably generalized to the present pattern, and that the degree of similarity is revealed through the amount of stimulus generalization.

We see, then, that the variables on which a measure of novelty must depend are difficult to define, let alone measure, without reference to stimulus generalization.

Moreover, it would be discouraging if we could never determine how new a stimulus is for a given subject without a complete account of his past life. We should like to tell how new it is by means of tests carried out now. And it would seem that such tests would have to work by ascertaining how far the stimulus in question evokes responses (including, of course, verbal responses) that can be attributed to generalization. For the reasons we have already reviewed, the study of the generalized responses aroused by a novel stimulus is bound to mean the study of *conflicting* generalized responses.

Variables Supplementary to Novelty

Before leaving novelty, we must observe that novelty, in any of the senses we have been discussing, is often accompanied by other properties, each of which may have its separate influence on the direction of stimulus selection or the strength of any stimulus-selecting process. The effects proper to them need, however, to be verified and measured separately. Yet they have rarely been isolated by experimenters, which makes it hard to determine exactly what the operative variable is in much of the literature in our present field of inquiry. The properties in question are as follows:

Change. Here we refer to a change or movement that occurs while the stimulus in question is acting on receptors. If a spot of green light were presented at intervals of a few seconds and then a red light ap-

22

peared in its place, we should have an instance of (short-term) novelty without change, contrasting with the sight of a spot of light changing from green to red before the subject's eyes.

The extent and rate of the change undergone by a pattern can be expected to have some importance in determining its stimulus-selection priority.

Surprisingness. A novel stimulus or a stimulus undergoing change may, in addition, be *surprising.* This implies more than that the stimulus was not expected or that it differs from what preceded it. It implies the existence of an expectation with which the stimulus disagrees.

About the oldest explanatory principle in psychology is one with variants known as *association by contiguity* (a concept that can be traced back to Plato and Aristotle), *redintegration* (Hamilton 1859), and *sensory integration* (Osgood 1957). The principle is stated by Osgood as follows: "The greater the frequency with which stimulus events A and B are associated in the input to an organism, the greater will be the tendency for the central correlates of one, a, to activate the central correlates of the other, b." In the days of introspective psychology influenced by associationism, the central correlates referred to were conscious ideas. In modern psychology, they are usually thought of as neural processes or as implicit responses.

The principle has somewhat different implications when applied to different cases. First, we must note that the statement that A and B are frequently contiguous or associated may mean either that they occur in close succession or that they occur simultaneously. Nineteenth-century associationists distinguished *successive* from *synchronous* association. In the one case, b will follow a, and in the other case, it will accompany a.

Another distinction lies between the phenomena that Osgood calls *evocative integration* and *predictive integration* (although the more specialized term "redintegration" may be preferable). The former may occur when the activation of b is especially strong, which may result from an all but inseparable association between A and B, from the presence of a large number of stimuli all of which are associated with B, or from some abnormal state of the organism, such as psychosis, hypnosis, or intoxication. The form in which b is activated will then be identical with the form it takes when B is actually at work, and the subject may then have a hallucination of B; he may behave in all respects as if B were there. But more frequently, the activation of b will be strong enough only for a priming or threshold-lowering effect (predictive redintegration). It will cause b to occur in response to a lower intensity of B than would otherwise suffice, or it will increase the intensity of b produced by a given intensity of B.

23

The prominence allotted to expectations and the manner in which they are interpreted vary widely among contemporary theories. Be that as it may, an expectation must consist of some process which "represents" the expected stimulus, i.e., it must have some properties that vary with those of the latter, and its strength must increase with the latter's probability. It may be aroused by some sign that has habitually preceded the expected stimulus in the past. Alternatively, it may be aroused less directly by some stimulus that has never preceded it in the past but is shown by some inferential process to signify its imminent appearance. It will usually also reflect how soon the expected stimulus will occur.

We are entitled to speak of an expectation of stimulus B only if we can point to some objective difference between behavior when B is expected and behavior when it is not, whether the difference appears before B is due or after. In human beings, expectations may be expressed in words, and interrogation may be used as a means of ascertaining what is expected and how strongly. But this will not always be possible, as expectations are far from always conscious.

Several indexes of expectation can be identified in mammals. As far as behavior preceding the expected stimulus is concerned, animals expecting B act in such a way as to prepare themselves for it, i.e., they perform responses that enable them to react more advantageously when B occurs, whether *preparatory* responses that ensure maximum benefit from its presence if its affective value is positive, or *avoidant* responses that minimize its impact if it is aversive. Overlapping preparatory and avoidant responses will be *anticipatory* responses, i.e., conditioned incipient or fractional versions of responses associated with B. Alternatively, the expectation may be revealed by the readiness with which B is *recognized* or with which another stimulus is *mistaken* for it.

We may ascribe the effects of surprise to conflict on the following grounds. Let us suppose that a stimulus A evokes an expectation of B but a stimulus X that contrasts with B occurs instead. At the time of X's occurrence, we shall thus have two responses or sets of responses aroused, one appropriate to X, evoked directly by X, and one appropriate to B, evoked by redintegration. If B and X are distinct, we can expect the responses corresponding to them to have some measure of incompatibility, so that conflict will result from the disparity between what is expected and what is experienced.

Incongruity. We are reserving the term "surprise" for cases where there is a stimulus inducing an expectation and a later stimulus that contradicts the expectation. *Incongruity,* on the other hand, exists when a stimulus induces an expectation which turns out to be disap-

24

pointed by the accompanying stimuli. The expectations involved will thus be due to *synchronous predictive redintegration*. Incongruity requires not merely a combination of stimuli that is novel but a combination differing from, yet having components in common with, one that the organism has learned to treat as more likely.

The distinction between incongruity and surprisingness will admittedly be difficult to make at times. We can think of incongruity, if we insist, as a special case of surprise, since the incongruous pattern contradicts expectations aroused by the whole mass of past experience. Alternatively, if the parts or properties of an incongruous pattern are scanned or apprehended in succession, even though the whole pattern is there at once, some properties will contradict expectations aroused by others that were perceived earlier.

UNCERTAINTY AND INFORMATION THEORY

The word "uncertainty" has acquired some notoriety through Heisenberg's "principle of uncertainty," also known as the "principle of indeterminacy," which dominates contemporary theoretical physics. This principle sets limits to the precision with which quantities like the position or the momentum of a particle can be measured or even discussed. If the value of a certain variable can only be placed within the range of values x to $x + \Delta x$, but not located more precisely, then Δx represents the uncertainty of the measurement. If Δx is the uncertainty of the *position* of a particle along one dimension, then the uncertainty of its *momentum* along the same dimension (Δp_x) is greater than or equal to $h/4\pi\Delta x$, where h is Planck's constant.

In economics and other fields where decision theory is of importance, there is much discussion concerning "decision making under uncertainty" (cf. Arrow 1951, Thrall, Coombs, and Davis 1954). Here "uncertainty" refers to situations where events have probabilities other than 1 or 0.

Two intuitively recognizable characteristics of uncertainty are thus exemplified by these two approaches. One is that uncertainty is greater, the greater the range of values that a variable may have or, in other words, the greater the range of alternative possibilities. The other is that uncertainty is greater, the further probabilities diverge from 0 and 1, so that the maximum of uncertainty is reached when an event has an equal chance of materializing and not materializing. Both of these characteristics are reflected in the measure of uncertainty that is most promising for our present area of inquiry, namely the one used in *information theory* (Shannon and Weaver 1949).

Information theory consists of a mathematical language for talking

25

about communication channels. As an example of the kind of situation for which it was originally designed, we may consider a telephone line, with an observer stationed at the receiving end. The observer is waiting for a signal to reach him, and, before it arrives, he has a list of classes to which it could belong and knows the probability of its belonging to each class. We can calculate a quantity that Shannon called *entropy* (H) but which is now coming more widely to be called *uncertainty*. It is equal to $-\sum_i p_i \log_2 p_i$ "bits," where p_i is the probability that the awaited signal will belong to class i. This measure has the two properties we mentioned: it reaches a maximum when all the p_i are equal, and, when they are equal, it increases with the number of alternative classes to which the signal could belong.

The observer may have not only a certain degree of uncertainty about what will be received at the output end of the line but also a degree of uncertainty, calculated in the same fashion, about what went into the input. In a perfect communication channel, there will be a complete one-to-one correspondence between input and output signals, so that the observer will have the same degree of uncertainty about both. But in an imperfect or "noisy" channel, the correspondence will be partial, so that the uncertainty about the input and the uncertainty about the output may have different values.

It soon became appreciated that information-theory measures may be usefully applied to many other situations than those which concern the communication engineer. Measures like uncertainty can be applied whenever we have an event selected from an *information space,* i.e., a set of alternative, mutually exclusive events with a probability assigned to each of them. Whenever we have events selected from two information spaces, we can treat them as input and output signals and apply other information-theory measures, which refer to the transmission of information and reflect the extent of the correlation or correspondence between the two spaces.

In psychology, we have, in fact, two information spaces which seem admirably fitted for treatment as input and output of a communication channel, namely the stimulus space and the response space. Many quantities that are of interest to the psychologist (e.g., how quickly a subject will respond to a stimulus, how accurately he will identify a stimulus, how likely he is to remember a stimulus correctly a few minutes after its disappearance) are very much affected not only by the nature of the stimulus that occurs but also by what stimuli (or responses) might have occurred instead and how likely they were. They depend, in other words, on the degree of uncertainty, as recent researches have abundantly demonstrated (G. A. Miller 1956, Broadbent 1958).

If we are to calculate the stimulus uncertainty or the response uncertainty, we must, however, first be able to describe the appropriate information spaces. This means, as we have seen, that we must be able (1) to draw up a list of stimuli (or responses) that might occur, (2) partition these into classes, and (3) assign a probability to each class. All of these raise perplexities immediately.

1. How do we identify events that might have occurred but did not? What it means to assert that this or that *would* have happened if so and so had been the case is still a question (the so-called problem of counterfactual conditionals) that logicians have not answered to their own satisfaction (Chisholm 1946, Goodman 1947). What it means to assert that this or that *might* have happened raises all the difficulties of this problem and others besides. The perennial problem or pseudo problem of free will hinges on the sense, if any, in which it can be claimed that, however a man acts, he might have acted otherwise.

From the point of view of an external observer, the problem of defining the stimulus and response spaces may not be so serious. For one thing, the external observer is quite likely to be an experimenter who has control, through his experimental arrangements, over the kinds of stimuli that can occur and how often or, through his instructions, over the responses that shall be open to the subject. In any case, he can base his list of alternative stimuli and responses on what happened in similar situations in the past or on any considerations that suit his purposes. He may very well have access to facts, revealing what stimuli and responses are possible, that are not available to the subject.

Any variables of psychological interest that depend on uncertainty are, however, bound to be more closely related to the uncertainty of the subject than to that of the observer. They will depend, in other words, on what stimuli or responses might occur, and with what probabilities, *from the subject's point of view,* and determining which these are is a more difficult and a less arbitrary matter.

First, the responses that *might* occur, as far as the subject is concerned, must be the ones that the subject was prepared to make before the stimulus was received, i.e., ones that were aroused in an implicit form by whatever conditions preceded the stimulus in question, although their overt expression will have been withheld pending the appearance of the stimulus. There is evidence that, when we imagine or think of a bodily movement, some of the processes that would be entailed in the performance of the movement take place; there are weak but detectable action currents in the muscles that would be used (Jacobson 1929), and there is also suppression of prevailing electroencephalographic (EEG) rhythms in the motor area of the cortex (Fessard and Gastaut 1958).

27

Similarly, the stimuli that might occur, in any sense that affects the subject's behavior, must be ones that the subject is expecting, i.e., ones that are represented by processes of some sort inside the subject. The data of learning experiments show that, when a subject expects a stimulus to which a definite response is attached, i.e., when the subject is exposed to cues that have frequently heralded such a stimulus, anticipatory responses will occur, at least in an implicit form. These anticipatory responses will include the response associated with the expected stimulus, evoked anticipatorily through conditioning, as well as preparatory and avoidant responses.

2. Next we have the question of how the set of stimuli that might occur, assuming that we can enumerate them, is to be divided into classes. The only meaningful answer is that stimuli that call for the same behavior in the situation in question should be counted as a stimulus class, whereas stimuli calling for different reponses should be placed in different classes. The point is well illustrated in an example given by Weaver (1948). Most bridge players would be astonished to find themselves holding thirteen cards of one suit, because they realize that this is highly improbable. Yet any hand that could possibly be dealt is just as improbable, since all combinations of thirteen cards are equally likely. The fact is, of course, that no player can have a separate response available for each of the millions of hands that are possible, at least not at the stage of the game that immediately follows the deal. Each hand is not represented, therefore, as a subdivision of the stimulus space, but hands are grouped together in broad classes according to their immediate effects on behavior, e.g., as bad, good, or freak hands, or as hands calling for the same opening bid. Some of the classes in these stimulus spaces will, of course, be much less probable than others.

The upshot of this argument is that the partitioning of the stimulus space must correspond to the partitioning of the response space.

3. When we put our final question, namely, "How are we to allot probabilities to the various classes of stimuli that the subject treats as ones that might occur?" the answer is clearly that probability in this connection must mean *subjective probability*. The subjective probability of an event is the strength of the subject's expectation that the event will occur, and this will be reflected in the strength of the corresponding anticipatory response.

So the conclusions to which we are proceeding are as follows: situations in which a stimulus that may belong to any of several alternative classes is impending, and in which a subject's behavior is affected by his degree of uncertainty about this stimulus, are situations in which responses corresponding to the various alternative stimulus classes are anticipatorily aroused. But, since each stimulus class calls for different behavior, these responses will be incompatible with one another. Therefore, *situations in which uncertainty is of psychological importance are situations of conflict.* If we are to use the formula $-\sum_i p_i \log_2 p_i$ as a measure of psychological uncertainty, then the p_i must represent the strengths of competing responses.

Novel stimulus patterns will generally arouse uncertainty, since there will be no way of telling what will follow them. The expectations that they induce will depend on what familiar patterns they resemble, and, especially if they are very novel, they are likely to bear a comparable degree of resemblance to many different familiar patterns, giving rise to discrepant expectations. Conditions that arouse uncertainty will, on the other hand, not necessarily be novel.

Measures of Information

Information theory provides, of course, not only a way of measuring uncertainty but also ways of measuring information. These sound as if they ought to be of interest to us, since stimulus-selection processes can be considered means of bringing the organism into contact with new sources of information and of determining which items of information, from the various sources that are accessible, shall be conducted through the organism's nervous system to emerge in the form of behavior.

There are several distinct measures that are relevant here.

1. *The Amount of Information in a Signal.* This measure depends solely on the probability or relative frequency of the class to which the signal belongs. The smaller this probability, the more information the signal contains, the amount of information in a signal of class i being equal to $- \log_2 p_i$ bits.

This quantity is sometimes regarded as a measure of novelty, which is an example of the confusions that can arise when concepts like novelty are not examined carefully. It is true that it reflects the rarity with which a particular kind of stimulus has occurred in the past, and this is admittedly one of the determinants that must figure in any measure of degree of novelty. But it does not reflect the other two determinants, namely, degree of resemblance with previous stimuli and time elapsing since the last occurrence of a similar stimulus. A stimulus can belong to a highly improbable class, and yet other stimuli of that class may have been experienced quite recently.

There is, on the other hand, a close relation between this measure of information and surprisingness (Samson 1951). A higher animal can be assumed to possess expectations corresponding to whatever are the most probable impending stimulus events, given the conditions of the moment, and these expectations will have strengths increasing with the probabilities of the events to which they refer. Stimuli with a low probability, and hence with a high information content, will thus conflict with the predominant expectations.

2. *The Rate of Transmission of Information.* This is a measure of the *average* amount (per signal or per unit of time) by which an observer's uncertainty about input signals is reduced when he receives output signals. It can be expressed as $H(X) - H_Y(X)$, where $H(X)$ is the initial uncertainty about the input, and $H_Y(X)$ is the average residual uncertainty about the input when an output signal has been received.

It can be regarded as a measure of the over-all correlation between input and output signals. Limitations of channel capacity are described in terms of the maximum rate of transmission of information, and so, if stimuli are treated as input signals and responses as output signals, this is the measure that is pertinent to occlusion conflict. If one knows only the responses of an animal, there is a limit to the inferences one can make about the stimulus situations in which the responses were performed. Responses cannot reflect more than a small fraction of the ways in which stimulus situations can differ.

3. *The Amount of Transmitted Information.* This measure has not so far played a large part in the use of information theory either by communication engineers or by psychologists. It is, however, likely to be the most meaningful measure of information as far as our present area of interest is concerned. It is the *actual* amount by which uncertainty about the input is reduced when a particular output signal has been received. We may define the *amount of information transmitted through an output signal of class j* as $H(X) - H(X|y_j)$, where $H(X|y_j)$ is the residual input uncertainty on receipt of an output of class j and equals $-\sum_i p(x_i|y_j) \log_2 p(x_i|y_j)$, x_i being an input signal of class i.

We can apply this measure whenever we have a stimulus event that reduces our uncertainty about some other inaccessible (possibly future) stimulus event. It can thus be regarded as a measure of the *extent by which conflict is reduced.* The amount of transmitted information will have as its maximum possible value $H(X)$, which will be realized when uncertainty about an inaccessible event is reduced to zero.

There will, however, be exceptional cases where uncertainty can even be increased by receipt of a signal, so that we should have to say that a negative amount of information has been transmitted! Suppose, for example, that there are three candidates, A, B, and C, contesting an election, with 90 per cent, 5 per cent, and 5 per cent chances of

30

winning respectively. A message stating simply that A had been defeated would then increase uncertainty from 0.57 bits to 1 bit, and the amount of transmitted information would be −0.43 bits!

The concept of "conflict," as we are using the term, is rather broad. Conflict, in our sense, must accompany virtually every moment of normal waking life in the higher mammals. Nevertheless, there must be more of it on some occasions than on others, and stimulus situations will obviously be conflictful to differing degrees.

Conflict, whether called by that name or some other, has already obtruded itself into several lines of psychological inquiry. Both Pavlov and Freud arrived independently at the conclusion that conflict produces neurosis, although the types of evidence on which they based this conclusion and the kinds of conflict they had in mind were very different. A whole host of writers, taking their cue largely from Freud's work, have interpreted many forms of normal behavior as devices for reducing or minimizing conflict. They include not only the dreams, parapraxes, and other relatively isolated departures from rationality discussed at length by Freud but also distortions of perception and thinking and pervasive and lasting personality traits. Conflict has frequently been cited as the principal source of emotion (e.g., Dewey 1895, Luria 1932, Darrow 1935, Hebb 1949, Brown and Farber 1951), whether emotion is thought of as violent motor activity, as autonomic activation, or as a disruption of ongoing processes. The difficulty with which an item will be committed to memory and how likely it is to be forgotten after an interval are widely recognized as dependent on the amount of interference among discrepant associative tendencies (Gibson 1940, McGeoch and Irion 1952). One of the most consistently mentioned of all the effects of conflict is an increase in reaction time (Berlyne 1957b).

These effects are all eminently quantitative. They can all exist in varying amounts, and the extent to which they occur can be assumed to depend on how much conflict there is. It looks, therefore, as if we shall sooner or later be obliged to distinguish and measure degrees of conflict (Berlyne 1957d).

Degree of conflict must not be identified with the *severity of the effects* of conflict. The severity of the effects will depend partly on the degree of conflict but also on other factors. For example, the kinds of responses that are competing will play a part: Lewin (1935) and Miller (1944) have shown why conflicts between approach tendencies should be less serious, and resolve themselves with greater ease,

31

than either conflicts between avoidance tendencies or approach-avoidance conflicts. There are also bound to be differences between individuals in conflict tolerance, so that some will be more disturbed by a given degree of conflict than others. It seems not unlikely that prolonged subjection to a particular conflict situation will mollify some of its effects by bringing long-term adaptive mechanisms into play and will even increase an individual's general conflict tolerance.

It may not be amiss, at this juncture, to remark that frustration and conflict, which are often treated as one entity, are not identical. Rosenzweig (1944) marks off *primary frustration*, in which an aroused response tendency is prevented from completing itself by the absence of the necessary goal object (e.g., the frustration suffered by a thirsty traveler in the desert), from *secondary frustration*, in which the goal object is available but some other factor prevents the organism from fully utilizing it. Secondary frustration can be either external (e.g., resulting from the presence of a physical obstacle) or internal. Conflict must necessarily produce internal secondary frustration, as at least one response tendency is either completely suppressed (in cases of complete incompatibility) or weakened (in cases of partial incompatibility). But other forms of frustration need not entail conflict in our sense of the word.

Determinants of Degree of Conflict

If we ask ourselves what properties a degree-of-conflict measure should have, there are three that suggest themselves immediately (Brown and Farber 1951, Berlyne 1954b, 1957b, 1957d). Degree of conflict must surely increase with (1) the *nearness to equality in strength* of the competing response tendencies, (2) the *absolute strength* of the competing response tendencies, and (3) the *number* of competing response tendencies.

Berlyne (1957b) has secured evidence that all three of these variables influence one of the most sensitive and easily measurable indexes of conflict, namely, the lengthening of reaction time. The experiments in question studied both *forced-choice* and *free-choice reaction times* (RTs). The forced-choice RT is what has traditionally been called *choice RT*: the subject is informed that any one of a number of specified alternative stimuli, e.g., lights of different colors, might appear. Each stimulus has its corresponding response, e.g., pressing a particular telegraph key, and the subject is to perform the appropriate response as soon as he has identified the stimulus. In the free-choice situation, several stimuli, each having its corresponding response, are presented together, and the subject is instructed to respond to any one of them.

32

Both forced and free choices can be assumed to entail conflict. The free choice means a conflict between response tendencies of about equal strength, while the forced choice means an unequal contest between a strong tendency to make the one correct response to the stimulus that occurred and weaker tendencies, resulting from stimulus generalization, to make errors, i.e., to make responses appropriate to other stimuli that might have occurred. In the experiments, free-choice RTs were found invariably to exceed forced-choice RTs, which confirms that reaction time increases with *nearness to equality of strength* among competing response tendencies.

Secondly, free-choice RTs were longer when two spots of moderately intense light constituted each stimulus than when single spots were employed. If we assume that two spots of light associated with the same response will arouse the response more strongly than one spot, we can see that the *absolute strength* of competing response tendencies also affects reaction time.

Both of these conclusions receive additional support from the regularly reported observation that forced-choice RTs increase as the stimuli that the subject is to discriminate become more similar. When this happens, incorrect response tendencies due to generalization will become both absolutely stronger and nearer equality in strength with the preponderant correct response tendency.

The influence of the third determinant, *number* of competing response tendencies, was likewise verified. Both free-choice and forced-choice RTs lengthened when the number of alternative responses was increased from two to four. Forced-choice RTs were found by previous investigators (Merkel 1885, Hick 1952) to undergo a negatively accelerated increase with the number of alternative stimuli.

A fourth variable that may seem to have a plausible claim to recognition as a determinant of degree of conflict is the *degree of incompatibility* between competing response tendencies. Most writers have concentrated on conflict between responses which are completely incompatible in the sense that one cannot occur at all if the other is being performed.

But Sherrington (1906) cites cases of partial interference between reflexes. For example, if both shoulder blades of a spinal dog are tactually stimulated, one hind leg will scratch but the other hind leg "is found to present steady extension with some abduction." Konorski (1948), extending the notion of partial antagonism to conditioned responses, cites the case of an electric shock which is made into a conditioned stimulus by reinforcement with food. Electric shocks elicit strong defensive reactions, which are antagonistic to alimentary behavior. Salivation in response to the shock is, however, not alto-

33

gether impossible. There is merely slower conditioning and a lower maximum than with other conditioned stimuli.

Nevertheless, degree of incompatibility does not appear to affect free-choice RTs. When the alternative responses were ones that cannot be performed together, e.g., pushing a key forward and backward with the right hand, the free-choice reaction was no slower than with two responses that can be performed together, e.g., pushing different keys forward with right and left hands. Forced-choice RTs were longer when the alternative responses were incompatible, but this can be explained by the fact that the initiation of a wrong response can be corrected more quickly when the other response is to be made with the other hand.

If we look back at our discussion of ways in which learned incompatibility can arise between responses (see Chapter 1), we find prospects of reducing degree of incompatibility to other more tractable variables. In the case of patterned fear conditioning, the degree of incompatibility might be identified with the strength of the fear response. In the conditioned-inhibition case, the degree of incompatibility may be identified with the net strength of the inhibitory influence of response R_1 on response R_2. Instead of speaking of a conflict between two partially incompatible responses R_1 and R_2, we might speak more conveniently of a conflict between two completely incompatible responses R_2 and R_{-2}, the latter being the inhibition of R_2 that is traceable to the arousal of R_1. The greater the degree of antagonism between R_1 and R_2, the greater the conflict, since the more nearly equal in strength R_2 and R_{-2} will be.

Degree of Conflict and Uncertainty

Assuming that we can disregard degree of incompatibility or reduce it to the other determinants, we can now state our requirements for a degree-of-conflict variable C as follows. We suppose that the members of a set of responses $\{R_1 \cdots R_n\}$ are simultaneously aroused in an organism, that these responses are such that no two of them can be performed at once, and that we can associate a value E_i with each R_i as a measure of its strength. The E_i may be one of the recognized manifestations of response strength, such as amplitude or speed of responding, or it may be some intervening variable, like Hull's (1943, 1952) "reaction potential," whose value can be inferred from these measures.

We require C to be a function of $(E_1 \cdots E_n)$ with the following properties:

1. C is a symmetric function of $E_1 \cdots E_n$, i.e., its value depends on the response strengths alone and not on which response has which strength.

2. C is a continuous function of $E_1 \cdots E_n$, i.e., if any of the E_i increases gradually, C will not undergo sudden jumps.

3. $C \geq 0$

4. If $n = 1$, $C = 0$

5. If $\sum_{i=1}^{n} E_i$ is held constant, C reaches an absolute maximum when $E_1 = E_2 = \cdots = E_n$.

6. If $E_1 = E_2 = \cdots = E_n$, and a response R_{n+1} with strength E_{n+1} is added to the set, C will increase.

7. If every E_i is multiplied by a constant $k > 1$, C will increase.

Now, since probability of occurrence is extensively used as a measure of response strength, either alone or in conjunction with other measures like amplitude and latency (reaction time), let us assume that we have some way of transforming each E_i into a probability p_i. The transformation must comply with the following conditions:

1. $0 \leq p \leq 1$

2. $\sum_{i=1}^{n} p_i = 1$

3. If $E_1 = E_2 = \cdots = E_n$, then $p_1 = p_2 = \cdots = p_n$

4. If one E increases with the others held constant, then the corresponding p will increase and the other p's will decrease.

We then find that the information-theory expression for uncertainty, H, which is $-\sum_i p_i \log_2 p_i$, satisfies the first six of the requirements for a degree-of-conflict function C. But it does not satisfy the seventh. It increases with the number of alternatives, and it increases when their strengths approach equality. But it does not vary with their absolute strengths. This is, of course, because the probability of a member of a set of competing responses can only reflect its *relative* and not its *absolute* strength.

In order to produce a measure that will satisfy all our requirements, we shall have to multiply H by a scaling factor, representative of the absolute strengths of the competing responses, such as ΣE. A possible degree-of-conflict function would then be $C = \Sigma E \times H$.

We can see that, according to this formulation, there can be a great deal of uncertainty without much conflict, if strong response tendencies are not in competition. For example, one man may be engaged in a battle between temptation and conscience, while another cannot make up his mind whether to buy a newspaper or not. In both cases, the two alternative responses may have equal probabilities of prevailing, so that the uncertainty will be 1 bit, but the psychological effects of

35

the two conflicts are likely to be of very different orders of gravity.

It should be noted that the uncertainty involved in our present discussion is an external observer's uncertainty about the subject's responses, whereas, earlier in the chapter, we were concentrating on the subject's own uncertainty regarding the stimuli he will encounter and the responses he will perform. These objective and subjective uncertainties are likely to co-vary, but they will not necessarily co-incide with each other.

An additional assumption that we must make is that there is some sort of threshold value that the relative strength, p, of a response tendency must exceed if it is to contribute to conflict. This is justifiable, for one thing, because there will usually, at any moment, be an enormous number of extremely weak responses aroused by generalization or by weak stimuli, and these cannot be expected to have any appreciable effect. Secondly, we shall be making use (see Chapter 11) of the supposition that addition of a new, very strong response to a set of relatively weak, conflicting responses would reduce the degree of conflict to a negligible quantity. But the very strong response would be adding to ΣE while it is diminishing H (by diminishing the p or relative strength of each of the other responses). There must be a point at which the suppression of the weaker responses is so complete that the strong swamping response can be made still stronger without increasing conflict. The reduction of response uncertainty to below a threshold value is what we mean when we speak of a conflict being *resolved*.

This assumption may seem, at first glance, to disaccord with everyday experience. There are times, it may be objected, when a person unvaryingly responds to a recurring situation with the same reaction (i.e., there is practically no uncertainty about his behavior) and yet suffers acute psychological distress, because there are factors present that cause him to perform that reaction with reluctance or that work in favor of alternative responses, even though these never attain fulfillment. These are likely, however, to be cases where the performance of the predominant reaction and the suppression of its possible competitors entail frustration or fear (see N. E. Miller 1944), whose effects must be differentiated from those of conflict pure and simple.

In the expression for C or degree of conflict that we have arrived at, the first term, ΣE, may be thought of as representing the "scale" of the conflict or the "importance" of the competing responses, while the second term, H, represents the uncertainty of the outcome.

The information-theory measure of uncertainty is a generalization of the notion of entropy, as used in statistical mechanics, a quantity which reflects the randomness of a system or the "imprecision of our knowledge about it" (Kittel 1958). Entropy may be regarded as a measure of how evenly the total energy in the system is distributed. Moreover, all other things being equal, the greater the entropy, the smaller the proportion of the energy in the system that is available to produce work.

So one might, whether as a suggestive analogy or as an assertion of a deeper correspondence, think of our ΣE as a representation of the total amount of energy invested in the competing response tendencies and of H as an index of how evenly this energy is distributed among them. One might, further, think of H, the uncertainty, as an index of the extent to which energy is drawn on by the competing response tendencies in the course of counteracting one another and thus rendered unavailable for behavior acting on the outside world.

There is, however, a striking contrast between the roles of entropy in physics and in psychology. In physical processes, there is a progression from less to more entropy. When entropy has reached its maximum, a system reaches equilibrium, and the process ceases.

As far as behavior is concerned, states of high entropy, uncertainty, and conflict are states of disequilibrium. The manifold influences that play on organisms from outside and inside would, no doubt, soon lead to a degradation of behavior paralleling the degradation of energy that follows from the principle of increasing entropy, were it not for special mechanisms that come into play when this biologically perilous development threatens. Maturation and learning lead away from the uncoordinated squirming of the newborn infant or the perplexed groping of an animal in an unfamiliar environment toward increasing uniformity and predictability of behavior (see Miller and Frick 1949). The processes of stimulus selection are likewise essential bulwarks against the menace of excessive entropy, although, as we shall see, they often work by allowing entropy to enter in manageable doses.

We may see this, if we so choose, as yet another instance of the ability of living creatures to form islands of temporary and local resistance in the tide of mounting entropy which, we are told, is carrying the universe to a "heat death." This is a theme on which many writers, from Helmholtz (1869) on, have expended eloquence. Schrödinger (1945) describes how organisms keep down or even decrease their own entropy by absorbing negative entropy from surrounding objects in the form of foodstuffs, oxygen, and heat. Wiener (1950) has dwelt on the intake of negative entropy in the form of information, the opposite of uncertainty. Animals are thus equipped to preserve their intricate organization for a while and postpone the time when they, like everything else, must succumb to disintegration.

Complexity is, without any doubt, the most impalpable of the four elusive concepts that we are attempting to delimit. One might say roughly that it refers to the amount of variety or diversity in a stimulus pattern.

It is, however, possible to enumerate some of the most obvious properties on which the complexity ascribed to a pattern will depend. Figure 2-1 will serve to illustrate.

1. Other things being equal, *complexity increases with the number of distinguishable elements.* Thus, Fig. 2-1*b* would be regarded as more complex than Fig. 2-1*a*.

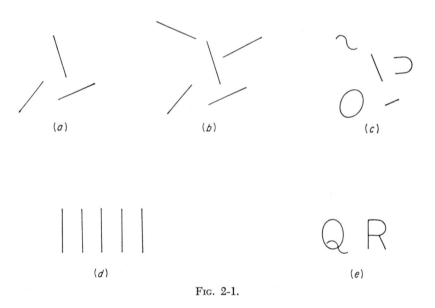

(*a*)　　　　　　　(*b*)　　　　　　　(*c*)

(*d*)　　　　　　　　　　　　(*e*)

Fig. 2-1.

2. If the number of elements is held constant, *complexity increases with dissimilarity between elements.* Thus Fig. 2-1*c* would be regarded as more complex that Fig. 2-1*b*. Complexity can be cut down by having identical elements in different locations (e.g., cyclic repetition or translational symmetry), by having elements that are identical except for orientation (e.g., reflexive—mirror-image—symmetry, rotational symmetry, and radial symmetry), or by having elements that have one property in common while differing in other respects. Conversely, complexity may be lessened by giving elements a similar

orientation (e.g., figures with regular or geometrical arrangement—cf. Fig. 2-1d).

3. *Complexity varies inversely with the degree to which several elements are responded to as a unit.* Thus Fig. 2-1e is less complex than Fig. 2-1c. A combination of elements may evoke a joint response either as a releaser for an item of innate behavior or as a configuration to which a learned response has become attached through patterning.

Spatial arrangement, especially proximity, is likely to determine whether elements will be treated as a unit or not. It might even be suggested that similarity between parts reduces complexity because similar elements tend to be grouped and thus to evoke a joint reaction, as was indicated by Wertheimer (1923). At any rate, we can see that complexity depends on the number of psychological parts rather than the number of physical parts. It depends partly on physical properties that will be the same for all normal subjects and partly on habit structures that will vary from subject to subject. A pattern may thus have different degrees of complexity for different individuals, but there will be some correlation between them.

Nevertheless, we cannot afford to snub complexity merely because of difficulty in establishing its exact identity. A variable more or less coincident with its opposite, namely, "goodness" of configuration, has been amply demonstrated by the Gestalt school to be an important property of perceptual figures. How "good" a figure is depends, they claim, on how effectively a perceptual organization that preserves it as a unit will fend off competing organizations, how unlikely the figure is to be misperceived in conditions of poor visibility, and how far attempts to reproduce the figure from memory will be immune from distortion. Attneave (1955) has shown that more complex visual patterns are more difficult to reproduce from memory and to recognize among similar figures.

But the problem of measurement arises for complexity no less inexorably than for the other concepts that we have been attempting to analyze. The Gestalt school, while eager to emphasize that figures can have varying degrees of "goodness," refrained from defining it and contented themselves with noting its dependence on such properties as simplicity, closure, regularity, and symmetry (Wertheimer 1923, Koffka 1935). They provided criteria for selecting the "better" of two patterns that differ only slightly, but they never laid down rules that would enable one to compare any two patterns for "goodness," let alone to measure their exact degrees of "goodness."

The interesting problem of adequately defining the simplicity-complexity or goodness-of-configuration dimension has remained a refractory one, although the urgent need for its solution has been keenly felt and ingenuity has been lavished on it from time to time. Some of the most assiduous attempts to deal with it have come from writers who were interested mainly in aesthetics, and they will be considered in Chapter 9.

Attneave (1957) asked a large group of airmen to rate polygons for complexity and found their judgments to depend largely on the number of independent turns in the contour, the presence or absence of symmetry, and the mean difference between the angles of successive turns in the contour. We require, however, a technique for measuring complexity that cuts across boundaries between classes of stimulus material and even across sensory modalities. Moreover, Attneave was investigating what determines the usage of the word "complexity" in an unspecialized population, and the question of how closely related this is to variables of psychological significance must be raised.

Complexity and Uncertainty

The most promising of recent attempts to treat goodness of configuration and complexity quantitatively, and the ones that are most germane to our present inquiry, are those that draw on information theory (Hochberg and McAlister 1953, Attneave 1954). As we have seen, the information-theory measure of uncertainty is equivalent to the average amount of information that will be received from a source or to the amount of transmitted information that is required for complete communication (reduction of an observer's uncertainty to zero).

Now there are various reasons for associating more complex (less "good") figures with more uncertainty. For one thing, figures with more parts can assume a greater range of alternative forms, since the parts can vary independently. And if there is to be some symmetry or other similarity between parts, the number of degrees of freedom (and hence the range of alternative figures meeting the specifications) will be reduced.

Another way of stating much the same fact is to say that more complex figures, whether they owe their greater complexity to their number of component parts or to their diversity, will need more data to describe them adequately. For instance, to identify a member of a population of squares in a Cartesian plane, two diagonally opposite points (four coordinates) must be supplied. If a population consists of irregular quadrilaterals, four points (eight coordinates) must be specified. If it consists of irregular pentagons, the number of points required goes up to five (ten coordinates). So complexity can be related to the number of alternatives, which is one of the determinants of uncertainty.

But uncertainty is affected also by the distribution of probabilities among the alternatives. And this likewise can be related to complexity. One manifestation of the uniformity of nature is the tendency for like to be grouped together with like. A consequence of this tendency is the fact that, once part of a pattern has been identified, the other parts are more likely to have certain characteristics than others (and, as a result of the uneven probability distribution to which this gives rise, uncertainty will diminish from its initial value). In particular, the other parts will more often than not resemble the part already revealed. The more repetition there is among the parts already revealed, the greater the probability that the repetition will continue. And in a pattern which owes its low complexity to its homogeneity, uncertainty about the rest of the pattern will fade rapidly as one similar component after another comes into view. We might think of a series of dots arranged in a straight line; the progressive uncovering of one dot after another from left to right will soon inflate the confidence with which the arrangement of the remaining dots will be predicted. If, on the other hand, we had a highly complex pattern of dots, such as a shower of raindrops might produce, the progressive uncovering of one dot after another from left to right would leave uncertainty about the positions of the remaining dots as high as ever.

We have seen how complexity is lessened if elements can be grouped together to form a combination that evokes a joint response. Combinations with this property will naturally be ones whose components tend to occur together more often than by chance. There will thus be a great deal of redundancy among them; the perception of one or some of them will enable a subject to predict, with a high degree of confidence, that the others will be perceived also. This is, of course, another way in which uncertainty can be reduced.

Complexity and Conflict

Pursuing the same line of thought in a somewhat more speculative direction, we can glimpse possible linkages between complexity and degree of conflict. Tachistoscopic experiments show that, at least in some conditions, subjects first identify the general class to which a perceptual figure belongs and then gradually narrow down its specific nature and minor details (Vernon 1952, pages 20 to 26). In the earliest phases of this perceptual process, there "runs a note of vagueness and uncertainty," and, later, "there is a trial of a succession of forms in order to find the appropriate one." We may thus surmise

41

that the first second of exposure to a stimulus pattern is marked by conflict between a number of competing perceptual or identifying responses. It would seem plausible that simpler figures would entail less prolonged and less intense conflict, both because they would be identified more quickly and because, once the general class to which they belong has been selected, there would be (as we have seen) fewer alternative members of that class to be selected from in the next stage.

Other accounts of perception picture it as a scanning process, in which parts of a pattern are responded to in turn. This must obviously occur when we have a visual display occupying a large area, since receptors must then be brought into contact with one portion of the display after another. According to some theories, there may be scanning even when receptors are steadily focused on a stationary pattern, the brain registering information from different points of the pattern in succession. Whenever some parts of a pattern are identified earlier than others, we can expect some degree of redintegration with reference to the parts not yet identified. The redintegration may be evocative or predictive, and it may take the form of expectations, preparatory responses, or anticipatory responses, perhaps of the neural processes described hypothetically by Hebb (1949). In a simple figure, one redintegrative process will probably predominate, whereas a partial perception of a complex figure, which may be completed in any of a vast number of different ways, would generate quite a numerous array of competing redintegrations and thus a great deal of conflict. If the perception of one part arouses an expectation that the other parts will resemble it, then a highly complex figure, by disappointing this expectation, may provoke the conflict characteristic of incongruity.

Further possibilities of conflict, increasing with complexity, come from eye movements. The assumption that visual patterns with more distinct parts arouse more numerous visual adjustments is central to both Birkhoff's and Rashevsky's theories of aesthetic value (to be discussed in Chapter 9). Birkhoff makes much of the feeling of effort or tension which accompanies perception and seems to be commensurate with the complexity of the perceived pattern. He calls this feeling the "psychological counterpart of . . . complexity" and ascribes it to proprioceptive feedback from motor adjustments. We may conjecture that the discomfort that accompanies perceptual activity, especially when it is directed at complex forms, depends rather on conflict between the discrepant fixations or other adjustments that are demanded by the many features of a complex form.

Piaget's (1961) theory of perception reveals yet another way in which more complex figures may give rise to conflict which is absent when "good" configurations are contemplated. He has shown that the size of a visual stimulus element on which attention is focused tends to be overestimated. Successive parts of a complex figure will, according to the theory, receive fixations in a random order, but larger or more prominent parts can be expected to receive the lion's share of them. The result is that different parts appear to expand and shrink in turn as the gaze wanders over the figure. There will be a net illusion consequent on the uneven distribution of fixations, but this illusion, being at the mercy of chance factors, will vary in extent from moment to moment and from occasion to occasion. The complex figure thus has a succession of incompatible and, we may infer, conflict-arousing appearances. A "good" or less complex figure is free from this instability because its component parts, being similar, tend to attract fixation equally often and to give rise to distortions that compensate one another and cancel out. The net illusion is thus zero, and the figure produces the same stable, uniform, conflict-free perception whenever it is examined.

Finally, we must recognize that reactions to distinct parts of a pattern, whatever form they take, may, if sufficiently numerous, give rise to occlusion conflict through limitations of channel capacity. There may be nothing impossible about buying a hat and a pair of shoes simultaneously. But if a person has a limited income, purchases will become more and more incompatible with one another as his list of coveted possessions grows.

Complexity and Novelty

To complete the cycle, it is not hard to find connecting links between complexity and novelty. The simplicity-complexity dimension can be used for the description of temporal as well as spatial patterns, and a succession of events that contains an item with short-term novelty will have a greater degree of temporal complexity than one that is purely repetitious. Furthermore, a pattern with a high degree of synchronous complexity will probably have a high degree of relative novelty. This is especially true in a society as replete with geometrically designed artifacts as our own. But animal and vegetable forms and even, as Köhler (1921) explains, inanimate nature approximate the circle, the straight line, and other simple configurations more frequently than any particular irregular pattern.

Quite apart from their relative commonness, regular, homogeneous patterns may act as though they were familiar if only because they approximate the central tendencies of large classes of irregular patterns. If the rectangles that we encounter are just as likely to have their horizontal sides longer than their vertical sides as vice versa, and if the lengths of their sides are normally distributed, the square will be most representative of the population by the least-square-deviation criterion. In the same way, the most representative member of the class of closed curves will be the circle, with its equality of curvature at all points.

COLLATIVE VARIABLES

In what follows, we shall need some way of referring collectively to the variables that we have been discussing in the present chapter. For want of a more satisfactory term, we shall call them *collative variables* since, in order to evaluate them, it is necessary to examine the similarities and differences, compatibilities and incompatibilities between elements—between a present stimulus and stimuli that have been experienced previously (novelty and change), between one element of a pattern and other elements that accompany it (complexity), between simultaneously aroused responses (conflict), between stimuli and expectations (surprisingness), or between simultaneously aroused expectations (uncertainty).

Chapter 3

ATTENTION

The first notion that we must examine in our review of processes contributing to stimulus selection is *attention*. It is a notion that bulked large in the introspective psychology of fifty or more years ago, but it has been rather overlooked by recent psychologists, chiefly because it was traditionally discussed as an aspect of conscious experience. Nevertheless, the problems that lie behind it are ones that the study of behavior will have to face sooner or later.

The word "attention" has had more varied usages than, perhaps, any other in psychology. It has, however, commonly been thought of as something with both *intensive* and *selective* aspects. On the one hand, it has been used to refer to processes that determine an organism's degree of alertness or vigilance, i.e., how effectively behavior is being controlled by the stimulus field as a whole. On the other hand, it has been applied to the processes that determine which elements of the stimulus field will exert a dominating influence over behavior. These are logically two distinct functions, but it is widely felt that closely related processes must be responsible for both.

The two aspects of attention can be described quite easily in information-theory language. First, there is the problem of how much information is being transmitted from the environment or from internal sources of stimulation (e.g., thoughts) to behavior. For example, a sleeping person displays the same unvarying behavior through a wide range of environmental changes, whereas the behavior of a highly alert person reflects the most minute variations in what is going on around him or inside him. Secondly, there is the problem of which items of incoming information will occupy the organism's limited information-transmitting capacity.

As we know from experience, attention can solve this problem with differing degrees of concentration. At a noisy cocktail party, one can participate adequately in one conversation at a time and take no notice of sounds coming from round about. Alternatively, one can attempt to converse with one person and simultaneously listen to what the people behind are saying. This, however, will inevitably mean missing or misunderstanding parts of both conversations. To put it more generally and behavioristically, there are times when behavior depends closely on stimuli coming from one source and remains un-affected by stimuli coming simultaneously from other sources, and there are times when it is under the partial control of each of a number of stimulus sources acting at once.

This corresponds to a range of variation that is always open when the input end of a communication channel is taking in more in-formation than the channel can conduct: the channel can transmit all the information contained in some input signals and lose all the information contained in the remainder, or it can transmit part of the information in all the input signals, giving rise to errors of transmission.

THE RETICULAR AROUSAL SYSTEM

The portion of the nervous system that is now believed to have most to do with alertness or intensity of attention is the *reticular formation* or *reticular arousal system* (RAS), a column of nerve cells extending through the lower brain (Moruzzi and Magoun 1949, Brodal 1957, Rossi and Zanchetti 1957). It is called reticular because it consists of a network (Latin *reticulum,* little net) of short fibers and cell bodies with many synapses, rather than a bundle of distinct tracts.

It includes both ascending pathways, leading up to the cortex, and descending pathways, which influence motor functions. How far it should, in fact, be regarded as a unified system and how far as a collection of nuclei is a matter on which neurophysiologists are not yet in full agreement.

The RAS receives collateral fibers (see Fig. 3-1) from the various sensory tracts as they rise toward the cortex, and it sends offshoots all over the cortex in its turn. It forms, therefore, one route by which excitation can reach the cortex from stimulated receptors. But its function as part of a *diffuse projection system* differs sharply from that of the more direct route constituted by the *specific projection system.* The latter preserves information about the exact location and quality of the stimulus all the way from receptor to cortical projection area. The diffuse projection system, in contrast, seems to take ac-count mainly of the urgency of stimuli and to ignore their finely discriminable properties. Stimuli from all parts of the body's surface and all special sense organs seem to affect it in much the same way, and, when it is excited, it may send impulses to alert the whole cortex.

The upper or thalamic portion of the reticular formation, sometimes

46

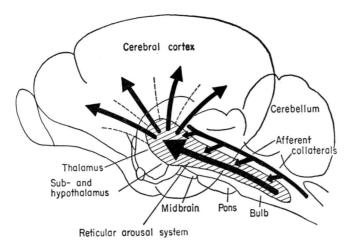

FIG. 3-1. Outline of a cat's brain, showing distribution of afferent collaterals to reticular arousal system. (From Starzl, Taylor, and Magoun 1951.)

called the *thalamic reticular system* or *nonspecific thalamic system,* has somewhat different properties from the lower or brain-stem (mesencephalic, pontine, and bulbar) portion. It is evidently more complicated both structurally and functionally. Different nuclei within it are connected with different parts of the cortex, and, unlike the brain-stem RAS, it can apparently alert broad areas of the cortex separately (Jasper 1954). In some conditions, stimulation of points within its boundaries can even have de-activating effects, so that some writers (e.g., Jasper 1954, Roitbak 1958) believe that it might inhibit some parts of the cortex while others are activated.

When the reticular formation is injured, somnolence or lethargy is apt to result. Its excitation, on the other hand, gives rise to the *activation pattern,* also known as the *arousal pattern* or as *desynchronization,* in the EEG: alpha waves—the regular, high-amplitude, medium-frequency oscillations (8 to 13 cps in human adults and many other mammals) that tend to dominate the EEG in waking but relaxed subjects—give way to fast, irregular, low-amplitude fluctuations. At the same time, the overt behavior characteristic of a wide-awake, alert animal appears.

When an animal is anesthetized or sleeping, the specific sensory pathways continue to transmit excitation to the cerebral cortex. But the animal does not react to external stimuli overtly, apparently because the cortex is not receiving its normal quota of excitation via the RAS. If a stimulus comes along that is capable of energizing the RAS—a stimulus that is unusually intense, like a loud noise of a

47

severe jolt, or one that has special significance, like the faint sound of crying that reaches a sleeping mother—the organism wakes up, and the stimulus begins to affect overt behavior.

Peripheral Effects

Excitation of the RAS has a multitude of peripheral effects, both motor and sensory. Stimulation of the thalamic reticular system produces an *arrest reaction,* the animal becoming immobile and irresponsive to external stimuli. Once an action has, however, been unleashed, stimulation of the RAS is likely to make it more vigorous.

Most of the brain-stem reticular formation contains points whose stimulation facilitates motor functions, but there is a motor-inhibitory area at its lower, or bulbar, end. These structures collaborate with the cortex and the cerebellum in the maintenance of general muscle tonus. They affect the tonic reflexes on which posture depends and the phasic reflexes that produce transitory bodily movements (Hugelin 1955b, Lindsley 1957a).

Stimulation of the RAS heightens the sensitivity of the eye, apparently as a result of photochemical changes instigated through fibers that carry impulses outward, counter to the mainstream of traffic, from the central nervous system to the retina (Granit 1955). It also seems, in the light of an experiment on monkeys performed by Fuster (1957), to make animals discriminate between objects with different qualities more reliably and faster, an effect which must depend on more central portions of the sensory apparatus.

The Arousal Dimension

In addition to the EEG changes that mark intense excitation of the RAS, referred to as the *arousal pattern,* psychologists (e.g., Duffy 1957, Malmo 1957) are beginning to recognize *degree of arousal* as a dimension or continuum, as one of the variables that would have to be assigned a value if the psychological condition of a human being or higher animal at any particular time were to be adequately described. It is a measure of how wide awake the organism is, of how ready it is to react. The lower pole of the continuum is represented by sleep or coma, while the upper pole would be reached in states of frantic excitement.

Emotional States

What are usually called emotional states are, it seems, states of high arousal (see Lindsley 1951). The visceral and somatic indications

48

of emotion appear when brain-stem structures adjacent to the RAS are directly stimulated. The EEG activation pattern is likely to occur in tracings taken from subjects who are momentarily apprehensive or suffer from chronic anxiety states.

It is highly significant that some dimension resembling degree of arousal is invariably recognized when attempts are made to classify emotional states. It figures in Wundt's (1896) classical tridimensional theory of feeling as the "excitement-quiescence" dimension and in Schlosberg's (1954) recent tridimensional theory of emotion as "level of activation." "Activity" is also one of the three factors defining the "semantic space" in which Osgood's "semantic-differential" technique for measuring affective aspects of meaning (Osgood, Suci, and Tannenbaum 1957) locates words, phrases, and other stimuli.

Autonomic and Humoral Activity

The RAS tends, moreover, to work in close conjunction with the sympathetic nervous system, so that indexes of EEG activation and vegetative changes indicative of sympathetic innervation commonly occur together. When various stimuli are applied to human subjects, the amplitude of the galvanic skin response (GSR), or rise in palmar conductance, is positively correlated with decrease in alpha waves and increase in faster EEG activity (Darrow, Jost, Solomon, and Mergener 1942). When subjects are engaged in solving multiplication problems, EEG frequency is positively correlated with heart rate (Hadley 1941).

Bonvallet, Dell, and Hiebel (1954) have demonstrated that EEG activation patterns coincide with rises of arterial blood pressure in cats and dogs under flaxedil (a drug inducing motor paralysis). Both phenomena occur simultaneously in the course of spontaneous fluctuations (being accompanied by pupillary dilatation) and also in response to nociceptive stimulation (of the sciatic nerve), stimulation of the splanchnic nerve, or an injection of adrenaline.

The active RAS appears also to inhibit the parasympathetic system. Arousing stimuli will provoke pupillary dilatation, even when the sympathetic nerve supply to the iris is cut off (Shakhnovich 1958).

It appears, in fact, that the activity of the RAS can be intensified by the direct action of substances circulating in the blood, as well as by nerve impulses reaching it from sensory pathways or from the cortex (see Chapter 7). The power of adrenaline alone to stimulate the RAS is proved by experiments in which the brain stem is transected at various levels (Bonvallet, Dell, and Hiebel 1954, Dell, Bonvallet, and Hugelin 1954).

Arousal, Vigilance, and Efficiency

It will be appreciated that the relation between arousal and vigilance can hardly be a simple one. The maximum of vigilance is likely to coincide with moderate arousal, as behavior is not likely to be maximally responsive to subtle differences between stimuli in states of either extreme excitement or somnolence. In information-theory language, transmission of information from the environment through behavior will be greatest with a moderately high degree of arousal.

An inverted U-shaped relation between arousal (as the independent variable) and some measure of efficiency (as the dependent variable) has been established in several situations (Freeman 1948, Duffy 1957). For example, higher scores on an auditory tracking task appear when subjects are moderately well motivated than when they believe they are merely helping to calibrate the apparatus or when they are over-motivated with promises of high remuneration coupled with threats of electric shock for failure (Stennett 1957*b*). The motivating conditions that make for the best performance are likewise marked by an intermediate rise in muscular tension and an intermediate intensity of palmar conductance. When a single subject is repeatedly tested, his quickest reactions are found to coincide with medium GSRs (Freeman 1940).

Cortical Activation

Alpha waves are normally present in the EEG records taken from subjects who are awake without being engaged in any particular activity, and alpha blocking is thus a convenient and clear sign of heightened arousal. Alpha activity and arousal are, however, not inversely proportional to each other. It is true that alpha waves are replaced by faster and more irregular waves when arousal becomes unusually intense. But they also disappear, making way for slower oscillations, when a subject becomes drowsy and falls asleep. The curvilinear relation between alpha activity and arousal is neatly confirmed in an experiment by Stennett (1957*a*). He put human subjects through a variety of situations designed to produce a variety of levels of arousal, ranging from resting to performing an auditory tracking task with monetary rewards and electric shocks depending on the score achieved. EEG tracings were taken, as well as recordings of palmar conductance. Maximum alpha-wave intensity appeared when conductance was at an intermediate level.

Both Eastern and Western neurophysiologists (see Buser and Roger

1957, Fessard and Gastaut 1958) are beginning to identify the highly activated state of the cerebral cortex (produced by impulses from the RAS and indicated by fast, irregular EEG waves) with the "excitatory" state that figures in Pavlov's theory, and the state of low activation (indicated by slow EEG waves) with Pavlov's "inhibitory" state. Non-Russian physiologists and psychologists were inclined for a long time to view these Pavlovian concepts askance. Konorski (1948) criticized Pavlov's failure to distinguish between excitation and positive excitability or between inhibition and negative excitability. Neurons are known to be capable of exciting and inhibiting one another through synapses, but these are localized processes, whereas Pavlov's excitatory and inhibitory states could spread over the whole cortex or major portions of it.

Recent discoveries have made the notions of widespread modifications in excitability more acceptable, although Pavlov's formulations require considerable reinterpretation and modification. States of high and low activation can certainly occupy the cortex as a whole (presumably if the brain-stem RAS is operating) or particular areas (presumably under the influence of the thalamic reticular system), and they appear to coincide with states of high and low excitability respectively.

EEG waves are now generally believed to be connected not so much with the familiar nerve impulse or "spike" as with the relatively slow electrochemical changes that have been shown to occur in dendrites and to affect the ease with which a neuron can be made to fire (Clare and Bishop 1955, Li, Cullen, and Jasper 1956).

Kennedy (1959) has suggested that EEG patterns may be at least partially due to mechanical vibrations of the brain, which could be altered by expansion and contraction of blood vessels. In case this suggestion turns out to be substantiated, we may note that changes in the blood supply to the brain may well be associated with changes in excitability.

THE DIRECTION OF ATTENTION

We shall find ourselves continually coming back to discussion of arousal in later chapters. Meanwhile, we must turn to the directing or selective aspect of attention, in view of its unmistakable relevance to stimulus selection.

There are actually three separate problems that can be regarded as problems of attention as a process of selection:

1. When an organism is receiving a number of stimuli associated

with incompatible responses, which will be the stimulus whose response is performed? We shall call this the problem of *attention in performance*.

2. When an organism is receiving a number of stimuli while performing a response in reinforcing conditions, i.e., conditions conducive to learning, which stimuli will become most strongly associated with the response? We shall call this the problem of *attention in learning*.

3. When a human being is receiving a number of stimuli, which stimuli will he be able to remember on future occasions? We shall call this the problem of *attention in remembering*.

It has often been assumed, if only tacitly, that the three problems are all one, so that the same principles will determine which stimuli shall predominate in performance, learning, and remembering. This assumption is plausible, but it does not necessarily have to be correct. It requires empirical evidence to establish it, and the necessary empirical evidence has certainly not been methodically gathered. We shall therefore take up the three problems in turn and review what experimental data we have that bear on them.

ATTENTION IN PERFORMANCE

Selective attention has traditionally been regarded as a phenomenon with two parts to it: the intensification of the process on which attention is being concentrated, and the holding in check of other, distracting processes. But whether there is intensification or inhibition depends on what is being compared with what. The process at the focus of attention seems to be intensified by comparison with those that are peripheral or by comparison with the same process before attention was drawn to it.

But we are interested mainly in the comparison between a process occurring in virtual isolation and the same process when it is competing with others. From this point of view, the most manifest effect is the weakening of the responses associated with the stimuli that are not receiving attention. One has only to think of a child engrossed in a game. He usually reacts with alacrity when his name is called, but now he gives no sign of hearing the name at all.

As for the stimulus on which attention is concentrated, we badly need more investigation of how it is affected by the competition that it overcomes. As far as we can see, its response is sometimes strengthened through an effort to overcome distraction, sometimes weakened by distraction, and sometimes left much as it would be without competition.

Subcortical Mechanisms. A number of recent neurophysiological experiments seem to throw valuable light on the inhibitory facet of attention. They demonstrate the existence of efferent fibers that can convey inhibitory influences from the central nervous system to the sense organs and sensory nerve centers. When the central nervous system is strongly alerted by a stimulus from one sensory mode, it can use these fibers to block the transmission of other sensory processes, so that the organism can devote itself more fully to events of overriding significance.

Such inhibitory fibers were found by Galambos (1956) in the auditory nerve of the cat. Their artificial excitation depressed the electrical activity that auditory stimuli produce in the cochlear nucleus, the first substation on the way from the ear to the cortex. Other experiments have implicated the RAS. It has been reported (Hernández-Peón, Guzmán-Flores, Álvarez, and Fernández-Guardiola 1956, Hernández-Peón, Scherrer, and Jouvet 1956, Hernández-Peón 1957) that stimulation of points in the reticular formation of the cat will block activity in sensory pathways whose receptors are simultaneously stimulated. Vision, learning, smell, and cutaneous sensitivity have all been shown to be susceptible to this effect, which can occur relatively early in the afferent process. In the case of vision, for example, it appears to intervene at the retina. Moreover, it can be produced by the sight of mice in a bottle, the smell of fish, or an electric shock to the paw, stimuli that we can assume to be highly arousing for the cat.

Desmedt and Mechelse (1958) have, however, succeeded in weakening cochlear-nucleus potentials in the cat by stimulating points in the brain stem outside the RAS. Desmedt (personal communication) suggests that this extrareticular path may be the sole route through which the cortex exercises control over what reaches it from the ear. The RAS may, he points out, occasion sensory blocking indirectly; when it is strongly activated, the RAS may act on the cortical end station of the extrareticular sensory-inhibitory pathway.

That sensory inhibition can occur at the behest of the cortex is confirmed in an experiment by Jouvet, Benoît, and Courjon (1956), in which depression of potentials in the medial geniculate nucleus (an auditory relay station) resulted from stimulation of points in the auditory, somaesthetic, and motor areas of the cortex. Desmedt and Mechelse (1959) have traced the extrareticular audio-inhibitory pathway back to a cortical area that borders on the auditory projection areas. It is an area that looks as if it might be an auditory association area, since its removal impairs ability to recognize patterns of sounds.

Hugelin (personal communication) has found that the auditory blocking that results from stimulation of certain points in the RAS depends on the *tensor tympani* and *stapedius* muscles of the middle ear. The effect is absent when these muscles are removed or when curare (which produces muscular paralysis) is injected. In these cases, it is thus a matter of orienting responses (see Chapter 4). On the other hand, Jouvet and Desmedt (1956) discovered points whose stimulation would continue to weaken cochlear-nucleus potentials resulting from clicks, even in animals that were curarized. So it seems that blocking can occur at the cochlear nucleus itself. Similarly, the anatomical studies of Shkol'nik-Iarros (1958) indicate that there are pathways proceeding directly from the visual cortex to the retinae, where they could presumably bring modulating influences to bear on visual excitation. It is, in fact, likely that sensory inhibition can be affected by centrifugal fibers at various levels of the nervous system.

Most of the experiments that demonstrate the obstruction of sensory processes below the cortex have, as we have seen, used cats as subjects. There is, however, a parallel experiment with human subjects by Jouvet (1957). Electrodes were introduced into the subcortical structures that connect with cortical sensory-projection areas, and the subjects' eyes were exposed to light flashing once a second. When the subjects were resting in silence, the subcortical electrodes exhibited a clear-cut response, consisting of a sharp positive deflection followed by a negative deflection, at the time of each flash. This response was intensified when the subjects were asked to count the flashes. When, however, their attention was called upon by stimuli of other modalities —a painful prick in the thigh, a question from the experimenter, an odor, a request to identify an object placed in the hand—the potentials corresponding to the flashes of light were attenuated or abolished. More recently (Jouvet and Lapras 1959), Jouvet has shown that asking the subject a question will, in the same way, diminish potentials in the thalamus corresponding to tactual stimulation of the face.

Before leaving subcortical mechanisms, we must recall the contribution that the thalamic reticular system may make to the selective activation of cortical areas.

Cortical Mechanisms. All these findings demonstrate that messages coming from stimuli that are not at the focus of attention can be blocked off before they reach the cortex. It will be noted, however, that they all illustrate selection between messages belonging to different modalities. There must surely be additional mechanisms for suppressing sensory processes after they have reached the cortex. These cortical mechanisms would account for selective attention when it depends on fine distinctions between stimuli belonging to the same modality and when the messages that oust others do not have such an overriding title to privileged treatment.

Sherrington (1906) used the term "induction" for the process whereby the performance of one reflex response promotes the performance of an allied reflex response and excludes that of an antagonistic reflex response. The concept was taken over and modified by Pavlov (1927), who applied it to the functioning of the cortex, and it played an ever more prominent role in his theorizing without ever having been fully assimilated by Western learning theory.

It originated in experiments on the alternation of excitatory and inhibitory conditioned stimuli. If an excitatory stimulus was applied immediately after an inhibitory stimulus, the amount of saliva secreted was notably greater than that stimulus would usually produce. When, on the other hand, the inhibitory stimulus followed the excitatory stimulus, the inhibitory effect was intensified. It became, for example, almost impossible to rid an inhibitory stimulus of its inhibitory properties, as long as it was presented in these conditions. These phenomena were called *positive* and *negative induction* respectively. Pavlov claimed them as evidence that excitation of one point of the cortex induced inhibition at neighboring points and vice versa. He later came to the conclusion that negative induction underlay *external inhibition*, the inhibition of a well-established conditioned response by any unusual, disturbing stimulus.

Milner (1957) has argued that something like negative induction must necessarily occur in the cortex. He reminds us that the axons of a typical cortical neuron have branches that make contact with several other neurons. Each of these neurons links up in its turn with several other neurons. The firing of one small group of neurons might therefore be expected to precipitate a chain reaction which would soon involve the whole cortex and make finely adjusted responses impossible. This can be avoided if the activation of one afferent neuron is accompanied by inhibition of others, so that the prepotent process can be safeguarded against interference. The weakening of the prepotent process through neural fatigue would diminish the inhibition of competing processes, which might account for the continual fluctuations to which attention is usually subject.

Rochester, Holland, Haibt, and Duda (1956) have been endeavoring to test Hebb's (1949) neurophysiological theory by programing a computer to simulate the formation of groupings of brain neurons. The results suggest that cell assemblies, whose existence could, as Hebb argued, explain many psychological phenomena, would not form

55

in the absence of inhibitory connections. It seemed, however, that they might come into existence and work in the way described by Hebb if Milner's hypotheses were realized.

In a similar vein, Beritov's (1956) theory of cortical functioning, inspired by neurophysiological findings from both Soviet and Western laboratories, contends that adaptation to environmental events requires excitation to predominate in some neuron chains, while other, especially neighboring, cortical areas are inhibited.

Both Milner and Beritov draw on facts about the histology of the cortex to describe in some detail how inhibition of potentially interfering processes might be effected. Their accounts do not agree, however, on which types of cortical neuron are inhibited by which. Nevertheless, their general idea receives some support from an investigation by Ricci, Doane, and Jasper (1957) in which microelectrodes were used to probe the activity of individual cortical neurons. This technique revealed that, when conditioned and unconditioned stimuli are applied, the general activation pattern recorded from the surface of the cortex is actually accompanied by firing in some neurons and a suspension of activity in others.

Phenomena reminiscent of negative induction, and similarly implying that a dominant cortical process can weaken other processes that are going on at the same time, are familiar in the field of perception. We have the phenomenon of *simultaneous contrast,* the apparent darkening of a gray surface on which a white object is placed. A strong contour, i.e., a line separating areas of sharply differing brightness, may make other contours and brightness differences in its immediate neighborhood invisible (Fry and Bartley 1935). We may also recall Rubin's (1915) demonstrations that part of a perceptual field usually forms a prominent figure while the rest becomes the much less vivid ground.

Experimental Design

The appropriate experiment for determining the laws that govern attention in performance is one in which we first make sure that a number of stimuli are associated with distinct but incompatible responses and then present all the stimuli together to ascertain which response occurs and thus which stimulus dominates behavior.

The preliminary stage might consist of presenting the separate stimuli in turn and verifying the occurrence, even perhaps measuring the strength, of the response corresponding to each. It might consist, instead, of subjecting the organism to a learning process, such that each of the stimuli becomes associated with a different new response. In the case of verbal instructions given to human beings, e.g., to press such and such a key on the appearance of a light with such and such

56

properties, we can safely assume that a strong association between each component stimulus and its corresponding response will be induced, without having to test in advance.

We then investigate the probability that each of the responses will be the first to occur when the stimuli are simultaneously active and competing, and we can also measure other variables indicative of response strength, such as latency and amplitude. The ideal is to be able to predict what will happen in a conflict situation from a knowledge of how strong the various alternative responses are when they are aroused alone. So far, none of the extant behavior theories or mathematical models for learning has been shown to do this successfully (Berlyne 1957b).

Some accounts of learning (e.g., Estes 1950, Bush and Mosteller 1955) are based on the notion that any response that is ever evoked must be competing with alternative responses. If the organism had not performed that response, it would have done something else instead. So any measure of response strength is a measure of how well the response is able to dominate other responses that are in competition with it. According to this view, situations in which only one response (e.g., bar pressing or salivation) is being studied, and the animal is either doing this or doing nothing in particular at any moment, do not differ radically from those in which an animal is clearly faced with a choice among responses, any of which he might perform (e.g., entering one of several maze alleys at a choice point).

If this kind of formulation is justified, we should expect that the factors determining response strength in general, such as number of reinforced trials or amount of reward per trial, will also influence the direction of attention in performance. But other determinants of attention, depending on properties of stimuli or relations between stimuli, can manifest themselves only when stimuli as well as responses are competing.

The kind of design that we have just discussed has not been used very often. Instead, it has frequently been assumed that whatever response has the greatest strength when the stimuli are presented separately will be the one most likely to prevail over others when the stimuli are all presented together. This sounds like a reasonable assumption, and there is at least one study that supports it. Honig (1958) trained pigeons to peck at a green (550 mμ) key on a variable-interval schedule, i.e., with the response occasionally resulting in the delivery of food. He then tested the birds when the key was illuminated with various other colors. It was found, in accord with the principle of stimulus generalization, that the new colors evoked lower rates of pecking than the original green color, the difference being greater the further removed from it they were. These generalization-test trials were interspersed with trials on which two keys of different colors were presented. The general finding was that a trial with paired stimuli produced about the same total response rate as the more effective member of the pair acting alone. But the responses were distributed between the two keys in proportion to the response rates they produced when presented singly. Discrimination training with single stimuli widened the difference between the response rates for positive and negative stimuli, and this enhanced difference was then reflected when the stimuli were presented in pairs.

That the factors determining which of several competing stimuli is most likely to capture attention should include the factors that determine how strongly a stimulus is responded to when acting alone is, however, by no means a logical necessity. We need many more experiments to tell us how far it happens to be so. In what follows, we shall review what data we have concerning the determinants of attention in performance. For many of the factors that are of most interest to us, such data are lacking, and so we shall have to use information about the effects these factors have on noncompetitive response strength as a source of hypotheses and of suggestive, but indirect and inconclusive, evidence on their role in attention.

Innate Factors. The ethologists have carried out many experiments to identify the precise properties that cause stimuli to evoke particular unlearned patterns of behavior. Usually they, like the psychologists, have compared the effects of stimuli presented in turn. But one ethological study which uses a stimulus-selection situation and demonstrates that the direction of attention can depend on the strength of an innate stimulus-response association is the study by Baerends (1955) of parental behavior in the herring gull. When a bird of this species is sitting on eggs in a nest, it will retrieve an egg that has fallen out by hooking the egg with the underside of its beak and rolling it back into the nest. Baerends, experimenting with models, was able to identify some specific stimulus properties that determine the strength of the egg-retrieving response. He did so by placing two models side by side on the rim of the nest while the bird was absent and observing which model it attempted to move first on its return. The probability that a model would be chosen turned out to increase with its size, the number of spots on it, the smallness of the spots, and the contrast in color between the spots and their background.

There have likewise been experiments on the pecking response of the chick. If chicks are confronted with two heaps of food, illuminated with light of different colors, they will be more likely to peck at the heap with the lighter or less saturated color (Hess and Gogel 1954).

These preferences cannot be a result of experience and learned association, since chicks peck at tan rather than green, whether they have
lived and been fed from birth in tan light or in green light. Similarly,
chicks tend to peck at the rounder and less angular of two objects that
are presented side by side (Fantz 1957). They will show this preference even during their first ten minutes of visual experience.

A large number of studies have shown that stimuli having the power
to release instinctive responses will dominate indifferent stimuli. Sometimes they will have priority only when the animal is in the motivational state necessary for the performance of the response. When the
male stickleback is sexually motivated, which can be seen from his
indulgence in nest building and from the bright red color of his underside, the sight of the characteristic swollen abdomen of an egg-bearing
female will take priority over other stimuli (Tinbergen 1951). When
birds are building nests, the sight of material that can be used in this
activity will outweigh other stimuli. Some stimuli, such as the sight
of a male intruder in a male animal's territory and the sight, sound,
or smell of a hereditary enemy, seem capable of ousting others from
attention at any time.

Turning to factors that perhaps affect learned as well as innate responses, we have to consider some that are well known for their power
to determine the strength of responses in general, as well as the collative variables discussed in Chapter 2.

Stimulus Intensity. Russian investigators (see Razran 1957) are continually insisting that more intense conditioned stimuli make for faster
and more effective conditioning. But their experiments have generally
used one intensity throughout the conditioning process. American psychologists have, on the other hand, been anxious to distinguish the
effect of stimulus intensity on learning from its effect on performance.
This requires a sophisticated experimental design in which groups of
subjects are first trained with different intensities and then tested with
the same intensity; significant contrasts between them must then be
attributed to differences in their experiences during training. The
usual finding has been that performance is better with more intense
test stimuli, but that the intensity used during training does not affect
the strength of the habit. Logan (1954) has suggested, with some
experimental evidence in support, that the influence of stimulus intensity on performance is a consequence of the greater distinctiveness
that results from the contrast between more intense stimuli and their
backgrounds.

These findings, as well as common experience, encourage the expectation that more intense stimuli will divert attention away from
others. An experiment verifying this was carried out by Berlyne

(1950*b*). The apparatus included a vertical board with a row of four square apertures. There were four telegraph keys corresponding to the four apertures, and subjects were required to press the corresponding key as soon as a circular spot of light appeared at one or another of them. If two apertures bore a spot of light at the same time, either of the appropriate keys was to be pressed. A series of single stimuli interspersed with pairs of stimuli was presented, and the pairs are, of course, critical for the study of attention. In one experiment, some of the pairs consisted of two spots of unequal intensities. In another experiment, some of the pairs consisted of spots of equal intensity but unequal size. The subjects made the response corresponding to the more intense stimulus on an average of 13.5 out of 16 trials, and the response corresponding to the larger stimulus on an average of 12.7 out of 16 trials. Size may be regarded as equivalent to intensity, if it is remembered that size determines the quantity of light falling on the retina.

Further confirmation of the role of intensity comes from a series of experiments on binocular rivalry by Breese (1899). He had his subjects look into a stereoscope which exposed the right eye to a red field bearing five black lines sloping diagonally from the upper left to the lower right corner and the left eye to a green field bearing black lines with the opposite slant. When the two fields were unequally lighted, the brighter one was seen about 60 per cent and the darker one about 40 per cent of the time.

Color. In an unpublished experiment, using the apparatus and procedure already mentioned, Berlyne found that a red or green spot of light was more frequently responded to than a white spot with which it was coupled, even though the colored filters let through less light than the white ones.

Sensory Mode. Anokhin (1949) developed a conditioning technique, called the *method of active choice*, that fits our paradigm for attention in performance quite well. A dog, strapped in a harness, is trained to take food from a container placed to one side of him on receiving a stimulus of one kind. He is then trained to take food from a container on the other side when he receives a stimulus of another kind. The two stimuli are then applied together to see which of the two containers the animal will then approach. Zachiniaeva (1950), using this method, associated approach to one side with an auditory stimulus and approach to the other side with a visual stimulus. When the stimuli were given simultaneously, the response to the auditory stimulus prevailed, even though this stimulus had been reinforced with bread and the visual stimulus with meat. Meat is strongly preferred to bread by dogs and consequently acts as a much more powerful reinforcing agent in general.

Affective Value. By the term "affective value" we mean association with rewarding or punishing situations. Some stimuli, e.g., food or pain, have an innate or primary reward (reinforcing) value or punishing (drive-arousing) value. These will usually be ones with a beneficial or noxious effect on the organism. Other stimuli, which are neutral or indifferent in themselves, will acquire affective value through frequent contiguity with primary rewards and punishments. They will be the ones to which contemporary behavior theory attributes secondary reinforcing properties or acquired reward value on the one hand and secondary drive-arousing properties or conditioned aversive properties on the other. Stimuli appear to acquire affective value through having affective reactions attached to them as classical or Pavlovian conditioned responses (Mowrer 1950, Skinner 1953). It looks, in fact, as if these affective reactions might involve the excitation of certain pleasure and fear centers in the lower parts of the brain (Olds and Milner 1954, N. E. Miller 1958).

An experiment by Schafer and Murphy (1943) illustrates the effect on attention of association with reward and punishment. It used figures like Fig. 3-2. It will be noted that either half of the circle can be seen as a face in profile. During a training phase of the experiment, the two halves were shown separately, each was given a name, and subjects were rewarded by receiving sums of money in the presence of the one profile and punished by having money withdrawn from them in the presence of the other. They were tested with tachistoscopic exposures of the whole circles, contain-

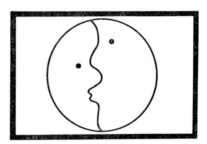

Fig. 3-2. (From Schafer and Murphy, 1943).

ing both profiles together, and instructed to name the face that they saw. There turned out to be a significant tendency for the face associated with reward to be reported more often than the other one. This experiment satisfies our requirements for the use of stimulus-selection language, since subjects were first acquainted with the competing stimuli separately—they were taught to apply a name to each stimulus —and subsequently tested with the stimuli in competition.

Any case of simultaneous discrimination, e.g., responses learned in the Lashley jumping stand or the discrimination box, might be cited as evidence that association with reward or punishment can determine to which stimulus an animal will respond. But in most of the relevant experiments, the stimuli are not first encountered separately, and so the appropriateness of stimulus-selection language is in doubt. An exception is Grice's (1948) experiment, in which animals were rewarded for approaching a white circle of a certain size. This treatment was found to increase the ease with which they would learn to approach that circle when it was paired with one of a different size.

The relation of punishment to attention is ambiguous. On the one hand, a tendency not to notice unpleasant or anxiety-producing facts about the environment has often been mentioned. It raises such subjects of hot dispute as the Freudian dynamisms, repression and denial, and recent experiments purporting to illustrate perceptual defense. On the other hand, wild animals will become instantly oblivious to the rest of the environment when a danger signal appears, and no pattern of behavior could be more essential biologically.

Smith and Hochberg (1954) did an experiment with Schafer and Murphy's two-profile figures in which they found that profiles whose presence in the training phase was accompanied by electric shock were less likely to be reported in the test phase. On the other hand, Cantril (1957) mentions a binocular-rivalry experiment, carried out by G. W. Allport, which points in the other direction. Zulus were exposed to a picture of a European and a picture of an Indian presented simultaneously to different eyes. The Indian was much more likely to be perceived, which is ascribed to the economic threat that South Africans of Indian extraction represent for Zulus.

We may speculate, pending the advent of adequate experimental data, that the influence of punishment on attention depends on how avoidable the punishment is. A warning signal may, innately or through learning, have a punishing or aversive quality. But if some timely reaction to it enables an organism to escape a severely punishing situation that would otherwise follow, we can understand why learning or the evolutionary process should make it preempt attention. If, on the other hand, the reaction it would evoke does not diminish impending danger and assuage fear but perhaps intensifies them, we can understand why response to another stimulus should receive preference.

The results of an experiment by Dulany (1957) are in line with these speculations. He prepared a number of cards, each of which bore a black circle, triangle, square, and diamond, with the relative positions of these figures varying from card to card. The cards were exposed tachistoscopically, and subjects were asked to indicate which of the four figures was most recognizable during a particular exposure by pressing a key corresponding to its position. Each subject had one or another of the figures as a "critical" figure and was allocated to a "defense" or "vigilance" group. The defense group received an electric shock to the leg whenever they pressed the key indicating the critical figure but not otherwise. The vigilance group were shocked if they indicated any figure but the critical figure. The outcome was that the frequency with which the critical figure was indicated as most recognizable diminished for the defense group and rose for the vigilance group. This diminished or heightened frequency, as the case may be, persisted when subjects were tested once again with electrodes removed and with an assurance that no more shocks would be forthcoming. Only two out of thirty-two subjects were able to state the principle that had determined the occurrence or nonoccurrence of shock.

This experiment thus shows how human beings will learn to ignore a stimulus whose response has meant inevitable punishment and to respond instead to other stimuli that are available. We require, however, additional experiments to tell us whether a stimulus that has often heralded painful experiences will be attended to in preference to neutral stimuli when the painful experiences can be averted by responding to it.

Motivational State. McDougall (1908) mentioned, as one of the signs that an instinct has been aroused, the tendency to perceive relevant objects more readily than others. When a strong drive activates an organism, we can expect a stimulus that facilitates the reduction of the drive to dominate behavior. The response associated with such a stimulus will presumably have been learned through the reinforcing effect of the drive reduction that it occasions. The internal stimuli stemming from the drive, coupled with the external stimulus, will then evoke that response intensely enough to make it dominate other responses that may also be aroused. Common experience confirms that the influence of the sight of food on the behavior of a hungry animal will outweigh that of most other stimuli. But systematic experimental studies of the phenomenon in situations of stimulus competition are lacking.

There are several experiments (see Allport 1955, Chapter 13) that show both affective value and motivational state to affect the way an ambiguous stimulus is perceived, i.e., which of a set of alternative responses to it will occur. But it has generally been a matter of competition between responses to one stimulus and not of competition between stimuli.

Indicating Stimuli. Attention can be directed by a type of conditioned stimulus that we may call the *indicating stimulus.* The sight of a pointing finger and an arrow painted on a wall are good examples.

Verbal formulas will do just as well, e.g., "Read out the first word on the second line!" or "Take the third turning to the left!" Alarm calls perform this function, apparently innately, in lower animals. They do not signify the direction in which the danger lies, but they cause other individuals of the species to cease whatever they are engaged in and to respond promptly to the danger signal as soon as they perceive it. Most, if not all, indicating stimuli that affect human beings must, however, owe their influence to learning.

In one of his experiments on binocular rivalry, Breese found that he could make either field dominate between 60 and 70 per cent of the time by instructing subjects to make an effort of will to hold it. Movements of the eyes directed to one point after another of the field in question seemed to contribute to the effect. Breese found himself unable to control dominance voluntarily once he had trained himself to refrain from eye movements, whereas telling subjects to move their gaze up and down the middle line of one particular field caused that field to be seen more often than the other.

An experiment by Broadbent (1952a) provides a striking illustration of our sensitivity to indicating stimuli when we cope with competing auditory stimuli. His subjects heard two recorded voices asking simultaneous questions about visual figures that were in sight. They had learned, during a preceding training period, to call one voice G.D.O. and the other Turret. One group was instructed to answer whichever voice prefaced its question with the call sign "S-1." They answered 48 per cent of the relevant questions correctly, 4 per cent of the relevant questions incorrectly, and 16 per cent of the irrelevant questions correctly. A second group was given an additional cue: during one experimental run they were instructed to answer voice G.D.O. only, and, during the second run, the experimenter pointed to the name of the voice to be answered on a visual display before each trial. This second group achieved a score of 70 per cent. Here we have three kinds of indicating stimuli, all of which caused subjects to respond to one set of stimuli and ignore the other. And we can see that the availability of two indicating stimuli improved their performance.

Novelty. In a series of experiments using the apparatus mentioned on page 60, Berlyne (1951) investigated the effect on attention in performance of stimuli that have recently undergone a change. In one experiment, there was a phase in which subjects had to make key-pressing responses to white circles, appearing singly or in pairs at any of the four apertures. In the second phase, white circles continued to appear at three of the apertures, but the fourth began to bear a white square. The trials of interest are, of course, those of the second phase in which a circular (or familiar) and a square (or novel) stimulus appeared simultaneously. There turned out to be a small but statistically significant tendency (13.9 responses out of 24) to respond to the novel stimulus. The same result (22.2 responses out of 32) was obtained in another experiment, which employed the same procedure except that the novel stimulus was a red circle and the familiar stimuli were white circles. It was also obtained (24.1 responses out of 32) in a third experiment, which used red circles as familiar stimuli and white circles as novel stimuli. Control subjects, for whom the first phase of the experiment was omitted, failed to show the phenomenon, and so it can be ascribed to the change that was effected between the first and the second phase for the experimental groups.

A fourth experiment studied the effect of a series of changes. The familiar stimuli were red circles, and after the first phase, one of these was changed successively to a white circle, a white square, a green circle, and a green square. A growing preference for responding to the changed stimulus was particularly marked in this experiment.

More recently (Berlyne 1957a), some of the outstanding questions about this phenomenon were answered by a further experiment. Whereas in the original study the novel stimulus always appeared at the same aperture, this new experiment was arranged so that novel or familiar stimuli could appear at any of the four positions. Nevertheless, the tendency to respond to the novel stimulus was still in evidence (27.0 responses out of 48), showing that processes occurring after the onset of the stimuli can determine the direction of attention. It was, moreover, found that the effect does not survive an interval of twenty-four hours between the two phases and that it does not occur unless subjects have to make the same response to the stimuli in the two phases.

A related phenomenon has been reported by Poulton (1956). His subjects had to listen for calls preceded by the name of a certain aerodrome control tower and to write down the airplane number that was mentioned in each call. Relevant calls might come over either of two loudspeakers, one of which was constantly busy with calls or conversations and the other of which was busy intermittently. Poulton reports that the second (usually idle) loudspeaker tended to capture attention whenever it was active. Fewer of the relevant numbers transmitted by it were misheard or omitted, and an irrelevant call emanating from this loudspeaker often caused the subjects to miss relevant information transmitted simultaneously by the busy loudspeaker.

The part played by novelty is, however, not a simple one. Engel (1956), in a binocular-rivalry experiment, found that upright faces were likely to predominate over upside-down faces that were presented to the other eye. Bagby (1957) also used the binocular-rivalry technique, pairing scenes from life in Mexico and life in the United States that were, as far as possible, corresponding in content but typical of their respective cultures, e.g., a baseball scene and a bull-fighting scene. The subjects were Mexicans and Americans matched for age, education, and social status, and each nationality tended predominantly to see whichever picture was representative of its own country.

These results seem to show familiar rather than novel stimulus patterns attracting attention. But, for one thing, we do not know how far affective value was the decisive factor in these cases. In any case, it may well be that stimuli to which strong, distinctive responses are attached draw attention away from unfamiliar stimuli with no special significance for behavior. Novelty may, on the other hand, tip the scales when a novel property is combined with other properties that are associated with a clear-cut response as in Berlyne's experiments. It is, of course, also possible that the laws governing dominance in binocular rivalry differ from those governing other forms of attention in performance.

Change. Breese, in one of his binocular-rivalry experiments, arranged for one of the monocular fields to be moved by a swinging pendulum and found that this increased the power of that field to dominate.

Complexity. In another experiment, Breese found that a green field with diagonal lines or some other figure on it would tend to dominate over a plain red field. When both fields bore differing patterns of lines, the one "which would be expected to induce the greatest amount of eye movement remained (longer) in consciousness."

ATTENTION IN LEARNING

The appropriate experimental procedure for the study of attention in learning is to have a number of stimuli simultaneously present when a response is performed and reinforced, and then to present the stimuli separately, noting how strongly associated with the response each has become. In this way, we ascertain what Hull (1943) called "the distribution of habit strength acquired by the several components of a stimulus compound."

According to some conceptions of learning (e.g., Spence 1936), all stimuli that have accompanied, or just preceded, the reinforced performance of a response should acquire increments of association with the response. But this assumption has been argued over at length, and at times acrimoniously, in the literature on discrimination learning in animals. Some writers have maintained that only those cues to which an animal is "attending" (Lashley 1942) or which are relevant to the

66

"hypothesis" that the animal is entertaining (Krechevsky 1932) during a trial will be involved in the learning process. Others have contended that the range of cues to which a response can become attached may shrink if an animal is strongly motivated, or if a habit based on a familiar cue has been overlearned (Bruner, Matter, and Papanek 1955).

It is obvious that the direction in which receptors are turned must limit the range of stimuli that can play a part in the learning process. It is also plausible that a discriminative habit may be easier to build up if the same cues have already figured in another discriminative habit (Lawrence 1950), since response-produced stimulation accompanying the cues may render them more distinct than they would otherwise have been. The bearing of stimulus-selection processes on discrimination is beginning to receive more consideration in current theoretical treatments, and with good reason.

Yet the facts and the most satisfactory concepts for analyzing them are by no means settled. In any case, discrimination-learning experiments do not, as a rule, follow the procedure we have mentioned as appropriate to attention in learning. To use an anthropomorphic description that can easily be translated into behaviorist language, it is hard to tell whether an animal has not noticed a cue or whether he has noticed it but confused it with its contrary. For this reason, the implications of these experiments for attention in learning are not too clear.

A few experiments have attacked the problem directly with reference to classical conditioning, using the following procedure. Two indifferent stimuli are presented simultaneously and closely followed by the appearance of food. The compound stimulus comes, as one would expect, to evoke conditioned salivation. The two components of the compound are then presented separately to ascertain the degree to which each has become associated with the response. Pavlov tells us that one of the components is generally found to elicit about as much salivation as the compound itself, while the other elicits little or none. One of the two stimuli "overshadows" the other, to use Pavlov's term, and assumes more or less the entire load of conditioning.

Determinants of Attention in Learning

Early experiments in Pavlov's laboratory (Pavlov 1927) showed that a tone produced by a tuning fork would overshadow the switching on of three electric lamps, and that contact with a cold object at zero degrees centigrade would overshadow tactual stimulation of the skin. Later it was established that the relative degree of association with the response depended not only on the modality of the components of the compound but also on their physical intensity. Kupalov

67

and Gantt (1928) found that a bright, 400-candlepower lamp or a cold (zero degree centigrade) stimulus would overshadow a faint sound, while, in experiments by Rikman (1928), a tactual stimulus was overshadowed by a loud tone but itself overshadowed a faint tone. Similarly, intensity determines how far each element in a compound becomes associated with the response when both are auditory. The sound of a whistle will overshadow the hum of a tuning fork, but if the compound consists of tones of different pitches but comparable intensity, the response will become conditioned to both of them about equally.

A cognate phenomenon has been observed in an instrumental-conditioning experiment by Vatsuro (1957). A dog was trained to run to a food trough in response to the combination of a bell and a light. The bell and the light were then presented separately, and the bell was able to elicit the response while the light had no effect. The dog was subsequently trained to perform the response to the light alone, but further applications of bell plus light caused the light to lose its association with the response.

Razran (1939b) did some similar experiments on salivary conditioning in human beings. His compound stimuli were patterns of red and green lights and occasionally other stimuli. When components were tested separately, the sum of their effects was generally either greater or less than the effect of the compound and not, as in the Russian experiments, about equal to it. But a large, bright component light elicited a stronger conditioned response than a small, dim one, thus confirming the importance of intensity.

There is thus some evidence that two of the factors known to influence attention in performance, namely, *sensory mode* and *stimulus intensity*, also influence attention in learning. The other factors have not been tested with the same procedure. We are therefore compelled to consider the influence of these factors on the strength of a learned response to a stimulus presented singly as a source of hints of what their role in attention in learning might be. That this is fraught with pitfalls is illustrated by the case of stimulus intensity. As we have seen, there is some evidence that intensity affects attention in learning. But in learning with single conditioned stimuli, it appears that intensity does not affect the ease with which a stimulus becomes associated with a response, although it affects the strength with which a response is performed.

The effect of the *novelty* of a stimulus on learning is a little equivocal. Gibson and Walk (1956) found it easier to build up a discriminative habit in rats when the shapes to be discriminated had, for some weeks before the training, been visible from the animals' home cages.

Forgus (1958) argues, however, that the benefits of prior exposure to cues may stem rather from the contrasts between the previous experience and the training experience. His rats had to learn to approach a triangle in preference to a circle as a means of reaching food and avoiding pain. Subjects whose home cages had contained a circle and a cornerless triangle for fifty-two days before the start of the training were appreciably superior to others that had been exposed to a circle and a complete triangle or to a circle and a triangle with broken sides. This result had been predicted from the assumption that attention would be drawn toward those features which distinguished the positive discriminative cue from the familiar figure that was most similar to it, i.e., toward its most novel features. In the case of the cornerless-triangle group, attention would thus be focused on the triangle's most distinctive and information-laden parts, namely its corners.

A number of East European studies suggest that stimuli which have lost their novelty have a reduced capacity to function as conditioned stimuli. Kostenetskaia (1949) presented indifferent stimuli without food during intervals between presentations of food. The indifferent stimuli acquired strong inhibitory properties in consequence. Konorski and Szwejkowska (1952) built up a conditioned alimentary response to one stimulus, S_1, and then interspersed appearances of another stimulus, S_2, amid presentations of S_1. Thereby S_2 turned into an inhibitory stimulus, and it was unusually hard to change into a positive conditioned stimulus when it later began to accompany food.

A more recent experiment by Sokolov and Paramanova (1956) is even more illuminating. They used Ivanov-Smolenski's verbal-reinforcement method. The subjects were human adolescents. The response was raising the hand, the unconditioned stimulus consisted of the words "Raise your hand!", and the conditioned stimulus was a sound. Most of the subjects for whom the conditioned and unconditioned stimuli were paired from the start learned readily to raise their hands on hearing the sound. But other subjects were exposed to the sound repeatedly before the conditioning trials began. In their case, the conditioning was slow, and with some of them it did not occur at all.

In all these investigations, stimuli of varying degrees of novelty were applied separately. What we need is a series of experiments in which more novel and less novel stimuli are combined during the acquisition of a learned response and then tested separately. We should then be able to see whether the less novel stimulus has become less firmly associated with the response. Hull (1943) suggests that this will be the case, pointing out that part of the stimulus situation in any learning process must include a number of ubiquitous background features, such as daylight. Such features must have figured in innumerable learning situations in the past and had many an accidental association with a response extinguished. These circumstances would tend, he says, largely to "blur out the capacity of such stimuli to be conditioned to any reaction in particular."

Kappauf and Schlosberg (1937) carried out an experiment in which they varied the interval between the onset of the conditioned stimulus (a buzzer) and the onset of the unconditioned stimulus (an electric shock lasting 1/3 second). Both stimuli terminated together. It was found that the longer the conditioned stimulus had been acting before the shock occurred, the less effectively it became conditioned to the gasping response originally elicited by the shock.

A comparison of this finding with those of Wickens, Gehman, and Sullivan (1959) shows up the dangers of concluding how strongly each of two stimuli will become associated with a response when they are presented simultaneously from a knowledge of the relative strengths of the associations they acquire when presented alone. Wickens's group applied the kind of design we have recognized as appropriate to problems of attention in learning to an experiment with human subjects. They first turned on conditioned stimulus $CS1$ (a light or a tone). After this stimulus had been on for a certain interval, which varied from 0 to 4,100 milliseconds for different groups of subjects, a second conditioned stimulus, $CS2$ (a tone or a light), began. The unconditioned stimulus, a shock to the hand, began 500 milliseconds after the start of $CS2$, and all three stimuli terminated together 100 milliseconds later. The response was the GSR.

The two conditioned stimuli were then presented singly without the unconditioned stimulus, in order to measure the GSR that each was able to evoke alone. The outcome was that the longer-acting stimulus, $CS1$, produced the more intense response when the $CS1$–$CS2$ interval was from 200 to 420 milliseconds and when it was 2,000 milliseconds. Otherwise, $CS2$ was more effective.

Particularly interesting, however, was the finding that, when the amplitude of the response was plotted against the length of the $CS1$–$CS2$ interval, the curves for the two conditioned stimuli were almost exact mirror images of each other. As the experimenters say, "It is as if a certain magnitude of response could be conditioned at any given time interval and . . . a certain amount of this response strength is controlled by one element of the complex, and control of the remainder is allotted to the other element." One is reminded of Pavlov's experiments with compound stimuli in which, as we have already mentioned, the sum of the amounts of saliva secreted in response to the two component stimuli presented separately was approximately equal to the amount secreted in response to the compound. One might also feel tempted to say that there is a limited quantity of attention in learning, so that the more attention one stimulus receives during the learning process, the less there is left for the other. This makes attention in learning seem similar in its properties to attention in performance and, as we shall see, to attention in remembering.

Experiments in which the duration of continuously acting stimuli is varied must, however, bring in special factors other than those that affect intermittent stimuli with differing degrees of novelty. There is, for example, the fall-off in the sensory-nerve discharge that is known to occur in the course of persistent stimulation.

One of Razran's experiments (1939b) showed more *complex* stimuli, i.e., alternate flashes of red and green lights, to acquire stronger conditioned salivary responses in human subjects than simpler stimuli, i.e., alternate flashes of two green lights. But the complexity of conditioned stimuli is yet another factor that requires investigation in experiments using stimulus compounds.

ATTENTION IN REMEMBERING

When a learned response consists of a symbolic representation of an event or object, we regard it as an instance of remembering. It has often been contended that much more of our past experience must have left traces in the nervous system, and thus be susceptible of recall, than the amount we can recollect at any moment would lead us to believe. The fact that apparently lost memories can be recovered in hypnotic trances or in psychoanalytic sessions, the fact that forgotten material is easier to relearn than material encountered for the first time, and the fact that interference from other processes can account for a great part of forgetting are cited as evidence.

Some have even spoken as if all our experience is retained in some form. But, since the central nervous system does not have enough capacity for all the information reaching sensory surfaces at one moment, it can hardly have enough to store the content of a whole lifetime.

Certainly, only some of the features of a complex stimulus situation will be recalled, and some features will be recalled more easily than others. The problem of attention in remembering is quite distinct from the problem of attention in learning. There it was a question of comparing the strengths of association of several stimuli with one response. Here there are several stimuli with a different symbolic response corresponding to each. There the stimulus used for the test was present during the learning. Here the stimulus that evokes the mnemonic response in which we are interested is not the stimulus that that response

71

represents but some other stimulus which identifies, or reminds the subject of, what is to be recalled.

The experimental procedure for attention in remembering involves exposing the subject to a number of stimuli simultaneously and then, after their removal, asking him to recall as many of them as he can. It has been used occasionally in the psychological laboratory, but it has perhaps played a more prominent role as a familiar party game than in a concerted attack on the variables affecting attention in remembering.

The exposure of a number of items in succession, followed by a request for recall of as many as possible, either in their original order or in any order, has been widely used. This is not quite the same as the procedure we have specified. For one thing, complicating influences on recall arise from temporal position and temporal order. But the two procedures are, admittedly, not so easy to differentiate sharply. Items that are experienced in succession are often stored for a few seconds or minutes in the immediate memory system. They then act as a collection of simultaneously available material so that they can be recalled in a different order (Broadbent 1958). On the other hand, the fixation of parts of a complex display in turn may well cause components of a simultaneous assembly of stimuli to be perceived one by one.

Another type of experiment on remembering that has compared ability to recall several simultaneously displayed aspects of a stimulus situation is concerned with *incidental learning*. Incidental learning is learning that is not demanded by previously received instructions, and the term has usually, though not invariably, been applied to remembering. Sometimes one group of subjects is instructed to memorize something, another group is exposed to the same material but is not so instructed, and the performances of the two groups on a recall test are compared. In other experiments, subjects are directed to memorize certain aspects of a display and then tested for their ability to remember other aspects of the display not mentioned in the instructions.

Experiments on incidental learning have generally aimed at measuring the amount of material incidentally learned or at discovering properties that differentiate incidental from intentional learning. The study of factors that determine what material will be most amenable to incidental learning has been somewhat neglected. The very use of the term and the comparatively meager investigation that has been directed to it illustrate the point that was made at the beginning of Chapter 1: the ease with which words can be used to cajole human beings into learning has deflected psychologists from the factors that make experiences "stick in the mind" in everyday life where instructions to remember are, more often than not, lacking and almost all remembering is, in the sense defined above, incidental learning.

It might be thought that the limitation to the amount of material that can be remembered stems from the limitations to the number of identifying responses that can be performed in a given interval of time. This seems particularly plausible when the identifying responses are subvocal verbal responses, since the vocal apparatus can hardly pronounce, even silently, two words at once. But it looks as if the limit is partly one of a number of *items* that can be memorized in a trial of fixed duration and partly one of the amount of *information* that can be absorbed (G. A. Miller 1956).

The quantity of information per item can be decreased, either by using sequences of items approximating those of ordinary conversational language, so that the nature of each provides some clue as to what the next one is likely to be (Miller and Selfridge 1950), or by restricting the range from which the subject knows the items to be chosen (Aborn and Rubinstein 1952). The number of items retained tend then to increase accordingly. If stimulus objects differ in several ways, e.g., in color and form, and if the experimenter's instructions lay stress on remembering one property accurately, the accuracy with which the other properties are recalled will diminish compensatorily (Bahrick 1954, Lawrence and La Berge 1956).

In some circumstances, however, especially when the amount of information per item is high, the limit is set by the number of items that can be recalled (G. A. Miller 1956).

Determinants of Attention in Remembering

Of possible determinants of attention in remembering, *intensity* does not appear to have been studied. Common experience and advertisers' practices suggest that inordinately large, bright, or loud stimuli will remain in the memory, but it is impossible to dissociate the effects of intensity from those of surprise without a carefully controlled experimental program.

Affective value has been studied but usually with items presented in succession. Much of the evidence is inconclusive, and many investigations have overlooked necessary controls, but the consensus is that affectively colored experiences are recalled more readily than neutral ones and pleasant more readily than unpleasant (McGeoch and Irion 1952).

Motivational states, and the enduring *motivational dispositions* that are often called "interests," have been extensively discussed as factors influencing what is remembered and in what form (e.g., Bartlett

1932). But their role in attention in remembering has had far from adequate examination.

It is a commonplace that a *verbal instruction* to memorize something, which can be regarded as a kind of conditioned stimulus, will promote the remembering of the material to which it refers. Postman, Adams, and Phillips (1955) have shown, for example, that subjects who are told to learn low-association nonsense syllables will recall more of them than incidental learners, who were exposed to the stimuli under a misapprehension that they were experimenters and not subjects. There are plenty of anecdotes scattered through elementary psychology textbooks to illustrate how human beings may sometimes fail completely to recall material to which they have been exposed countless times in the absence of a motive to learn or an expectation that their ability to recall it would be tested.

The potency of verbal instruction is impressively, but not surprisingly, demonstrated by Kreuger's (1932) experiment. He set his subjects to learn twelve pairs of unrelated nouns, testing retention after each learning trial by presenting the stimulus items in a different order. When no special instruction was given, the first three and the last three pairs were learned most quickly, in accordance with the well-known and well-established *serial-position effect*. This effect was, however, overcome when subjects were told to learn the middle six pairs first, since these were then mastered earlier than the others. The serial-position effect could, on the other hand, be intensified by instructing the subjects to begin by concentrating on the first and last three pairs.

One of the classical experiments that is almost always mentioned in any discussion of the direction of attention is the one by Külpe (1904). Visual displays containing nonsense syllables were exposed briefly. Different groups of subjects were directed in advance of the exposure to pay attention to identifying the syllables, to identifying their spatial arrangement, to identifying the colors in which the syllables were printed, and to counting the syllables, respectively. After seeing the display, all subjects were asked to record all four kinds of data, and, as one would expect, they were able to record the facts that they had been told to watch for much more accurately than the others. This experiment has often been criticized, and it certainly falls short of our modern ideas of satisfactory experimental design. In particular, it does not make clear how far the difference in ability to recall the four kinds of data was due to what was happening while the subjects were looking at the display and how far it was due to processes that occurred between seeing the display and writing down the answers to the questions (Lawrence and Coles 1954).

Nevertheless, similar experiments by Chapman (1932) and Brown

(1954) verified that subjects are capable of more accurate recall when they are told beforehand which parts or aspects of a visual display they will be required to remember than when they are told afterwards. The same conclusion is supported by studies with auditory material (Broadbent 1958).

A Russian experiment, which forms an interesting variant of Külpe's, suggests a close relation between attention in remembering and attention in performance. Leontiev and Rozanova (1951) did not instruct their subjects to remember anything in particular. Instead, they imposed tasks that required attention to certain aspects of a display but not to others. The material comprised an array of cards bearing words. The tasks were, for different groups of subjects, to remove cards indicated by the experimenter, to remove words beginning with the Cyrillic letter U, to state which initial letter was most frequent, and to collect cards bearing names of animals. Subjects were then questioned about the words on the cards, and the general finding was that they could recall facts to which they had had to attend in order to accomplish their tasks, but not to others; e.g., subjects who had had to remove cards bearing words beginning with U could recall the positions of these cards, but they could recall no other initial letters and could specify few of the words beginning with U.

The effect of *novelty* on attention in remembering is a complicated matter, because novel stimuli cannot have had so many opportunities to participate in learning processes as familiar stimuli. It is notorious that familiar, meaningful words or figures are easier to remember than others. Responses will adhere to them from past experiences with them, and the response-produced stimulation that results from these will make them more distinctive and thus less susceptible to interference. They may also have been able to build up, and become capable of arousing, unified neural processes such as Hebb (1949) describes.

Nevertheless, items that are *surprising* may well have an advantage in remembering. Wilcocks (1928) confirmed this in an experiment with successive presentation. A series of eighteen nonsense syllables was presented five times but in different orders. A new syllable was inserted into the series during its fifth presentation, and then the subjects were instructed to write down as many of the syllables as they could recall. In spite of its having appeared only once while the others had appeared five times, the new syllable was recalled more often than the others.

Oddity (the property of being in a minority) seems to affect the organism in a similar way. Wilcocks presented a visual display bearing a number of letters for fifteen seconds and then asked subjects to write down those they recalled. In one experiment, one letter was moving while the rest were stationary, and in another experiment the reverse was true. The letter that differed from the rest was recalled more effectively in both cases.

Essentially the same phenomenon is known as the von Restorff effect when it appears in serial learning. Von Restorff (1933) discovered that an item that differs strikingly from others in a series, e.g., a number in the midst of nonsense syllables or vice versa, will be recalled more frequently than one that resembles the majority of the series.

The von Restorff effect has been explained in various ways in accordance with various theoretical tastes. However, Green (1956, 1958a) has provided evidence that the crucial factors are novelty and surprise. Even in a list containing just as many syllables as numbers, a number will be recalled more readily if it comes unexpectedly after a series of syllables and vice versa. Isolating a syllable, by causing it to be followed as well as preceded by numbers, does not add to this effect. Green attempted to verify that surprise as well as novelty favored recall by repeating the procedure with other subjects who were informed beforehand about the structure of the lists. This diminished the effect slightly but not significantly. A later experiment (Green 1958b), in which surprisingness was neatly coupled with lack of novelty, was, however, successful. Subjects were set to learn a list of letters which were projected on a screen in different colors. The critical item was a yellow *H*. This was a surprising item for one group of subjects, since it was the second *H* to appear and no other letters had been repeated, while this was not so for another group. Significantly more members of the former group were able to recall the color of this critical letter, which was, of course, an instance of incidental learning.

The effectiveness of surprise is illustrated also in an experiment by Berlyne (1954c). Subjects read through a series of disconnected statements about invertebrate animals, including answers to questions that had previously been put to them. They were asked to indicate which statements they found surprising. When they were later asked the questions again, the surprising answers were remembered with greater frequency than the others.

Finally, we may refer to a result obtained by Leontiev and Rozanova. In one of the series of experiments mentioned above, a word-bearing card that had been present for several trials was replaced by another card which bore the same word surrounded by a black border. The word was thereupon recalled by most subjects, even though it did not figure in any of the tasks required of them and the word had never been recalled in earlier trials.

As for *conflict* of another kind, there is Lanier's (1941b) finding that words reported to have mixed affective value, i.e., to "arouse both pleasant and unpleasant feeling states," are more likely to be recognized as having been encountered during a previous experimental session than words classified simply as pleasant, unpleasant, or indifferent. Of the "mixed" words, those recognized had evoked larger GSRs than the others when they were first presented.

CONCLUSIONS

While our knowledge of the laws to which the various forms of attention are subject is glaringly deficient, the evidence we have to go on tends to favor the view that the determinants of attention in performance, attention in learning, and attention in remembering are similar. They seem to include many of the factors that affect response strength in general. Moreover, the collative variables that are a special concern of ours seem to play a part in all three. Nevertheless, we could do with more data regarding the role of certain variables, notably stimulus intensity, negative affective value, and familiarity.

We can thus provisionally assume that all three forms of selective attention depend on common processes, and we can henceforth speak of *selective attention* in general.

Chapter 4

EXPLORATORY BEHAVIOR:
I. ORIENTING RESPONSES

The processes that subserve selective attention, that hand over the reins to one or another of the stimuli that are competing for control over behavior, fall into two classes.

First, there are evidently central processes which influence the fate of sensory information after it has left the sense organs and while it is passing through the nervous system on its way to the effectors. As we saw in the last chapter, there are neurophysiological mechanisms that can obstruct some items of incoming information and smooth the way for others. Our ability to pick out one series of sounds from a hubbub must depend on central filtering, since we know of no way in which the ear could do the necessary sorting. And although attention is normally concentrated on the part of the visual field that is projected on the fovea, we can exceptionally attend to something that is seen peripherally (cf., Fraisse, Ehrlich, and Vurpillot 1956).

But there are other processes which intervene earlier and affect the nature of the stimulation reaching the sense organs. We shall conform to what is now a general practice and refer collectively to these responses that alter the stimulus field as *exploratory behavior*. Such a connotation differs from that of the word "explore" in ordinary English, but it is perhaps nearer to the original wide usage of the Latin word *explorare*.

Exploratory responses can help one stimulus to win the contest for attention by raising its intensity and weakening or eliminating its most formidable rivals. Thus the schoolteacher, when she asks the class to attend to what she is saying, is not content to rely on central filtering processes but expects her pupils to be seated in front of her with faces and eyes turned in her direction.

Nevertheless, exploratory behavior is by no means confined to the service of selective attention, all three forms of which—attention in performance, attention in learning, and attention in remembering—mean selection from elements that are actually present in the stimulus

78

field. Exploratory responses are subject to no such limitation. Their principal function is, in fact, to afford access to environmental information that was not previously available. They do so by intensifying or clarifying stimulation from objects that are already represented in the stimulus field, and thus reducing uncertainty about the properties of those objects, or else by bringing receptors into contact with new stimulus objects.

Either way, they widen the scope of stimulus selection enormously, since they enable stimuli that are not at present acting on receptors to be placed in command of behavior. They are required whenever conflict cannot be resolved by central filtering alone but only through changes in the stimulus field.

VARIETIES OF EXPLORATORY BEHAVIOR

Exploratory behavior can be divided into three categories according to the nature of the responses that comprise it. When exploratory responses consist of changes in posture, in the orientation of sense organs, or in the state of sense organs, we shall call them *orienting responses*. When they consist of locomotion, we shall refer to them as *locomotor exploration*. When they effect changes in external objects, by manipulating them or otherwise, we shall call them *investigatory responses*.

We shall find it convenient to divide up our material according to this classification, but the criteria on which the classification is based are, admittedly, superficial and somewhat arbitrary. Only future experimentation, on both behavioral and physiological levels, can tell us where the natural affinities and oppositions within exploratory behavior lie. Even from our present vantage point, however, it seems likely that certain distinctions which cut across our threefold classification and have been quite woefully overlooked in the extant literature on exploration will prove more substantive.

One of these is the distinction between *extrinsic* and *intrinsic* exploration. The stimuli to which a subject gains access through extrinsic exploration are sought only as cues for the guidance of some succeeding response with an independent source of biological value or reinforcement. The stimuli made available by intrinsic exploration are, in contrast, sufficient in themselves, regardless of their immediate practical value. Confusion between the two is a common basis for dramatic irony in literature. Othello's request to see Desdemona's handkerchief, for example, is made to look like an intrinsic investigatory response. It is, however, actually extrinsic investigation, since his purpose is to elicit from her a reaction, indicative of guilt or innocence, that will

79

determine his subsequent treatment of her. Extrinsic exploratory responses are often called *observing responses*, after Wyckoff (1952).

Next, there is the distinction between exploration that is aimed at stimuli coming from one particular source, providing information about one particular object or event, and exploration that has no such direction. The former, which we shall call *specific exploration*, is characteristic of a human being who sets out to find a piece of lost property or the solution to an intellectual problem. A person who seeks entertainment, relief from boredom, or new experiences will be satisfied with stimuli from any of a wide range of sources, provided only that their collative properties are just right. This we shall call *diversive exploration*.

Lastly, there may well be material differences between exploratory responses yielding further stimulation from stimulus objects that are already acting on receptors and exploratory responses that bring the subject into contact with objects that are not already represented in the stimulus field. We shall call these *inspective* and *inquisitive* (Latin *inquirere*, to seek) responses respectively. The distinction between them is the one that colloquial speech draws between looking *at* and looking *for* something.

We shall differentiate between exploratory responses and responses through which knowledge is acquired, although the two may often coincide. Discussion of the latter, which we shall call *epistemic responses*, will be left to Chapters 10 and 11.

THE ORIENTATION REACTION

In a celebrated and frequently quoted passage, Pavlov (1927) refers, with some enthusiasm, to what he called the "investigatory" (*issledovatel'ski*) or "what-is-it?" (*chto takoe?*) reflex. He writes:

> It is this reflex which brings about the immediate response in man and animals to the slightest changes in the world around them, so that they immediately orientate their appropriate receptor organ in accordance with the perceptible quality in the agent bringing about the change, making full investigation of it. The biological significance of this reflex is obvious. If the animal were not provided with such a reflex its life would hang at every moment by a thread. In man this reflex has been greatly developed with far-reaching results, being represented in its highest form by inquisitiveness—the parent of that scientific method through which we hope one day to come to a true orientation in knowledge of the world around us.

At other times, Pavlov used the terms "orientation" (*orientirovochny*) reflex and "adjusting" (*ustanovochny*) reflex for the same phenomenon, while his contemporary and compatriot, Bekhterev (1928), spoke of it as the "concentration reflex" (*refleks sosredotocheniia*). These various names have been used more or less interchangeably by Russian physiologists and psychologists, although they have recently been tending to reserve the term "investigatory" or the compound "orienting-investigatory" for the more elaborate and energetic forms of exploratory behavior that we have placed in the other categories.

Orienting behavior has been recognized by Russian experimenters as a worthwhile topic for research ever since Pavlov paid his respects to it. But advances in neurophysiological knowledge and recording techniques have caused the Pavlovian concept of an orientation reflex or orientation reaction to be modified and extended and given a new impetus to its investigation in Soviet laboratories. Among those, too numerous to mention, who have worked in this area, Sokolov (1954, 1957*b*, 1958) has concentrated on it most systematically and gone farthest toward a theoretical synthesis of his own and other men's findings.

The major conclusion yielded by these investigations is that outwardly visible orienting behavior—the postural changes and receptor adjustments that we have agreed to class as orienting responses—forms part of a whole constellation of physiological processes, permeating the entire organism, that can be elicited by the onset, termination, intensification, weakening, or modification in any other way of any kind of stimulation. The components of this many-sided orientation reaction, as revealed by the experiments of Sokolov and others (including American investigators, e.g., Robinson and Gantt 1947, Davis *et al.* 1955, Dykman *et al.* 1959), are as follows:

1. *Changes in Sense Organs*

   a. The pupil of the eye dilates.
   b. Photochemical changes, lowering the absolute threshold for intensity of light, occur in the retina.

2. *Changes in the Skeletal Muscles That Direct Sense Organs*

   a. The eyes open wide and turn toward a source of visual stimulation; this action is often accompanied by movements of the head, the trunk, and even the whole body.
   b. The head turns toward a source of sound.
   c. Animals prick up their ears.
   d. Sniffing occurs, especially in animals that use their olfactory sense much more than man.

3. *Changes in General Skeletal Musculature*

   a. Ongoing actions are temporarily arrested.
   b. General muscle tonus rises, increasing readiness for activity in the

skeletal muscles. Kvasov (1958) has called this phenomenon the "what's-to-be-done?" (*chto delat'?*) reflex by analogy with Pavlov's "what-is-it?" reflex.

c. There may be diffuse bodily movements and vocalization (reported in the dog by Robinson and Gantt 1947).

d. There is an increase in muscular electrical activity, detectable with the electromyograph (Davis *et al.* 1955).

4. *Changes in the Central Nervous System*

a. Alpha waves, when present, disappear and give place to faster, more irregular EEG activity.

b. When slower EEG waves, representative of drowsy and somnolent states, are present, they are replaced by alpha waves.

c. If, however, fast waves in the beta (14 to 30 cps) or gamma (over 30 cps) range are already present, the orientation reaction will not produce an EEG change.

5. *Vegetative Changes*

a. The blood vessels in the limbs contract, while those in the head expand.

b. The GSR (an increase in the electrical conductance of the palm and the sole) occurs.

c. There are cardiac and respiratory changes, whose exact nature varies. Petelina (1958) distinguishes a "compression" reaction, with breathing momentarily interrupted, or at least becoming slower and shallower, and with a reduction in the pulse rate, from a "stimulation" reaction, marked by deeper and quicker breathing and faster heartbeats. The compression reaction was evoked in dogs by the first presentations of a tone, while the stimulation reaction occurred in response to later presentations of the tone and to the first presentations of a flash of light. Vestibular sensations, produced by rotating the chamber in which the animals were placed, evoked the stimulation reaction when they began and the compression reaction when they ceased. American experimenters (e.g., Robinson and Gantt 1947, Dykman *et al.* 1959) have likewise found that, while a novel stimulus will generally provoke a change in heart rate, the direction of the change may vary from subject to subject or even from time to time in the same subject. Davis *et al.* (1955) report that, in human subjects, tones cause respiration to become greater in amplitude but lower in frequency and that the first few presentations of cutaneous stimuli are followed by a decrease in amplitude and an increase in frequency, whereas later presentations increase amplitude and decrease frequency.

Most of these changes are readily recognizable as phenomena associated either with excitation of the RAS or with excitation of the sympathetic nervous system. The close collaboration that evidently exists between these two systems has already been remarked on in the last chapter. Both Western (e.g., Buser and Roger 1957, Fessard and Gastaut 1958) and Russian writers have, accordingly, been quick to connect the new, broad conception of the orientation reaction with the activation or arousal pattern. Direct stimulation of either the reticular formation or the hypothalamus of the waking cat will, in fact, produce typical manifestations of the orientation reaction (Grastyán, Lissák, and Kékesi 1956).

FUNCTIONS OF THE ORIENTATION REACTION

Efferent Aspects

The functions of many of the elements of the orientation reaction are obvious when one realizes that the reaction is generally called forth by environmental events that may require prompt and energetic action. The skeletal musculature is mobilized for swift execution (3b, 3c, and 3d). Any activity that is already under way is stopped, so that it will not interfere with any measures of overriding priority that may be called for, and motor resources are held in check pending the receipt of enough information to select the most effective course of action (3a and perhaps the compression reaction discussed in 5c).

Afferent Aspects

The changes in the internal state of sense organs and in their orientation intensify the stimulus that provoked the orientation reaction. But it is important to note also that they provide access to new sources of stimulation for the same sensory mode and that they affect the reception of stimuli that concern other sensory modes. The turning of the head in the direction from which a sound is coming, for example, not only makes the source of sound equidistant from both ears, which is an optimal condition for hearing; it also enables the eyes to pick up visual stimuli from the same location. Furthermore, virtually every stimulus occasions a range of processes that sensitize the whole receptor equipment of the organism. Pupillary dilatation, for instance, is elicited not only by visual phenomena—reduction in illumination and change of color—but also by auditory, olfactory, gustatory, tactual, and electrocutaneous stimulation (Liberman 1958, Shakhnovich 1958). Similarly, acid on the tongue, the sound of a whistle, and the stroking of the skin with a hair all intensify the action currents that are normally detectable in the external eye muscles.

Sokolov thinks that some of the vegetative components of the orientation reaction are likewise connected with processes that enhance receptivity—that the respiratory changes facilitate olfaction and that the GSR has to do with changes that raise cutaneous sensitivity. Darrow (1936), however, saw the increase in perspiration that produces the GSR as a mechanism for enabling the palms and the soles to grip better.

Kvasov (1958) claims that every sensory mode has its "propriomuscular" apparatus, belonging to a muscular system that is distinct from the commonly recognized skeletal and visceral musculatures; the propriomuscles are controlled by their corresponding sensory areas in the cerebral cortex and not by the motor areas in the frontal lobe. Propriomuscles include, of course, the internal muscles of the eye that control the width of pupillary aperture and the shape of the lens, the external muscles that move the eyeball, the muscles that move the outer ear and those that alter the tension of the eardrum, the muscles in the nostrils and nasal passages, and the muscles that move the tongue. In addition to these more obvious instances of propriomusculature, there are the muscle spindles and the muscles at the roots of hairs, whose contractions, according to Kvasov, promote kinesthetic and cutaneous sensitivity, respectively.

Not all of these propriomuscular responses have been shown to participate in the generalized orientation reaction, evoked indiscriminately by all kinds of stimulus change. But it seems not unlikely that all do so.

Once a stimulus that is capable of provoking the orientation reaction has been delivered through one sense, it is manifestly important to have the organs of other senses sensitized, since an event that stimulates one receptor will usually emit supplementary information to which other receptors are responsive. There is no lack of evidence, especially in recent Russian work, that this reciprocal sensitization among different modes occurs (see Sokolov 1958). The absolute threshold for luminous intensity can be lowered by applying auditory, tactual, and other stimuli, while the auditory threshold falls in response to visual stimuli that evoke eye movements. These increases in sensitivity coincide with the manifestations of the orientation reaction.

There is, of course, a perplexity here that only future research can clear up. We have mentioned studies showing that the advent of a dominant stimulus can both raise and lower sensitivity to stimuli

84

arriving at other receptors. Moreover, direct stimulation of the RAS has been claimed to have both facilitatory and inhibitory effects on sensory channels, just as it can have both facilitatory and inhibitory motor effects. It is possible the intensity of the orientation reaction decides which direction the sensory effect will take. Sensory inhibition has been produced in cats by stimuli of special biological significance, such as the sight of a mouse or a painful prick (see Hernández-Peón, Scherrer, and Jouvet 1956), whereas Sokolov detected visual sensitization during the action of novel but biologically indifferent sounds. It is noteworthy that these sounds were most effective in increasing visual sensitivity when they had been repeated a few times, i.e., when their novelty had worn off a little. Likewise, Makarov (1952) found that painful electric shocks would lower visual sensitivity at first but raise it after a while.

Central Aspects

One of the most distinctive signs of the orientation reaction is simultaneous vasoconstriction in the extremities and vasodilatation in the head. Sokolov believes that this represents the diversion of blood from the periphery to the brain, which must be ready to analyze incoming information and organize emergency action.

Evidence that an enhancement of visual analyzing capacities coincides with alpha-wave blocking has come from East (Sokolov 1954, 1958) and West (D. B. Lindsley 1957b). It will be remembered that, in a waking subject, an increase in arousal means a change in the EEG pattern toward *less regularity* and *higher frequency*. Both of these may help.

Lindsley cites data from his own and other laboratories, seeming to indicate that the alpha wave mirrors a cycle of excitability, such that optimal response to a visual stimulus can occur only at the moment when the wave is in a certain phase. It looks, in fact, as if the transmission of impulses from the eye to their cortical destination is interrupted until this phase is reached. In a state of high arousal, the electrical activity of the cortex is irregular, which must mean that the cyclical changes of state in different cortical units are no longer synchronized. Different units will then reach their optimal phase at different times, so that any incoming volley of impulses from the optic nerve can, as soon as it arrives, find some unit somewhere that is able to process it immediately, and response to visual information will thus be expedited.

The increase in EEG frequency seems likewise to betoken an increase in what Sokolov calls the "lability" of the visual cortex, i.e., the speed with which neural units can recover from one burst of activity to undertake another. The cortex of the cat or the monkey will normally respond with two separate potentials to flashes of light 100 milliseconds apart, but with a single potential when the interval between the flashes is reduced to 50 milliseconds. If, however, the reticular formation has just been stimulated, two distinct responses will occur even with the shorter interval (D. B. Lindsley 1957*b*). Sokolov reports consonant observations with *photic driving*. This is the name given to a phenomenon which appears when the eyes are exposed to rhythmical flashes of light; at frequencies within a certain range, the EEG waves will come to coincide with the flashes. Sokolov's group used light flashing at 9, 18, and 27 cps. Normally, the most marked photic driving appeared at 9 cps, but conditions evoking a strong orientation reaction, e.g., the occurrence of a loud sound, caused the maximum to shift upwards to the higher frequencies. The increased lability that all these data demonstrate indicates an increase in visual resolving power—in the number of discrete visual stimuli that can be registered in a unit of time and thus in the rate with which information coming in through the optic inlet can be utilized.

DYNAMICS OF THE ORIENTATION REACTION

It is difficult to disentangle the roles of heredity and learning in the formation of the orientation reaction. Many of its components, especially the less overt ones, certainly appear to be innate. Generalized movements and inhibition of ongoing activities like sucking appear in human infants within the first hours after birth as responses to loud sounds (see Bronshtein, Itina, Kamenetskaia, and Sytova 1958). But their precise functional significance is obscure. The ability to follow an object accurately with the eyes takes some time to become established. This could very well be a matter of maturation. But the ability could conceivably be the product of learning, if maintaining the image of an object on the fovea acts as a reward. In adult human beings and other mammals, we can be sure that learning has the major say in determining what conditions will evoke the orientation reaction as well as what actions will follow its evocation.

What is most interesting about the orientation reaction, however, is the way in which, learned or unlearned, it conforms to many of the principles that have been found to govern learned responses in general. It contrasts with most innate behavior patterns, particularly in the ease with which its association with a stimulus can be switched on and off.

Extinction

The orientation reaction gradually disappears if the stimulus eliciting it is repeated at intervals of a few seconds or minutes. Further repetitions will produce a chronic extinction, the reaction extinguishing more and more quickly on succeeding days. Popov (1921) found that this chronic extinction was still in evidence after seventeen days, but Robinson and Gantt (1947) found some degree of recovery after two months. Continued repetition of a stimulus that has ceased to evoke an orientation reaction will bring about a more and more generalized inhibitory state, affecting quite different responses and eventually bringing on sleep (Chechulin 1923). The efficacy of continuing or rhythmically repeating stimuli as aids to the induction of a hypnotic trance is, no doubt, another aspect of this property. Pavlov (1927) used prolonged conditioned stimuli without reinforcement to provoke the various hypnotic phases in dogs.

Stimuli with Signal Value

The orientation reaction becomes especially resistant to extinction or, if it has already been extinguished, it revives when a stimulus is given *signal value*. One way to accomplish this is to apply the stimulus a few times shortly before a biologically important condition, such as pain or the presence of food. Another easier way that works well with human subjects is to impose, through verbal instruction, a task requiring them to note the presence of the stimulus and its properties. For example, subjects can be told to press a button whenever the stimulus is detectable or to rate the intensity of the stimulus on a five-point scale. Maruszewski (1957) restored extinguished GSRs and EEG activation patterns to sounds by telling subjects to count how often long and short sounds occurred or to raise one hand on hearing a short sound and the other hand on hearing a long sound. The orientation reaction will also return temporarily when stimuli become intense enough to cross the pain threshold.

In such circumstances, the orientation reaction is likely to persist for a long time, extinguishing only when the response required by an assigned task becomes entirely automatic. If a discrimination is imposed (so that stimuli of one kind are followed by a biologically important event but stimuli of a slightly different kind are not) or if the instructions require subjects to perform different responses according to the properties of the stimuli, the orientation reaction to both positive and negative stimuli will become extremely persistent and strong. The more difficult the discrimination, the more this will be so. Similarly, the orientation reaction will be singularly intense and last more or less indefinitely if a stimulus with signal value is hard to detect, e.g., because it is near the absolute threshold.

In view of these phenomena, it is worth noting the finding of Galambos, Sheatz, and Vernier (1956) that the electrical discharge in the cochlear nucleus that is provoked by a click becomes markedly more frequent, more intense, and more widespread when the click is paired with an electric shock. This is presumably due to facilitatory influence conveyed by special efferent fibers.

Experiments by Grastyán, Lissák, Madarász, and Dunhoffer (1959) with cats and by Polezhaev (1959b) with dogs seem to signify that there can also be qualitative differences between the orientation reactions evoked by signal and nonsignal stimuli. When an unfamiliar stimulus is first experienced, an animal is likely to stop whatever it is doing (cf. Pavlov's external inhibition and the arrest reaction associated with stimulation of the thalamic reticular system) and either to look up in no particular direction or to direct short, abrupt orienting movements of the head toward the source of stimulation. Breathing is momentarily interrupted or becomes slower. Polezhaev reports an increase in EEG amplitude during these phenomena (which he names the "reflex of biological caution"), but the Hungarian experimenters report desynchronization in both the hippocampus and the neocortex. When the formerly indifferent stimulus has been paired with food a few times, another pattern of behavior emerges. Prolonged systematic searching movements are directed toward the conditioned stimulus or, later, toward the place where food appears. Simultaneously, there is desynchronization in the neocortex, while slow waves are recorded from the hippocampus.

ADAPTIVE AND DEFENSIVE REACTIONS

The kinds of stimuli that evoke the orientation reaction are capable also of evoking other reactions, which, while they embody phenomena resembling those of the orientation reaction and interact with the latter in interesting ways, are sharply distinguishable from it. They fall into two categories, namely, *adaptive* (*adaptatsionny*) and *defensive* (*oboronitel'ny*) reactions (Sokolov 1957a, 1958).

1. Adaptive Reactions

Adaptive reactions act in the opposite direction to the orientation reaction, since they tend either to diminish the impact of a change in stimulation—to desensitize, in other words—or to restore excitation to some optimal level.

The most familiar examples are those which occur in the eye. A decrease in illumination causes pupillary dilatation, which raises the influx of light, and the photochemical retinal process of dark adaptation, which heightens retinal sensitivity; an increase in illumination reverses these changes by making the pupils contract and the retina undergo the threshold-raising process of light adaptation. The partial restoration of alpha-wave activity as light continues to stimulate the eye is, according to Sokolov, a more central visual adaptive response.

If hot or cold objects are applied to the skin or the temperature of the air rises or falls, adaptive responses take the form of a general dilatation of superficial blood vessels (facilitating the loss of heat) or their general constriction (facilitating the retention of heat), respectively.

One must delve a little deeper to detect auditory adaptive responses, but Hernández-Peón and Scherrer (1955) report a falling off of potentials recorded from the cochlear nucleus, the first substation reached by the auditory tract on its way to the brain, with successive presentations of a repetitive click. The potentials recover their strength after the clicks have been paired with electric shocks. The way in which cutaneous, gustatory, and olfactory sensations lose their intensity when prolonged or repeated suggests that the neural mechanisms of other senses may be subject to similar processes.

The general rule is that the orientation reaction marks the first onset of a stimulus and is later replaced by adaptive responses. This is, for instance, the case with thermal stimuli. A continuous hot or cold agent evokes orientation for a few seconds, but adaptive responses then appear, giving way to a brief recurrence of the orienting reaction when the agent ceases to act. If hot or cold agents are applied repetitively, later applications will come to evoke their adaptive responses immediately, without being preceded by orientation. The two kinds of reaction are easy to distinguish, since the vascular component of the orienting reaction involves vasodilatation in the head and vasoconstriction in the hand, whereas the plethysmograph registers similar changes in both areas—constriction in response to cold and dilatation in response to heat—during the adaptive phase.

The effects of visual stimulation are rather more complicated. In exceptional circumstances, a sudden increase in illumination may momentarily provoke the pupillary dilatation that is part of the generalized orientation reaction. Usually the influx of light produces, right from the start and simultaneously, peripheral adaptive responses (contraction of the pupil and light adaptation of the retina) and the central component of the orientation reaction (alpha blocking). The result is that the visual threshold is raised while light is actually stimulating the eye. The threshold is found to be lowered a few seconds after a brief flash has ceased, but if intense illumination is prolonged, alpha blocking and pupillary constriction gradually diminish, probably because the retina is becoming less responsive as light adaptation proceeds. On the other hand, a sudden plunge into darkness evokes peripheral adaptive responses (expansion of the pupil and retinal dark adaptation) and a brief central orienting reaction (alpha blocking) which work in the same direction, namely, toward heightened visual sensitivity. Subsequently, if darkness continues, alpha waves become intensified and general drowsiness may supervene.

Unlike the orientation reaction, adaptive responses are localized phenomena, being confined to those sense organs and parts of the central nervous system that are associated with the particular modality to which the stimulus belongs. They contrast with the orientation reaction further in taking different forms for stimuli of different qualities, in producing opposite effects when a stimulus starts and ends, in continuing throughout the action of a stimulus, and in failing to extinguish with repeated evocation. Adaptive responses can, however, be inhibited and replaced by the orientation reaction if an extraneous stimulus obtrudes itself or if the stimulus to which they are attached acquire signal value. (See Fig. 4-1).

2. Defensive Reactions

Defensive reactions resemble adaptive responses in that they act to counteract stimulation. Yet they share with the orientation reaction a generalized and pervasive character. The stimuli that evoke them are those with extremely high intensity or with a painful quality.

As Sokolov uses the term, "defensive reactions" include running away or withdrawing part of the body from a noxious agent, as well as aggressive movements aimed at its removal or destruction. But there are other, more immediate physiological processes that form the organism's first line of defense and bear the same relation to these more active measures as orienting responses bear to other varieties of exploratory behavior. There is, for example, the response of becoming immobile. There is blinking, which protects the eye from, say, a puff of air but also occurs in response to bright flashes of light, loud noises, or pain. Then there are gasps, constriction of blood vessels, and various humoral processes.

The clearest way to distinguish orientation changes from defensive reactions is, once again, to measure vascular changes in the head, since these take the form of dilation in the former case and constriction in the latter, whereas the blood vessels of the hand constrict

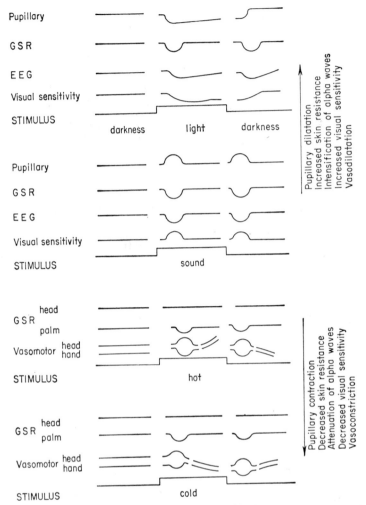

FIG. 4-1. Examples of orientation and adaptive reactions. (Adapted from Sokolov 1957a and Sokolov 1958.)

in both cases. Figure 4-2 shows the results of an experiment by Sokolov on the interaction between the two kinds of reaction with varying intensities of electrical stimulation to the skin. The intensity is measured in "conventional units," a measure which is directly proportional to voltage. It will be seen that the weakest stimuli of all evoke neither reaction; they are, in other words, subliminal. Then follows a range of intensities with more and more intense stimuli evoking the orientation reaction for more and more trials before extinction. Next comes a range of intensities which evoke the orientation

91

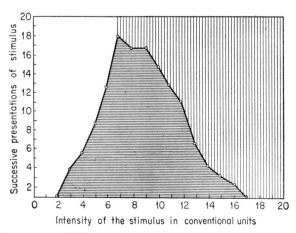

FIG. 4-2. Orientation and defensive reactions as a function of stimulus intensity and number of presentations: (1) □ no reaction; (2) ⊟ orientation reaction; (3) ⦀ defensive reaction. (From Sokolov 1958.)

reaction for the first few presentations and the defensive reaction thereafter, the change from the one to the other coming earlier and earlier as intensity grows. Finally, the most intense stimuli of all evoke the defensive reaction from the start, without going through a phase of evoking the orientation reaction. It seems likely that much the same thing would happen with varying intensities of other kinds of stimulation, although they would presumably have to become extremely strong before they gave rise to defensive reactions.

When a stimulus acquires signal value, the range of intensities evoking an orientation reaction undergoes a marked expansion in both directions (see Fig. 4-3), encroaching on both the intensities that were formerly too weak to evoke any reaction at all and the intensities that were formerly high enough to evoke defensive reactions instead.

In this connection, it is worth noting that activation of the RAS, either by direct electrical stimulation or by the injection of adrenaline, was found by Hugelin (1955a) to inhibit a nociceptive reflex (opening of the mouth in response to an electric shock to the tongue) in the cat. It is as if the alerted nervous system had to sacrifice processes dealing with local threats in order to reserve their equipment for information gathering or urgent action in the interest of the whole organism.

THE ORIENTATION REACTION AND AROUSAL

Two distinctions introduced by Sokolov may prove instructive with regard to the relations between the orientation reaction and the arousal dimension.

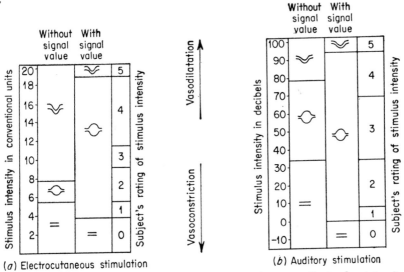

(a) Electrocutaneous stimulation   (b) Auditory stimulation

Fig. 4-3. Orientation and defensive reactions as a function of stimulus intensity and presence or absence of signal value. The upper curve of each pair represents the blood vessels of the head and the lower curve the blood vessels of the hand. Examples from two subjects. (From Sokolov 1958.)

Phasic and Tonic Orientation Reactions

First, he extends to orientation reactions Sherrington's (1906) distinction between *phasic* and *tonic* skeletal reflexes. For Sherrington, phasic reflexes were those that produce transient bodily movements, while tonic reflexes were the ones that serve to alter or maintain posture. The phasic orientation reaction is the complex of short-lasting changes that follow the onset, termination, or sudden modification of a stimulus. It is, in fact, the orientation reaction with which we have been chiefly concerned so far. Tonic orientation reactions, on the other hand, take the form of longer-lasting and more gradual rises in the indexes of arousal.

An intense or sudden stimulus, especially if it is painful or has signal value and is repeated a few times, will, quite apart from provoking phasic orientation reactions, drag upward the dominant frequency of background EEG activity and the prevailing level of skin conductance. It will rouse a subject from sleep or drowsiness, and it will intensify phasic alpha blockings and GSRs when they occur. If, however, an indifferent stimulus recurs at short intervals, the attenuation and eventual disappearance of the phasic orientation reaction goes hand in hand with a decline in background skin conductance and EEG frequency.

93

The tonic orientation reaction seems clearly enough to constitute a long-term shift in the level of arousal, whereas the phasic orientation reaction amounts to a fleeting jump. To use Stennett's (1957a) apt analogy, the one is related to the other as a tide is related to a wave. This does not, of course, exclude the possibility that there may be other, more fundamental differences between them, e.g., that one of these reactions may have some components that the other does not have.

Generalized and Localized Orientation Reactions

Sokolov's second distinction is between *generalized* and *localized* orientation reactions. The immediate effect of any sharp change in the stimulus field is of the former kind: the generalized orientation reaction alerts the organism's total sensory equipment, whatever the modality to which the provoking stimulus belongs. But as the change is repeated, the processes affecting other senses disappear with relative quickness, and localized orientation reactions, corresponding to the sense that is being stimulated, remain for some time longer.*

Both visual and tactual stimuli, for example, initially evoke alpha blocking and the GSR as components of a generalized reaction. But, with successive flashes of light, the GSR extinguishes early and the EEG activation pattern in the visual cortex persists, whereas the GSR outlasts other components if tactual receptors are repeatedly excited. If kinesthetic stimulation is produced by moving the subject's arm up and down, the localized reaction, which continues after other components have faded, is the blocking of the Rolandic rhythm, the bow-shaped waves (*rythme en arceau*) that are recorded from the motor cortex in some subjects and have approximately the same frequency as alpha waves.

The generalized orientation reaction is attributed (Fessard and Gastaut 1958, Sokolov 1958) to the lower or brain-stem section of the RAS which, it will be recalled, belongs to a nonspecific projection system, while the upper or thalamic reaches of the RAS, which are apparently able to activate cortical areas separately, are held to be responsible for the localized reactions.

---

* Sharpless and Jasper (1956) distinguish a "tonic arousal reaction," which is slow to occur, slow to subside, easy to habituate, and dependent on the lower RAS, from a quicker, briefer, habituation-resistant, "phasic arousal reaction," dependent on the thalamic RAS. This seems, however, to be closer to Sokolov's generalized-localized dichotomy than to his usage of the terms "tonic" and "phasic."

Nomenclature

Kvasov (1958) quarrels with the practice, well established among other Russian writers, of using the expression "orientation reaction" to cover all the changes that regularly supervene when a startling stimulus is received. Some of these changes clearly modify incoming stimulation and augment its yield of transmitted information. They are thus entitled to be regarded as exploratory behavior. But others do not seem to be directly concerned with receptivity at all. They seem rather to consist of processes that are likely to come in useful in quite different ways, e.g., by facilitating action or thought, on occasions when stimuli that call for close scrutiny are present.

We shall, however, conform to what has become current usage in both Eastern European and Western countries and refer to the whole complex as the orientation reaction. We shall reserve the term "orienting response" for processes that focus, direct, or sensitize receptor organs and thus have an unmistakable exploratory function. These latter will include responses of the propriomusculature, which Kvasov thinks should alone be called orienting responses. But it seems reasonable also to include responses of the skeletal musculature that orient receptors by changing posture, as well as any photochemical, humoral, or vegetative responses that might elevate sensitivity.

The term "arousal reaction" is usually and most properly applied to the change that turns a sleeping animal into a waking one, whereas the orientation reaction is a process that occurs in an animal that is awake but not at its most alert. Both the arousal reaction and the orientation reaction can be assumed to entail a steep rise in the level of arousal.

Many of the orienting responses that are embodied in the orientation reaction contribute to the intensive aspect of attention. They expand the inflow of information from the environment as a whole. They might, like the retinal-sensitization response or the pupillary-dilatation response, draw increased information from one particular source. But they do not diminish the information that is entering through other channels, whether or not the latter is filtered out by central attentive processes. Other orienting responses, such as shifting the gaze or turning the head or running the fingers over an object, have a stimulus-selecting function. They increase or introduce information from one source at the expense of information from other sources.

It may be remarked in passing that the other kinds of exploratory behavior, namely, locomotor exploration and investigation, can have only a selective function. When an animal changes its location, it must inevitably move its receptors away from some stimulus objects while bringing them nearer to others. And when changes are effected in an external object, information derived from its new state replaces information that would have been obtainable from other states in which it might have been.

The Role of the Cortex

Subcortical structures must be able, to some extent, to control orienting responses, since Pavlov and his followers found them to occur with appreciable strength in decorticate animals. But since selective orienting responses can vary quite subtly with the nature and position of the stimuli that evoke them, it seems probable that they normally call on the fine discriminating powers of the cortex. It is noteworthy, therefore, that the stimulation of a particular point in the visual cortex of the monkey will make the eyes move to fixate the corresponding point in the stimulus field (Walker and Weaver 1940). Likewise, in a series of experiments on cats and monkeys, Lagutina (1955, 1958) found in all cases that stimulation of the visual cortex would evoke head turning and eye movements, stimulation of the olfactory cortex would evoke head turning and sniffing, and stimulation of the auditory cortex would evoke pricking up of the ears, as well as nonspecific accompaniments of the orientation reaction, such as pupillary dilatation and respiratory disturbance.

DETERMINANTS OF SELECTIVE ORIENTING RESPONSES

We must now turn to the question of what factors direct selective orienting responses toward one stimulus object rather than another. We must consider available experimental evidence bearing on this question, but, once again, we shall find it lamentably inadequate. Most of it is, for fairly obvious reasons, concerned with visual orientation.

1. Intensity

Developmental psychologists (e.g., Piaget 1936) have regularly reported that infants fixate and follow patches of bright light from a few weeks after birth. On the other hand, Berlyne (1958b) failed to find any preference in three- to nine-month-old babies for looking at a white rectangle rather than at a gray or black one, perhaps because the differences in intensity were, in this case, not great enough. Harlow (personal communication) reports strong preferences for looking at white objects in newborn monkeys.

2. Color

The influence of color on visual fixation in infants has been investigated by Valentine (1914) and by Staples (1932). Valentine presented two different colored strands of wool side by side and noted how long each was fixated. Staples used a similar procedure with paper disks. It appears that infants have definite color preferences by about the fourth month and that they are more likely to look at chromatic colors than at gray. There is no exact agreement between these two writers on the order of preference, but, in general, infants prefer to look at the warm hues in the long-wave half of the spectrum. A baby chimpanzee tested by Fantz (1958a) was, however, more inclined to fixate blue than red.

Brandt (1944), using an eye-movement cinecamera, found that adults spend more time looking at red and white designs than at black and white ones and also that they spend more time looking at that member of a pair of hues which they say they like better.

3. Indicating Stimuli

Human life supplies countless demonstrations that orienting responses can become attached to signals through learning. Verbal formulas like "Look at what he is doing!" and "Listen to this!" and pointing with the finger are obvious examples. The sight of another person performing an orienting response will often do just as well. There is the time-honored practical joke in which a man stops in the middle of a busy street with eyes focused on the sky—and then walks off, leaving a staring crowd.

Several Russian experiments have shown how a conditioned orienting response can become associated with a stimulus that has regularly preceded another, even though both stimuli are biologically neutral. Narbutovich and Podkopaev (1936) exposed dogs to several repetitions of a flash of light followed by a tone, and the light came to evoke head turning toward the source of sound. Similarly, a tone sounded just before a flash of light evoked head turning toward the bulb. The same phenomenon has been demonstrated in the 2½-month-old human infant, with a tone as the conditioned stimulus and a flash of light to the right of the head as the unconditioned stimulus (Kasatkin, Mirzoiants, and Khokhitva 1953).

A specially vivid illustration of the principle is the experiment of Alekseeva (1956). She allowed a dog to wander freely about a room instead of being harnessed to a stand, as is more usual in conditioning experiments. The room contained a table onto which the dog could climb to take food. A metronome beat for a few seconds before food was placed on the table, so that climbing was rewarded only after receipt of this signal. The sound of the metronome was preceded in its turn by the switching on of a light bulb for ten seconds. With repetition of this sequence of events, the dog developed a ritual that consisted of going up to the light bulb and licking it, then, when the light went on, standing on a carpet in front of the table with head and eyes turned toward the metronome, and finally jumping up onto the table when the beating of the metronome began.

Dzhavrishvili (1956) has even obtained backward conditioning of an orienting response in the dog. The turning on of a lamp was followed several times by the ringing of a bell. Afterward, the sound of the bell without the prior presentation of the visual stimulus evoked head turning toward the lamp.

4. Novelty

An experiment by Berlyne (1958a) verified that novel stimuli are more likely to attract visual orienting movements than stimuli that have appeared repeatedly in the recent past. Pairs of pictures of animals were projected side by side on a screen for ten seconds. For ten trials, one animal reappeared constantly on one side, whereas a different animal appeared every time on the other side. It was found that subjects spent more and more of the ten seconds fixating the novel pictures on the varying side and less and less fixating the recurring picture.

This experiment was, of course, concerned with short-term novelty. Long-term novelty may be most potent in eliciting fixations when it is present to an intermediate degree. Piaget's (1936) observations of infants aged five weeks and more led him to state: "The subject looks neither at what is too familiar, because he is in a way surfeited with it, nor at what is too new, because this does not correspond to anything in his schemata (for instance, objects too remote for there yet to be accommodation, or too small or too large to be analyzed, etc.)."

The attraction of fixation in both infants and adults by moving or continuously changing objects is a familiar phenomenon but one which has received little systematic study.

5. Surprisingness

In experiments on learning, orienting behavior is often found to be strengthened by an unheralded change in experimental conditions. It may appear in a particularly marked form in the dog when conditioned stimuli that have habitually been presented in a certain order are, for once, presented in a different order (Soloveichik 1928). If two stimuli have to be discriminated, either because one but not the other is followed by pain (Vinogradova 1958, with human subjects) or because they indicate that different instrumental responses will be rewarded (Polezhaev 1958, with dogs), orienting behavior is elicited when one stimulus follows an unbroken series of repetitions of the other stimulus. If a dog has been trained to treat several stimuli as positive or negative alimentary conditioned stimuli, it is likely to look round when a negative stimulus follows a succession of positive stimuli (Narbutovich 1938).

Looking up and looking about occur, together with other signs of emotional disturbance, when an animal is made to expect one kind of food and is supplied with another kind instead. This has been reported when rats, having previously found bran mash in the goal box of a maze, are given sunflower seed (Elliott 1928), when dogs, having previously found bread in a food box after hearing a bell, find meat there (Anokhin 1958), and when monkeys, having seen a banana being placed under a cup, find lettuce when they lift the cup (Tinklepaugh 1928). Except in the case of Anokhin's dog, these changes were from a more acceptable to a less acceptable food, so that frustration may have been the essential factor rather than surprise.

6. Complexity, Uncertainty, Incongruity

In Berlyne's (1958b) experiment with three- to nine-month-old infants, already mentioned in connection with stimulus intensity, patterns representing different degrees of complexity were also presented. The outcome was that, in each of the series of patterns shown in Fig. 4-4, the pattern on the extreme right was significantly more likely than the others to attract first fixations. It is worth noting that Fantz (1958a, 1958b) found a preference in both an infant chimpanzee and a group of human infants for looking at a chessboard pattern rather than at a square of solid color. These preferred patterns contain much more contour than the ones with which they were paired, and this fact may well be the key. Many of the receptors in the retina— the so-called on- and off-receptors—become active only when light begins or ceases to impinge on them. And the eyes are generally in motion, whether in the course of large-scale traverses of the visual field or in the course of the minute, fluttering, nystagmic movements that the eyes are constantly making. Consequently, patterns with more contour will bring the on- and off-receptors into play to a greater extent and thus have a higher stimulation value.

In human adults, on the other hand, orienting responses are influenced by other forms of complexity which are not always reflected

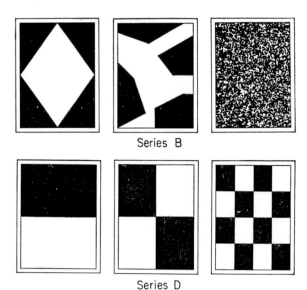

Series B

Series D

FIG. 4-4. (From Berlyne 1958b).

in the amount of contour and whose effect must therefore depend on more central factors. In another experiment, Berlyne (1958a) exposed adult subjects to pairs of figures, each appearing for ten seconds. The pairs of figures belonged to six series (exhibited in Fig. 4-5). One

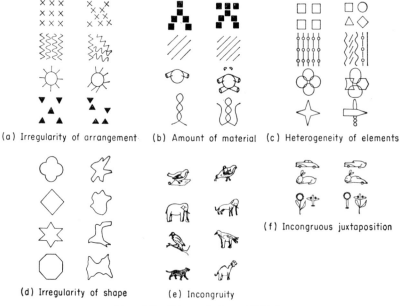

(a) Irregularity of arrangement   (b) Amount of material   (c) Heterogeneity of elements

(d) Irregularity of shape   (e) Incongruity   (f) Incongruous juxtaposition

FIG. 4-5. (From Berlyne 1958a).

member of each pair (shown on the right) in series A to D differs from the others in some respect which gives it greater complexity: irregular arrangement in series A, amount of material in series B, heterogeneity of elements in series C, and irregularity of shape in series D.

The variables can alternatively be described in terms of novelty and information-theory concepts. In series A, C, and D, the more complex figure is the less familiar; it is less like things that the subject will have encountered before. This is because, in general, a particular type of regular pattern will be found more often than a particular type of irregular pattern, especially in a society with as many artifacts as our own. There would seem to be no way of separating these variables except by testing subjects who had been reared in an abnormal, nightmarish environment where irregular patterns preponderated. Turning to information theory, the more complex patterns in the same three series contain less redundancy and hence more uncertainty (relative and absolute). The more complex patterns of series B contain more absolute uncertainty; more information would have to be supplied for their complete description.

Series E and F dealt with a different, if related, variable, namely incongruity. One of the animals in each pair of series E is made up of parts that we have been trained to believe will not be possessed by the same creature, such as three heads or anatomical features characteristic of different species. They are more novel than the others, since animals or pictures resembling the latter but not the former will have been seen before. They may be regarded as stimuli evoking conflict, because the perception of one part conflicts with expectations aroused by other parts, or because the animal portrayed possesses attributes that we have learned to consider incompatible. Likewise, the incongruous animals contain more uncertainty. The normal animals are such that knowledge of the nature of one part enables the nature of the rest to be predicted easily, but this is not true of the incongruous ones.

Series F was added for purposes of control. If series E alone had been used, it would not have been clear whether any effect obtained was due solely to the unusual combination of elements in the incongruous animals or whether the spatial arrangement played a part. Thus it would not have been clear whether it was a matter of seeing an elephant's head and a lion's hind legs in unwonted proximity, or whether it was a matter of seeing a lion's hind legs where an elephant's hind legs were expected. In series F, therefore, both pictures of each pair contained the same material, and it included items not often found in juxtaposition. But in one picture of each pair, part of one object was incongruously attached to part of the other.

101

In every single pair of series A to F, the more complex or incongruous figure was fixated for a significantly higher proportion of the total exposure time than the other figure.

It might be objected that, during the first ten seconds of exposure to a pair of figures, subjects must barely have time to identify them. Consequently, if more time is spent fixating more complex or incongruous stimuli, it may simply be that those stimuli are harder to identify and thus require longer inspection. The theoretical importance of the findings may be severely limited if the tendency is confined to the first few seconds after stimuli appear. A similar experiment with material from categories A to E was therefore carried out (Berlyne 1958c), but this time the pairs of figures were exposed for two minutes each. Nevertheless, with two-minute exposures as with ten-second exposures, more time was spent looking at the more complex or incongruous figures.

A third (unpublished) experiment used other pairs of figures, one member of each pair once again being more complex than the other, but all the figures were markedly more complex than any used in the experiments that have just been mentioned. This time there was great variability among subjects, and the fixation times for the two pictures of each pair were not significantly different. This finding is difficult to interpret and points to the need for more investigation of the whole problem. It may mean, for example, that orienting responses tend not so much to be attracted to complex parts of the stimulus field as to shun features with low information content and that they distribute themselves more or less evenly among features whose information content exceeds a certain threshold. Alternatively, it may mean that the most eye-drawing level of complexity differs from subject to subject but is never in the neighborhood of the lower extreme.

7. Conflict

Polezhaev (1959a) established associations in dogs between various stimuli and various incompatible activities, e.g., feeding, avoidance of pain, vomiting, postural reflexes. The simultaneous appearance of stimuli associated with two of these activities generally gave rise to vigorous orienting behavior directed at both stimuli in turn.

Orienting movements were also recorded by Bykov (1958) in the course of conditioning experiments with dogs. The conditioned stimuli, consisting of various sounds, acted for fifteen seconds, at the end of which time food was delivered into a tray. When a negative differential stimulus—a sound that differed from the familiar conditioned stimulus and was not reinforced—was introduced, orienting behavior was temporarily called forth by its novelty. However, after a few experiences with the new stimulus without reinforcement, there was a marked intensification of orienting behavior not only when the negative stimulus was presented but even when the positive stimulus occurred. It died down in both cases after twenty or so trials. The same temporary resurgence of orienting behavior took place when a negative stimulus was transformed into a positive stimulus by being followed by the delivery of food, and when a positive stimulus was changed into a negative stimulus by ceasing to be reinforced.

The most reasonable explanation for these findings, and the one put forward by Bykov, is that both positive and negative stimuli in a differentiation situation come, for a time, to possess both excitatory and inhibitory properties. The positive stimulus will have not only an excitatory property due to its reinforcement but an inhibitory property due to generalization from the negative stimulus, while the negative stimulus will be inhibitory as a result of its nonreinforcement and excitatory by generalization. Similarly, a stimulus undergoing a transformation from a positive to a negative status or vice versa will be in the process of acquiring one property while not yet having lost the other. All these stimuli will thus be ambiguous or conflict-inducing. Further training relieves the conflict as excitation or inhibition establishes its predominance, and the orienting behavior consequently dies down.

In Chapter 2, we deduced that a discriminative task will induce conflict between correct and incorrect response tendencies and that the degree of conflict will increase with the similarity between the stimuli that have to be discriminated. Evidence that more difficult discriminations occasion more numerous and prolonged orienting responses is therefore of interest.

Vinh-Bang (Piaget and Vinh-Bang 1959) filmed eye movements while asking subjects to state which of two lines was longer. He allowed subjects to look at the figures for as long as they wished before making a judgment and found that the time taken (occupied by eye movements) was greater when the difference between the lines was smaller. Phillips (1957) allowed her subjects to lift two weights in turn as many times as they wished before judging which was heavier. Here again, subjects lifted the weights more often when they were more nearly equal.

Chapter 5

EXPLORATORY BEHAVIOR:
II. LOCOMOTOR EXPLORATION

Locomotor exploration appears to be universal among higher vertebrates and present to some degree in other branches of the animal
kingdom that are capable of locomotion. Yet it has been studied
systematically in rather few species. By far the greater part of the
relevant literature is concerned with the rat. This animal has many
advantages as an experimental subject for this area of research. Apart
from the qualities that have made him the favorite subject for animal
psychology in general and the extensive knowledge about so many
aspects of his behavior that has been acquired in consequence, his
small size and nimbleness make him especially suitable for experiments
in which locomotion is studied.

There have been a few investigations of locomotor exploratory behavior outside the mammalian class. Darchen (1952, 1954, 1957) has
done some with the German cockroach *Blatella germanica*. His work
is of special interest, not only because it is concerned with an animal
that is only remotely related to the rat or the human being, but
also because of the striking parallels between his findings and those
which experiments on mammalian exploration have yielded. The
strength of exploratory approach behavior in birds, especially among
the crows (family *Corvidae*), has often been commented on, although
mostly in anecdotal form.

Most of the experiments on locomotor exploration that have been
carried out to date have used mazes, alleys, and open spaces and
have taken the amount of movement between parts of the apparatus
as a measure of exploratory activity. Such experimental situations are
natural ones for animal psychologists to select, being ones that have
proved their usefulness for the study of an immense variety of problems. Moreover, a great deal of the running around that animals do
in such apparatus must clearly have an exploratory function.

But there are many reasons why the maze and similar pieces of
familiar equipment are not too suitable for the study of exploration.

For one thing, perambulation serves a variety of functions at different times, and it is not easy to establish the part played by exposure to stimuli. Montgomery (1953b) showed that rats that have recently been deprived of opportunities for physical activity do not traverse maze alleys more restlessly than others that have just been removed from an activity wheel. He claimed this as evidence that an activity drive is not at work. But the possibility that perambulation provides some kind of motor exercise that is not provided by running in treadmill fashion in an activity wheel is not entirely set aside, and, in any case, there are a whole host of variables that are known to affect the mobility of the rat.

More serious are the conceptual difficulties that are raised by attempts to measure the amount of exploration an animal devotes to his environment as a whole rather than to a particular portion of it. Is a rat that moves rapidly from one set of stimuli to another exploring more or less than an animal that spends a long time in one place before passing on? Is a visitor in an art gallery who remains fixed for an hour in front of one painting doing more or less looking than one who spends an hour on fleeting glances at all the items in the exhibition?

A further difficulty is of especial importance in view of the subtle interaction that appears to exist between tendencies to approach and tendencies to withdraw. When an animal is moving through a maze alley, he is inevitably moving away from one set of stimuli in the act of moving toward the next. But how can the relative significance of these two facts be unraveled?

It seems preferable, on the whole, to resort to a method in which the animal's exploration of one particular stimulus object can be measured separately. And we are on surer ground still if we record as exploration those approach movements toward the object which are followed by some distinctive orienting response. Craning the head forward and sniffing fulfill this requirement very well in animals like the rat. The technique of exposing a prominent stimulus object (or more than one) and observing the number of times an animal goes up to it and how long it spends in contact with it has been used in experiments by Berlyne (1950a, 1955) and Darchen (1952, 1954). Nevertheless, studies measuring perambulation have yielded most of the findings that we have at our disposal, and there can be little doubt, in most cases, that the activity recorded was mainly exploratory.

Before about 1950, there were reports on just a few experiments on exploration scattered about the literature. These were aimed almost entirely at demonstrating that activity with an apparently exploratory function will occur even in the absence of familiar drive states, such as hunger or thirst, and tangible incentives, such as food or water. Dashiell (1925) reported that satiated rats would wander about a maze of the pattern (Fig. 5-1) that has been named after him.

Nissen (1930) found that rats would cross an electrified grille in a Columbia obstruction box to reach a Dashiell maze containing miscellaneous objects which presumably heightened its power to attract exploration. They would show more willingness to cross the grille than would satiated animals with a food or water incentive or sexually aroused animals with nothing beyond the grille but a small empty compartment. He concluded from these observations that there is an exploratory drive, although its strength, as estimated from the number of grille crossings that it would motivate, was inferior to those of maternal, thirst, hunger, or sex drives. A similar conclusion was drawn by Mote and Finger (1942) when they found that satiated rats would run down an alley to an unfamiliar, empty goal box, although they would not do so with as much speed as satiated rats that had previously been fed in that goal box.

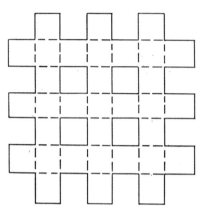

FIG. 5-1. The Dashiell maze. (From Dashiell 1925.)

The more recent experiments have started from the assumption that the existence and remarkable strength of exploratory tendencies are by now amply established, and they have accordingly proceeded to the detection of factors influencing the quantity of exploration.

DETERMINANTS OF INSPECTIVE LOCOMOTOR EXPLORATION

Novelty

We must first consider inspective exploration, which may well be the commonest kind in natural environments. What usually happens is that an animal sees an object in the distance, and this sight evokes the response of approaching the object, with the result that visual stimulation emanating from it is intensified and supplemented, while olfactory, auditory, or tactual stimulation may also be brought into play. The one property of objects that most readily comes to mind as evocative of such behavior is novelty. The study of the relations between novelty and exploration is, of course, inseparable from the

106

study of the diminution in exploration of an object as it loses its novelty.

Time since Last Presentation. Experiments attacking the problem from four different angles have established that exploration increases with the time that has elapsed since an object was last encountered.

COMPARISON OF EXPLORATION OF NOVEL OBJECTS WITH EXPLORATION OF FAMILIAR OBJECTS IN THE SAME SUBJECTS. In an experiment by Berlyne (1950a), rats were allowed to explore three identical objects —wooden cubes or cardboard cylinders—for five minutes, and they were then put back into the situation ten minutes later, to find one of the cubes replaced by a cylinder, or vice versa. During this second trial, they spent significantly more time exploring the novel object than exploring the other, familiar objects.

Thiessen and McGaugh (1958) trained hungry rats in a Y maze with food rewards for eighty trials. On the eighty-first trial, a new maze arm was added, and the rats showed themselves more inclined to enter this new arm than the arms with which they were already acquainted.

Berlyne and Slater (1957) gave rats eight trials per day for three days in a T maze. The goal boxes were empty except for visual figures attached to the rear wall, but, whereas one goal box bore the same (familiar) figure every time, the other goal box always bore a different (novel) figure each time it was entered. Moreover, the rats were exposed to the familiar figure outside the maze for ten minutes before each trial. The outcome was that they explored the novel figures for a higher proportion of the time spent in the goal box than they explored the familiar figures.

COMPARISON OF EXPLORATION BY SUBJECTS FACED WITH A NOVEL OBJECT WITH EXPLORATION BY SUBJECTS FACED WITH A FAMILIAR OBJECT. In Berlyne's (1950a) experiment, rats confronted with one novel and two familiar objects during their second exposure to the situation explored the familiar objects for less time than did other rats without the experience of the previous trial, which were meeting all three objects for the first time.

Another experiment (Berlyne 1955) showed how rats that have been exposed to a cube outside the experimental situation for five minutes immediately before the experimental trial will, during the first minute of the trial, make fewer approaches to the cube than rats that have not had this preliminary exposure.

Thompson and Solomon (1954) tested rats in a box in which there was a card bearing a black and white vertically striped pattern. After a two-minute interval, the animals were returned to the box for a second trial. A control group found the same pattern as before; an experimental group found the striped pattern replaced by a triangle. The experimental group explored their pattern more than did the control group during the second trial.

COMPARISON OF EXPLORATION WITH SUCCESSIVE EXPOSURES TO THE SAME OBJECT. In the first (1950a) of these two experiments by Berlyne, the two familiar objects present during the second trial were explored less than they had been during the first trial, when they had, of course, been novel.

In another experiment (Berlyne 1955), it was found that if rats are repeatedly placed in a box containing a wooden cube for three-minute trials at ten-minute intervals, the number of approaches to the cube in the first minute will decrease from trial to trial.

THE TIME COURSE OF EXPLORATION WITH PROLONGED EXPOSURE TO AN OBJECT. When an object is accessible to an animal for a continuous period of several minutes, exploration is regularly found to decline with time according to a concave-upward curve. This has been shown in the rat with exploration of a maze (Montgomery 1953a) and exploration of a wooden cube (Berlyne 1955). It has also been shown in the cockroach with exploration of a stick (Darchen 1952). Sometimes, when rats find themselves in a limited space to which they are not habituated, a brief initial rise in exploration has been observed to precede the ultimate decline (Thompson and Solomon 1954, Welker 1957). This raises the question of interaction between fear and exploration, which will be taken up in due course.

Degree of Resemblance between Test Situation and Previous Situation. So far, we have concentrated on whether an animal has previously encountered an object, how long ago, and for how long, as determinants of how novel the object is. Other experiments have taken as their independent variable the degree to which an object or situation resembles or contrasts with a previously encountered object or situation. This (as will be remembered from Chapter 2) is also a determinant of degree of novelty, and, when its effects are studied, similar conclusions are favored.

Montgomery (1953a) used black, gray, and white mazes. He placed his rats in one of the mazes for an exploration trial and then immediately afterward returned them to the same maze for a second trial or gave them a second trial in a maze of a different albedo. The amount of exploratory movement in the second trial increased with the difference in albedo between the first maze and the second maze. This shows that the decline in exploration will show generalization from one class of stimuli to another commensurate with the similarity between the two.

Montgomery used the number of 12-inch sections entered as his measure of exploration and exposed rats to alleys of different albedoes in succession. Dember and Millbrook (1956) made their rats choose between entering arms of different albedoes that were simultaneously accessible. In the first trial, one arm of their T maze was gray, and the other either black or white. In the second trial, which took place two minutes after the first, the arms were either both black (if the first trial had white and gray arms) or both white (if the first trial had black and gray arms). The rats tended to enter whichever arm had undergone the greater change in albedo.

On the other hand, Berlyne (1955) found that exposing a rat before a trial to a cube of a different albedo from the cube to be explored did not produce any different effect from exposing it to one of the same albedo. But this may have been expecting too much from the animal's powers of discrimination and generalization.

Darchen (1952) replaced a vertical white stick that his cockroaches had been exploring by a green one; this provoked a resurgence of exploration, such as replacement by a similar stick failed to provoke.

Duration of Exposure to Previous Situation. The length of time for which the stimulus situation replaced by a novel stimulus situation was active appears to influence exploration in the cockroach and deserves to be tested with mammals. Darchen (1957) found that cockroaches would explore a colored cube more promptly if it was introduced after they had spent sixty minutes in an empty box than if it was introduced after fifteen minutes.

Long-term Decrements. Experiments mentioned so far have demonstrated that exploration undergoes a short-term decrement as the time for which an animal has been exposed to a stimulus object increases. After an absence from the object, when the object has had a chance to recover its short-term novelty, its exploration is at least partly restored. However, the question arises of whether there is a long-term or permanent decline as well as a short-term decline. If there is, then long-term or complete novelty will be an additional determinant of the amount of exploration. It will show itself if exploration after a twenty-four-hour interval recovers to something less than its initial strength. If trials follow one another twenty-four hours apart, it will be revealed by a decrease over days.

The evidence on this point is not so unequivocal as one might wish. Montgomery (1953a) obtained remarkably similar scores on successive days of testing in a Y maze. But in other experiments using a Y maze, Zimbardo and Montgomery (1957a) obtained a between-trials decline in activity whenever a forty-eight-hour interval separated the trials.

Danziger and Mainland (1954) observed rats in a circular enclosure, giving group A a two-minute trial on each of twenty consecutive days and group B a single, continuous forty-minute trial. Group B's movement from one part of the enclosure to another underwent a large decrement in the course of the forty minutes, but group A's movement did not decrease from day to day.

Berlyne (1955) failed to find any effect when a cube that rats had not seen for twenty-four hours but had explored on five or more successive days previously was replaced by a cube of a markedly different appearance. On the other hand, there was a sharp drop in exploration of an empty alcove after the first of a series of daily trials.

In Berlyne and Slater's (1957) experiment with the T maze whose goal boxes contained cards bearing visual figures, there was a significant decrease in time spent sniffing at the figures, whether novel or familiar, from day to day.

An experiment by Williams and Kuchta (1957) is especially interesting because it subjected rats to one ten-minute trial per day. On the first four days, the experimental group explored a Y maze with three black arms and, on the next three days, a maze with one white and two black arms. During the trial on which they first met the white arm, these animals devoted a higher proportion of their exploration to this arm than did a control group that had had access to the white arm from the start. But their exploration of the white arm diminished thereafter. It is noteworthy that the control group, having two black arms and one white arm throughout the seven days of the experiment, explored the white arm to much the same extent every day. This suggests strongly that surprisingness plays a part, as well as novelty pure and simple. A white maze arm located where a black arm has regularly been found in the past is evidently more effective in attracting exploration than is a completely unfamiliar white arm. The phenomenon is only temporary, although the expectations underlying this surprisingness will evidently outlast twenty-four hours.

In general, this body of research suggests that exploration has a special role during the first minute or two of each exposure to a situation and during the very first exposure to it. Most of a rat's exploratory activity takes place at the beginning of a trial, although there are usually bursts of renewed exploration from time to time thereafter. Berlyne (1955) found that the proportion of exploration occurring during the first minute increases from one daily trial to the next, and also that many of the experimental variables had a significant effect only on the amount of exploration in this first minute. Exploration in the later part of a trial seems to be much more fortuitous,

110

depending largely on where a rat happens to be wandering and what happens to strike his eye.

Similarly, the day-by-day decline in exploration is usually found to be steep at first, then more gradual. R. H. J. Watson (1954) reports that rats are less active and emotional after their first experience in an experimental situation, even when several weeks elapse between the first experience and the second. It makes sense, perhaps both in the light of human behavior and biologically, that an animal should spend considerable time "getting his bearings" and "taking a look around" when he first finds himself in unfamiliar surroundings and that he should spend a short time recognizing or identifying a familiar situation every time he enters it.

Change. There has been an isolated attempt to introduce a change while subjects are present. Darchen (1952) suddenly increased the intensity of illumination while his cockroaches were exploring and found this to produce a temporary rise in exploratory activity. A sudden dimming did not, however, work in the same way.

Complexity

After novelty, the property of objects most commonly connected with exploration has been complexity. Novelty and complexity are not always too easy to keep apart, as the most complex environments will generally offer the greatest wealth of novel sights and smells—at least for an animal with such a limited range of experiences as the typical laboratory rat. For example, we cannot be at all sure how far it was novelty and how far complexity that made the Dashiell maze filled with miscellaneous objects so effective a lure in Nissen's experiment (1930).

With novelty controlled as far as possible, complexity appears to increase inspective exploration. Berlyne (1955) allowed some rats to explore an empty alcove and others to explore the same alcove containing a gray cube. All the animals had previously seen a black or an unpainted cube in the same location, but none had ever seen the alcove empty before; therefore novelty would be expected to favor exploration in the latter situation. Nevertheless, the cube, which added to the complexity of the stimulus field, provoked a significantly larger number of approaches in the first minute.

A somewhat more decisive test of the complexity variable was devised by Dember, Earl, and Paradise (1957), who used a maze shaped like a figure eight. One of its loops had walls bearing horizontal black and white stripes. The walls of the other loop were painted in vertical black and white stripes or else they were completely black or

111

completely white. Vertical stripes were deemed more complex than horizontal, and horizontal stripes more complex than plain walls, since they presented a much higher number of distinct black or white units to the animals' eyes. Rats were placed in this maze for one hour on each of two or more successive days. On the first day, some animals stationed themselves in the more complex section and some did not. Those that did not showed, on the second and later days, a marked tendency to prefer the more complex section. An interesting interaction (see Dember and Earl 1957) between novelty and complexity is thus indicated. A complex stimulus pattern became more attractive as it lost its novelty. Perhaps it should also be noted that the vertical stripes might have owed their influence to their excitation of a higher level of retinal activity (due to their persistent activation of on- and off-fibers as the subjects' eyes moved past them).

An attempt to control novelty was likewise made in an experiment by Williams and Kuchta (1957). Their Y maze had one white arm containing various black objects (a toy mouse, a chain, etc.); the other was white except for black stripes equal in area to the black objects in the other arm. The rats tended to enter the arm with the objects more frequently while exploring the maze freely. It was found, once again, that the preference for the more complex stimuli increased from the first to the last day of testing.

Finally, in an experiment by Welker (1957), rats explored an enclosure whose walls bore five cubes and five irregularly shaped objects. Welker reports that the irregular objects were approached more frequently than the cubes.

Intensity and Contrast

In general, many species of animals appear to approach moderately intense stimuli and withdraw from extremely intense ones (Maier and Schneirla 1937). This is especially noticeable in invertebrates, from amoebae upward, that have definite taxes, since a taxis will quite frequently change from positive to negative as a stimulus becomes stronger, though remaining unchanged in quality. It is, no doubt, a useful arrangement from a biological point of view. An intense stimulus means a great alteration in environmental conditions. Since the survival of most animals requires their environment to remain constant within nice limits, there must be a high probability that an intense stimulus heralds danger. Mild stimuli, on the other hand, may come from potential sources of food, potential mating partners, and other positive incentives. The precise intensity of light that is maximally attractive is, however, likely to vary with the species, depending on how prone it is to nocturnal or diurnal activity, for example.

It is not surprising, therefore, that data on the relation between luminous intensity and exploration vary in import. Berlyne (1955) found that rats would explore a gray cube about as much as a white cube; whether the cube resembled its background in albedo or contrasted with it made no difference. And Montgomery (1953a) failed to establish any difference between the amount of exploratory perambulation in white, gray, and black mazes. It has, however, frequently been reported that rats will prefer to enter dark rather than light maze alleys if given the choice.

When cockroaches have spent an hour on a dimly lit tray and a light is then suddenly introduced at one end of the tray, they are likely to move toward the light but to avoid the area of maximum illumination in its immediate neighborhood (Darchen 1954). When they are placed in a square enclosure, they will spend more time in the central, most strongly illuminated area when the illumination is faint than when it is intense (Darchen 1957). Sensory adaptation evidently plays a part, since there is more and more exploration of the central area under intense illumination as time goes on, and it is explored more extensively when a cockroach has been preadapted to strong light.

Poverty of Immediately Preceding Environment

Charlesworth and Thompson (1957) examined the effect of keeping rats in an impoverished environment before exploration. Some of their animals were confined in normal living cages, from which they could see out; others were confined for three, six, or nine days, in darkness or in light, in an empty box with opaque walls. There turned out to be no significant differences among subjects with different treatments when they were given an opportunity to explore a novel chamber. All groups were about equally prompt in entering the chamber and inclined to spend about equal amounts of time there.

This finding, coupled with Montgomery's (1953b) report that exploratory behavior is not intensified by restricting opportunities for bodily exercise before the test, seems to indicate that the vigor of inspective locomotor exploration depends on processes unleashed by the objects that attract inspection and not on motives generated by prior deprivations. We must, however, be chary of drawing far-reaching conclusions from negative findings; and if this particular conclusion is valid, then inspective locomotor exploration differs in this respect from investigatory behavior, as we shall see in Chapter 6.

Affective Value

Positive. The fact that animals will move toward stimuli with positive affective value is familiar to psychologists and has been illustrated

113

by numerous investigations of secondary rewards or conditioned reinforcers. A classical example is Grindley's (1929) experiment with chickens. One group of subjects was allowed to run down a straight alley, at the end of which they saw some grains of rice that a glass cover prevented them from consuming. The speed with which they traversed the runway increased to a maximum in successive trials, although not nearly so sharply as the speed of another group of chickens that could eat the rice. Then their speed sank back to its original level, showing that the sight of the rice was losing its secondary reward value.

How far movements toward stimuli with secondary reward value can be classed as exploration is, of course, a moot point. It is, however, of obvious biological advantage to an animal that it should advance in search of further information when it meets stimuli that have previously accompanied opportunities for gratification.

Negative. The position with regard to negative affective value is bound to be more complicated. Animals are strongly inclined, as a rule, to keep away from places where they have been hurt or frightened. But the learning that attaches fear and withdrawal responses to stimuli associated with pain and emotional stress necessitates some exposure of receptors to these stimuli. If the stimuli are weak or indistinct, exploration may be necessary to identify them; then fear or avoidance can be conditioned to them, and such responses, once conditioned, can be brought into play on encountering the stimuli again. The selection of the most effective means of escape or avoidance will likewise be impossible without the receipt of adequate information about the stimuli, even at the cost of protracting exposure to them.

Rats, in an experiment by Keehn (1959), readily learned to press a bar as a means of averting an electric shock, but they showed no significant inclination to take action to prevent the appearance of a signal indicating the imminent danger of shock. An animal that deprived itself of warning signals would, of course, not be able to distinguish times when avoidant responses are called for from times when they would be superfluous. Exploratory activity that seeks out stimuli associated with pain or fear will insure still more effectively against unnecessary alarm and exertion, as well as against the possibility of selecting the wrong reaction.

Thus a fleeing animal will slow down or stop from time to time and look back at its pursuer. The resulting impediment to the flight is presumably more than offset by the possibility that locating the pursuer may enable a more promising line of escape to be adopted or that finding the pursuer to be out of sight may permit the exertion to be discontinued.

Darwin (1874) tells of a monkey that was shown a box containing

114

a snake. The monkey shrank back in terror but, nevertheless, could not refrain from returning periodically to lift the lid of the box and peep inside. The biological advantage of this behavior is not self-evident, but it is certainly reminiscent of what we observe in human beings, especially children.

Hudson (1950) allowed rats to eat in the vicinity of a distinctive visual pattern and later gave them an electric shock at the same location. He reports, though on the basis of informal observation rather than systematic measurement, that this provoked vigorous exploration in the direction of the pattern. It is particularly interesting, however, that animals that had an opportunity to explore the vicinity of the pattern immediately after being shocked either steered clear of that vicinity or covered the pattern with sawdust when retested a day or more later, whereas other animals that had the pattern instantly removed from view after the shock, and were therefore deprived of an opportunity to explore, showed no tendency to avoid the pattern thereafter.

A difficulty about Hudson's experiment, apart from the lack of precise recording of exploratory responses, is that the subjects were fed and shocked successively in the presence of the same stimulus object, which means that conflict might have affected the findings.

These difficulties were avoided in an experiment (Berlyne 1958d) by Berlyne and Walley which seems, like Hudson's experiment, to suggest that objects that have become associated with danger are often explored before they are shunned. They gave their rats a fifteen-minute trial on each of three succeeding days in a box having a distinctive diagonally striped pattern at the rear of an alcove. The proportion of the time that a rat spent with his head inserted into the alcove was automatically recorded. One group of rats received a single brief shock on making their first exploration of the alcove on the first day; another group received no shock at all. The result was that the shocked animals explored the alcove significantly less than did the nonshocked animals throughout the experiment. It is interesting, however, that they performed a significantly higher proportion of their total exploration during the first three minutes on the first day, i.e., soon after the shock had been administered. On the third day, half of the rats in both groups received a shock on making their first exploratory response. This produced some reduction in subsequent exploration. But a shock received on the first day was appreciably more influential in reducing exploration on the third day than a shock on the third day. It is, of course, hard to establish conclusively that insertions of the head into an alcove have an exploratory function. For example, it might be thought that the shocked animals in this experiment were trying to push their way into the alcove immediately after the shock as an escape response. But this seems unlikely in view of the circumscribed dimensions of the alcove.

Nature and Nurture

It would be surprising if an animal's exploration were not subject to the influence both of its heredity and the kind of environment in which it has been reared.

The value of exploration in particular circumstances will undoubtedly vary with the pattern of life of a species. Within a species, it is bound to vary with the condition of sense organs, central nervous system, and locomotor equipment, all of which, we have good reason to believe, are amenable to some degree of genetic determination.

We know that an individual animal's previous experience will affect exploration, at least to the extent of determining how novel particular stimulus patterns are. But apart from this, the broad characteristics of the environment will surely leave an effect on the strength of exploratory behavior in general, or of the exploratory behavior attracted by specific types of situation. There is some evidence to bear out these suppositions, although it is meager in view of the scope of these problems.

Heredity. In so far as the amount of movement among sections of a maze represents exploration, hooded rats explore more than black rats and black rats more than albino rats (Carr and Williams 1957). Thompson (1953*b*) and McClearn (1959) have demonstrated consistent differences in what appears to be exploratory activity among inbred strains of mice. Of the two strains tested by McClearn, one was more active on four different tests, which involved running about in an open field, running around barriers, climbing through a hole in a wall, and climbing over barriers, respectively. Moreover, the performance of hybrids of the two strains was intermediate on the running tests and similar to that of the less active strain on the climbing tests. As McClearn acknowledges, the exploratory nature of the activity measured in these situations remains to be verified.

Previous Environment. Thompson and Heron (1954*a*) studied the influence of the richness of the environment in which dogs have been reared on level of activity in an empty room and in a maze. They found that dogs that had undergone severe restriction (having been reared in small wooden boxes, lighted only on alternate days) were more active than moderately restricted dogs (having been reared in roomier cages with opaque walls but continuously illuminated). In its turn, the activity of the moderately restricted dogs exceeded that of normal dogs (having been reared in cages from which they could see out all

116

the time and from which they were taken out occasionally). These investigators conclude that the activity they were observing must, at least in part, have been exploration, as it diminished markedly after a few minutes' exposure to the experimental situation.

Of course, the severely or moderately restricted dogs differed from normally reared dogs in being deprived of opportunities for both activity and varied stimulation, so that it is, unfortunately, impossible to assess the relative contributions of these separate factors. Moreover, the greater mobility of the restricted animals might mean that they were giving individual features of the environment less prolonged or thorough inspection, and this could be interpreted as a reduction in exploration. Later, Thompson and Melzack (mentioned in Zimbardo and Montgomery 1957a) tested dogs in a complex environment rather than in an empty room; in these circumstances, the normal dogs were more active than the restricted ones.

Somewhat similar experiments with rats likewise indicate an interaction between the poverty of the previous environment and the complexity of the environment in which exploration is being tested (Montgomery and Zimbardo 1957, Zimbardo and Montgomery 1957a). In a Y maze, there were no significant differences in behavior among "normal" rats reared in spacious wire-mesh cages, "behaviorally deprived" rats reared in much smaller wire-mesh cages, and "sensorily and behaviorally deprived" rats reared in small cages made of sheet metal. But a fourth group of rats, reared in special free-environment cages, containing marbles, colored blocks, and elaborate toys, explored a Y maze significantly less than normal rats. The authors suggest that animals will generally engage in vigorous exploratory activity only in an environment which is notably more novel or more complex than the one to which they are most accustomed. It is difficult to assess the contributions of novelty and complexity in these experimental findings, as these variables are confounded. But the interaction between the two variables (Dember and Earl 1957) that we have already considered may well be at work.

Miscellaneous Determinants

Thompson and Heron (1954a) recorded more activity from their *younger* subjects (their dogs ranged from nine months to four years), and *female* rats have been shown to explore more than males (Thompson 1953a, Thompson and Kahn 1955, Zimbardo and Montgomery 1957a).

The effects of *intelligence* are less well defined. Strains of rats bred respectively for "brightness" and "dullness" on the Hebb-Williams maze have been compared (Thompson 1953a, Thompson and Kahn

117

1955). The exploration of the two groups did not differ significantly in an elevated rectangular maze, but the dull rats explored more in an enclosed T maze.

Bright and dull rats were also compared in a test for retroactive facilitation and inhibition. Experimental animals in both groups were subjected to a test in a gray Y maze between two tests in a black T maze; control animals from both groups were allowed to rest in a black plywood cage between the two T-maze trials. The effect of the interpolated Y-maze experience was to increase exploration of the T maze in the second test for bright subjects and to decrease it for dull subjects. The bright subjects manifested retroactive inhibition (the exploration-reducing effect of the first T-maze exploration was, in some measure, erased) and the dull subjects manifested retroactive facilitation (the exploration-reducing effect of the first T-maze exploration was, in some measure, enhanced). This difference seems to point to a superior ability on the part of the bright rats to distinguish the two mazes.

The larger exploration scores of dull rats in the first T-maze test were largely the outcome of a much less pronounced fall in activity from the first to the second half of the trial. They remind us of the more intensive activity shown by dogs brought up in restricted environments (Thompson and Heron 1954b), since such dogs are, when tested, less intelligent than normal dogs (Thompson and Heron 1954b). They are also reminiscent of the lower extinguishability of orienting reactions in "inferior" organisms, which will be discussed in some detail in Chapter 7.

It would appear that less intelligent rats explore more assiduously because of a deficient capacity to retain traces of past experience. This would make the interior of a maze both initially more novel, because residues of similar stimuli received before would be less in evidence, and slower at losing its novelty in the course of continued exploration.

Blinded rats perambulate in a Y maze and in an open enclosure more than normal rats (Glickman 1958), which suggests that they must make up for their loss of visual stimulation by using increased mobility to enrich the stimuli reaching other senses.

In the cockroach, exploration increases with *temperature* (Darchen 1952). *Morphine* injections increase the time that the rat spends in exploratory contact with black cubes and slows down the decline in exploration that comes with habituation (Beach 1957). This observation can be related to the fact that morphine increases general activity and also to the fact that it seems to lower thresholds of reactivity to stimuli, e.g., it heightens startle reactions.

INTERACTION WITH OTHER ACTIVITIES AND
THE DRIVES CORRESPONDING TO THEM

Eating and Drinking

There is strong evidence for an antagonistic relationship between exploratory and eating responses; when a hungry animal is allowed access to food in the presence of unfamiliar stimuli, the tendency to explore is often strong enough to overcome eating.

When Majorana (1950) placed hungry rats in a T maze whose right-hand goal box contained food, he found that, once having found their way to the food, they would interrupt their feeding for comparatively long periods of time in order to explore their unfamiliar surroundings in the maze.

The proportion of time spent exploring or feeding may be altered by manipulating factors that can be expected to affect the relative strengths of the two responses. Chance and Mead (1955) removed rats from their living cages and then returned them to the cages, where food was now available. The delay between their return and their starting to eat, and the amount eaten within ten minutes, were used as indexes of the extent to which exploratory responses had interfered with feeding. Latency increased, and the rate of feeding varied inversely, with the number of changes made to the interior of the cage during the rats' absence. Addition of new objects was more effective in this way than withdrawal of familiar objects; but, whether objects were added or withdrawn, the greater the change, the greater the interference with eating. Likewise the interference increased as the degree of novelty of the cage was increased by lengthening the period of absence from it from ten minutes to five days. But the interference could be diminished by making the period of prior starvation longer.

Comparable results were obtained by Zimbardo and Montgomery (1957b), who subjected rats to one ten-minute trial in an unfamiliar checkerboard maze which was divided into nine square compartments. Hungry rats for which food was present and thirsty rats for which water was present in each of the compartments explored less than similarly motivated rats that found the maze empty. The proportion of time spent on exploration varied inversely, and the proportion spent on eating or drinking increased, with the number of days of deprivation before the experiment. Signs of conflict were noted in those animals that had access to food or water, taking the form of "incipient consummatory attempts," i.e., movements toward the food or water that were interrupted before they resulted in ingestion.

119

Hunger and Thirst

What information we have about the effects of hunger and thirst on exploration in the absence of food or water is rather perplexing. In the Dashiell maze (Fig. 5-1), hungry rats have been observed to enter more units in a one-minute trial than satiated rats (Dashiell 1925). In Thompson's rectangular maze (1953a), there were no significant differences among rats deprived of food for zero, twenty-four, and forty-eight hours. However, there was a significant interaction between hours of deprivation and sex: exploration of males increased with hours of deprivation, whereas twenty-four hours of deprivation produced the most exploration in females. In contrast, Montgomery (1953c) found that satiated rats explored a Y maze more actively than rats deprived of water for twenty-four hours or of food for twenty-four, forty-eight, or seventy-two hours, with no noteworthy differences emerging among these deprived groups.

A possible explanation for these contradictory findings has been proposed by Adlerstein and Fehrer (1955). They pointed out that the apparatuses in which deprivation turned out to increase exploratory activity offered more copious and varied stimulation than those in which the opposite effect appeared. In support of their contention, they performed an experiment in which hunger increased the amount of exploration in a complicated multiple-alley maze. But Zimbardo and Montgomery (1957b) rebutted them by noting that, in this last experiment, the hungry rats were apparently tested at about their accustomed feeding time, which fact would suffice to make them restless. They performed another experiment in which exploration of a quite complex maze varied inversely with the severity of hunger and thirst.

The best hopes of resolving the confusion come from investigations in which the possibility of an interaction between hunger and novelty of environment, overlooked by previous experimenters, is taken into account. Fehrer (1956) reminds us how necessary it is that hunger should impel an animal to leave familiar surroundings and explore far afield. She supports this point with an experiment in which rats were given a chance to leave a box in which they had spent twenty-four hours and enter an exploration box that was unfamiliar to them. In these circumstances, hungry animals spent more time in the exploration box than satiated ones. But hunger or satiation did not affect the visits to the exploration box of other rats, for which both boxes were equally novel.

Zimbardo and Miller (1958) have produced a similar effect with a smaller difference in novelty between two parts of an apparatus. They measured the speed with which rats would leave one gray compartment to explore another adjoining one. If the second compartment was accessible as soon as the subjects were put into the first, satiated animals would enter it earlier than hungry ones, although this difference disappeared as daily trials succeeded one another. But, of animals delayed in the first compartment for two minutes and so given ample opportunity to explore that compartment before a door leading to the second one was opened, the hungry ones moved over sooner.

We may be inclined to wonder why, from an evolutionary point of view, hungry animals should move from one novel location to another equally novel one less readily than satiated animals. It may be that hungry animals must spend enough time in an unfamiliar area to ascertain whether food is available there before they move on. Alternatively, it may be that hunger strengthens a large number of response tendencies (see Chapter 7), including the tendency to examine novel environments, making them more resistant to extinction. If the tendency to examine one section of a piece of apparatus must be extinguished before an animal is impelled to pass on to the next section, this process would then take longer to complete with a hungrier animal. It would also follow that hungrier animals would change to the next section with greater alacrity if it became accessible after the tendency to examine the first section had had time to extinguish somewhat. This is the explanation, rather different from Fehrer's, that is offered by Zimbardo and Miller.

One lesson that is underlined by this whole body of research has been touched on at the beginning of this chapter. It is that the measurement of exploration through the degree of mobility in a maze does not enable us to distinguish what animals are moving away from and what they are moving toward; techniques which permit this distinction might well lay bare relationships that the other technique obscures.

A second lesson is the desirability of bearing in mind ecological factors. It is driven home further by two other experiments. Petrinovich and Bolles (1954) found that it was easier to train thirsty rats than hungry ones in the habit of always entering the same arm of a T maze. But when reward depended on alternating between arms on successive trials, hungry animals learned better than thirsty ones. The experimenters related their finding to the fact that wild animals are likely to find water continually at the same place, while food will rarely be found at the same place repeatedly, because of depletion or through the scaring away of prey. Since the subjects of the experiment were laboratory rats which never had to hunt for their food, the implication is that the selective advantage of varying movements when hungry and repeating them when thirsty may have caused these tendencies to be inherited. Nevertheless, an experiment by E. L. Walker (1956) shows that thirsty animals will be more likely to alternate between the arms of a Y maze if a water reward follows either response.

That similar effects may be produced as well, or instead, by learning is indicated by a finding of Grossberg and Sprinzen (mentioned by Estes and Schoeffler 1955). They allowed two groups of rats to find food on a table top for two weeks, but one group always found the food in the same places and the other group found it in places that constantly changed. When tested subsequently in a Y maze, the latter group were more prone to alternate between the arms than the former.

Fear

It is well known that the novel, the strange, the unfamiliar is apt to repel and to provoke the emotional disturbances that we regard as indexes of fear. Yet in other circumstances, the same phenomena may elicit indexes of pleasure, attract animals toward them, and be eagerly sought out. The properties of objects or situations that we have seen to be most potent in prompting exploration resemble those that we might expect to provoke "fear of the unknown." We might thus expect novel stimulus patterns to attract and repel in turn or to arouse some degree of conflict or vacillation between approach and withdrawal.

Common observation bears this out. If an unfamiliar object, such as a human hand, is introduced into a rat's cage or if a strikingly novel toy is laid in front of a human infant, the contest between the two opposite tendencies is likely to be clearly perceptible. The subject will survey the object from a certain distance, apparently alert and delicately poised, perhaps even oscillating, between advance and withdrawal. If the object moves or undergoes some other sudden change, the subject will be startled into a hurried retreat. But if it remains stationary and innocuous, the subject will sooner or later begin to edge slowly forward until it can be closely inspected.

What is apparently behavior of the same kind has been observed in birds. Chaffinches react to the sight of a predator by "mobbing" it, a characteristic response pattern which includes moving up to within a few feet of the predator, making short flights alternately toward and away from it, and uttering peculiar "chink" sounds (Hinde 1954, Marler 1956). Mobbing is a rather mysterious form of behavior. It might be thought that it serves to frighten the predator away. But mobbing does not always have this effect and may even make a chaffinch more vulnerable to attack than it would have been otherwise. It may warn other chaffinches or lure a predator away from the chaffinches' young. But Hinde and Marler suggest strongly that mobbing is at least partly a form of exploratory behavior, with the vacillatory

122

movements reflecting a conflict between approach and escape. A tendency to observe sources of danger from a distance makes good biological sense. A prominent component of mobbing is visual fixation of the predator with the medial fovea of each eye in turn, and mobbing exhibits the same short-term and long-term decrements with prolonged exposure to the eliciting stimuli that have been found in the exploratory behavior of the rat. Marler reports that chaffinches are likely to respond to any strange object with behavior closely resembling mobbing and give a "subjective impression of curiosity or inquisitiveness." Having done this, they appear to "avoid (the object) or its location for a time."

Lorenz (1956) supplies a particularly graphic description of the competition between flight and exploratory approach in the raven:

> A young raven, confronted with a new object, which may be a camera, an old bottle, a stuffed polecat, or anything else, first reacts with escape responses. He will fly up to an elevated perch and, from this point of vantage, stare at the object literally for hours. After this, he will begin to approach the object very gradually, maintaining all the while a maximum of caution and the expressive attitude of intense fear. He will cover the last distance from the object hopping sideways with half-raised wings, in the utmost readiness to flee. At last, he will deliver a single fearful blow with his powerful beak at the object and forthwith fly back to his safe perch. If nothing happens he will repeat the same procedure in much quicker sequence and with more confidence. If the object is an animal that flees, the raven loses all fear in the fraction of a second and will start in pursuit instantly. If it is an animal that charges, he will either try to get behind it or, if the charge is sufficiently unimpressive, lose interest in a very short time. With an inanimate object, the raven will proceed to apply a number of further instinctive movements. He will grab it with one foot, peck at it, try to tear off pieces, insert his bill into any existing cleft and then pry apart his mandibles with considerable force. Finally, if the object is not too big the raven will carry it away, push it into a convenient hole and cover it with some inconspicuous material.

We can see how the exploration of novel objects is combined with fragments of behavior connected with eating and fighting. This recalls Lagutina's (1958) experiments with cats and monkeys, in which stimulation of most cortical points produced both implicit signs of the orientation reaction and overt orienting responses but, when certain points were stimulated, these responses were combined with alimentary or defensive responses.

The contest between caution and boldness in the reactions of monkeys and apes to novel stimuli dominates the observations of Dolin,

Zborovskaia, and Zamakhover (1958). These Russian experimenters introduced various objects—geometrical figures, tin boxes, toys, smaller animals—into the living cages of their subjects and watched from behind a one-way screen. The first reaction was invariably one that they call the "inhibitory reaction": the subject kept his distance from the stimulus object, remaining frozen in one posture, staring and often gaping. This phase then gave way to a phase of active exploration: the subject approached the object, looked at it from all sides, sniffed at it, touched it, handled it. There were often traces of alimentary, aggressive, or sexual behavior. The exploratory phase might last for over an hour, but if the novel object continued to be present, periods of active exploration would alternate with periods of passive staring in a trancelike state. The inhibitory reaction was likely to be more prominent with certain individual subjects, with living stimulus objects, and on the first day that the object was encountered.

The strength of the fear that can sometimes overcome any tendency to explore a novel environment is best seen when animals have access to a device for relieving fear. Harlow and Zimmermann (1958) have ascertained that an infant monkey, reared away from its natural mother and in the presence of a cloth-covered model, will come to treat the model as a mother substitute. When such an animal is placed in a room full of novel objects, but without the model, it is likely to "freeze in a crouched position" or "run rapidly from object to object screaming and crying." If the model is present, it will cling to it. After a few trials with the mother substitute, fear will die down sufficiently for exploratory tendencies to come to the fore. The monkey will use the mother substitute as a "base of operations" and "will explore and manipulate a stimulus and then return to the mother before adventuring again into the strange new world."

The common technique of placing an animal in a maze where it is showered with novel stimuli from all quarters, and recording its wanderings, is especially inadequate for the study of interactions between exploration and fear, when movements toward and away from novel features of the environment need to be contrasted. Methods which allow the animal a choice between remaining in familiar surroundings and venturing afield into new territory are much more enlightening in this connection.

Such a method has been applied by two experimenters. The first is Montgomery (1955). He established that elevated maze alleys are more fear-inducing than enclosed alleys by testing rats in Y mazes with varying proportions of arms of the two varieties. Animals offered the choice spent much more time in enclosed arms and entered them more frequently, to the extent of giving up the usual tendency of a rat in a Y maze to enter different arms in turn (spontaneous alternation). Elevated alleys are presumably more apt to arouse fear than enclosed alleys because they present a much more complex assortment of novel stimuli.

In another experiment, subjects were tested with one of the walls of the living cage opened up to give access either to an elevated or to an enclosed alley. The amount of time spent in elevated alleys increased from the beginning to the end of each 10-minute trial. This also happened with the enclosed alley on the first day, but thereafter its exploration showed the familiar within-trial decrease. Both types of alley evoked fear, manifested by retreats to the rear half of the living cage, but the elevated alley evidently evoked more fear and consequently more severe approach-avoidance conflict. Prolonged exposure to the sight of either type of alley seems to have led eventually to a gradual elimination of the avoidance tendency, but this occurred earlier with the enclosed alley. A day's rest between trials restored the avoidance tendency to some extent.

The other experimenter who has performed this kind of experiment is Welker (1957). As novel stimulus stimulation, he used a large rectangular enclosure. He subjected his rats on some days to forced trials, placing them directly in this box with no exit; on other days, they had free trials, in which they were able to enter the enclosure as often as they liked from a familiar carrying box. Much more exploration of the enclosure, measured by movement between the sectors of its floor, was recorded on forced trials. Forced exploration declined steeply through the course of each five-minute trial. Free exploration showed no such trend, but it increased steadily from day to day without ever reaching the levels characterizing forced trials.

Bindra and Spinner (1958) carried out an experiment in which they tested rats' reactions to their environment as a whole but made more detailed observations of their behavior than is usual. They prepared three test cages, representing three degrees of dissimilarity to the animals' living cages. There was actually some confounding of variables, since the more novel a test cage was, the more complex it was also.

Of the various responses that they recorded, sniffing went down with increasing novelty and complexity of the environment, whereas grooming went up. The amount of locomotion did not differ significantly among the three test cages, nor did the amount of freezing (i.e., sitting "rigidly motionless, or slightly trembling, in a hunched or prone position, with eyes open"), although there was more freezing in the two most novel environments. Within the fifteen-minute test periods, locomotion and sniffing declined from beginning to end, freezing increased steadily, and grooming rose to a maximum after about twelve min-

125

utes, decreasing thereafter. The authors stress that there were considerable individual differences and that not all the subjects followed these predominant trends.

The locomotion and sniffing responses can be identified as locomotor exploration and orienting behavior, respectively. Freezing is commonly accepted as a manifestation of fear, since it is a frequent response in animals to threatening situations; it has the obvious biological advantage of making a threatened animal less conspicuous or, at least, minimizing stimuli that would provoke attack in an enemy. Grooming bears all the marks of *displacement,* the tendency of an animal subjected to conflict or frustration to engage in some activity that is part of its repertoire but apparently irrelevant to the needs of the moment (see Tinbergen 1951). Since the rats in the experiment were most inclined to groom when exploratory behavior was waning and freezing was on the increase, it seems likely that displacement was due to a conflict between these two responses. Significantly enough, there was less grooming during the early part of the test period, when exploration dominated, and toward the end, when freezing dominated.

The factors that determine whether exploratory or fearful reactions will come to the fore when an animal encounters some unusual pattern of stimulation are complicated and call for much more study.

To a large extent, it seems to be a matter of how novel or complex the stimulation is. Extreme novelty or complexity tends to induce avoidance, and moderate novelty or complexity to induce approach. But another factor that evidently makes a great deal of difference is whether an animal is plunged into the midst of a totally unfamiliar environment or whether its environment contains both relatively novel and relatively familiar elements.

In the latter case, the general tendency is for the animal to keep its distance from the novel elements at first, with perhaps a few scattered exploratory forays, and then to become more and more inclined to expose itself to novelty as time goes on. But when an animal is attacked by novel stimuli from all sides, it does not have the same choice. There is then likely to be intensive exploratory activity initially, with a subsequent rapid decline. The observations of Bindra and Spinner show that this exploration may be replaced by behavior indicative of fear. Other investigators have been content to record the decrease in exploration without noting whether it gives way to a tense or a relaxed state. The fear is, of course, occurring at a stage when the animal would not yet have been ready for much spontaneous approach to the novel stimulus objects if it had had the alternative of remaining in familiar surroundings.

Much of the exploration that an animal indulges in when it is totally immersed in novelty may, Welker (1959) contends, really consist of looking for a way out. During the last few trials of his experiment (1957) mentioned earlier, when he had attached small cubes and other objects to the walls of the enclosure, the rats had more contact with these objects during forced than during free trials, and the objects most frequently explored were those on both sides of the doorway. In a later experiment (1959), he provided an avenue of escape from the test box into a small dark box, and the rats were quick to make use of it. When the illumination of the test box was dimmed, they would reenter.

It is clear, however, that not all the locomotor exploration of the rat can consist of attempts to find a path leading to a familiar or a dark environment. The power of stimulus objects to attract exploration does not depend solely on low luminosity or association with exits. And the rats that are most mobile when immured in a novel enclosure spend more time, and not less, in the enclosure than others when access to familiar living cages is open (Hayes 1960). They do not, therefore, seem the most eager to find an exit.

There have been a few experiments in which variations in fear were produced by other means than by varying the novelty or complexity of the environment to be explored.

Montgomery and Monkman (1955) failed to produce any effect on exploration of a Y maze by frightening rats before their entry into the maze, whether by strong auditory stimulation or by electric shock. The sounding of a buzzer while the animals were in the maze reduced activity temporarily, and administering a shock in the course of exploration provoked a large increase in activity during the shock and a depression of activity thereafter. These last effects of painful or startling stimuli are, of course, well known and by no means special to exploratory behavior.

Montgomery (1955) compared tamed and untamed rats, finding the former more ready to make exploratory sorties from their living cages into an adjacent maze alley. Barnett (1958) has shown that wild rats are apt to avoid novel objects that are placed in their living cages, even to the extent of not eating if the food can be obtained only by going near them. In these circumstances, tame rats will approach and explore the novel objects without delay, and their feeding is not disturbed. It is known that wild rats differ physiologically from laboratory-bred rats in several ways, including ways that can be expected to make them more susceptible to fear. For example, they have considerably larger adrenal glands.

That the strength and direction of locomotor responses can be affected by stimuli that do not present themselves until the responses have been completed has been demonstrated in experiments of three types.

Successive Exploration of the Same Path

In the first type of experiment, there is only one path that an animal can explore, and the strength of the locomotor response is compared on successive trials. It is exemplified by an experiment of Chapman and Levy (1957). Female rats, satiated with food, were allowed to run along a straight runway to an empty end box on each of nine consecutive days. The end box was so constructed that the animals could not see what was in it before they entered it. On the tenth day, the brown masonite that had previously covered the floor and walls of the end box was replaced by a pattern of black and white stripes. The result was that the rats ran out of the starting box much faster on the eleventh and succeeding days. The running is thus a clear example of inquisitive locomotor exploration, and it was evidently reinforced by the stimuli that followed its performance on the tenth day.

It is not possible to say how far the phenomenon was due to novelty and how far to surprisingness. The response was much stronger on the tenth day than on the first day, when the masonite was novel, but fear of the unfamiliar environment may have interfered with running on the first day. The operative factor might have been the failure on the tenth day to find stimuli that had repeatedly been present in the end box hitherto and had thus become expected.

Choice of a Path Offering Different Stimuli from Trial to Trial

The second type of experiment allows a choice between a path that leads to different stimuli on different occasions and a path that always leads to the same stimuli. In a maze used by Krechevsky (1937b), for example, there were two paths leading to food, one a standardized path of alternative left and right turns and the other a path which varied in its pattern of turns from trial to trial. He found that normal rats will take the varying path more frequently than the other, even if it is longer. They will, moreover, tend significantly to take whichever of the two paths they did not take last time.

Havelka (1956) has shown that some rats, but not all, show a consistent preference for visiting areas where the location of food is randomly varied from trial to trial rather than areas where the same quantity of food is always available at one and the same spot.

Spontaneous Alternation

In the third type of experiment, there is a choice between a path leading to stimuli that the animal has recently experienced and a path leading to other stimuli.

A Dashiell maze (Fig. 5-1) offers twenty paths of equal length from a starting box at one corner to a goal box at the diagonally opposite corner. Rats trained in such a maze will vary their routes among these twenty in a series of trials (Dashiell 1930).

One of the most consistently reported of all observations about rats is that they will alternate between the two arms of a T maze or Y maze on successive trials, if entries into both arms are equally rewarded. A tendency to shift from one response to another has likewise been noted in human beings and in animals of other species when several responses with comparable consequences are available. The literature is reviewed by Dember and Fowler (1958).

This phenomenon certainly seems to be relevant to stimulus selection in general and locomotor exploration in particular, since it is apparently a matter of seeking variety and shunning monotony. But we must be cautious. In most of the experiments in question, the responses were means of securing food or some other extrinsic reward; exploration was clearly not their sole function, although it could have been a subsidiary one. Secondly, the apparatuses were so designed that the animals were varying their responses as they varied the stimuli to which they exposed themselves. The relative importance of these two facts is hard to determine.

However, the latter difficulty has been resolved in two similar experiments by Glanzer (1953b) and Montgomery (1952) in which a cross-shaped maze like the one depicted in Fig. 5-2 was used. If a rat is started at S on one trial (with N blocked off) and at N on the next trial (with S blocked off), he will then have a choice between performing a different response (a turn in a different direction) from the last time or entering a different arm (repeating the same response). Goth Glanzer and Montgomery established that rats vary the arm entered rather than the response per-

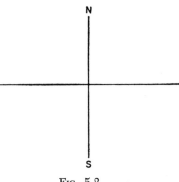

Fig. 5-2.

129

formed. Their procedures differed, however, in two respects: (1) Montgomery's animals received food at the end of whichever arm they entered, where Glanzer's received none, although they were hungry; and (2) Glanzer's animals could see into both arms from the choice point, while Montgomery's had their view of the arms blocked by one-way doors.

Even though alternation is shown to be a matter of changing stimuli rather than changing responses, we must still be circumspect about claiming that it has an exploratory function. It will be noted that the stimuli encountered *before* entering the two arms differ as well as those encountered *after* entering. In fact, if the arms are visible from the choice point, the stimuli to which a rat is exposed before entering an arm will resemble those to which he is exposed after. This fact underlies the *stimulus-satiation hypothesis* with which Glanzer (1953a) attempts to explain alternation, i.e., the hypothesis that, with each moment that an animal continues to receive a stimulus, the tendency to make any response to that stimulus diminishes. This explanation implies that the direction of locomotion is determined by the stimuli that *precede* entry into an arm. However, whether or not Glanzer is right, we can ascribe an exploratory function to alternation only if we can show that the responses are affected by the nature of the stimuli that result from them and *succeed* them.

There are several experimental findings that provide the necessary demonstration. If the proprioceptive feedbacks from left-turning and right-turning responses are made more distinctive by requiring the rats to contort their bodies in distinct ways when entering the two arms, there will be a tendency to alternate responses as well as stimuli (Walker, Dember, Earl, Fawl, and Karoly 1955). Proprioceptive stimulation can, of course, occur only after a response has been selected. Similarly, Walker (1956) showed that the tendency to alternate is stronger in thirsty rats when a water reward follows the response than when there is no reward. Lastly, Sutherland (1957) showed that alternation is greater when the two arms lead into different goal boxes than when they converge on the same goal box.

We are thus justified in counting alternation behavior as a form of exploratory behavior. Whether it is inspective or inquisitive depends on whether all the sources of stimulation that will act after an arm has been entered are or are not already acting at the choice point. Whether the presence of the consequent stimuli at the time of selecting the response makes a difference or not is a question that calls for some research. So far, both the inspective and the inquisitive forms of alternation seem to obey similar principles. We shall, therefore, con-

130

sider them together with regard to the influence on them of the stimuli that occur after the response has been executed.

Novelty. Alternation appears to be principally a means of gaining contact with stimuli that have short-term novelty in preference to ones that have not. We can see this from the fact that alternation is more likely when the intervals between successive trials are short (Dember and Fowler 1958). Moreover, the tendency to alternate can be strengthened by confining rats in the goal box for ten minutes after entry into it, thus prolonging exposure to the stimuli resulting from the response (Glanzer 1953*a*).

A rat will tend to enter a maze arm that provides novel stimuli, even without having run into a different arm shortly before. For example, Glanzer (1958*b*) and Sutherland (1957) have shown that if a rat is placed in one arm or its goal box and exposed to the stimuli therein without having reached them from the choice point, it will still be likely to enter the other arm on being allowed a free choice shortly afterward.

If satiated rats are permitted to see into two black (or white) arms, with entry into them prevented by glass partitions, and then placed in the maze again to find one arm changed from black to white (or vice versa) and the partitions removed, they will then be more likely to enter the arm whose albedo has changed (Kivy, Earl, and Walker 1956). The strength of this preference is much greater when the initial exposure lasts fifteen or thirty minutes than when it lasts one minute, suggesting that the *degree* of short-term novelty plays a part.

Dember (1956) performed an experiment resembling the one by Kivy, Earl, and Walker that has just been considered, but he exposed his rats to a black and a white arm during the preexposure period and made the arms either both white or both black for the free-choice trial. In these conditions, the animals preferred to enter the arm that had been changed. It presented the same albedo that had been received from the other arm during preexposure; but the combination of, say, right arm and whiteness brought together stimuli that had been received separately earlier, so that an effect of *relative novelty* is indicated.

A relation between relative novelty and inquisitive exploration is likewise indicated by the results of Krechevsky's experiment (1937*a*), which was mentioned earlier in this chapter, and those of an experiment by Hebb and Mahut (1955). It will be remembered that Krechevsky's subjects showed a preference for entering a path whose precise pattern of turns varied from one trial to the next. Yet this variable path and the alternative unvarying path consisted of similar

131

lengths of maze alley and right and left turns. It was merely the combination of these items that was novel in the variable path. Hebb and Mahut offered their rats a choice on each trial between running along a short straight alley to a goal box containing food and taking a much less direct route through a maze with manifold twists and turns and culs-de-sac. When the indirect, labyrinthine path was left unchanged from trial to trial, it was followed 12 per cent of the time. But when it was continuously altered so that similar elements were encountered in a succession of different arrangements, it was followed 42 per cent of the time.

It is no simple matter to differentiate the effects of short-term absolute novelty, short-term relative novelty, surprisingness, and incongruity. The last two present the difficulty that, when a number of stimulus elements are simultaneously accessible, it is usually impossible to know whether the animal receives them all at once as a spatial pattern or samples them in turn as he runs past them; i.e., changes his receptor orientation. The effects of the last two variables could be segregated from those of the first two by comparing a situation which has presented an uninterrupted succession of different patterns with one in which a certain combination of stimuli has remained fixed for many trials (sufficient for expectations to be formed) and is suddenly changed.

A hint that *surprisingness* or *incongruity* may add its quota to the vigor of inquisitive exploration can be extracted from a second experiment by Hebb and Mahut (1955). A group of rats had been put through 150 trials in which the direct straightway and the alternative route through the maze were both available. The maze was constantly altered from one trial to the next, but, throughout these 150 trials, it was composed of barriers that were so arranged that a rat was bound to come up against one after another of them in his attempts to find the exit. Then, for an additional 50 trials, the barriers were placed in a corner where they were visible but offered no impediment to locomotion. At the beginning of this series of trials, there was a steep but temporary rise in the proportion of entries into the maze. Moreover, the entries into the maze at this juncture were far more numerous in this group than in another group of rats that had had the barriers in the corner throughout the experiment. However, we badly need experiments in which the effects of all these distinct, though related, variables are isolated and compared.

An experiment by Denny (1957) demonstrates that the *long-term novelty* as well as the short-term novelty of stimuli consequent on a response can affect the probability of repeating that response. He used

132

a T maze with one black and one unpainted arm (the effect was not obtained when the arms were similar). Hungry rats were given forty-eight trials, two a day, so arranged that each subject was forced to visit one arm on four of each successive block of six trials and the other on two. All responses were rewarded with food. On the day following the completion of this course of training, and again a week later, the animals were given two free trials, during which both arms were open. They then showed an overwhelming preference for entering the arm other than the one they had been forced to visit during two-thirds of the training trials.

Complexity. In an experiment by Berlyne and Slater (1957), rats tended to enter a maze arm that led to complex stimulation (in the form of visual figures attached to the wall of the goal box and objects laid on its floor) when the other arm led to an empty goal box. The goal boxes were invisible from the choice point.

Kittens, studied in a similar maze by Miles (1958), learned to enter an arm leading to a manipulable object—a rubber ball, a small box, crumpled paper, or torn towelling—rather than one leading to an empty goal box. They also learned to find their way to a door that allowed them to leave the maze and explore the room, in preference to making for a goal box that contained a familiar, but empty, food dish.

Extraneous Drives. Chapman and Levy (1957) found that, in the case of twenty-two-hour-hungry rats, novel or surprising stimuli that became effective after a running response did not significantly affect the speed of the response on subsequent trials, although, as we saw earlier, they made a striking change in the behavior of satiated rats. And De Valois (1954) found variability in a maze offering several paths to decrease when thirst or electric shock were present at high intensities.

It will be recalled that, according to Walker's (1956) experiment, the tendency to alternate is intensified when rats are thirsty and rewarded with water. Whether all forms of reward would have this effect, as Walker (1958) hypothesizes, remains to be verified. Experiments by Farber (1948), Fowler and Fowler (quoted in Dember and Fowler 1958), and others make it seem likely that responses followed by the relief of pain and fear will be repeated with unusually low variability, accounting for the rigidity, stereotypy, or fixation that so many writers have recognized as a consequence of frustration or stress.

Brain Operations. Rats that have undergone brain operations which resulted in the removal of part of the cerebral cortex do not evince the preference for a variable path over a standardized path that is characteristic of a normal rat, except when the variable path is the shorter (Krechevsky 1937c). Brain-damaged rats likewise show less variability of route in a Dashiell maze (Krechevsky 1937a).

LOCOMOTOR EXPLORATION AND LEARNING

Whether inspective locomotor exploration is learned or not is an extremely difficult question to answer. The tendency to approach novel stimulus objects is so universal within and among species, and it is in evidence so early in life, that an answer would necessitate an elaborate investigation with animals reared for some time after birth in highly artificial conditions, precluding exploration. But this would be impossible without a drastic curtailment of opportunities for normal development such as, we now know, must have the most widespread deleterious effects on the whole organism. Without completely identifying, and somehow controlling for, these effects, an accurate answer is not possible. Supposing that this treatment produced abnormally weak exploratory tendencies, it would be impossible to state whether it was because the animals were prevented from learning to explore or because they had suffered some more far-reaching impairment.

Exploratory locomotion obviously does not follow the pattern of inborn reflexes that are activated by stimuli with specific physicochemical properties and give rise to uniform response sequences. Its flexibility in concomitance with environmental circumstances recalls that of the appetitive movements that so often lead up to more rigid consummatory activities in the predominantly instinctive behavior of lower animals (Tinbergen 1951). There could conceivably be some sort of innate feedback mechanism that steered animals toward parts of the environment with properties that warrant exploration.

On the other hand, it is possible that locomotor exploration consists of learned responses. They may be called forth by some kind of disturbance provoked by sufficiently novel or complex external stimuli, and they may be reinforced by the adaptive reduction of the disturbance through continued or intensified exposure to the disturbing stimuli. Perhaps improved descriptions of both the unlearned and the learned elements in behavior will one day make these two hypotheses seem less far apart.

The problems raised by inquisitive exploration are quite different. Exploration that serves to bring a previously inaccessible object into view must be guided by cues that indicate the direction in which the object is to be found. We have seen that a path is less likely to be entered when the stimuli to which it leads have recently been encoun-

tered. This means that the cues at the entrance to the path must interact with traces left in the nervous system by recent experiences.

To demonstrate instrumental learning, however, we need more than
proof that events following previous performance of a response have
affected the probability or strength of its future performance. We must
also show that the effects of these events are lasting, which is generally
taken to mean that they persist over an interval of at least twenty-four
hours. This was the case in the experiment by Chapman and Levy
(1957) and also in the one by Denny (1957). In the latter case, however, the exploratory response was inspective, and there was also a
food reward. A further hint of a long-term trend comes from Montgomery's (1952) experiment, in which the tendency to alternate was
not statistically significant on the first day but rose to a significant level
thereafter.

Other experiments have been inconclusive on this point. Berlyne and
Slater (1957) found no significant preference at all between entering
an arm leading to a novel visual figure and an arm leading to a familiar one. That the rats could distinguish the two figures and their
degrees of novelty is shown, however, by their tendency to spend more
time sniffing at the more novel one. It has been found that rats will
readily learn to enter a Y-maze arm leading to a Dashiell maze rather
than one leading to a cul-de-sac (Montgomery 1954, Montgomery and
Segall 1955). But it is difficult to determine what property of the
Dashiell maze was responsible for the effect. One possibility is that
the Dashiell maze was preferred to the cul-de-sac because it was
roomier and allowed the rats to circulate freely without having to turn
around in cramped quarters. This is especially plausible in view of the
fact that rats will learn to shun blind alleys in favor of less constricting
areas if given the choice (MacCorquodale and Meehl 1951, Berlyne
and Slater 1957).

Nevertheless, as the next chapter will show, the rat, like other mammals, will learn an arbitrarily selected response quite readily if that
response is followed by certain nonvital stimulus consequences. It
would seem highly probable that, if such responses as bar pressing can
be learned in this way, locomotion can just as well. But experiments
on locomotor exploration have evidently not yet identified the essential variables.

Chapter 6

EXPLORATORY BEHAVIOR:
III. INVESTIGATORY RESPONSES

Orienting responses and locomotor exploration work by effecting changes in the subject and not in the environment. They alter the states of sense organs, the positions of parts of the body relative to one another, or the position of the whole body relative to the environment. The result is a change in the spatial and other relations between the subject's receptors and the stimulus object and consequently a change in the nature of the stimulation received from the object. But neither the object itself nor anything else but the subject's body need be modified at all by the behavior.

In the case of investigatory behavior, these restrictions no longer hold. The only way in which an animal can control the stimuli acting on its receptors, apart from changing its own posture or location, is by effecting some sort of change in the environment. This can be done by acting either on the object in which the stimuli originate or on other objects intervening between the stimulus object and the subject's receptors.

Acting on the stimulus object itself is likely to take the form of manipulation. The only notable exceptions will occur when the stimulus object is another organism and investigatory behavior consists of aiming stimuli at that organism's receptors for the sake of information or entertainment that will be derived from its reactions. The use of questions to draw words from a human being is a case in point.

Manipulatory investigation, except when it is evoked in darkness, will generally be prompted by visual stimuli emanating from the object, and it will have the function of wresting further stimuli from the same object. It will thus be classifiable as inspective exploration. The stimuli that are added as a result of the investigatory responses may also be visual. Picking up the object and carrying it closer to the eyes may intensify or clarify the original visual excitation. Other operations may expose hidden aspects, external or internal, to the view or induce changes of form. Again, manipulation may cause the object to start acting on receptors of other modalities by moving it within range of tactual, olfactory, or gustatory receptors or by eliciting sounds from it.

Other investigatory responses affect some part of the environment that influences the transmission of signals between the object of interest and the subject's sense organs. Moving aside something that conceals the object would seem to be the commonest case in wild animals, although primates can certainly investigate objects by poking at them with sticks or by throwing things at them. Modern technology supplies a multitude of devices for making available, through manual operations, an immense range of stimuli that would otherwise be inaccessible, e.g., the telephone, the telescope, and the television set. As we shall see, experimenters interested in investigatory behavior have found it instructive to place such artificial stimulus-producing contrivances at the disposal of lower animals, although nothing of the sort could exist in the wild.

Most investigatory responses that bear on intervening objects will be inquisitive, since stimuli from the object of interest will normally be blocked until these responses have taken place. But some inspective forms are made possible by human artifacts. Placing binoculars in front of the eyes to examine something already seen with natural vision and turning the knob to bring the scene into focus are examples, as are switching on a light to see what has been making a noise in the dark and operating the volume control of a radio set.

There is one peculiarity of investigatory behavior that is momentous in its consequences and marks it off quite sharply from orienting behavior and locomotor exploration. This is the fact that an organism that is effecting changes in external objects as a way of modifying the stimuli reaching its own receptors is simultaneously modifying the stimulus field for any other organism that is in the vicinity. Changes in one individual's sense organs, posture, or location can alter only the relations between the perceived object and the individual's own sensory equipment. The relations between the object and another individual's sensory equipment must remain untouched.

Investigatory behavior, especially in the richness and variety that it possesses for human beings, can thus create what contemporary philosophers call "public" or "intersubjective" sense data. It can form the basis for massive collective activities in which whole societies can enjoy the products of individual investigatory accomplishments.

Human investigatory behavior includes much of the creative activity on which science, art, and entertainment depend. It also includes some of the behavior that is necessary in order to partake of what has been created in those fields, although orienting responses and

137

locomotor exploration will often suffice. Art and science have, however, other aspects which will be considered in Chapters 9, 10, and 11.

EXTRINSIC INVESTIGATORY RESPONSES

Most of the vital activities of animals in natural life conditions have to rely on the use of discriminations, whether acquired through learning or innate. Previous experiences may have revealed a correlation between the presence of certain stimulus patterns and the probability that a certain response will be rewarded, so that the response will be withheld in the absence of these patterns. Alternatively, certain instinctive responses have survival value if and only if they are performed in the presence of certain stimulus patterns; through evolutionary pressure, they may come to be released only by the appropriate sign stimuli. These discriminative stimuli will often not occur unless the organism does something to make them occur. Thus, behavior through which an animal is brought into contact with discriminative stimuli—positive or negative—which would not otherwise be forthcoming is necessary to guide subsequent behavior and to enable the animal to select advantageously between various courses of action or even between acting and refraining from action.

Orienting and locomotor responses will, no doubt, bear the brunt of this requirement in the wild. But there are times when they may be assisted by investigatory behavior—for example, when an animal pushes aside vegetation to see whether its quarry or its enemy is in the neighborhood or when it manipulates an object to find out whether it has a consistency and texture associated with edibility.

Many responses of both human beings and animals must combine investigatory with other functions. When a monkey, in the usual discrimination-training experiment, picks up one of the objects that are placed before him, his action may enable him to pick up food that was lying under the object. But it is also an action that provides him with information about the relations between the properties of the objects and the chances of finding food beneath them. This information will influence his later choices, improving his prospects of receiving an alimentary reward on future trials. Similarly, there have been vehement disputes over the precise effect on a human subject of hearing the experimenter say "Right!" in a verbal-learning experiment. Does the word reward by satisfying some such motive as a desire to excel or a desire to win the experimenter's approval, or does it merely inform the subject that he has responded correctly? Most of the usual experimental techniques make it difficult for us to segregate the informative from other functions of a response or to ascertain how far the provision of information acts as a reward.

There have been a few recent experiments in which this difficulty was circumvented by making observing and executive responses distinct. One of them is a demonstration experiment devised by Skinner (1957). A pigeon is placed in a box containing four keys and a colored area. The colored area bears one of four hues during each trial, and when the pigeon pecks at it, the names of the four hues appear in printed form on the four keys. To be rewarded with food, the pigeon must then peck at the key bearing the name corresponding to the hue of the colored area. The receipt of the reward thus depends, as it must in so many natural situations, on the performance of two responses in succession; the first response serves simply to present a discriminative stimulus identifying the form that the second response must take if it is to be effective.

In this last experiment, the investigatory response enables the animal to select a response that will be reinforced on every trial. Without it, there would be no way of selecting the correct key, and the animal could only peck at random—with the result that it would be fed on no more than one out of every four trials. Wyckoff (1952) has concentrated on an investigatory response that does not affect the number of food rewards that can be obtained but which, nevertheless, comes convincingly close to a great deal of human information gathering. A pigeon was trained to obtain food by pecking at a red key. Sometimes the same key was colored green, but the pecking response was then never reinforced, so that the pigeon built up a discrimination. In a later part of the experiment the key was white, and there was a fifty-fifty chance that pecking would produce food at the end of a particular period of thirty seconds. But if the pigeon stepped on a pedal, the key would become either red or green, indicating whether or not pecking during that period would be of avail. The investigatory pedal-stepping response was learned quite readily, even though, superficially, its only usefulness lay in sparing the pigeon the effort of a futile peck. When reinforcement was nondifferential, i.e., when food was obtainable through pecking regardless of the color of the light, the pedal-stepping response was performed infrequently.

Kelleher (1958) has demonstrated much the same phenomenon in chimpanzees. The investigatory response consisted of pressing a telegraph key, which was followed by the appearance of either a red light, indicating that food could be secured by pressing a second key, or a blue light, indicating that pressing the other key would be profitless. Performance of the investigatory response occurred in accordance with

139

the principles that are known to govern instrumental learning, although the rate of responding was higher during positive than during negative periods. The investigatory response was extinguished when the colors of the lights ceased to correspond with the availability or nonavailability of a food reward for pressing the other key.

Extrinsic investigatory manual responses in human beings have been studied by Holland (1957, 1958) in a series of experiments intended to bridge the gap between instrumental learning in animals and human occupations that require a prolonged watch for infrequent signals, e.g., those of the radar operator and the factory inspector. Holland's subjects were set the task of recording deflections of a pointer by pressing a key that reset the pointer. Most of the time they were in darkness, but they could provide themselves with 0.07 second of illumination by pressing a second key. Their behavior paralleled that of the rat or the pigeon that is trained to press a bar or peck at a panel for food in a Skinner box; the sight of a deflection of the pointer evidently acted as a reinforcer. When deflections appeared at fixed intervals of four minutes, the investigatory responses more or less ceased for a while after each occurrence and then rapidly picked up again as the end of the interval approached. With a fixed-ratio schedule (such that a deflection appeared during, say, every two hundredth flash of light) investigatory responses followed each other with practically no break. When deflections ceased altogether, the frequency of the investigatory response gradually dropped off in accordance with the usual extinction pattern.

These experiments represent rather isolated excursions into an enormous and largely neglected field of research. But they are concerned with investigatory behavior that subserves other activities, thus ignoring some of the problems raised by intrinsic investigatory behavior, with which the ensuing discussion will be primarily concerned.

INTRINSIC INVESTIGATORY RESPONSES IN MICE AND RATS

In the early 1950s, several investigators discovered, apparently independently and in some cases by accident, that an increase in illumination will act as quite a potent reinforcing agent for the bar-pressing response in the rat (Girdner 1953, Henderson 1953, Hurwitz 1956). Webb (Meehl 1950) and Girdner (1953) noted a similar effect with a rat's bar-pressing response followed by an indifferent sound, while Kish (1955) found changes in illumination to reinforce bar pressing in the mouse.

These discoveries were bound to perturb the psychological world somewhat. For one thing, it had been widely accepted that light is aversive to the rat and that a reduction in illumination will function as a reward (Keller 1941, Hefferline 1950, Flynn and Jerome 1952), and there had been many reports that rats have a strong tendency to enter black maze alleys in preference to white ones. An antipathy for light seemed reasonable in view of the rat's nocturnal propensities. Moreover, versions of drive-reduction theory that identified drive reduction with minimizing stimulation had wide currency (e.g., Miller and Dollard 1941).

It is, of course, known that animals will learn to perform operations that expose them to secondary reinforcers, i.e., to indifferent stimuli that have repeatedly accompanied a primary reinforcing condition such as the ingestion of food. Skinner (1938), for example, was able to produce a rising rate of bar pressing in a rat simply by having the response cause a clicking sound that had previously attended gratuitous deliveries of food pellets. It is tempting to suppose that the reward value of visual stimuli in the above mentioned experiments may also have been acquired through habitual feeding in light.

But this explanation does not square with the results of an experiment by Roberts, Marx, and Collier (1958). They found that changes in illumination were equally reinforcing for rats that had been fed in complete darkness since they were thirty days old (having been reared in extremely dim light until they reached that age) and rats that had always been fed in the proximity of fairly intense light.

Another hypothesis is that rats subjected periodically to increases in illumination will become more active or reactive because of the increased stimulation. This may cause them to press a bar more frequently than they would in a more uniform environment, thus giving a spurious impression that the response was being strengthened by its consequence. The hypothesis has been tested and found wanting in an ingenious experiment by Kling, Horowitz, and Delhagen (1956). They used two groups of rats, one of which was exposed to increased illumination while the bar was being pressed. Each member of the second group was paired with a member of the first group, and it received increased illumination when and only when its partner was receiving it, regardless of its own responses. According to the activity hypothesis, both groups of rats, since they were exposed to identical stimulation, should have been equally active. But the first group pressed the bar significantly more often, demonstrating that it is the coincidence between the response and the change in illumination that strengthens the former.

Another experiment refuting the hypothesis is that of Barnes and

141

Kish (1958). Mice had access to two bars, both of which could be pressed but only one of which delivered an increase in illumination. They pressed this bar significantly more often than the other.

Although this type of experiment represents investigatory behavior in its simplest possible form, stripped of all inessentials, complications abound even here, and few of the variables that need to be isolated have been methodically examined in the short time that the phenomenon has been known. If we consider only the nature of stimulus event consequent on the response, we have to consider the intensity of the illumination preceding the change, the intensity of the illumination following the change, and the direction and extent of the difference between the two. Then there are many factors in the animal's previous history that might have effects.

Direction of the Change. There is a measure of apparent contradiction in the literature on the question of how the reinforcement values of increases and decreases in luminous intensity compare. The more unexpected effect, namely that of increases, has by now been amply and repeatedly confirmed. A change from light to darkness has been reported to reinforce bar pressing (Keller 1941, Hefferline 1950, Roberts, Marx, and Collier 1958) and running responses (Flynn and Jerome 1952) in the rat. On the other hand, Hurwitz failed to raise the rate of bar pressing in rats when the response was followed by the extinction of a light, and Barnes and Kish (1958) met with the same failure in an experiment on mice.

The conditions of these various experiments differed, of course, in several ways. It is difficult to compare the initial intensities of light, since different writers used different manners of describing the illumination. But it would seem, by and large, that the removal of light was successful as a reinforcer when the light was fairly intense, and that those experimenters whose results were negative used fairly dim light. Keller noted, in fact, that the response rate increased with the intensity of the illumination that was removed. Roberts, Marx, and Collier (1958) found both onset and termination of light to have some reward value but the onset to have significantly more.

There is an experiment by Myers and Miller (1954) which uses quite a distinct technique from the rest of these experiments. They placed rats in a box that was divided into two compartments by a closed door. Pressing a bar caused the door to open, allowing access to the second compartment. Stimuli from the second compartment reached the subject as soon as the door opened, although the animals invariably indulged in locomotor exploration, i.e., running into the second compartment, which must have altered the stimulus field more radically. Nevertheless, the pressing of the bar must count as an investigatory response and, in spite of the complication of the subsequent locomotor exploration, there can be little doubt that much the same phenomenon is involved as in the experiments on changes in illumination. Myers and Miller obtained clear evidence for learning in the course of daily trials, taking the form of a progressive increase in the promptness with which the bar was pressed. But the learning was much more pronounced when the response allowed the rats to move from a black compartment to a white one than when the move was from white to black. So, once again, a change that intensifies visual stimulation turns out to be more effective than a diminution.

Intensity before and after the Change. Experiments in which the intensity of illumination before the change, the intensity resulting from the change (which we may call the *stimulus consequence*), and the extent of the change are varied and tested separately are badly needed but lacking. We have already mentioned the influence of the initial intensity on responses resulting in darkness (Keller 1941).

Henderson (1953), trying out stimulus consequences of various intensities, found the frequency of bar pressing to be highest with 16.56 millilamberts and lower with intensities above and below that level. In a similar experiment by Levin and Forgays (1959) using three consequent intensities, rats aged about seventy days showed maximum responsiveness at 1.76 millilamberts, the intermediate intensity, while the maximum for one-hundred-and-ten-day-old rats came at 33.04 millilamberts, the highest of the three intensities used. It seems likely that the results for the older group would also have undergone a reversal if a still higher intensity had been tried. It may be that for any particular animal there is some strength of stimulation that is optimally reinforcing, with lower and higher strengths less so, the actual optimum depending on various factors, including age.

But these two experiments confound the intensity of the stimulus consequence with the extent of the change, since the response was always performed in darkness. There may be a particular degree of change that is optimally rewarding, rather than a particular level of illumination.

Some attempt to segregate these variables was made in an experiment by Thomson (1955). Four intensities of light were used. Each intensity served both as an initial level of illumination and as a stimulus consequence for an equal number of trials, all sixteen combinations appearing equally often. The results revealed no influence of the initial level of illumination, but there was some evidence for an increase in the rate of bar pressing with the intensity of the stimulus consequence. Thomson's data are, however, not conclusive on this point.

In an experiment by Kish and Antonitis (1956), mice were allowed

143

to move freely among four platforms. One of the platforms made a click and sank slightly when a mouse landed on it, and this was the one on which the animals spent about 40 per cent of the time, although they went to it less and less on successive days' trials. Barnes and Kish (1957), using the same apparatus, found that mice would learn to go to a platform whose depression turned off intense noise and to keep away from a platform whose depression switched on intense noise. A comparison of these findings suggests that weak auditory stimulation is rewarding and intense auditory stimulation is aversive, but there is, unfortunately, another variable that was not controlled: the sound was transitory in the former case and continuous in the latter.

Novelty. There are two questions that must be kept apart in discussing the role of novelty, namely, "What is the effect of varying the novelty of the stimulus consequence?" and "What is the effect of varying the novelty of the change that results in the stimulus consequence?"

With regard to the novelty of the consequence, Myers (personal communication) carried out two experiments, using the box with two compartments. In one of them, rats in one group were placed for five minutes before each trial in the compartment that was to be made accessible by bar pressing. Those in another group were placed instead in the compartment from which they were to start. In the second experiment, a blinking light was present in the second or stimulus-consequence compartment. One group of rats had a similar light in their home cages for one week before the experiment began and also between trials. Another group never saw such a light outside the stimulus-consequence compartment. There was, therefore, in both experiments, a great difference in the novelty of the stimuli resulting from the response for the two groups of subjects. Nevertheless, all the animals learned the response, and neither experiment yielded an appreciable difference in performance between groups.

Premack, Collier, and Roberts (1957) had three groups of rats that were kept in darkness for twelve, twenty-four, and forty-eight hours, respectively, before the experiment. The rate of responding increased monotonically with the length of deprivation. This may appear to be evidence for an effect of novelty of stimulus consequence, since any visual stimulation would be more novel the longer the animals had remained in darkness. But the finding needs to be interpreted with caution. It may signify, not that visual stimuli are generally rewarding in proportion to their novelty, but that, for an animal that has had no visual stimulation at all for some time, visual stimulation has a reward value proportional to the duration of the deprivation. Alternatively, what is important may be the fact that the animals had no *change* in visual stimulation for so many hours. Roberts, Marx, and Collier (1958) found no difference in the performance of rats that had been kept in darkness before undergoing the experiment and others that had been reared in an environment that was constantly lit by a forty-watt bulb but was equally unvarying as far as intensity of illumination is concerned.

It is also possible that the decisive factor is not the deprivation of light as such but the deprivation of stimulation of any kind or of stimulus change of any kind during the period of darkness. This last possibility seems rather likely in view of findings with monkeys that are to be mentioned later. A crucial experiment to arbitrate between these hypotheses would be one in which animals were deprived of visual but not auditory stimuli before the experiment, their performance with a visual stimulus consequence being compared with that of animals deprived of all stimulation.

Whether the novelty of the change resulting from the response has any influence may be judged from the presence or absence of decrements in response strength with repetition, as with locomotor exploration. Here the findings have been confusing. Some experimenters have noted a steep decline within experimental sessions (Girdner 1953, Kling, Horowitz, and Delhagen 1956, Thomson 1955) and some have found no such trend (Hurwitz 1956, Levin and Forgays 1959).

Some experimenters have noted a decrease from one daily session to the next (Girdner 1953, Kling, Horowitz, and Delhagen 1956), while others have noted a steady increase over daily sessions (Hurwitz 1956, Levin and Forgays 1959). The attempt of Myers and Miller (1954) to train rats to press a bar when this response made it possible to pass from a white to a black compartment or vice versa succeeded only when trials were spaced a day apart. With massed trials about three minutes apart, there was no learning, which is additional evidence that the stimulus change loses its reinforcing power in losing its novelty.

It is interesting that rats, whether satiated and in darkness (Girdner 1953) or thirsty and in light (Schoenfeld, Antonitis, and Bersh 1950), will press a bar repeatedly, even when no special observable consequence follows the response. The frequency undergoes the familiar decline within and between trials, as with a visual stimulus consequence. This seems to mean that kinesthetic or tactual consequences or (when the animals are tested in the light) the sight of the bar moving may, like a change in illumination, have an initial reward value but subsequently pall.

Although it is not possible to explain exactly why one trend appeared in one experiment and another in another, it must be remembered that the experimental conditions have varied widely and in

145

many respects. If the stimulus change consequent on the response acts as a reward, and if it loses its reward value with repetition, the first fact should produce a progressive increase in response strength due to learning, while the second should counteract it by promoting extinction. The exact form of interaction between these processes, and which process outweighs the other, can be expected to vary with circumstances.

A further consideration is that the experiments in which a day-to-day decrease has been found have generally been ones in which animals were given a pretest in the apparatus without the stimulus consequence, and those in which an increase has appeared have generally omitted the pretest. One is reminded of the increase in locomotor exploration that often results from initial fear aroused by a new situation and is eventually followed by a decrease. It is possible that a change in illumination begins by inducing some fear, particularly in animals that are tense because they find themselves in an unfamiliar environment, and that this fear gradually gives way to a rewarding effect. The implication of this surmise is that even those experiments that produced a consistent increase in the strength of the investigatory response would have produced a decline if continued much longer.

Girdner (1953) had groups of subjects for which the increase in illumination began to result from the response on the first, second, fourth, and seventh days of the experiment, respectively. Before then, the response had no effect on illumination, but the animals were, of course, able to become familiar with the apparatus. The reinforcing effect of the stimulus consequence on the first day of its introduction was assessed by comparing the response rates that it induced with the response rates of a control group (which continued to have no stimulus consequence) on corresponding days. According to this test, its effect increased with the time elapsing before its introduction, except when this time exceeded three days. This argues for an additional measure of reinforcement attributable to *surprisingness,* since the change in illumination was equally novel for all groups, but they had had varying degrees of exposure to the situation with no change. The decay of surprisingness may also have something to do with the between-trials decline in response rate that has been noted when animals have had pretests with visual stimulus consequences. The sharp rise on the first day with the stimulus consequence can be seen clearly in the curves provided by some writers (e.g., Hurwitz 1956, Kling, Horowitz, and Delhagen 1956).

Hunger. The reward value of increases in illumination has been demonstrated separately with hungry (e.g., Hurwitz 1956, Marx, Henderson, and Roberts 1955) and satiated (e.g., Girdner 1953, Kish 1955)

146

animals. There have been some attempts to compare the strength of the investigatory response in hungry and satiated rats, with other conditions held constant. Hurwitz and De (1958) failed to find significant differences between animals deprived of food for six, twelve, and twenty-two hours, but two other studies have confirmed that the presence or absence of hunger makes a difference. In a dark box, rats that have not eaten for twenty-two hours will press a bar more frequently than satiated rats if the response is followed by five seconds of light (Forgays and Levin 1958). If light remains on for as long as the bar is held depressed, the response is more frequent with two hours of food deprivation than with satiation and greater still with twenty-three and one half hours of deprivation (Davis 1958).

Such differences seem to be due to the well-known tendency of hunger to raise the general level of responsiveness (Skinner 1938, Campbell and Sheffield 1953). Certainly, these experiments do not isolate the effect of hunger on performance from any effect it might have on the reward value of the stimulus consequence, as evidenced by the speed of learning.

Heredity. In the experiment by Kish and Antonitis (1956), mentioned earlier in this chapter, one strain of mice landed on the platform that made the click substantially more often than did another strain. But the difference appeared only during the first three days of testing. The former strain showed a greater decline in the frequency of the response with successive days until, from the fourth day on, the performances of the two strains were comparable. From this fact, the authors infer that the interstrain difference was unlikely to be one of general reactivity. We have, however, no way of knowing how far it was peculiar to investigatory behavior.

Tentative Conclusions

It seems clear that a change in visual or auditory stimulation favors the learning of a preceding motor response, and that the phenomena we have just been considering are not due to a transient feedback effect. This is shown by the increase over successive days of trials revealed by at least some experiments (Hurwitz 1956, Levin and Forgays 1959, Myers and Miller 1954) and by the fact that the response retains some considerable strength and extinguishes only gradually, once the stimulus consequence has been withdrawn (Hurwitz 1956, Kish 1955, Kling, Horowitz, and Delhagen 1956).

The principal reinforcing agent would appear to be the change itself rather than the stimulus resulting from the change, and the reward value of the stimulus change appears to increase with its short-term, and possibly also its long-term, novelty. Although the fact of

147

change seems to outweigh all others in importance, the reward value of a particular change may also depend on how nearly the extent of the change approximates some optimal intermediate value or on how nearly the stimulation that is introduced by the change approximates an optimal intermediate intensity. The reward value also varies with duration of sensory deprivation immediately preceding the experiment, although it is impossible at this juncture to say exactly what kinds of deprivation have this influence.

INTRINSIC INVESTIGATORY RESPONSES IN MONKEYS AND APES

The superior cerebral, visual, and manual equipment of the primates enables them to make much finer discriminations between perceptual patterns, as well as more finely coordinated manipulatory responses, than can lower mammals like the rat. It seems also to be a general rule that animals with more highly developed nervous systems are more given to investigatory and playful behavior generally. These facts would seem to imply that monkeys and apes will be especially fruitful subjects for investigation. There are, however, dangers inherent in the very scope that their investigatory activity offers. They will be sensitive to so many subtle variations in what is going on within their stimulus field that it will often be difficult to disentangle the contribution of each single factor. Those who have had opportunities to observe monkeys and apes at close hand for prolonged periods invariably dwell on their addiction to looking, mauling, prodding, licking, and generally squeezing every drop of possible entertainment from whatever crosses their path (see, e.g., Köhler 1921, Yerkes and Yerkes 1929).

Inspective Manipulation. Welker (1956a) exposed young chimpanzees to a series of stimulus situations, each of which involved the presence of two or more manipulable objects in front of the cage. The animals were confronted with each situation for a series of six-minute sessions, usually one per day, until satiation appeared. Then another situation was presented for a number of sessions, and so on.

The amount of playful handling of the objects declined steeply in the course of each session, and, although there would be a considerable recovery at the start of the next session, there was also a decline from session to session. Each animal showed some consistent preferences among objects belonging to the same situation, but the directions and strengths of these preferences varied widely from one subject to another.

Short-term and long-term novelty were thus the variables shown most conclusively by this experiment to prompt investigation. The importance of novelty has also been confirmed by other experimenters.

Voitonis (1949) left various objects in cages occupied by groups of monkeys—sacred baboons and pig-tailed macaques. Each object was eagerly played with when it first appeared, but interest in it gradually faded. As soon as the object was replaced by one that differed from it in shape, color, or size, the new object would attract energetic investigation for a while in its turn.

Inhelder (1955) introduced four zoo animals—two monkeys, a hyena, and a rhinoceros—to a variety of novel objects and observed them playing. His findings were similar to those of Welker and Voitonis. The animals lost interest in an object when it had been present for some time, but they would resume playing with it if they chanced upon some new way of using it, or if it were withdrawn for a time and then reintroduced.

A second experiment by Welker (1956b) brought out the importance of complexity. The chimpanzees were more responsive to multicolored, mottled rectangular blocks than to rectangular blocks of uniform color, and more responsive still to blocks that were heterogeneous in color and shape.

A rather similar technique was employed by Rensch (1957) with two monkeys—a smooth-headed capuchin and a common guenon—and a chimpanzee. He scattered test objects randomly on the floor of the cage and observed which ones the subjects picked up and handled. There were distinct preferences for colors, but apart from a preference for chromatic colors over gray, they varied between subjects and even from time to time in the same subject, a phenomenon compared by Rensch to "aesthetic vogues." When stimulus patterns of varying complexity were tried, there were preferences, but their implications were not too clear-cut, and they were not always statistically significant. A circular piece of white cardboard was picked up more frequently than pieces with irregular outlines. When black patterns painted on white rectangles were exposed, regular geometrical designs were generally more attractive than untidy and irregular designs. But this tendency was rather puzzlingly reversed in the case of one pair of patterns painted on larger rectangles. One member of the pair consisted of sixteen black strokes arranged in a matrix and the other of similar strokes haphazardly distributed. It may well be that once again we have apparently contradictory findings that the existence of some optimally satisfying intermediate degree of complexity would explain.

Welker's project also yielded information on variations of investigatory behavior with age (Welker 1956a, 1956c). During the first minute of a session, three- to four-year-old and seven- to eight-year-old animals played with the objects to a comparable extent, but the younger

149

animals showed much less satiation as the session continued. Two out of three of the younger animals showed no significant decline in investigation between sessions. Chimpanzees aged ten to twenty-six months, unlike three- to four-year-olds, spent more time looking at objects than handling them. After several sessions, however, they would begin to overcome their timidity and indulge in more and more manipulation. The fear of novel stimuli that we remarked on in the last chapter thus seems once again to be at work, with exploration growing in strength as fear becomes allayed through habituation. It also appears that the propensity for playful manipulation in chimpanzees, as apparently in man, reaches its maximum between infancy and adulthood.

Drawing. The scribbling and drawing for which monkeys and apes will occasionally show a taste must be considered investigatory behavior. Much of it, like the corresponding behavior at a certain stage in the human child, appears to be indulged in principally for the tactual and kinesthetic sensation that comes from rhythmic, sweeping movements. But there are signs that the visual products also are of some importance in the chimpanzee.

One female, the famous Alpha (Schiller 1951), showed some conformity to human notions of aesthetic value as well as to Gestalt principles of perceptual organization. When given a piece of paper bearing a circle, for example, she tended to keep her drawing within the bounds of the circle, showing some appreciation of figure-ground relations. And she scribbled in the vicinity of the gap in an incomplete circle, as if she were attempting to achieve "closure."

Opportunity for Manipulation as a Reward. Harlow and various collaborators have shown experimentally that complex manual operations can be self-reinforcing for the rhesus monkey; opportunities to perform them will promote learning, revealed by a rise in the frequency of performance and by the substitution of successful for unsuccessful actions, without reinforcement from any other source.

One of the operations that figured in these studies consisted of solving a complex manual puzzle, an arrangement of interlocking pieces that could be dismembered by undoing a series of fastening devices (a hasp, a hook, a pin, etc.) in a particular order. In one experiment (Harlow, Harlow, and Meyer 1950), an experimental group of animals had the puzzle left assembled in their home cages for ten days. The puzzle was periodically put together by the experimenters so that subjects could have repeated experiences of undoing it. A control group had the unassembled pieces in their cages for the same period. Both groups were subsequently tested, at first with food obtainable by pulling the puzzle to pieces and then with no food obtainable. In both situations, the experimental animals were clearly better at solving the puzzle than the control animals, which shows that their previous practice with no extrinsic reward had produced some learning. They actually performed better without food than with food, as its presence made them go straight to the later stages of the solution instead of going through the necessary preliminary stages first.

In order to gauge the resistance to extinction or satiation of this behavior, two monkeys were allowed five chances to open the puzzle on each of twelve days and then, on the thirteenth day, they were able to open it up to ten times an hour for ten successive hours. The outcome was that the proportion of successful attempts to solve the puzzle went up from day to day until the laborious last day, when there was a progressive decline in the number of devices opened although the rate of trying remained more or less constant.

The potency of whatever reward is at work is thus dependent to some degree on *short-term novelty*. The behavior can also be impaired by *brain operations* (Davis, Settlage, and Harlow 1950).

Discriminations can be based on the presence or absence of opportunities for manipulatory activity, as an experiment by Harlow and McClearn (1954) illustrates. The apparatus consisted of a board with a number of screw eyes inserted into it. Some of the eyes could be taken out of their holes, and others could not, movable and immovable ones being colored differently. Three monkeys were faced with a board of this sort for a one-hour trial on each of four successive days, and the percentage of responses aimed at the movable eyes mounted from day to day.

A rather similar series of experiments has been carried out by Rokotova (1953) in Russia. She was able to train a chimpanzee to pull a lever by using as reinforcing agent the receipt of miscellaneous objects (a different object for every trial) with which the animal was allowed to play for a short time. She interpreted this behavior as "a conditioned reflex based on the unconditioned investigatory reflex," but it is clearly a case of instrumental conditioning. When the response was reinforced after a white light but never after a blue light, the chimpanzee learned rapidly to withhold the response on receiving the negative stimulus. He likewise formed a discrimination between two buzzers, only one of which indicated the availability of a plaything. Extinction, conditioned inhibition, and speedy restoration of an extinguished response after renewed reinforcement were also brought about.

Voitonis (1949) demonstrated that opportunities to handle objects can motivate more impressive forms of learning than these. His monkeys became quicker and quicker at opening a puzzle box (fastened with a strap secured by nails and buckles) that contained nothing but stones. They would likewise learn to use tools without extrinsic incentives. They caught on to the use of a bucket to haul sand out of a well, an achievement that they could later adapt to draw water for drinking. In Birch's (1945) experiments, chimpanzees did not arrive at the response of pulling an object toward them with a T-shaped stick until they were able to familiarize themselves with the sticks in the course of investigatory play.

It might be thought that manipulatory behavior and its attendant stimuli acquire reward value through association with feeding and other primary rewards, since primates are bound to have performed many manipulatory operations in the course of satisfying their physiological needs. But this hypothesis is rendered unlikely by an experiment of Harlow, Blazek, and McClearn (1956), who found manipulation of a fastening device to be self-rewarding (improving with practice in the absence of extrinsic reinforcement) even for infant monkeys that had always been fed by hand.

In all these experiments, there is the difficulty that the response to be learned was followed not only by changes in the stimulus field but also by further manual responses. We do not know how far the motor processes were rewarding in themselves (and to the extent that they were, we do not have true exploratory behavior) and how far reward depended on the stimuli, including perhaps the kinesthetic stimuli, that resulted from them.

That playful manipulation is governed, at least in some measure, by the nature of its sensory outcome is supported by Welker's (1956a) experiment with chimpanzees. Five subjects showed a significant preference for handling objects that moved on pivots rather than objects that were identical except for being rigid. Objects whose manipulation caused a light to go off or a bell to sound were likewise markedly preferred by one subject, although the result for the other subjects was inconclusive.

Nevertheless, the possibility of handling an object is important for monkeys. Voitonis (1949) exposed his monkeys for a number of days to a specially designed chest of drawers and noted how often, and for how long, each of the twelve drawers was held open. Drawers that were empty or that could not be opened far enough to investigate their contents were soon avoided. Those that contained visual but nonmanipulable objects, e.g., a toy windmill or a flashing bulb under glass, were quite popular; one containing a ball that could be felt, but not brought into view, by thrusting a hand through a hole in a board, was about equally popular. But drawers that held pebbles or balls that could be picked up and removed were by far the most frequently opened.

A drawer whose opening caused a bell to ring was not particularly attractive to Voitonis's monkeys, as, in general, auditory stimuli were not. However, sounds were sought out by some bear cubs that Voitonis studied, as well as by a baby chimpanzee subject of Ladygina-Kots (1935).

Inquisitive Investigation. Other experiments achieve a more stringent demonstration of the reward value of sights and sounds by making stimulus consequences independent of manipulatory behavior once they have been introduced. The power of the stimuli in question to *reinforce* an investigatory response is also separated from any power they may have to *evoke* such a response, by withholding them until the response has been executed.

Thus, Moon and Lodahl (1956) have shown that a change in illumination will reinforce lever pressing in the rhesus monkey, as it will in the rat and the mouse. A change from a 60-watt lamp to a 15-watt lamp and the opposite change were about equally effective.

Monkeys will also learn to open a door with the possibility of looking out of the box in which they are confined as the sole incentive, and they will form a discrimination between colors characterizing a door that can be opened and another door that will not yield to pressure (Butler 1953).

Experiments in which monkeys are free to push and hold open a door ad libitum for long periods have shown how astonishingly resistant this behavior is to extinction or satiation. Three normal animals continued to repeat the response for nine, eleven, and nineteen hours respectively before giving it up (Butler and Harlow 1954). Six animals tested for ten hours on each of six consecutive days spent about 40 per cent of the time looking out. The frequency and duration of holding the door open showed no consistent trends either during or over daily trials, suggesting that the animals worked to maintain a "relatively fixed amount of daily visual . . . experience" (Butler and Alexander 1955).

This kind of investigatory behavior, like behavior leading to manipulation, is affected by *brain operations.* Amygdaloid injuries lower the speed of performing the correct response in a discrimination test, while temporal injuries appear to prevent monkeys from acquiring the discrimination in the first place. In a free-responding situation, however, monkeys with temporal or frontal ablations continue the investigatory response with a persistence comparable to that of normal monkeys.

Butler (1954) has compared the reinforcing power of a number of

153

different sensory experiences. The frequency of door-opening responses was lowest when the door gave out onto the empty room, higher when it exposed a display of fruit and other food, higher still for the sight of a toy train in motion, and highest of all for the sight of another monkey. In a second experiment, the sound of the train was a more potent incentive than the sound of a monkey, and both produced less response strength than when the response made the train or the monkey visible.

All these incentive conditions varied in so many respects that it is hazardous to make any generalization from the data, apart from concluding that not all stimulus consequences are equally rewarding. In particular, the sights and sounds emanating from another monkey might have special innate or acquired rewarding properties. It looks, however, as if the alternative incentive conditions might represent different degrees of *complexity* and, if so, some hint of a positive relation between complexity and reward value might be sensed.

Another experiment by Butler (1958) provides some evidence for a relation between investigatory reward value and *affective value*. Monkeys opened a door more readily to see another monkey than to see an empty cage, but less readily to expose themselves to the frightening sight of a dog. Similarly, there were differences among sounds in their effectiveness as reinforcers of a lever-pressing response. Cries from a solitary monkey were more effective than white noise, but emotional noises from the monkey colony and the barking of a dog were considerably less so.

Data pointing in the same direction were secured by Harlow and Zimmermann (1958). They tested infant monkeys in an apparatus of the kind devised by Butler. The animals pressed the lever more readily when it afforded them a glimpse of a real mother monkey or a cloth-covered model than when it allowed them to see a wire-netting model or an empty box, although all these incentives were effective to some degree. It will be recalled from the last chapter that infant monkeys accept a cloth-covered model as a mother substitute in default of a natural mother.

INTRINSIC INVESTIGATORY RESPONSES IN HUMAN INFANTS

The earliest clear forms of human investigatory behavior noted by Piaget (1936) consist of *secondary circular reactions,* which first emerge between the ages of three and six months. Orienting responses, directed at brightly illuminated areas or at objects with special associations, such as human faces and feeding bottles, appear within a few weeks of birth. These do not require the capacity for maintaining flexible relations between behavior and environmental events that matures later.

The term "circular reaction" was introduced by Baldwin (1895) to describe the repetitive and, to a superficial glance, self-reinforcing actions that are prominent in the infant, such as babbling and thumb sucking. These actions appear to be kept up for relatively long periods because the stimuli produced automatically by their preceding performance have the power to evoke a repetition; hence the circularity. It may also be that the same stimuli, being consequences of the response, act as reinforcers. But whether the actions in question result from instrumental conditioning due to such reinforcement, in which case they might qualify as investigatory responses, or whether they result from innate connections or from some form of classical conditioning, is still an open question.

Piaget distinguishes these *primary circular reactions*, which involve merely the direct influence of one action on another action of the same organism, from the later developing *secondary circular reactions*, which fit events in the environment into the circuit.

The kind of situation which Piaget regards as the prototype of the secondary circular reaction is as follows. The infant is lying in a crib fitted with a hood. A rattle hangs down from the hood, and a string the infant is able to reach is attached to the rattle. Having pulled the string in the course of random play and thus caused the rattle to swing and to sound, he reiterates the movement and resorts to it whenever he is placed in the crib as a procedure for making "interesting sights last." For the next few months, any action that chances to bring on an unforeseen happening is likely to be repeated and incorporated into a growing stock of resources for controlling external events. Once he has assimilated one of these response patterns, the child will generalize it to other stimulus situations and to other interesting sights. For example, when Piaget waved a watch about at some distance from the crib, one of his daughters reverted, as soon as the spectacle stopped, to the tried and tested device of pulling the string.

These reactions are unmistakable instances of instrumental conditioning, evidently reinforced by "interesting" environmental changes. Skinner (1951) likewise claims that instrumental conditioning can easily be demonstrated in the human infant by making almost any such change, e.g., switching a light on and off, follow any simple motor response. Investigatory responses of this sort are, according to Piaget, the child's first experiences of being able to influence external agencies by carrying out appropriate bodily movements. After all, he has little occasion to acquire instrumental responses to any end except the

155

provision of what we should regard as entertainment, both because his capacities are too limited for him to secure more vital satisfactions through his own efforts and because a rich repertoire of parental behavior is at hand to forestall biological distresses. Crying, which appears to be innate in certain circumstances and learned in others, is about the only contribution his own skeletal musculature can make to the cause of self-preservation, apart from emergency reflexes. A whole mass of more serious instrumental responses appears later in life; when the child is ready for them, they are able to build on the discriminations and coordinated responses that the investigatory secondary circular reactions have put at his disposal.

At five to seven months (Piaget 1936), a child will pull away a piece of cloth that is put over his face and blocks his view, a response clearly reminiscent of the door-pushing response by which a monkey frees himself from a monotonous stimulus field. The human child removes the obstacle to vision with intense glee, and, after a few more months have passed, the behavior turns into the indefatigable peek-aboo game, in which the visual field is recurrently blocked off by covering up the face or hiding behind a door for the sheer pleasure of having everything reappear.

Then comes a stage where the child is beginning to discriminate, and respond to, spatial and temporal relations between phenomena, and where he can fit two pieces of behavior, originating as secondary circular reactions, into a well-coordinated chain. This stage starts at eight to ten months. It is the stage where an object that is out of sight will be looked for in the place where it is usually to be found. If an object disappears behind a screen, the child will move the screen away or walk round it. This is an important step forward, Piaget stresses, as it implies the beginnings of some conception of a permanently existing object, i.e., some process whereby the child represents an object to himself after it has left the visual field, and anticipates its reemergence.

It may also be observed that this behavior is inquisitive, whereas the secondary circular reaction is inspective. And looking for a particular object behind a screen is specific exploration, while removing a cloth from the face is presumably diversive. In the former case, the child "knows what he is looking for" and is liable to be disappointed if his expectations are violated, but removing the cloth is a way of seeing anything that might be going on. Specific inquisitive behavior can be expected to appear later than the other form of investigation, since it presupposes a capacity for recognizing a signal that heralds a new absent stimulus and for somehow identifying what will follow.

While this is going on, the child comes to use his stock of secondary

156

circular reactions for sounding out the properties of new objects. On encountering something unfamiliar, he brings into play what resources he has for arriving at an "understanding" of it. The only understanding of which he is capable at this stage has, of course, nothing conceptual or intellectual about it. It amounts simply to learning what can be done to or with the object and what behavior to expect from it. So, when he finds himself face to face with a novel object, he is likely to begin by inspecting it visually and tactually, using the orienting responses that were his first resources for observation. Then he will probably try out one after another of the secondary circular reactions that have been applied with satisfactory results to similar objects. If the reaction extracts from the new object the same sensory consequences as it has extracted from familiar objects in the past, the new object is, to use Piaget's expression, "assimilated with old schemata." In behavioristic terms, this would mean that, by evoking responses and expectations similar to those evoked by certain familiar objects, it will be assigned to the same acquired-equivalence class; it is henceforth treated like them through mediated or secondary stimulus generalization.

Sometimes, however, performing a familiar operation on a new object leads to different, and thus surprising, results, or perhaps some accidental variation in the reaction produces an unexpected sensory experience. The child then repeats the operation as if trying to acquaint himself with the intriguing new properties that lie unsuspected in the object. He may thus acquire a derived secondary circular reaction on the basis of the old one, giving rise to what Piaget calls a new "schema," i.e., a new stimulus-response association with a corresponding expectation of outcome.

Finally, at the age of eleven months or so, the *tertiary circular reaction* shows itself. The secondary circular reaction was essentially repetitive. Having stumbled upon a method for bringing on some amusing occurrence, the child avails himself of it in much the same form over and over again. But now he performs the action in a somewhat different form each time. He varies his responses in order to observe the corresponding variations in the outcome. He drops a ball from different heights and at different places to see how the way in which it falls is thereby affected. He hits the tablecloth, the plate, the glass, and the fork with his spoon to see how differently they sound. He can thus be described as actively experimenting. This is not yet the systematically planned experiment of science, but it is already a matter of contriving changes in antecedent conditions to identify the associated changes in consequent events. It results in an incomparable broadening of the child's acquaintance with the behavior of external objects and with the relations between their behavior and his own, since he is no longer limited to fortuitous discoveries but actively brings about the stimulus patterns that will be most informative.

This description of the sequence the child passes through before the advent of speech and its attendant symbolic functions opens up a vast new universe of investigatory possibilities, and it is, of course, only a beginning. Piaget's account of this prelinguistic period is derived mainly from observations of his own three children. On the whole, they seem to agree with reports of other developmental psychologists and with common experience of infant behavior. But only the enormous program of rigorous experimentation whose necessity is indicated by Piaget's work can answer some of the outstanding questions and check some of the tentative conclusions. We can, however, provisionally trace the role of some of the collative properties of stimulus patterns that we are interested in.

Change of more or less any kind seems to be what first prompts orienting or secondary circular behavior. The strength of secondary circular behavior seems also, although we have only common observation to go on, to depend on the novelty (short-term and complete) of the consequent stimulus pattern. With regard to a particular pattern, it seems to follow a time course similar to the one we have so often noted in orienting behavior and locomotor exploration: the response wanes with massed repetition, reappears if the evoking stimulus is reencountered after an interval, but shows a downward trend with each reappearance until it is no longer called forth at all. As the work of Bühler and her associates, to be discussed in Chapter 8, illustrates, a simple, indifferent sensory event has only a brief reign as a source of infantile delight. During the first months of life, its appreciation is beyond the infant's rudimentary powers, or its impact is harsh enough to be alarming. And after a few more months, it is relegated to the realm of the vapid and the stale.

At the stage where old investigatory responses are tried on new objects, other factors, which we are not now in a position to delineate precisely, come into the picture. For instance, it cannot be clear without further experimentation how far the new object evokes the secondary circular reaction through generalization alone—in which case it would evoke it, if anything, less powerfully than the original evoking stimulus would if it were present instead at that moment—and how far it evokes it with special effectiveness because it is new and puzzling and challenging. In the latter case, implying properties peculiar to stimuli that are not too near to the original stimulus yet not too far, some sort of excitatory-inhibitory conflict would seem to be at work to increase the probability of the response. The prolonged exercise of a derived secondary circular reaction, once it has been discovered, may mean that surprisingness of the outcome is rewarding, but only as long as it remains surprising, or that it provokes some sort of discomfort which is relieved as the outcome ceases to surprise.

Responses which remove obstructions to vision seem to point to rather different sources of motivation, although they must involve the same intellectual acquisitions as the other forms of investigatory behavior that arise simultaneously with them. The removal of something covering the eyes may be a response to anxiety that animals, understandably enough from a biological point of view, innately experience when their vision is obstructed, or else to boredom brought on by meagerness of stimulation. Alternatively, or in addition, it may depend on the reward value of a sudden influx of visual excitation. The response of finding or unmasking a concealed object may be purely extrinsic investigation, motivated by whatever would motivate behavior directed at the same object if it were not concealed—as when a child tries to find a toy that he was playing with until it went out of sight. But there may be a supplementary reward value to regaining something after its disappearance, perhaps from the assuagement of frustration or from the fulfillment of an expectation (the relief of "anticipatory tension," Mowrer 1950). If something is known to be hidden but its identity is not known—a state of affairs notoriously unbearable to children, though usually when they are older than the infants we have been discussing—we have special effects attributable to the conflict that accompanies uncertainty. Bühler (1928) speaks of the "strange" and the "hidden" as the two breeding grounds for curiosity.

This cursory account shows how many intricately entangled problems are already thrown up by the scanty data that we have about investigatory behavior in infancy, and yet these problems must be simplicity itself compared to those that we must penetrate on the way to the corresponding behavior in adult human beings. It is, however, hopeful to recognize that rigorous variable-isolating experiments could easily be designed to take care of practically all the unanswered questions that we have reviewed.

INTRINSIC INVESTIGATORY RESPONSES IN HUMAN ADULTS
AND OLDER CHILDREN

Experimenters have found that visual stimuli will reinforce instrumental responses quite effectively in human children and adults without being required for the guidance of some later response. Ivanov-Smolenski (Ivanov-Smolenski, Gurevich, Skosyrev, and Soloveva 1933) has made extensive use of a method that he calls "conditioning with orienting reinforcement." It has been particularly successful and convenient to apply with school children. The response consists of pressing a rubber bulb (attached to a kymograph which registers the response automatically) on receipt of a simple visual or auditory conditioned stimulus. The reinforcement is supplied by a tachistoscopic glimpse of a picture. O. R. Lindsley (1956) has also used exposures of pictures to reinforce the pulling of a plunger in psychotic patients, and he has obtained quite high response rates with some subjects. Certain of the pictures that he used were nudes, which may, in more than one sense, have made the underlying motivation less pure.

Both Ivanov-Smolenski and Lindsley have been interested in showing similarities between the conditioned responses produced by such reinforcers and those that have been studied with more familiar experimental arrangements, or in studying aspects of learning processes in general that could equally well have been studied with other kinds of reinforcement. Neither of them has systematically varied the reinforcing pictures with a view to finding properties that make some pictures occasion more investigatory responses than others. There is, on the other hand, a series of experiments by Berlyne (1957c) in which precisely this was done.

In these experiments, the subject was seated in a darkened room, facing a tachistoscope. Every time that he pressed a lever, a figure in the tachistoscope became visible for 0.14 second. The instructions emphasized that the experiments were concerned solely with ascertaining how interesting certain pictures were, and that no questions about the figures would be asked at any time. The subject was free to expose himself to as many glimpses of a particular figure as he liked, and when he had seen enough of one figure he was to say "yes," whereupon the experimenter would replace it by a new figure.

Each subject took part in four experiments, designed to reveal the influence of different variables on the number of lever-pressing responses per card (see Fig. 6-1). The variables and the results follow.

Incongruity. Incongruous pictures of animals and birds (i.e., animals 2 and 4 and birds 3 and 5) elicited significantly more responses than pictures of normal animals and birds.

Complexity (Absolute Uncertainty). There was a series of six figures developing, by progressive addition of material, from a circle into a picture of a bear, and a similar series developing from a circle into a picture of a clown. It will be seen from Fig. 6-1 that the figures numbered 6 in both series are markedly more complex than those numbered 2 to 5, while those numbered 2 to 5 are more complex than those numbered 1. In information-theory terms, these three groups of figures differ in the amount of information to be absorbed before they

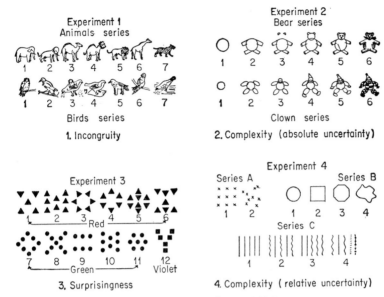

Experiment 1
Animals series

1 2 3 4 5 6 7

Birds series

1 2 3 4 5 6 7

1. Incongruity

Experiment 2
Bear series

1 2 3 4 5 6

Clown series

1 2 3 4 5 6

2. Complexity (absolute uncertainty)

Experiment 3

1 2 3 Red 4 5 6

7 8 9 10 11 12
Green Violet

3. Surprisingness

Experiment 4

Series A

1 2

Series B

1 2 3 4

Series C

1 2 3 4

4. Complexity (relative uncertainty)

FIG. 6-1. (From Berlyne 1957c).

can be identified (i.e., the uncertainty or entropy). The mean numbers of responses per card varied significantly between the three
groups, increasing with the degree of complexity. Whether a series
was presented in numerical order from 1 to 6 or in a random order did
not make any difference.

Surprisingness. There were twelve cards bearing geometrical figures
of colored spots. Figures 1 to 6 were composed of red triangles, figures
7 to 11 of green circles, and figure 12 of violet squares. Surprisingness
can be imputed to figure 7 and figure 12, since they both deviated
sharply from prominent characteristics shared by at least five figures
immediately preceding them, and these surprising figures elicited significantly more investigatory responses than figures 2 to 6 and 8 to 11.

Complexity (Relative Uncertainty). There were three series, each
containing figures with differing degrees of redundancy. Redundancy
is, in information theory, equal to 1 minus relative uncertainty, and
relative uncertainty is the ratio of the uncertainty in a set of signals
to the maximum uncertainty that there could be. Redundancy thus
measures the extent to which the information carried by different signals overlaps or is duplicated. Redundancy increases, and relative uncertainty thus decreases, when parts of a visual figure resemble one
another, since the existence of one part with certain properties makes
the existence of other parts with those properties more probable (Attneave 1954). Orderly arrangement, similarity in shape, symmetry, and

161

fewness of changes in contour are all inversely related to relative uncertainty, which is thus a measure of complexity.

In series A, one figure comprised nine crosses in a matrix pattern, and the other comprised nine crosses in an irregular arrangement. Series B contained a circle, a square, an octagon, and an irregular closed curve, all of approximately equal perimeter. The figures in series C were made up, respectively, of five parallel straight lines, two straight and three wavy lines arranged symmetrically, two straight and three wavy lines arranged asymmetrically, and five contrasting lines. In all cases, figures with more relative uncertainty attracted more investigatory responses, and the differences were significant throughout.

Questioning of subjects revealed that they usually continued to press the lever until they had identified the figures, and then ceased. We might expect that each tachistoscopic exposure would transmit an approximately equal quantity of information, so that more complex or uncertainty-laden figures would require more exposures to be recognized. It would then be understandable that they should occasion more investigatory responses. It is of interest, however, that the subjects, without instructions obliging them to do so, persisted spontaneously in exposing themselves to the figures until uncertainty had been eliminated.

Although all four experiments occurred equally often in all four temporal positions, there was a slight but significant tendency for later experiments to give rise to more responses per figure. The means increased, in fact, with a concave-downward curve reminiscent of the usual learning curve. It looks, therefore, as if the exposures to the figures provided some reinforcement for the response.

An age difference of some consequence was revealed when experiment 1 and slightly modified version of experiments 2 and 3 were tried with five-year-old children and with 0.014-second exposures. On the average, the children responded 12.1 times per figure, while four advanced undergraduates tested with the same exposure time responded 2.3 times, on the average, to the same figures. The children failed, moreover, to respond to surprising or incongruous figures more frequently than to others. Without further experimentation, it is not possible to say whether this was due to their age or to the shorter exposure. It seems plausible that five-year-old children may be insufficiently familiar with the appearance of normal animals to be affected by pictures of incongruous ones, and that their ability to form expectations may be deficient, making them less susceptible to surprise. Their resistance to satiation is reminiscent of that observed by Welker in young chimpanzees.

162

Chapter 7

TOWARD A THEORY OF EXPLORATORY BEHAVIOR:
I. AROUSAL AND DRIVE

Having now reviewed evidence on the working of stimulus selection in animals and of the simpler forms of stimulus selection in human beings, we can no longer shirk some of the theoretical questions that they raise. Unfortunately, we are not yet in a position to come out with a clear-cut theory that will explain all the data that we have reported in previous chapters, and it would be rash in the extreme to found far-reaching conclusions on them. Although some effects seem to emerge repeatedly in a number of different experimental situations, there are plenty of seeming inconsistencies between experiments; there are effects that have been reported once only and in none too convincing circumstances; there are experiments in which several distinct independent variables have been confounded; and, above all, there are glaring gaps in the evidence at one crucial point after another.

Any theoretical suggestions that we can venture at this point must thus be highly tentative and roughly outlined. They must inevitably be speculative. This need not make them scientifically disreputable as long as they point insistently to lines of experimental research. It may not be possible, however, to couch some of them in the form of rigorously testable statements until a great deal more spadework has been done to refine concepts, justify classifications, and contrive measuring techniques.

There is a certain amount of controversy in psychological circles about the necessity of theory. But no better corroboration than the present state of the literature on exploratory behavior could be found for a moderate position, according to which much valuable information can be accumulated by more or less haphazardly trying out one promising-looking variable after another, but a point of diminishing returns and needlessly inconclusive effort is soon reached unless specific questions, arising out of attempts at theory, are on hand to take over the helm.

In what follows we shall be echoing and piecing together a number of ideas that more and more writers are beginning to voice in different forms and terms. That several students of an area of science simultaneously find themselves drawn toward certain hypotheses is, of course, no proof at all that the hypotheses are correct. But it indicates that the hypotheses are timely, that the data force them on our consideration at this juncture, and that they should be worked out in further detail and thoroughly assayed before progress toward more definitive theories can be made.

The proposition that all behavior is motivated is, many psychologists feel, amply substantiated and generally accepted. It is commonly taken to mean that every piece of behavior can be traced to a particular drive or combination of drives. The fact that much exploratory behavior occurs in the absence of "organic" drives, such as hunger, thirst, sexual appetite, or pain, has seemed to some writers to justify the conclusion that the existence of special exploratory or manipulatory drives must be recognized. But the advocacy of this conclusion has not always been accompanied by a clear statement of the implications that it is meant to bear.

Other writers have tended toward the opposite extreme, asserting that experimental findings on exploratory behavior have completely discredited current theories of motivation, especially those based on the concepts of drive and drive reduction.

It is true that this type of theory has often been coupled with a picture of the animal organism as a being whose whole behavior is ultimately a collection of devices for keeping stimulation down to a minimum (Freud 1915, Miller and Dollard 1941). It is a picture that has been severely battered by the growing body of knowledge about exploration. Even without formal experiments, anybody who has had to spend half an hour with an unamused child must have had his faith in the proposition that animal life has torpor as its principal goal rudely shaken. The abandonment of the postulate that all behavior is aimed at escape from stimulation would replace the would-be sluggard of an animal, wanting nothing so much as to be left undisturbed, with a fidgety busybody, filled with a craving for entertainment and an eagerness to see what is going on.

The substance of a scientific theory, however, lies not in its graphic content but in its cold, fleshless, abstract structure. How far theories that discourse of drives and drive reduction can accommodate the newly recognized phenomena of stimulus selection cannot be judged by how far these phenomena fit the pictures associated with the theories. The shattering of a picture may accompany a comparatively minor change in the wording of a postulate. Nor is the fact that these theories, as they now stand, fail to predict the facts about stimulus selection a sufficient reason for rejecting them out of hand. A failure to predict all the facts that will ever be known is a common shortcoming of scientific theories. We can decide which is the most advisable strategy at the present stage of inquiry—whether to add to the postulates of an existing theory, to modify them, or to discard them altogether and start completely afresh—only after methodically examining concepts and assumptions with the new facts in view.

THE CONCEPT OF DRIVE

The concept of drive, which dominates contemporary discussions of motivation, resolves itself into three logically distinct concepts. We may distinguish them as $drive_1$, $drive_2$, and $drive_3$.

$Drive_1$. There is first the notion of drive as a condition that affects the *level of activity*. It is customary to speak of the "energizing effect of drive" in this connection. Its most celebrated expression is found in Hull's (1943) postulate that the strength (reaction potential) of any response that is aroused will increase with the total amount of drive that is present, from whatever sources.

The actual manifestations of high $drive_1$ will depend on whether an animal is receiving some stimulus that brings out one clear-cut dominant response or whether it is in a situation that is not capable of canalizing behavior. This latter condition will obtain when discomfort strikes a newborn infant (except in the few cases that can be disposed of by a specific innate reflex), when an animal finds itself in a novel environment lacking stimuli that can release instinctive behavior sequences or habits, when an animal is in a restricted environment (e.g., an empty box or a prison cell) where instinctive or habitual response patterns are thwarted, or when an animal is asleep. In such circumstances, high $drive_1$ will be reflected in a diffuse, more or less random restlessness (Richter 1922, Wada 1922). This effect seems to be especially pronounced when some stimulus like illumination is introduced, so there has been some controversy over whether $drive_1$ is reflected by a level of activity or a level of reactivity (Campbell and Sheffield 1953, Hall 1956).

In situations containing a releaser for instinctive consummatory responses or a cue that causes one learned response sequence to predominate, high $drive_1$ will manifest itself through the intensification of the prepotent response. Hull's postulate implies that the strength of any response that is aroused will be multiplied by a factor representing drive strength. The difference in strength between the prepotent response and its competitors (its net reaction potential) will therefore be multiplied by the same factor; an increase in $drive_1$ will

165

thus mean an increase in the vigor, persistence, or reliability with which that response is elicited.

The close resemblance between the manifestations of $drive_1$ and those of arousal will hardly have escaped the reader. High $drive_1$ and high arousal are both associated with restlessness, heightened reactivity of the skeletal musculature, and general agitation. There appears to be an inverted U-shaped relation between arousal and efficiency, as we saw in Chapter 3. Likewise, there are several experiments to show that maximum efficiency of learning and performance occurs with moderately high drive and that overmotivation causes a deterioration.

The activation of the descending facilitatory reticular system is known to intensify specific reflex responses and may well affect learned responses likewise. Indexes of heightened arousal in the form of rarer alpha activity, reduced amplitude of alpha waves when present, and lowered skin resistance have been shown to accompany at least one organic drive condition, namely lack of sleep (Armington and Mitnick 1959, Malmo 1958). Heart rate, another index of arousal, increases with hours of water deprivation (Bélanger and Feldman, cited by Malmo 1959). Three other prominent drive conditions—excess of carbon dioxide, hunger, and sexual deprivation—modify the chemistry of the blood in ways that sensitize the reticular formation (Dell 1958), and the responsiveness of the reticular formation to adrenaline and noradrenaline, hormones whose secretion has much to do with fear and anger (Funkenstein 1956), has been clearly demonstrated (Dell 1956).

So it will require no great temerity to regard $drive_1$ and arousal as intimately related. Nor will it require great originality, as several writers have been drawn toward the same step (e.g., Hebb 1955, Lindsley 1957a, Morgan 1957, Malmo 1958).

Sometimes, as when an animal is beset by fear or pain (see Sheffield 1948, Brown and Jacobs 1949), the prepotent response consists of ceasing to move; so an increase in $drive_1$ can then be expected to engender a lowering of activity. It may be worth remembering, in this connection, that the RAS contains inhibitory as well as facilitatory descending portions. Increasing the performance level (net reaction potential) of the dominant response will, however, usually mean increasing the level of motor activity.

Drive$_2$. The second notion represents drive as an *internal condition that makes certain overt responses more likely than others.* It differs from $drive_1$ in its selectivity. $Drive_1$ is thought of as a factor that indiscriminately strengthens all response tendencies that happen to be aroused; $drive_2$ strengthens "relevant" response tendencies, i.e., those which are biologically useful in the conditions characterizing the arousal of a $drive_2$ state, at the expense of others.

Normally, a $drive_2$ will produce the specific behavior corresponding to it only in the presence of appropriate releasers or cues. An exceptionally high level of $drive_2$ will, however, widen the range of external stimuli that will serve, so that an animal will eat, for example, or will make sexual advances to, all sorts of unsuitable objects. When $drive_2$ climbs to really extreme intensity, the behavior corresponding to it may burst forth independently of external stimuli, becoming what ethologists call "vacuum activity" or "explosion activity" (Tinbergen 1951).

$Drive_3$. The third notion identifies drive as a *condition whose termination or alleviation is rewarding*, i.e., promotes the learning of an instrumental response.

This notion covers the states that earlier psychologists used to call "aversions" (as distinct from "appetites"), i.e., states in which the organism is motivated to escape from something. They would also include Skinner's (1953) "aversive condition," as well as the *Trieb* (inexactly translated as "instinct") of Freud's (1915) middle period.

The influential brand of behavior theory sponsored by Hull (1943, 1952), and advocated with particular vigor by Dollard and Miller (1950), holds that all learning depends on the action of rewards and that all rewards are instances of $drive_3$ reduction. We shall provisionally assume a more noncommittal position.

We shall accept the statement that the learning of at least some responses is affected by events that follow their performance. This statement is amply established by a vast body of data on learning in the Skinner box and in other situations, whereas a case has been building up for the view that some learning, notably classical or Pavlovian conditioning, depends solely on events preceding or accompanying the performance of the response. Secondly, we shall agree that at least some rewards can legitimately be described as forms of $drive_3$ reduction. This means that their reward value proceeds from the attenuation of a condition of the organism that can be measured or detected in some independent way.

Events that satisfy this criterion must necessarily be ones that are not invariably rewarding. There must be times when the $drive_3$ that they are capable of reducing has a zero value and so cannot be reduced further. This fact makes it possible to regard a "drive for x" as a condition in which x is rewarding. For example, the presence of food will not reinforce responses in a glutted animal, and it seems that the reward value of an opportunity to eat increases with hours of deprivation (Lewis and Cotton 1957).

Furthermore, it must follow that any rewarding events that satisfy the criterion for $drive_3$ reduction must eventually lose their efficacy if they are repeated indefinitely without replenishment of the drive. If the drive is one that builds up with deprivation—hunger, thirst, sexual deprivation, or many others that ethologists have identified in submammalian classes—the rewarding event may have an unvarying potency, provided that its repetitions are separated by long enough intervals. But a reward that does not pall with massed repetition, if such there be, can be justifiably regarded as $drive_3$-reducing only if something happens between one occurrence of the rewarding event and the next to replenish the drive.

The Identification of $Drive_1$, $Drive_2$, and $Drive_3$

One of the working assumptions of S-R reinforcement theory, as developed especially by Hull (1943, 1952) and his associates, has been that $drive_1$, $drive_2$, and $drive_3$ can be identified—that conditions in which general activity is increased are also conditions that make certain unlearned responses more likely than others, or else furnish internal conditioned stimuli for learned responses, and are conditions whose relief will be rewarding.

This is a bold assumption of the sort that is justified in the early stages of an inquiry, and it has been responsible for many valuable experiments. But it cannot be claimed that the assumption has been verified, even in the case of all recognized sources of drive. It is difficult to verify. For one thing, the indexes by which we can judge the strength of $drive_1$, $drive_2$, and $drive_3$ (namely, the level of activity, the strength of prepotent responses, and the degree to which learned responses are reinforced) are all potently affected by variables other than those which are recognized as determinants of drive. Miller (1955, 1956) has shown that attempts to measure the same drive through different operations do not always yield comparable results. The position is, in fact, analogous to that confronting the tester of intelligence. The outcome of any test imposed on a subject must depend not only on the factor of general intelligence—if it exists —but on factors specific to the task, or even specific to the occasion on which the task is performed. Thus, only the collation of results yielded by a large collection of tasks can provide a trustworthy estimate of intelligence. A similar approach is indicated for the estimation of drive level or, for that matter, arousal.

The identification of the three notions of drive has important implications regarding the nature of reward. It involves the hypothesis that agents that reduce $drive_3$ are also agents that reduce $drive_1$ and $drive_2$.

To take up first the relation between reward and $drive_1$, it is clear

168

that the attainment of the rewards that have been most closely studied —food, copulation, escape from pain, etc.—is generally followed by a marked decline in activity and in other outward signs of arousal.

Turning to the relation between reward and $drive_2$, we have already recognized that a reward can properly be categorized as $drive_3$ reduction only if there is an independent way of showing that some internal condition is being weakened. Relevant instrumental and consummatory responses more often than not supply the most convenient measures not only for $drive_2$ but also for $drive_3$. Their characteristic decline with repeated elicitation supplies evidence that a variable qualifying as a drive in both senses is being reduced. For example, we are entitled to conclude that the introduction of food directly into a rat's stomach through a fistula reduces hunger ($drive_2$ and $drive_3$) on the grounds that it makes the animal less inclined to eat (Berkun, Kessen, and Miller 1952) and is able to reinforce a turning response (Miller and Kessen 1952).

There are, however, plenty of instances in which rewards do not follow these patterns—even among rewards that lose their efficacy when an organism becomes surfeited with them. One might, of course, point to the unmistakable reward value that exploratory behavior, exercise, and play often possess to illustrate how the enjoyment of rewarding events may accompany a rise in general activity (arousal? $drive_1$?). In other cases the receipt of a reward may, at least temporarily, increase the vigor of instrumental and consummatory activity ($drive_2$?). Proverbial wisdom intimates that *l'appétit vient en mangeant* (see Flugel 1948), a process to which Hebb (1949) refers, somewhat more prosaically, as the "salted-nut phenomenon." A rat runs more speedily to a goal box that contains water if it drinks a few drops immediately before the trial, although the response is slowed down if it drinks appreciable quantities (Bruce 1938). Incomplete sexual activity, interrupted while still in the phase of rising intensity, will reinforce a maze habit in the rat (Sheffield, Wulff, and Backer 1951).

We must, however, be cautious about the conclusions that we derive from such facts, especially regarding the role of arousal. It is true that an increase in arousal seems generally to mean an increase in overt activity, but the reverse need not necessarily hold. As we shall see later, there are reasons for suspecting that overt activity may help to keep arousal lower than it would be otherwise. There can be a "cat-on-hot-bricks" process: arousal remains relatively low while a certain response is being performed and rises as soon as the response ceases.

This may be coupled with a "vicious-circle" process: the stimuli issuing from each successive experience of the reward tend, innately or through conditioning (see Reid 1958), to move the intensity of ensuing arousal, instrumental behavior, or consummatory behavior up a notch, outweighing the effects of drive reduction. Something of this sort appears to happen over long periods with drug addictions: the picture is one of a craving that mounts progressively with continued indulgence, and yet each dose of the drug paradoxically relieves the craving. A similar mechanism acting over a much shorter period may account for the peculiar properties of salted nuts and their erotic counterparts.

That arousal may be closely linked with $drive_2$ and $drive_3$ is suggested by the close link that evidently exists between arousal and $drive_1$. There are, no doubt, states of high arousal, taking the form of general excitement and emotional tension, in which activity is disorganized and diffuse, so that the selective strengthening of one line of behavior that characterizes a $drive_2$ is lacking. On the other hand, we have seen that the RAS has the power not only to raise over-all sensory keenness but to give some sensory processes priority by blocking others. It is also known that the RAS can exert both facilitatory and inhibitory influences on motor centers; the possibility that it may help to promote certain behavior patterns at the expense of others cannot, therefore, be excluded.

Apart from this, high arousal will generally be accompanied by physiological processes and external stimuli that vary with the conditions that precipitated the rise in arousal. These will make certain overt responses predominate over others.

As for $drive_3$, we shall adopt the hypothesis that *decreases in arousal are rewarding*. This seems, at first sight, to be irreconcilable with facts of which we have been constantly reminded in earlier chapters, namely that human beings and higher animals spend most of their time in a state of relatively high arousal and that they often expose themselves to arousing stimulus situations with great eagerness. However, as our discussion of the working of arousal proceeds, we shall endeavor to show that the hypothesis is compatible with these and other facts. Our first step is to consider factors that determine the level of arousal.

DETERMINANTS OF AROUSAL

Systematic searches for properties determining the degree to which stimuli generate arousal would ideally either register events in the RAS directly or use several of the recognized indexes of arousal simultaneously. Studies of this kind have been confined to a few problems, so that again we shall have to rely on patchy evidence, in many cases concerned with single phenomena that have been linked with arousal—EEG changes, GSR and other vegetative processes, muscular tensions, general motor activity, and the outward signs of emotional turmoil. Moreover, some determinants are suggested by common experience and remain to be tested experimentally.

There are certainly risks attached to this kind of evidence, since these several indexes may be subject to influences other than the level of arousal. One thing that will be impressive, however, is the way in which we shall be encountering once again the variables that we have repeatedly come across as determinants of the various kinds of exploratory behavior. Their involvement with arousal supports our contention that arousal underlies exploration.

For convenience, we present the relevant variables under three headings.

1. *Intensive Variables.* We have seen that collaterals from sensory tracts converge on the RAS in such a way as to destroy information about the location and quality of the stimulus. This information is, apparently, largely lost in the lower or brain-stem parts of the system but partially preserved in the upper or thalamic parts. But such an arrangement would certainly be expected to perpetuate information about the *intensity* of stimulation, reflected in the frequency of nerve impulses and the number of fibers activated.

Russian investigators have regularly found that the intensity of various manifestations of the orientation reaction increases with the intensity of the stimulus. For example, the vascular component varies directly with the strength of auditory stimuli, except that it is more pronounced with stimuli near the absolute threshold than with somewhat stronger stimuli (Vinogradova and Sokolov 1955). The promptness with which alpha waves are suppressed increases with the intensity of visual stimuli (Sokolov 1958). The amplitude of the GSR increases with the intensity of visual stimulation, the amplitudes of the GSR and of finger-volume contraction increase with the intensity of electrocutaneous stimulation, and the amplitudes of the GSR, of finger-volume contraction, of breathing, and of muscular action potentials increase with the intensity of auditory stimulation (Davis 1930, Hovland and Riesen 1940, Davis, Buchwald, and Frankmann 1955, A. K. Popov 1958). Rats are more restless in light than in darkness (Campbell and Sheffield 1953), and their restlessness increases when illumination is intensified (Lubow and Tighe 1957). However, none of these studies isolates the effect of the intensity following the introduction of the stimulus from that of the difference between the intensities preceding and following the change.

Size seems commonly to act as an equivalent of intensity. Increasing the extensity of a patch of light is often tantamount to increasing luminosity, i.e., as far as absolute thresholds are concerned. Either way, one increases the total flux of energy that impinges on the retina. Alternatively, one may think of the larger patch as a source of stimulation for a greater number of receptor units, facilitating spatial summation, while the intenser patch induces a higher rate of firing in fewer units, facilitating temporal summation. The effects of large but variegated stimulus objects which do not produce homogeneous stimulation in neighboring receptors—objects such as a large animal or a large building—cannot be explained in the same way. But there is probably a high correlation between size and biological importance. And if we assume, as so many writers have in one form or another (e.g., Freud 1905*a*, Lipps 1903, Piaget 1945, Werner and Wapner 1952), that we respond to perceived objects with some sort of empathetic or imitative reaction, involving both the nervous system and the musculature, then we can assume that this reaction and the response-produced stimulation resulting from it will be intenser with larger objects, making for higher arousal.

Chromatic colors seem to be more arousing than nonchromatic colors, possibly because grays, browns, and blacks are more likely to be found in relatively unimportant, unvarying background objects. And among the chromatic colors, the emotional impact of the warm hues toward the red end of the spectrum generally outweighs that of colder hues at the other end. This phenomenon has never been completely explained, but one can point out that green and blue are likely to predominate in natural environments of aquatic animals and of terrestrial animals living among vegetation under the open sky. The warm colors, rarer and more concentrated, will more likely represent something that requires action. Fire is an obvious example.

For human beings, *high-pitched sounds* seem to be more exciting than low-pitched sounds, all other things equal. There is perhaps a reversal when the uppermost register is reached, although special stresses are induced by squeaks and whistles that approach the higher threshold for pitch. In experiments by Zagorul'ko and Sollertinskaia (1958), using tones of between 20 and 5000 cps, the amplitude of the orientation reaction (measured by cardiac, respiratory, muscular, and EEG changes) was greatest at 800 cps in pigeons and at 500 cps in dogs. It may be relevant that the frequency of impulses in the auditory nerve increases with the frequency of the stimulating sound waves up to 2000 or more cps, making pitch resemble intensity in at least one aspect of the nervous system's response. Differences in arousal value between timbres, e.g., between the strident tones of brass instruments and the soothing tones of wood winds, have long been recognized and exploited by musicians.

We can expect that stimuli belonging to different *sensory modes* will vary in their power over the arousal system. Painful stimuli produce the most widespread and intense cortical arousal patterns in anesthetized cats and monkeys, followed by proprioceptive, auditory, and visual stimuli, in that order (Bernhaut, Gellhorn, and Rasmussen 1953). In an experiment with human infants, the orientation reaction (indicated by an interruption of sucking) was most reliably evoked by auditory stimuli, followed by visual, vibratory, olfactory, tactile, and thermal stimuli (Bronshtein, Itina, Kamenetskaia, and Sytova 1958). In another experiment (Petelina 1958), the respiratory and heart-rate indexes of the orientation reaction in young dogs were found to be more pronounced and more resistant to extinction with auditory than with visual stimuli and with visual than with vestibular stimuli (resulting from rotation).

Since the relative importance of the different sensory modes varies widely from species to species, it is only natural that comparative studies should reveal contrasts. In fact, we find that olfactory stimulation induces orienting movements of the head in the newborn pup from the first day of life—long before other forms of stimulation have this power—which contrasts with the human infant's relative indifference to odor (Nikitina and Novikova 1958). Orienting activity in the carp (intensification of swimming movements) and in the pigeon (head turning and the hiding reaction) is called forth more strongly by visual than by auditory stimuli (Vedaev and Karmanova 1958).

2. *Affective Variables.* We have already discussed the relations between drive and arousal, and (see Chapter 3) the striking overlap between the vegetative and motor processes that have recently been identified as manifestations of the orientation reaction and those which have long been counted among the concomitants of emotion.

Alpha waves commonly disappear from the EEG tracing when a subject is exposed to fear-inducing conditions, e.g., when he is apprehensive about the unfamiliar EEG-recording procedure or when he imagines himself in some terrifying predicament (Loomis, Harvey, and Hobart 1936, D. B. Lindsley 1951). Patients suffering from chronic anxiety states tend to have flat and relatively alpha-free EEG patterns (Cohn 1946, Lindsley 1951) and to show greater irregularity in breathing, heart rate, neck-muscle activity, and finger-muscle activity than normal persons when they are subjected to stressful situations, e.g., a painful stimulus or a difficult size-discrimination test (Malmo 1957).

These studies, like most of the work that psychologists have done on emotion, concentrate on the unpleasant forms of emotion. We shall venture the hypothesis that pleasant emotional excitement and rewarding stimuli also heighten arousal, although probably less sharply than states of distress and punishing stimuli. There is one piece of confirmation for this hypothesis in the observation, made by Yoshii and Tsukiyama (1952), that the EEG waves of the rat take on a higher frequency when the rat, placed in a maze, approaches a goal box containing food.

The hypothesis implies that rewarding conditions, if sufficiently intensified, will provoke high arousal and thus be distressing. This may seem paradoxical and implausible at first sight, but we may recall that human beings who find themselves glutted with unanticipated good news frequently weep and evince extreme agitation. The fact that their behavior in such circumstances may be indistinguishable from behavior appropriate to misfortune is a standard source of comedy on the stage. We may also mention the overstimulation syndrome in young children. It is remarkable how often a day out or a birthday party, intended to provide an unbroken string of pleasures, will end with a bout of crying and bad temper.

3. *Collative Variables.* A direct demonstration that the intensity with which a stimulus produces arousal increases with its *novelty* is furnished by Sharpless and Jasper (1956). They inserted needle electrodes into the brain stems of cats. Loud sounds, lasting about three seconds, were presented at intervals of a few minutes while the cats were asleep. At first each stimulus evoked a burst of irregular high-frequency waves, resembling those that denote high activation in EEG tracings, with durations of up to three minutes or more. With succeeding stimulations, the arousal reactions tended to become shorter and shorter until, by about the thirtieth trial, they failed to appear at all. On the following day, the arousal reaction reappeared, but habituation was more rapid, showing that long-term novelty plays a part. However, a few days' rest abolished all signs of previous experience with the stimuli.

Habituation was highly specific to the stimulus. When the reaction to a tone of one pitch was habituated, other pitches would still provoke arousal. Similarly, habituation to a falling tone was not transferred to a rising tone except when lesions were made in the upper portions of the RAS. Removal of the auditory cortex did not destroy the specificity of habituation to a particular pitch, but it eliminated the ability to distinguish between rising and falling tones.

It is only to be expected that fine distinctions between patterns will require the specialized capacities of the cortex, whereas grosser discriminations may be accomplished by subcortical structures in lower mammals. It is worth noting, especially in view of our later discussions of the role of the cortex in the habituation of arousal, that Sharpless and Jasper did not remove the whole cortex.

The thalamic arousal reaction turned out to be more resistant to habituation than the mesencephalic arousal reaction, which harmonizes with Sokolov's remarks on the greater persistence of localized, as compared with generalized, orientation reactions.

Both transient and longer-lasting habituation—effects varying with short-term and long-term novelty—have also been observed in two of the most sensitive indexes of arousal, EEG alpha-wave blocking and GSR. N. A. Popov (1953) presented brief tones to waking human subjects. Alpha suppression appeared initially in response to a tone, but it ceased to appear after several repetitions of the tone in close succession. It reemerged after a day's delay but took less and less time to habituate on successive days. Likewise, when Wilson and Wilson (1959) presented repetitive flashes of light, they found the duration of the alpha suppression provoked by each flash to decline steeply over the first thirty seconds and to remain fairly constant for up to thirty minutes thereafter. A twenty-minute rest after five minutes of stimulation caused the duration to rise again, but not to reach its original value.

Seward and Seward (1934), applying five electric shocks at one-minute intervals to human subjects, found the resulting GSR to fall off from trial to trial within days and also over days. It is a general finding (see Woodworth 1938) that words which produce marked GSR changes because of some emotional significance lose this property when repeated.

The orientation reaction is, it will be remembered (Chapter 4), brought on by the onset, offset, or modification of any stimulus. We may anticipate that the *degree of change* (i.e., the degree of dissimilarity between what is present at the beginning and end of the change) and the *suddenness of change* (i.e., the speed with which the change is effected) will affect the amplitude of the reaction, although experiments in which these variables are systematically tested are lacking. Melzack (1952) found that harmless novel objects with moving parts would elicit outward signs of fear (crouching, turning away) in the dog.

There are, on the other hand, a great many experiments illustrating the importance of *surprisingness*. Two are reported by Sokolov (1957b). In one of them, subjects were instructed to forbear from blinking in response to a combination of a sound and an air puff. They succeeded in doing so, but both blinking and the orientation reaction were restored (disinhibited) when the sound was unexpectedly presented alone. In the second experiment, a loud and a faint sound were repeated in combination until the orientation reaction disappeared. It returned when the loud sound was heard alone.

Desai (1939) found that surprise, created in a variety of ways (e.g., by presenting subjects with pictures of animals immediately after they had seen eight cards bearing numbers and had been instructed to press a key on recognizing each stimulus pattern, or by suddenly turning on a light while subjects were engaged in tapping), would induce a GSR and an arrest of ongoing movements.

The orientation reaction is especially apt to appear in conditioning experiments whenever experimental arrangements that have persisted for a number of trials are unexpectedly altered. For example, the vascular component appears in human subjects when a sound that has regularly been followed by electric shock is presented without the shock, or when positive and negative differential stimuli have previously been presented in one order and the order is then changed (Vinogradova 1958). Yoshii and Tsukiyama (1952) found that withdrawing food from the goal box of a maze produced fast EEG waves in rats, although lower frequencies made an appearance as extinction of the running habit proceeded. Unfortunately, in this latter experiment it is impossible to distinguish the contribution of frustration from that of surprise.

That *incongruous* stimulus patterns are apt to disrupt behavior and to occasion dramatic emotional outbursts has been demonstrated by Hebb (1946, 1949). He was able to provoke what he describes as "paroxysms of terror" in chimpanzees simply by letting them see an anesthetized chimpanzee, a skull, a clay model of an isolated chimpanzee head, a human attendant wearing the coat usually worn by another attendant, and so on.

Perhaps the most enlightening data of all on this point come from the protocols provided by Charlotte Bühler's group from their studies of human infants. Bühler, Hetzer, and Mabel (1928) observed more negative reactions (i.e., reactions indicative of displeasure or fear) to *partially strange* stimulus patterns (e.g., a distorted voice coming from a familiar face, a mask over the face of a familiar person speaking with a normal voice) than to *completely strange* patterns (e.g., the unusual voice or the mask alone).

We may also cite Haslerud's (1938) experiment on avoidance reactions in chimpanzees. He introduced novel objects into the visual field while the subjects were eating, finding that stationary objects provoked a greater percentage of avoidance reactions, and longer-lasting signs of caution, in fully grown than in immature individuals.

This seems to imply that the possession of a body of experience with which a novel object is discrepant, a body of experience that the young would not have had time to acquire, augments the alarming properties of novelty. Likewise, Bühler (1931) notes that negative reactions to strangeness in human infants increase with age up to eight months, showing that the disturbance is not at a maximum at the time when all stimuli are novel.

Experiments clarifying the relations between arousal and *conflict* pure and simple are scanty. Lowell (1952) subjected rats to an approach-approach conflict by placing them on a platform from which two elevated runways led in opposite directions and simultaneously presenting a light which had previously been associated with food at the end of each runway. This elicited faster running than a situation in which the animals were attracted predominantly in one direction by a single light.

Polezhaev (1958, 1959a) trained dogs to raise a paw in response to the sound of a metronome as a means of avoiding electric shock. The appearance of a piece of meat while the metronome was ticking evoked an exceptionally prominent orientation reaction, evidenced by quicker and deeper breathing and by EEG desynchronization, as well as by active looking and listening. This is attributed by Polezhaev to conflict between antagonistic alimentary and defensive responses, and he mentions that other pairs of stimuli associated with incompatible activities had the same effect.

There is, however, a need for some control to exclude the possibility that surprise alone was the responsible factor. This difficulty arises in all experiments in which the effects of conflict are sounded by unexpectedly applying a combination of stimuli, associated with incompatible responses, that have hitherto been applied separately. It must be shown that the difference between the conflictful and nonconflictful situations persists after the former have been repeated often enough to lose their surprisingness.

An experiment by Lanier (1941a) did not have this particular drawback. He had his subjects classify each word in a list as "pleasant," "unpleasant," "indifferent," or "mixed," and he simultaneously recorded GSRs. The "mixed" words had both pleasant and unpleasant aspects; so Lanier concluded that they will have involved "affective conflict." It turned out that the "mixed" words evoked more intense GSRs than those of the other categories. They also took longer to categorize.

We saw in Chapter 4 how the various accompaniments of the orientation reaction become singularly resistant to extinction in the presence of positive or negative differential stimuli. We also saw that they may continue more or less indefinitely if the difference between

177

the positive and negative stimuli is a fine one. Similarly, the orientation reaction is particularly strong when stimuli are weak enough to be near the absolute threshold. The vascular component is more intense and persistent with barely audible sounds than with sounds that are a little louder (Vinogradova and Sokolov 1955), and barely visible light blocks alpha rhythms more persistently than light of higher intensities (Mikhalevskaia 1957). These effects are presumably due to conflict between excitation and inhibition, resulting from the resemblance between, and consequent generalization from, the conditions that call for a response (supraliminal stimulus or positive differential stimulus) and those that call for the response to be withheld (absence of stimulus or presence of negative differential stimulus). After all, difficult discriminations form one of the best-known means of creating experimental neuroses in animals.

There is, however, one experiment whose results do not fit in too well with our postulated relation between conflict and arousal. Yoshii and Tsukiyama (1952) found that, as a rat ran through a maze, its low-frequency background EEG waves increased in amplitude from the starting box until just after the choice point and then gave way to faster waves. If we assume that the stimuli coming from the choice point must have induced conflict since they were associated with two incompatible turning responses, this is not what we should expect. It is, however, impossible with present knowledge to tell what factors are at work in this situation. The rats were fed whichever way they turned so that any conflict must have been of a mild approach-approach type. Other studies (cf. N. E. Miller 1944) point to a steady increase in drive as a rat comes nearer and nearer to a location where he has regularly been fed.

Milerian's (1955) discovery that melodies would provoke more prolonged alpha blockings than simple tones—at least if subjects said they were interested—may be offered as evidence for a connection between arousal and *complexity*.

Other experiments seem relevant to *uncertainty*. Smith, Malmo, and Shagass (1954) had subjects listen to a recording of an article which was deliberately made hard to hear in spots. There was an initial increase in the tension of muscles in the arm (measured with the electromyograph), but it subsequently dropped. Wallerstein (1954) obtained a similar result with subjects who listened to the reading of a philosophical essay: there was a rise in muscular tension followed by a fall after the first few minutes. Persons with no specialized knowledge of philosophy would presumably not have much uncertainty about what would come next, once they had ascertained "what sort of stuff" it was. All subsequent patterns of sound likely to ensue would be equivalent for them. Bartoshuk (1958) found that increases in forehead-muscle tension were correlated with lowness of EEG amplitude (indicative of high arousal) during the first hearing of a story, but not during the second or third hearing. But EMG gradients, like other indexes, are likely to depend on other factors besides arousal.

We shall henceforth refer to all these properties of incoming stimuli with power to affect arousal as *arousal potential*.

INTERACTION BETWEEN THE RAS AND THE CEREBRAL CORTEX

As our inquiry into the relations between arousal and exploratory behavior proceeds, it will be helpful to bear in mind the constant and far-reaching interactions between the RAS and the cerebral cortex that research is bringing to light. It is by now well established, thanks to a number of anatomical and physiological studies, that there are fibers transmitting impulses downward from the cortex to the RAS, as well as ascending fibers by which the influence of the RAS is brought to bear on the cortex.

Various experimenters have made it clear that the stimulation of virtually any point of the neocortex can produce activation of the RAS (see Bremer 1954). If the RAS receives stimulation simultaneously from sensory pathways and from the cortex, the outcome may be facilitation or interference, according to the pathways brought into play (Hernández-Peón and Hagbarth 1955). It is only natural to conclude that influences from the cortex play a part whenever the arousal value of a stimulus pattern depends on (1) subtle differences whose detection must require the highly developed analytical powers of the cortex, or (2) meaning based on learned associations. This conclusion receives some support from Bremer's observations that a meaningful auditory pattern—a human voice calling—would normally wake up a sleeping cat and change the EEG tracing to one characteristic of activation. It would not produce this effect, however, in a cat whose auditory cortex had been removed, although a tactual stimulus would still do so.

The inhibitory influences that the cortex exerts on the RAS promise, however, to be even more important for our present preoccupations than the facilitatory influences.

It was observed quite early in Pavlov's laboratory (and it has been regularly confirmed ever since) that when the cortex has been removed, it is difficult, if not impossible, to extinguish orienting responses and the various accompaniments of the orientation reaction by repeatedly presenting a stimulus. Orienting responses are also ab-

179

normally resistant to extinction and abnormally quick to recover from extinction in individuals with defective cortical functioning, e.g., in premature and hydrocephalic infants (Bronshtein, Itina, Kamenetskaia, and Sytova 1958), in some patients with brain injuries and neuroses (Briullova 1958), and in some psychotics (Traugott, Balonov, Kaufman, and Lichko 1958).

The most obvious implication of these facts—that the extinction and, generally, the inhibition of the orientation reaction depend on the activity of the cortex—is corroborated by a number of other experiments. In one carried out by Vinogradova and Sokolov (1955), repetition of a tone led first to a weakening of the vascular component of the orientation reaction and then to its resurgence with shortened latency and heightened intensity when the subjects had reached a somnolent state. Even more revealing is an experiment (Roger, Voronin, and Sokolov 1958) on the effects of combining a flash of light with proprioceptive stimulation, produced through passive movements of the arm. Prolonged repetition of the combination of stimuli led to the extinction of the GSR and to the appearance in the EEG record of slow, high-amplitude waves, indicative of drowsiness or sleep. But continued proprioceptive stimulation later came to provoke a renewal of the GSR and a return of faster waves, in the alpha and beta range, to the cortex. In other words, the monotonous stimulation first put the subjects to sleep and then woke them up! Or more precisely, the repetition of the stimuli led first to extinction of the orientation reaction and later to cortical inactivation which, in its turn, meant the withdrawal of inhibitory influences from the cortex and consequent reactivation of the RAS.

As we saw in Chapters 3 and 4, EEG activation and vegetative changes dependent on the sympathetic nervous system generally occur together in the stimulated organism. When, however, human subjects are awake but resting without stimulation, heart rate and palmar conductance are *negatively* correlated with the indexes of cortical activation (high EEG frequency and low EEG amplitude), which again seems to imply that the cortex and the subcortical structures concerned in arousal can interact antagonistically (Darrow, Pathman, and Kronenberg 1946).

The susceptibility of the RAS to inhibition of cortical origin has been demonstrated more directly by Hugelin and Bonvallet (1957a, 1957b, 1957c, 1958). Their experiments were performed on cats with transsections at the junction between the brain and the spinal cord (i.e., *encéphale isolé* preparations). The object was to study the effects of RAS stimulation on a monosynaptic myotatic reflex involving contraction of the jaw muscles. The afferent nerve subserving the reflex was stimulated every 1.5 seconds while the RAS was under continuous stimulation, and the discharge in the motor nerve was recorded.

The result of reticular stimulation was a sharp increase in the magnitude of the motor discharge. This was followed after a few seconds by a return to the original magnitude or less, even though the RAS continued to undergo stimulation. That the curtailment of the motor facilitation was the work of the cortex is shown by the fact that the facilitation persisted in animals that were decorticated, that had the cortex frozen, or that were injected with chloralose (which inactivates the cortex).

A particularly instructive finding was that the phase of facilitation did not occur at all, and the reflex remained unaffected, when the RAS was subjected to a stimulation whose intensity gradually rose from zero, instead of to a stimulation whose full force was applied from the start.

The conclusions warranted by this series of experiments are reasonably clear. We know that the activation of the RAS sends facilitating impulses down to motor units and activating impulses up to the cortex. It seems that the activation of the cortex causes it to send inhibitory impulses back to the RAS to counteract the influence of whatever has been acting on the RAS and to restore the original level of arousal. A sudden, intense activation catches the cortex off its guard, as it were, and causes equilibrium to be momentarily upset. If, however, the activation of the RAS is gradual, the cortex has time to adjust its inhibitory feedback and prevent the process from getting out of hand.

This picture has several interesting implications bearing on matters that are of concern to us. First of all, it enables us to understand more satisfactorily the relations between the orientation reaction and the level of arousal or, in Sokolov's terms, between the phasic and tonic orientation reactions. The former seems to represent a transient escape of the arousal system from cortical control, while the latter is likely to be the result of a progressive adjustment of the equilibrium between reticular arousal and corticireticular inhibition.

Secondly, we can see why surprise is such a potent factor in raising arousal. If the cortex has some previous notice of impending arousal potential, e.g., through the presence of a warning signal, it should be able to forestall a disturbance of equilibrium by increasing its inhibitory influence in anticipation.

Direct evidence that the diminution of arousal depends on inhibitory processes transmitted from cortex to RAS has been secured by Jouvet and Michel (1958). These processes are presumably different from the corticireticular inhibition that we have just been discussing. When a normal cat is awake, relatively fast waves can be recorded simultaneously from its cortex and its RAS, and slow waves appear in both structures when it goes to sleep. Jouvet found that, although decorticated cats would alternate between wakefulness and sleep as judged by muscular tension and relaxation, the RAS continued over periods of up to ninety days to exhibit fast waves, typical of fairly high arousal, and never once went over to slower electrical activity. In cats that retained a portion of the cortex, however small and wherever located, RAS activity could be depressed.

We may also note that stimulation of certain cortical areas may persistently inhibit the potentials that are normally evoked in the RAS by auditory stimuli, while processes in the specific sensory pathways remain unaffected (Jouvet, Benoît, and Courjon 1956).

At the cost of some speculation, we can discern one way in which the orientation reaction might be intensified and prolonged by conflict. From what we know of the thorough dependence of most complex neural processes on subtle collaboration, and especially synchronization, between incoming impulses, we may deduce that the simultaneous instigation of conflicting chains of events will result, at least initially, in blockage, mutual impediment, and, in short, the absence of a definite response. As we saw in Chapter 3, it looks as if the launching of one piece of adaptive behavior is generally accompanied by the inhibition of structures that might bring other response processes into play. If two response processes are activated simultaneously and with about equal strength, the most likely outcome is that each of them will succeed in inhibiting the other so that neither will come to fruition.

If this stultification of cortical functioning hinders or delays the processes that are responsible for restraining and ending high arousal, the RAS will keep the organism mobilized and exceptionally receptive to incoming information. It will thus stave off the catastrophic paralysis that would otherwise threaten. The RAS would then be comparable to a receptionist who puts into effect a routine policy for dealing with an obstreperous visitor and continues with it until the boss has either made up his mind on what to do with him or decided he is not worth worrying about.

AROUSAL TONUS AND ANTICIPATORY AROUSAL

Animal organisms differ from inanimate objects in their ability to keep a highly intricate structure intact through a diversity of environmental vicissitudes. They owe this ability to their capacity for adjustment. They undergo internal changes in correspondence with the environmental events that impinge on them; these changes, occurring

182

principally in the muscular, endocrine, and nervous systems, preserve or rapidly restore the nicely determined and delicately balanced internal conditions on which survival depends.

But each act of adjustment is achieved at a cost, which may be minute in comparison with the threat at which it is directed but telling in its cumulative effect. The cost comes from at least two sources. First, there is general wear and tear on bodily equipment which, if calls for intensive action follow one another without respite, may form an internal threat to the organism's well-being rivaling any threat that can originate from without. Everybody is familiar with the effects of overwork, overexertion, and overstrain. Particular organs that are unremittingly brought into play, whether they be sense organs, muscles, or neural units, will suffer fatigue effects, entailing a temporary decline in efficiency and, in extreme cases, lasting damage. In addition to localized impairment, there may be the diffuse "general adaptation syndrome" described by Selye (1946): heightened resistance to a prolonged stress is gained at the expense of greater susceptibility to other stresses that might come along, and ultimately, if the "stage of exhaustion" is reached, of abnormal vulnerability to all stresses with the possibility of psychosomatic ailments and eventually death.

The second source of cost is the risk that every act of adjustment entails. There is always the possibility that the response selected at a given instant will be the wrong one, that it will come too late, that it will be ineffective, or will even make matters worse.

Arousal Tonus

There are a number of ways in which these two dangers can be minimized. One of them is to maintain a *chronic tonus*, a state of preparedness that anticipates emergencies by keeping in constant action the processes that must form part of the answer to any threat. If there is a measure of alertness as a continual background, the stressful effects of action will be reduced, since it must be less wearing to change moderate exertion into maximum exertion than to leap to maximum exertion from zero. The risk of failure will also be lessened since, with a "head start," action can be speedier.

For example, a degree of muscle tonus is maintained by a normal, waking human being, even when he is resting. A state of generalized muscular relaxation would imperil prompt action. A state of high muscular tension would not only be exhausting but would reduce the plasticity of the response mechanism. So moderate tension is maintained as the most advantageous compromise. The actual level of tonus varies. When the need for rest becomes pressing or when the

183

chances of a call to action are unusually low, more or less complete relaxation may be appropriate, although most human beings in our culture find it notoriously difficult to achieve such a state or even to understand what it is like. But in circumstances where stress is unusually plentiful and long-lasting, motor units may be tuned up to a tautness that would threaten physical or psychological health if continued indefinitely but can be sustained with impunity for short periods.

The principle of chronic tonus, which is so familiar in so far as it affects muscular tension, seems likely to apply to other aspects of the organism's functioning, including arousal, and for the same reasons. It may help to answer the question why arousal in a normal, waking animal has a moderately high level. This level (which we shall call *arousal tonus*) may represent something like the average level of arousal required of the organism in its particular circumstances, susceptible of modification if the circumstances alter.

Expectation

The second device which cuts down the cost of adjustment is *expectation*. If the event that calls for action is part of a regularly recurring sequence of events, its predecessors can serve as warning signals. Expectations open the way to preparatory and avoidant responses or to prior selection of a response by reasoning, all of which will raise the chances of success when the heralded event arrives. Expectations may diminish stress by making adjustment less abrupt and by obviating the increment of arousal that is contributed by surprisingness. Expectations will usually be accompanied by high arousal as well as by responses (mostly implicit) that identify the particular event that is expected.

Anticipatory Arousal

But there will be times when the precise nature of an impending occurrence cannot be anticipated, either because premonitory cues are lacking or because their significance has not been learned. In such cases, an executive response cannot be preselected. But those component processes of the orientation reaction that come into play in coping with any urgent situation and do not depend on the specific properties of the situation can, perhaps, be mobilized in advance. This is a third mechanism, that of *anticipatory arousal*. It requires the presence of a pattern of cues indicating how arousing, novel, conflictful, important, etc., the experiences of the next few moments are going to be, without telling exactly what they will contain. They must be cues that have preceded a variety of events with a common arousal value and so have become conditioned to a particular strength of the orientation reaction.

Anticipatory arousal will reflect the individual's uncertainty in both the usual and the information-theory sense, since the information theorist's measure of uncertainty is precisely a measure of the *expected* or *average* amount of information that is about to emerge from a channel. The actual amount of information that comes may exceed or fall short of this value, but the uncertainty represents the best estimate than can be made from a knowledge of the range of possibilities and their probabilities. Anticipatory arousal will, however, depend on more than uncertainty. It will reflect the individual's estimate of how important the impending event is likely to be, how much surprise he must brace himself for, how far it is likely to demand some vigorous action that cannot be identified beforehand, how close an examination it will require. It may take the form of a general alertness or vigilance. If it is particularly intense or combined with the distinctive accompaniments of fear, it will appear as a state of general foreboding, apprehensiveness, or, to give the word a connotation it sometimes has, anxiety.

Without affording all the advantages of a specific expectation, anticipatory arousal will permit speedier and more energetic action when the anticipated event has been detected, as a result of the heightened sensitivity of receptor organs and the reduced strain that comes with less sudden mobilization. If the anticipated event has unpleasant aspects that nothing can mitigate, if it is, for example, a piece of irrevocable bad news, anticipatory arousal will make it easier to withstand the shock, perhaps by producing some anticipatory habituation.

The benefits of anticipatory arousal are plain, and processes that would make it possible have been illustrated in a number of experiments. Indifferent stimuli that occur shortly before stimuli apt to provoke violent orientation reactions will elicit various components of the orientation reaction through conditioning. The GSR has become one of the responses used most commonly for the study of human conditioning. It will attach itself quite readily to any stimulus that precedes an electric shock or a loud sound. Circulatory changes produced by electric shock have been conditioned. And conditioning of EEG arousal patterns, whether localized and characteristic of a particular kind of arousing stimulus or diffuse, has been carried out by a whole series of investigators. The most frequently used method has been sound-light conditioning. A sound, which has first been repeated alone enough times to extinguish its own orientation reaction, is paired with a flash of light, beginning a few seconds before the

185

light appears and continuing until the light goes off. After a number of trials, the desynchronization that was formerly contemporaneous with the light occurs anticipatorily as soon as the sound begins.

Arousal patterns are also easily associated with verbal stimuli. Milerian (1955) was able, for example, to obtain a pronounced alpha-blocking response simply by saying to his human subjects, "Listen to the sound!" The response ceased as soon as he said, "That's enough!" even though the sounds continued.

By taking advantage of warning signals that herald stimulus events with high arousal value, the following beneficial conditions could, in fact, be secured: (1) Arousal increases before the heralded event makes its impact, thus preparing the organism for prompt action and optimal receptivity to information. (2) Arousal increases gradually rather than sharply, thus minimizing the disturbance of internal equilibrium. (3) Arousal does not rise unnecessarily high once the anticipated event has appeared, thus minimizing wear and tear and upheaval. (4) Arousal falls to a normal or optimal level as soon as the rise in arousal has performed its functions.

In the last chapter we discussed cortical facilitation of RAS activity. If this were conditioned to warning signals, it could ensure the first and second of the conditions listed above; and cortical inhibition of RAS activity, if brought into play anticipatorily through conditioning, could ensure the third and fourth of them.

Anticipatory arousal will be at least partially relieved when the impending event occurs and can be identified, since, whatever other cause for disquiet remains, the contribution of uncertainty to the arousal level will be removed. Times of anticipatory arousal will be times when exploratory behavior, serving to accelerate and maximize the receipt of information about the impending event, will be strongly reinforced by arousal reduction and thus strongly evoked.

BOREDOM

Earlier in this chapter we considered properties of drive states in general. If we wish to mark off one drive from another, we have to specify what conditions arouse or intensify the drive and what conditions reduce it. Drives aroused by different conditions will be reduced in different ways because they will involve not only processes that are common to all drives but also processes that are specific to themselves. These other processes will be sources of distinctive internal stimulation, whether acting on receptors or directly on the central nervous system, and this stimulation will cooperate with external stimulation to furnish discriminative signals, guiding the organism toward activity that promises to alleviate the drive.

There is evidently one kind of drive that is reduced through divertive exploration and aroused when external stimuli are excessively scarce or excessively monotonous. Both of these are conditions in which arousal potential will be exceptionally low, since monotony means lack of novelty, surprisingness, uncertainty, and complexity. In information-theory language, both will mean a meager influx of information—in the one case because signals are lacking and in the other case because signals are highly predictable. The drive in question is what we usually call *boredom*.

Boredom is particularly likely when stimuli lack short-term novelty, i.e., when a stimulus is repeated many times in immediate succession. But it may also be brought on by a shortage of long-term novelty, e.g., by having the same menu for dinner day after day, or of surprisingness, e.g., when life is varied but highly predictable.

Sensory deprivation has been used to induce boredom in quite a spate of recent experiments, beginning with one by Bexton, Heron, and Scott (1954). These investigators paid students $20 a day to remain in an isolated cubicle, wearing translucent goggles that excluded patterned vision and cardboard cuffs and heavy gloves that minimized tactual stimulation, and with no auditory stimulation apart from an unchanging hum. This treatment produced a large number of interesting phenomena, from hallucinations to a deterioration in intellectual abilities. But the most significant facts for us were that subjects could stand no more than a few days of the treatment, despite the high rate of pay and the complete lack of exertion. They resorted to desperate and far-fetched measures for providing themselves with increased stimulation, e.g., by talking or whistling to themselves or tapping the cardboard cuffs together. When given the opportunity, they would call again and again for stimulation that they would normally have eschewed as intolerably dull, e.g., a recording of a stock-exchange report or of an antialcohol speech intended for an audience of young children. They showed growing irritability and other signs of emotional stress and, in short, found the experience unpleasant in the extreme.

Karsten (1928) is responsible for another of the surprisingly few laboratory studies of boredom. She concerned herself with a phenomenon which she named *psychische Sättigung* (translatable either as "mental satiation" or as "mental saturation"). She had her subjects perform monotonous, repetitive, and essentially uninteresting tasks, telling them that they were to work as long as they felt like it and to stop when they no longer wanted to continue. The experimenter acted in such a way, however, as to encourage subjects to go on as long as possible. The tasks included drawing small vertical strokes, putting thimbles in holes, reading the same short poem over and over again, drawing a simple figure repeatedly, etc.—all of them tasks that could be carried on indefinitely with little physical effort.

As the experiment proceeded, the quality of the performances deteriorated; mistakes became commoner, and larger units of speech or of drawings broke up into meaningless elements. But more interesting from our present point of view was the mounting struggle, often carried on with quite diabolical ingenuity, to achieve some variety within the bounds of the instructions. The strokes were drawn, for example, with varying rhythms, with the pencil held in different ways, with their shapes varied so as to approximate a series of meaningful patterns, with the task interpreted in new ways, e.g., as a test of speed. Coupled with this trend was a growing distaste for the task and everything associated with it, a tendency to think of other things that would be more pleasant to do instead, aggressive feelings toward the task, the experimenter, or even the subject's self, expressed verbally and in outbreaks of mild violence, and finally a refusal to go on.

Karsten insists that muscular exhaustion could not have been behind the final halt or the other phenomena, since the subjects would readily use the same muscles for other responses, provided that their "meaning" was different. For example, they would brush back their hair or draw strokes in a different pattern after declaring that the arm was too tired to do anything more. Having just been writing a and b until they felt they could no longer do so, they were still capable of writing a and b as parts of their names and addresses. It would seem, therefore, that the monotonous stimulation resulting from the monotonous activity was responsible for the aversive quality of the situation, and that changes in "meaning" made it less stressful by somehow varying the pattern of stimulation that followed the response. It is worth remembering that even physical fatigue is now mainly attributed to central inhibitory processes in which kinesthetic feedback stimuli probably play a large part, rather than to physicochemical changes in muscles that preclude their contraction (see Berlyne 1951). So factors at work in boredom and factors at work in fatigue may turn out to be closely akin.

A Hypothesis

It is tempting to suppose that the conditions that make for boredom will produce exceptionally low arousal, and that low arousal, as well as high arousal, must therefore be aversive. Such a hypothesis has been put forward by several writers (e.g., Hebb 1955). Nevertheless, we shall stand firm against the temptation and refrain from adopting this hypothesis. Instead, we shall suggest, though with even more diffidence than accompanies our other theoretical suggestions, that boredom works through a *rise in arousal*.

There are several reasons for this seemingly implausible suggestion. First, we may point out that a human being or an animal in the throes of agonizing boredom does not look like a creature with low arousal. On the contrary, he shows the restlessness, agitation, and emotional upset that usually coincide with high arousal. Introspection corroborates this impression.

A state of low arousal is a state of drowsiness or sleepiness characterized by high-amplitude, low-frequency EEG waves. A host of Russian experiments, from Chechulin (1923) to Roger, Voronin, and Sokolov (1958), have shown that the repetition of an unvarying stimulus until overt and implicit components of the orientation reaction have been extinguished brings on just such a state. It is common knowledge that a lack of stimulation also has the tendency to put people to sleep.

Being lulled to sleep is not generally reckoned an unpleasant or distressing experience. Sleepiness is unpleasant and distressing, it would seem, only when there is some strongly motivated activity with which it interferes, e.g., when there is something that one needs urgently to be doing or when one is sitting in the front row at a lecture given by an acquaintance.

Lastly, we may recall the experimental literature reviewed earlier, showing how inhibitory impulses from the cortex may curb or dampen arousal and how the inactivation of the cortex as a result of monotonous stimulation may release the RAS from this restraint and allow arousal to flare up again. Sokolov, thinking of these findings, remarks that low arousal must correspond to a "definite level" of cortical activity. High cortical activation is associated, whether as cause, effect, or both, with high arousal, and minimal cortical activity is associated with the liberation of the RAS from cortical surveillance. We may ask whether, in an animal that is not ready for sleep, minimal arousal may not likewise correspond to an intermediate level of arousal potential in external stimuli.

Lying motionless in a quiet dark room is agreeable and conducive to sleep when one is tired or ill. It is extremely trying to have these conditions forced on one when one is healthy and has had enough sleep. The subjects of Bexton, Heron, and Scott usually fell asleep quickly after being placed in the cubicle. But they could not sleep

189

indefinitely, and the situation became intolerable only when they were no longer able to sleep.

We may therefore surmise that sensory deprivation becomes aversive when internal factors cause a rise in arousal and the lack of stimulation renders the cortex incapable of keeping arousal within bounds. An endogenous rise in arousal may be the result of physiological processes with an inherent rhythm—in all likelihood closely related to the sleep-waking rhythm, which, while it is certainly susceptible to cultural conditioning, must have limits imposed on it by physiological factors. Internal stimuli, e.g., from thoughts, may also contribute to endogenous arousal, since they are so prone to emerge in the absence of external foci of attention in normal, waking human beings.

Some psychoanalytic writers have maintained that the unpleasantness of boredom is due to anxiety-producing thoughts, which adequate external stimulation would help to crowd out of consciousness. There may well be something to this hypothesis if we interpret anxiety widely as arousal rather than as something invariably linked with psychosexual problems or physical dangers. The way in which young children can become frantically afraid of the dark is also worth bearing in mind.

Bexton, Heron, and Scott took EEG tracings in the course of their experiment, and a general finding was that frequencies tended to become abnormally low. Heron (personal communication) says that periods of irritability and unpleasantness were transitory but "tended to become more frequent, to last longer and to be more intense as the experiment progressed." The EEG, he reports, tended to be flatter (generally taken as a sign of desynchronization and thus of heightened arousal) during these periods. Except in one subject, delta waves (waves in the 1–3.5 cycles per second range, often recorded during sleep) were absent during spells of anxiety and tension. J. A. Vernon, who has performed other sensory-deprivation experiments, supplies the information (personal communication) that skin conductance, which we have seen to be an index of arousal, was notably greater after four days of confinement than before.

Turning to the question of boredom produced by monotonous stimulation, as illustrated by Karsten's research, we may first observe that, while repetitive stimulation often brings on sleep, there are times when it does not. Whether it brings on sleep seems to depend on its arousal value, especially its intensity. We can be put to sleep by a droning voice or by a lullaby, which is usually sung softly and slowly and has an undulating melody without abrupt transitions. But a loud fast-ticking clock, a dripping tap, and Chinese water torture are hardly soothing. A mother may quiet a disturbed infant by stroking his forehead or patting his back gently, but rhythmically prodding him in the eye would not work so well. The proprioceptive stimulation that comes from motor activity seems similarly (whether because of its intensity or for some other reason) to be inimical to sleep however monotonous it may be. It is difficult to put oneself to sleep by singing oneself a lullaby, counting sheep aloud, or stroking one's own forehead. Repetitive passive movements can, nevertheless, produce drowsiness, as the experiment of Roger, Voronin, and Sokolov shows.

So it may be that when monotonous activities are forced on a subject or monotonous stimulation is too strong to be soporific, boredom results because the stimulation acts on the RAS to keep arousal high and at the same time incapacitates the cortex from performing its normal moderating function, so that habituation does not take place. When attempts to escape from the situation are thwarted by social pressure or other obstacles, conflict and frustration can be expected to push arousal still higher.

Another possibility, however, is that monotonous stimulation raises arousal through the intervention of a special protective mechanism, such as the one that produces physical fatigue and causes us to desist from a repeated bodily movement long before muscles are incapacitated. In this event, boredom from monotony and boredom from sensory deprivation would work rather differently.

Yet a further possible explanation is that neural fatigue, which we can expect to supervene when monotonous stimuli bring the same neural units into action over and over again, disturbs the timing of processes in the central nervous system. This could be presumed, as Hebb (1949) says, to have disorganizing effects like those of conflict.

Whatever process is responsible for the aversiveness of monotonous stimuli must clearly be capable of remaining persistently attached to the stimuli in question through some sort of conditioning. If men are served two alternating daily menus for periods of up to three weeks, the foods figuring in the menus become increasingly unpalatable, as shown both by subjects' ratings and by the amounts left uneaten (Siegel and Pilgrim 1958). They become distasteful even though forty-eight hours intervene between successive servings of the same item, and after an interval of three and one-half to four months they are still rated as unfavorably as at the conclusion of the experiment.

We have already touched on the possible affinity between boredom and fatigue, and everyday language recognizes such an affinity by applying words like "tired" to both. It is of interest that Japanese experimenters have found fast EEG waves to result from physical fatigue (produced through enforced swimming) in the rat, and a phase of fast

191

waves followed by a phase of slow waves to accompany "mental fatigue" (resulting from a time-estimation test) in human beings (Yoshii, Tsukiyama, and Horiuchi 1953).

Our hypothesis that the torments of boredom are associated with an upsurge of arousal and our general assumption that diminutions of arousal are rewarding do not, of course, imply that a rise in arousal can never be accompanied by positive affect. We have already in this chapter mentioned ways in which it could be, and, in the next chapter, we shall be considering another. It also seems plausible that a highly arousing environment is more uncomfortable when one is in a state of low arousal than when one is fully mobilized to cope with it. So an upward adjustment of arousal tonus in response to a lasting increase in arousal potential, actual or anticipated, may well be rewarding, even if its subsequent cancellation is also rewarding.

Chapter 8

TOWARD A THEORY OF EXPLORATORY BEHAVIOR: II. AROUSAL POTENTIAL, PERCEPTUAL CURIOSITY, AND LEARNING

The properties of stimuli that we have grouped together as *arousal potential* are ones whose intensification seems, on the whole, to entail a rise in arousal. But they seem also to overlap with properties that enable the cortex to moderate arousal. The relation between arousal and arousal potential can, therefore, hardly be a straightforward one.

When arousal potential is inordinately low, arousal may mount. An environment with exceptionally low collative properties may occasion the upsurge of arousal that seems to mark boredom. When the intensity of a stimulus falls almost to the threshold, there will be an increment of arousal due to conflict.

At the other pole, exceptionally high arousal potential may possibly lead to a steep drop in arousal. Many societies have ceremonies that induce ecstatic and trancelike states by stirring up vehement emotion and overwhelming the senses, and even in the most sedate communities, one may now and then be dazed and bemused by too much excitement. These phenomena may well involve the "supramaximal inhibition" that figures in Pavlov's writings as a protective device, intervening when extremely strong stimuli overtax the excitatory capacity of the nervous system.

Furthermore, we have noted that arousal, except in sleep or abnormal conditions, is maintained at a level considerably above the lower extreme of the arousal dimension. We have called this level arousal tonus. We may think of this tonus as the minimum level of arousal of which the organism is capable at a particular time over a wide range of conditions. The location of the tonus level will depend on the pattern of corticireticular interaction, with, no doubt, other subcortical structures playing their part also. This interaction will, in its turn, depend on internal factors, such as those that control the sleep-waking cycle, and external factors, such as how often the environment has been issuing calls for urgent action.

The arousal tonus, we suppose, will require a particular rate of influx of arousal potential to maintain it. If the influx of arousal potential either exceeds or falls short of this rate, arousal will rise above the tonus level, increasing drive. Then a return to the tonus level will be rewarding, and any responses that promote such a return, whether by rectifying the excess or deficit of arousal potential or by compensating for it, will thus be reinforced and likely to recur in such circumstances.

Our hypotheses imply, therefore, that, for an individual organism at a particular time, there will be an *optimal influx of arousal potential*. Arousal potential that deviates in either an upward or a downward direction from this optimum will be drive inducing or aversive. The organism will thus strive to keep arousal potential near its optimum, which will normally be some distance from both the upper and the lower extreme.

Several assumptions resembling this one have appeared in the recent literature, although the description of the variable possessing an optimum varies from writer to writer. The notion of an optimal, intermediate, actively sought value has been applied to the quantity of stimulation (Leuba 1955), the rate of "perceptualization" (i.e., "the process of perceiving and assimilating new data, new relationships, new meanings") (McReynolds 1956), the flow of information from the environment (Glanzer 1958a), the level of stimulus complexity or novelty (regarded as equivalents) (Dember and Earl 1957), the extent of departure from an adaptation level (conceived as a value of some stimulus variable that an organism has been experiencing for some time or is, through some other process, expecting) (McClelland, Atkinson, Clark, and Lowell 1953), and the level of activity of the RAS (Hebb 1955).

It is easy to see why reductions in arousal potential should so often be welcomed, since they are the most obvious means of producing a fall in arousal. Exploratory behavior, however, seems to intensify stimulation from sources of high arousal potential, and there would seem to be three reasons why stimulation with relatively high arousal value should be sought out:

1. The stimulation may move the influx of arousal potential back toward its optimum when it has fallen below, thus reducing boredom. This will apply principally to *diversive* exploration.

2. Continued exposure to the stimulation may reduce arousal. This will apply principally to *specific inspective* exploration and to *specific inquisitive* exploration following *anticipatory arousal*.

3. A temporary increase in arousal may be sought for the sake of the drop in arousal that follows it. This will apply principally to other cases of *specific inquisitive* exploration.

We shall now consider processes underlying the second and third of these. Without departing too far from normal usage, we shall use the term *perceptual curiosity* to refer to states of high arousal that can be relieved by specific exploration and in which, therefore, specific exploratory responses are likely to occur.

THE RELIEF OF PERCEPTUAL CURIOSITY
BY SPECIFIC EXPLORATION

As we have noted in previous chapters, animals will sometimes withdraw from novel or conflict-inducing objects and sometimes approach and inspect them. Exploration is more likely to occur when arousal potential is only slightly supraoptimal and thus easily brought back to its optimum, or when an animal is surrounded by arousing stimuli with no way of escape. Human beings may also flee from extremely weird or overwhelming complex situations. But, because of their symbolic capacities, they will be more sparing in recourse to withdrawal. Even when withdrawal is evoked, it will rarely be the end of the story. The human aptitude for symbolic representation in memory and thought means that novel, conflictful, or complex stimulus patterns will continue to haunt the nervous system through their internal correlates even after they have left the stimulus field. So the only way of disposing of their disturbing effects, since it is also the only way of coping with their symbolic representatives as well, will ultimately be through exploratory or epistemic (see Chapters 10 and 11) activity. Symbolic processes will likewise enable absent or imaginary patterns to excite curiosity before they are actually encountered, so that they are either sought for or created in the real world.

We must go on to ask how it happens—as it evidently does—that arousal may be reduced by continued, or even intensified, exposure to the very stimulus complex that is responsible for its rise.

First there is, of course, the process of *habituation* that is known to moderate the orientation reaction when an initially novel stimulus with no special significance is repeated or protracted and so loses its novelty.

When arousal has been boosted by intense stimulation, it can be brought down again by the sensitivity-reducing adaptive responses that Sokolov has shown to succeed the orientation reaction (see Chapter 4). When these are inadequate, there is Pavlov's supramaximal inhibition, which is assumed to shield the organism from the deleterious consequences of excessive excitation and has been identified not only in conditioning experiments but also in the course of recent EEG work (see Buser and Roger 1957). There is the spontaneous re-

195

laxation that so often supervenes when emotional tension has been forced up to the limits of endurance, the "purgation of the passions by pity and terror" which Aristotle saw as the main purpose of tragic drama.

In contrast, high arousal produced by stimuli associated with pain or danger to life is markedly resistant to habituation by repetition or prolongation, whether the stimuli owe this action to heredity (e.g., fear of predators in birds, Thorpe 1956) or learning (Solomon and Wynne 1954, Wolpe 1958). And it makes biological sense that this should be so.

Similarly, habituation cannot suffice to remove all disturbances due to conflict. If, however, exploratory behavior does not merely maintain the stimulation unchanged but rather makes accessible details or aspects of the stimulus object that were originally imperceptible, curiosity can be relieved through *recognition*. The fluctuating stimulation resulting from varied inspection eventually turns up a stimulus property that evokes a definite and prepotent response, overt or implicit, that is already in the organism's repertoire. In other words, the object is recognized as assignable to some familiar category, classifiable under some familiar concept, or capable of being placed in some familiar ordering scheme. Uncertainty is lessened because the input category is identified and the transmission of information is completed. The release of some definite cortical response, which is stronger than any competitors that were initially aroused with it, reduces conflict. It results, presumably, in the subdual of arousal through corticifugal pathways.

Next we must consider cases where the deadlock is broken through the *learning of a new response*. An "understanding" of a strange object may be arrived at through vocal or muscular imitation of the object's characteristic sounds, movements, shape, or size (Freud 1905a, Piaget 1945, Werner and Wapner 1952). Guernsey's intensive study (1928) shows how infantile imitation of various actions rises with age and then wanes, finally disappearing when the imitative response has been fully mastered. Alternatively, understanding may come through verbal formulas, descriptive or explanatory naming (see Chapter 10), and through motor responses adapted to the manipulation, use, or control of the object. All these will be overt at first and later shrink to implicit token responses. They may emerge from the individual's own trial and error or thought processes. They may be taken over from the demonstration or verbal instruction of another individual for whom the object is not strange or perplexing. If it is strong enough, the newly acquired response will break the deadlock which is delaying arousal reduction by overcoming its competitors and thus reducing conflict.

Hebb's theory (1949) suggests a neural process which may under-

196

lie adaptation to relatively novel or incongruous patterns. At first, simultaneous presentation of two stimulus properties that have rarely or never been encountered together, and the simultaneous activation of the neural networks (cell assemblies) corresponding to them, will disrupt cortical activity. This can happen for a number of reasons. The two cell assemblies might very well have component neurons in common; firing in one cell assembly may therefore leave a particular neuron in a refractory state just when it is needed to play its part in the firing of the other assembly. Alternatively, if stimulus property A' replaces a stimulus property A that is the usual accompaniment of property B, the absence of A may mean the lack of a particular afferent input that is a necessary condition for the smooth functioning of a cell assembly corresponding to $A + B$. After the unfamiliar combination of properties has been experienced for some time, the disruption can be obviated by the formation of a new cell assembly corresponding to the new pattern, $A' + B$, perhaps incorporating the units shared by the two older A' and B assemblies; the new assembly can, in its turn, become associated with definite motor or verbal responses peculiar to the new pattern. If something like this happens, it is evident that these modifications can take place quite rapidly, since, at least in human beings, a single, quite brief exposure to a strange pattern will often suffice to rob it of its strangeness.

THE AROUSAL JAG

The premises on which the concepts of drive and reward are based may, at first sight, seem to imply that rises in drive level will never be actively pursued. But closer examination will show this not to be so. It is true that a $drive_3$ or aversive state is commonly thought of both as something whose removal is rewarding and as something whose onset is punishing. The latter property means that animals will learn to refrain from responses that are habitually followed by the onset of the state or to perform avoidant responses that prevent the state from supervening in circumstances in which it would otherwise do so. However, the definition of $drive_3$ to which we are committed states solely that the termination or reduction of the drive will be rewarding; it does not follow logically from this that its induction must have punishment value.

It is commonly postulated that any indifferent stimuli regularly preceding aversive states will have conditioned to them a secondary drive of fear (anxiety) (Dollard and Miller 1950, Mowrer 1950) or conditioned aversive properties (Skinner 1953) whose alleviation will reinforce preventive action. This hypothesis has been amply substan-

197

tiated in the case of anticipated pain. Experimental data have also inspired the suggestion that "fear of fear" (Mowrer and Viek 1948) and "fear of hunger" (Ullman 1951) can be attached to warning signals and account for avoidance. But the evidence for these reasonable extensions of the theory is not too plentiful so far.

We can, however, point to many facts contradicting the assumption that aversive or drive$_3$ states are *invariably* avoided and implying that they may even be welcomed in some conditions.

Even in the case of pain, we have masochistic behavior in human beings and experiments like the one by Masserman (1946) in which a cat eagerly presses an electrified lever to obtain food. There have been several experiments with rats in which electric shocks actually strengthen responses that occur simultaneously with, or just before, the shocks (Hamilton and Krechevsky 1933, Muenzinger 1934, Gwinn 1949). Further experiments support the view that the responses in question are reinforced by the subsequent reduction of pain or fear (Farber 1948, Mowrer 1950).

As for fear, one has only to visit the nearest fairground to appreciate the economic value of being tossed and flung through the air, and posters advertising the latest horror film will graphically depict the allurements of being scared out of one's wits.

Much the same point can be supported with regard to hunger or thirst. Various devices from a walk to an anchovy are employed to work up an appetite. As for the sex drive, any comment would be supererogatory.

We are far from being in a position to characterize in detail the conditions in which increases in drive are sought and to differentiate them from those in which they are avoided. But as far as we can see at present, the important ones are (1) that the drive is aroused to a moderate extent, and (2) that the arousal is promptly followed by relief.

Both of these conditions have been cited by Hebb (1949, 1955) as those in which arousal or emotion will be pleasurable, and they are implied by Meyer's (1956) hypothesis that emotion is pleasurable when we feel that the situation is under control.

Some psychoanalytic writers might be inclined to assume that if fear, pain, or other forms of distress are actively courted, it must be for the sake of self-punishment as a means of assuaging guilt feelings. This may conceivably be a contributory condition at times, but the evident importance of quick relief in most of the pertinent cases argues against this view. If mountaineers were habitually suspended over abysses for days on end instead of for a few minutes at a time, their number might well be smaller than it is, although the pastime would, no doubt, still find a few devotees.

There is, however, another psychoanalytic interpretation of apparently self-persecuting behavior that is closer to ours. This is the theory of "belated mastery" (Fenichel 1945), according to which experiences that originally produce anxiety are repeated as a means of gaining control over them. As Fenichel puts it,

> An expenditure of energy is associated with the anxiety or the fearful expectation felt by a person who is uncertain whether he will be able to master an expected excitation. The sudden cessation of this expenditure brings its relieving discharge which is experienced by the successful ego as a "triumph" and enjoyed as functional pleasure. . . . When a child is tossed in the air by an adult and caught [and] is certain that he will not be dropped, he can take pleasure in having thought that he might have been dropped; he may shudder a little, but then realizes that this fear was unnecessary. To make this pleasure possible, conditions of reassurance must be fulfilled. The child must have confidence in the adult who is playing with him and the height must not be too great.

This is precisely the kind of process that we shall assume to occur in connection with arousal. In fact, we shall assume that it is at work whenever a momentary rise in arousal potential, such as a pleasant surprise or a colorful spectacle, is rewarding in the absence of a previous and independently produced spell of severe supraoptimal arousal. Such slight and transitory jumps in arousal will become pleasurable as a consequence of the drop in arousal that quickly terminates them. Consequently, behavior that is regularly followed by such *arousal jags,* as we shall call them, will be learned.

We ought, however, to mention another type of neural mechanism that might underlie the arousal jag. Experiments have shown that direct electrical stimulation through implanted electrodes of certain points in the lower brain will provide quite powerful reinforcement for lever-pressing responses in the rat and the monkey (Olds 1956, Brady and Conrad 1956). The points in question include some within the boundaries of the reticular formation. W. W. Roberts (1958) has shown that current applied to certain points in the posterior hypothalamus has a peculiar property: a cat will learn to enter one maze alley if this response is followed by the switching on of the current, and to enter another alley about ten seconds later to have the current switched off. This alternation between seeking the onset of the stimulation and seeking its termination may occur even when the cats are confined in each alley for three minutes after entering it, so that the reward value of the onset seems to be independent of that of the offset. When the stimulating voltage was relatively weak, the attractiveness of its commencement was very much in evidence and escape responses were desultory. But an increase in the voltage strengthened the escape responses and depressed the stimulation-seeking responses.

The stimulation used in this experiment has, therefore, rewarding properties at first and aversive properties later. The former, it is interesting to note, are most manifest when the stimulation has just come on and when it has a moderate intensity. It is possible that the effects of activating other points in the brain stem, including those points in the RAS that have been shown capable of mediating reward, may follow the same pattern and thus account for the reward value of arousal jags.

THE QUEST FOR INTERMEDIATE AROUSAL POTENTIAL

We can now take up supporting evidence for our assumption that human beings and higher animals will normally strive to maintain an intermediate amount of arousal potential. Some of this evidence comes from experiments and some from everyday experience of human behavior. At many points, we shall have to make do with verbal and other manifestations of pleasure and displeasure as indications of what is rewarding and what is aversive. This seems, on the whole, to be justified, but it has by no means been justified beyond question.

Intensive Variables

It has been noted often enough that many forms of stimulation are pleasant at medium intensities and turn unpleasant when their intensities are higher. It was, in fact, laid down by Wundt (1874) as a general rule that the curve representing hedonic tone as a function of stimulus intensity has the shape depicted in Fig. 8-1.

Solutions of sour, salty, and bitter substances taste pleasant when their concentrations stand a little above the absolute gustatory threshold, but as their concentrations are increased still further, they become more and more unpalatable (R. Engel 1928). Sweet solutions were judged pleasant by most of Engel's subjects even at the highest concentration he tried (40 per cent of cane sugar), but, as he recognized, it would surely be possible to find solutions of other substances, e.g., saccharine, that would be so sweet as to be disagreeably sickening or cloying. Rats will drink more saccharine solution than plain water when the concentration is slightly above threshold, but their preference

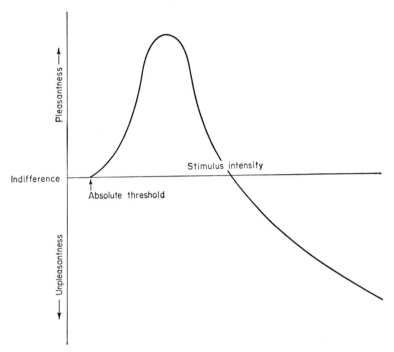

FIG. 8-1

for the solution wanes and then becomes negative as the sweetness of the solution rises (Beebe-Center, Black, Hoffman, and Wade 1948). When the difference between the amount of the solution and the amount of water drunk is plotted against the concentration of saccharine in the solution, a curve remarkably similar to the one in Fig. 8-1 is obtained. The reactions of rats to different salt solutions show a similar pattern (Weiner and Stellar 1951). And Lehmann (1892), whose human subjects had their fingers in water heated to various temperatures, obtained reports of pleasant warmth between 35 and 40 degrees and of definite unpleasantness or pain above 45 degrees centigrade.

Wundt's hypothesis and these experiments seem to fit our inference that moderate arousal potential will be maximally rewarding. Similar experiments could well be carried out with other qualities of stimuli but are so far lacking. However, as McClelland, Atkinson, Clark, and Lowell (1953) argue, how attractive a particular stimulus intensity is may depend on what the organism has been experiencing in its recent or distant past. It may, in other words, depend on the degree of change, novelty, surprisingness, or complexity that it introduces.

Affective Variables

We have already dwelt on the human proclivity to seek emotional experience and excitement either in real life or vicariously through art or entertainment. The self-inflicted stress seems generally to be relatively mild or else short-lived. Some emotional athletes may seem able to withstand virtually unending drafts of hectic turbulence. In these cases, however, we may suspect that the turbulence undergoes wide fluctuations with frequently interspersed recessions, or else that some psychopathological process is operating. The emotions that can be elicited by dramatized fiction may also appear to be quite violent at times, but the unreality of their source, the fact that it is "only a story," surely provides a safety valve that normally prevents them from exceeding manageable bounds.

Collative Variables

Change and Complexity. The circumstances in which stimulus changes will have a positive affective value have been examined by McClelland, Atkinson, Clark, and Lowell (1953), who offer an original theory to account for the facts as they see them. According to this theory, "positive affect is the result of smaller discrepancies of a sensory or perceptual event from the adaptation level of the organism; negative affect is the result of larger discrepancies." The theory is not worked out in sufficient detail to define the nature and value of adaptation levels in all instances. Sometimes, the adaptation level seems to be a value of a stimulus variable that an animal has been experiencing for some time. At other times, it seems to approximate a central tendency of values experienced in the recent past or in the animal's life history, being comparable to Helson's (1948) notion of an "adaptation level" as a factor determining absolute psychophysical judgment. Alternatively, the adaptation level may be a value that is expected in an impending stimulus or some value "based on symmetry, balance, and so forth."

These authors cite an experiment by Alpert (1953) in which subjects were first exposed to homogeneous visual fields of red light. A spot in the middle was then, for a series of two-second trials, made more or less intense than the rest of the field by varying amounts. When the background intensity was low, central spots that were slightly brighter or dimmer were generally judged pleasant and those that were very much brighter were generally judged unpleasant. When the background intensity was high, central spots that were very much dimmer, slightly dimmer, or slightly brighter were alike judged pleas-

202

ant. The intense background illumination seems, therefore, to have had an aversive quality, as a result of which a much dimmer central spot was rewarding in spite of its large discrepancy from the background.

It will be remembered (from Chapter 6) how the literature on investigatory behavior in the rat provides some hints that moderate changes in the intensity of illumination are rewarding but that, over and above this effect, highly intense light is aversive. An experiment by Haber (1958) reveals a similar pattern in human affective reactions to thermal stimulation. Whereas Lehmann's experiment, mentioned above, started from the normal skin temperature, Haber used various temperatures as adaptation levels. His subjects had first to immerse both hands in water of a particular temperature, and then to place the two hands in water of differing temperatures. They were to indicate which hand was more uncomfortable by withdrawing it from the water. The results showed clearly that water at the adaptation temperature, or very much warmer or colder, was generally more uncomfortable than water whose temperature differed from the adaptation level by 1 to 3 degrees in either direction. Nevertheless, this rule did not hold when adaptation levels exceeded normal skin temperature by more than a few degrees: the adaptation temperature was then judged more comfortable than any temperature above it.

The theory offered by McClelland and his associates has clearly much in common with our own, and it is aimed at much the same neglected problems. When an adaptation level is represented by the stimulation that an organism has just been receiving, as in Haber's experiment, then the extent to which a new stimulus departs from it will represent the degree of *change*, which is in our list of determinants of arousal. When the adaptation level depends on stimuli received in the organism's near or distant past, the extent of a deviation from it can be identified with *short-term* or *long-term novelty*, respectively. And when it is a matter of a disparity between two portions of a stimulus field, as in the experiment by Alpert, we can speak of *complexity*. Thus, wherever there is a moderate departure from an adaptation level and therefore, according to the McClelland theory, a rewarding state of affairs, there will be what we should characterize as a moderate amount of arousal potential.

There are, however, some differences between the McClelland theory and our own. One is that, whereas that theory appears to assume the existence of a large number of separate adaptation levels for different stimulus properties, we envisage a single arousal level to which many stimulus properties will contribute. Moreover, we are making assumptions, admittedly tentative, about the physiological correlates of arousal, and we also recognize a wider variety of determinants of reward or punishment value. We are not, however, putting forward our theory in preference to McClelland's because we believe that ours is more likely to be correct. On the contrary, our theory, being more comprehensive, is less likely to be correct. It is just that when a body of initial data has been gathered about an area of inquiry and it is time for the first attempts to work out unifying assumptions, the bolder a theory, the more useful it may prove in suggesting and guiding experiments. Its imprudences and callownesses can always be remedied later, once methodical inquiry is under way.

Novelty. Some of the most instructive studies on the affective value of novelty, apart from studies directly aimed at exploratory behavior, are those carried out under the direction of Charlotte Bühler (already mentioned in Chapter 7). We may first mention a finding of Bühler, Hetzer, and Mabel (1928). As typical of the behavior of a six-month-old child exposed to a strange stimulus, they furnish the following protocol of reactions (with durations) to four successive experiences, lasting thirty seconds each, of a falsetto voice:

> 1st exposure: Cry of fear, movement indicative of displeasure (35 seconds).
>
> 2nd exposure: Movement and vocalization indicative of displeasure (20 seconds).
>
> 3rd exposure: Listening, no vocalization indicative of displeasure, slight signs of attention (15 seconds).
>
> 4th exposure: Interested looking in the direction of the sound (15 seconds).

Löwenfeld (1927) observed the reactions made by infants up to eight months of age to various novel sounds (a rattle, a whistle, a hand clap, a tuning pipe, and a bell). At one month, the reactions were predominantly expressive of negative affect, but the frequency of such negative reactions declined steadily with age. Indexes of positive affect began to appear in the third month, rose to a maximum at six to seven months, and then fell off. Neutral reactions became more and more frequent from the second month and finally preponderated over others.

There is no way of knowing for certain how far changes due to maturation lay behind the changes in reaction with age. Presumably they played some part, since Bühler, Hetzer, and Mabel failed to elicit positive reactions from subjects under two months by repeating their auditory stimuli. But the parallel between the passage from negative to positive reactions with increasing age and the analogous development with successive repetitions of an unfamiliar stimulus suggests that degree of novelty is the operative variable in both cases. As each new month of an infant's life enlarges his acquaintance with sounds and with stimuli in general, unfamiliar sounds such as those used by Löwenfeld will contrast less and less with the contents of previous experience.

Bühler (1928), in summing up her conclusions from this series of researches, describes how a stage where the unfamiliar generates displeasure ("shock," "disturbance of equilibrium," and "fear") and the familiar generates pleasure is gradually replaced; as more and more stimuli lose their novelty and are "digested," the familiar gives rise to boredom and the unfamiliar to the satisfaction of *Neugier* (conventionally translated as "curiosity," but literally "desire for the new").

An experiment by Alpert (1953) shows that this process is not peculiar to infants. He exposed adult subjects a number of times in succession to a pattern of sounds with an unfamiliar rhythm. The pattern was first adjudged unpleasant, and then, after several repetitions, pleasant, and finally, after more repetitions, indifferent. Countless innovations have met with the same sequence of reactions in the history of music and other arts.

In our review of animal experiments (especially in Chapter 5), we noted that stimulus objects are often avoided by adult animals at first; then, when their novelty has worn off a little, they are approached and sought out, finally becoming indifferent.

On the other hand, Harlow (personal communication) states that the newborn monkey "responds positively to almost all visual stimuli. Fear responses to large, intense stimuli apparently 'mature' some time after 20 days of age." The seeming discrepancy between his findings and those of Bühler's group could be due to interspecies differences, to age differences (Bühler's and Löwenfeld's subjects were already several weeks old), or to differences in the kinds of stimuli used (Bühler's group used mainly auditory stimuli with a sudden impact).

Conflict and Uncertainty. In Chapter 6, we referred to an experiment by Wyckoff (1952) in which a pigeon learned to step on a pedal, although the only outcome of this response was a cue (the red or green coloring of a white key) indicating whether or not pecking at the key would be rewarded with food. These results seem to harmonize with our hypothesis about the relation between conflict and arousal. The state of the pigeon while the key is white (and pecking has a fifty-fifty chance of being rewarded) is manifestly one of uncertainty, and the main function of the pedal-stepping response may be said to consist in transmitting information, reducing the uncertainty by one bit.

We may also suppose that the white key induced a conflict between pecking and not pecking, expecting and not expecting food, excitation and inhibition. The coloring of the key that resulted from stepping on the pedal must then have attenuated the conflict by strengthening one of the competing tendencies and weakening the others.

When the discrimination was reversed, Wyckoff found that the frequency of the pedal response would temporarily decrease. This also fits our interpretation, since each color would then go through a stage of evoking both excitatory and inhibitory tendencies, and seeing the key colored would thus exacerbate rather than relieve conflict.

The results of Kelleher's (1958) experiments (see Chapter 6) may be interpreted in a similar fashion.

An experiment by Prokasy (1956) is somewhat analogous to those of Wyckoff and Kelleher. He trained rats in a T maze. After turning right or left at the choice point, the animals had to turn a corner to enter a chamber in which they were delayed for thirty seconds. A door then opened, admitting them to a goal box which contained food on half the trials and was empty on the other half. The only difference between the two arms of the maze was that on one side the delay chamber was black when the goal box contained food and white when it did not (or vice versa), whereas on the other side the color of the delay chamber, though also black and white equally often, was not correlated with the presence of food. The rats acquired a significant preference for the former or "consistent" side. One might infer that entry into the "inconsistent" arm will have meant uncertainty, conflict, or anticipatory arousal, which entry into the "consistent" arm avoided.

Uncertainty is manifestly one of the burdens that the human frame is least equipped to stand. Even when the uncertainty concerns something of relatively minor importance, its pressure can become irresistible. There are, no doubt, people who could be left alone in a house a day before their birthday, knowing that a present is lying unwrapped in a certain drawer, and who would withstand the temptation to look. But they would not encompass the whole human species.

During the 1955 British general election and the 1956 American presidential election, broadcasting corporations went to great trouble and expense to procure the services of expert commentators and electronic computers. As results came in from the different areas of the country during the course of the night, the best available forecasts of the final outcome were continuously supplied. It is hard to see what practical use could have been made of these forecasts in the middle of the night, especially when one thinks that listeners could have gone to bed and known the final outcome for certain almost at their next moments of consciousness. Yet the deep-seated human reluctance to wait an unnecessary moment for information about what the future holds, even when there is no way in which one could act on the information, sustains a gamut of professions from that of the political columnist to that of the astrologer.

Grave dangers can be faced with signal courage if the outcome depends on unpredictable natural occurrences or on the doings of an inaccessible enemy, though, even then, human beings have always been partial to omens and auguries as means of treating the unforeseeable as foreseeable. It is significant that vocations like those of the miner, the air pilot, the actor, and the professional sportsman, in which there are unremitting risks of disaster, whether from injury or death or from loss of reputation through poor performance, are notoriously conducive to superstition.

If, however, there is any hope of knowing in advance whether some feared (or even gratifying) event will occur—if, for example, it depends on a decision made by some person close at hand or on information that is available to such a person—there is almost no price that will be too much to pay, and no stratagem that will be too tortuous, for the puniest hint of which way things will turn. This is so even when it is fully realized that the news may not be pleasing. There is such a thing as the "comfort of knowing the worst." After intensively interviewing a fair number of convicts, Farber (1944) found one of the major sources of suffering in prison to be uncertainty about how much time would have to be served. Those prisoners who had hopes of a parole suffered much more than those who knew that they would never be released.

Nevertheless, our assumptions imply, and common knowledge attests, that some moderate degree of uncertainty can serve to make life less dull. Uncertainty, as well as fear, may be sought through physically dangerous pastimes. But the behavior that seems most clearly to the point here is gambling, especially gambling with stakes that are not large enough for their loss to be serious, although they are large enough not to be ventured for nothing.

Skinner (1953) has emphasized the analogy between human gambling and the behavior of the rat or the pigeon under variable-ratio schedules of reinforcement. In both cases, we have a response that will be rewarded on the average once in so many times, but how many responses will be unrewarded before the next reinforcement occurs is unpredictable at any moment. This treatment produces astonishingly high resistance to extinction and induces the rat or the pigeon, like the human gambler, to perform many consecutive responses without a single reward.

But although the analogy is striking and cannot be accidental, it can hardly be the whole story. Many human beings appear to gamble with immense zeal before they receive their first winnings. And even when they win, there is often so long an interval between placing a bet and collecting the pay-off that reinforcement must come through symbolic processes (expectations) whose mode of operation must be a major determinant in the pattern of behavior responses.

Economists and decision theorists have been puzzled by the prevalence of gambling because of its apparent irrationality. Since bookmakers and the proprietors of casinos assure themselves of a profit, whoever partakes of their services must be accepting a negative mathematical expectation, i.e., his expected winnings (the amount he can win multiplied by the probability of winning it) must fall short of the amount staked. There have been various attempts to circumvent this difficulty. It can be done, for example, by assuming that utility does not increase linearly with monetary value (Friedman and Savage 1948) or that subjective probability does not increase linearly with objective probability (Edwards 1955). Consistent models can apparently be founded on these assumptions, although they do not always incorporate neatly shaped curves, and the curves tend to vary from person to person.

Some decision theorists have, therefore, been led to speak of the 'utility of gambling' as such. And we may surmise that this utility derives from the rise and subsequent fall in arousal due to uncertainty.

It is, of course, not easy to separate the role of fear (or anticipation of reward) from that of uncertainty in either gambling or physically dangerous pastimes. We have identified degree of conflict as a quantity that increases both with "importance" (what is at stake, ΣE) and uncertainty (see Chapter 2). The two can be studied apart only by manipulating expected gains or losses while holding probabilities constant, and vice versa.

This has been done in a series of interesting but avowedly pioneering experiments by Edwards (1953, 1955). In one experiment, he asked his subjects to select from a set of imaginary or real bets having equal expected values but differing in the probability of winning or losing. When expected values were positive or zero, but in either case held constant, he found a pronounced tendency to prefer bets with a 0.5 chance of a favorable outcome. It is noteworthy that this is the condition in which the events are equally probable and thus uncertainty is at a maximum for two alternatives. In another experiment, he varied what we have called the importance factor, by varying the amount that could be won or lost while holding the expected values constant. He found that this factor affected preferences, though in different directions for different individuals and generally not so much as the probabilities.

Most mass gambling appears to satisfy either or both of the conditions we have suggested for the attractiveness of an arousal jag: the stake is fairly small, so that its loss will not be disastrous, and the uncertainty is relieved fairly quickly.

There are, no doubt, habitual gamblers and financial speculators who will readily risk ruin. But in many cases, the mathematical expectation will actually be quite high or the risk will be taken in games where the outcome of each venture is soon revealed and the tension soon relieved. There may be others for whom neither of these conditions is fulfilled, just as there are those who will inflict injury on themselves or commit suicide with no uncertainty of outcome. But these will provide subject matter for abnormal psychology.

EQUIVALENCE OF VARIOUS FORMS OF AROUSAL POTENTIAL

We have been thinking of the level of arousal as subject to the influence of a large number of variables whose effects will be additive and thus interchangeable. It follows that an individual whose arousal has already been raised by one kind of arousal potential can be aroused far beyond the tonus level by what, for other individuals, would be a quite comfortable measure of arousal potential from a different source. Anxious people, for example, will be distressed by an amount of novelty, change, or complexity that others would take in their stride. Observation of neurotics or of normal individuals at times of unusual stress gives very much this impression. And some less commonplace deductions from the assumption of equivalence between sources of arousal have received some confirmation.

We must first mention two experiments by Smock (1955a, 1955b) on the interaction between stress and intolerance of ambiguity. The subjects of both experiments were divided into two groups, one of which was encouraged to feel insecure and the other to feel relaxed by the experimenter's attitude. In the first experiment, the subjects looked at a series of figures, each beginning with a pattern of meaningless marks and developing into an easily recognizable picture by progressive addition of materials. They were to guess what the final product of a series would be as soon as they were ready to do so. The insecure group tended to voice guesses earlier than the relaxed group, and, since their guesses were often made prematurely with inadequate information, they were often incorrect and so delayed the attainment of the right responses. In the second experiment, an incongruous picture, e.g., of an old woman in company with a young man, of a half-male-half-female person, was given a succession of one-second exposures, well out of focus at first and then becoming gradually clearer. The group that had been subjected to stress re-

209

quired more exposures than the other group to identify the picture.

Brim and Hoff (1957) have devised a verbal test of "desire for certainty." It consists of thirty-two statements about matters of common interest, in which a probability value must be filled in. An example is this statement: "The chances that an American citizen will believe in God are about —— in 100." Subjects are to supply the missing probability and also to indicate on a five-point scale the certainty with which they do so. An item is scored by subtracting the probability percentage supplied from 0 or from 100, whichever is nearer to it, and then multiplying this difference by the certainty rating. In the experiment that is of interest to us here, the administration of the test was preceded by a test based on Gottschaldt's (1926) celebrated experiment in which simple forms were hidden in complex figures and had to be discovered. One group of subjects were given far more Gottschaldt tasks than they could possibly complete in the time allowed, a procedure designed as a "frustration condition." The remainder had tasks that were few enough and simple enough to produce a "satisfaction condition." The frustrated subjects then obtained significantly higher scores on the desire-for-certainty test.

An experiment by McReynolds and Bryan (1956) had neuropsychiatric patients as subjects, which might raise doubts about the generality of the findings, but it favors much the same conclusions as the others. Subjects were first shown a series of cards bearing designs or pictures and told that each design or picture would appear twice. For one group of subjects (the L group), all had actually appeared twice by the end of the series, but the remainder (the H group) had seen twenty out of sixty only once when the series was interrupted. Therefore the H group had, to use McReynolds' terminology, a "higher level of unassimilated percepts." All subjects were then given a sorting test. They were shown a collection of wooden pieces, each of which had a word printed on its underside. There were triangular pieces which, subjects were informed, bore words standing for the "more familiar sorts of things," and odd-shaped pieces which, they were told, bore names of the "more novel, unusual sorts of things." The pieces were to be dropped into three slots marked "animal," "vegetable," or "mineral," according to the objects named on them. Time was allowed for less than half of the pieces to be sorted, so that how many unusual and how many familiar object names were encountered depended on the order in which subjects chose to pick up the pieces. The outcome was that the H group exposed themselves to significantly fewer unusual object names than the L group.

To turn to an animal experiment, Thompson and Higgins (1958) used a maze with black and white compartments, first habituating

210

their rats to either the black or the white compartment. At a later stage, some of the rats were shocked at the choice point and some were not. It was found that those which had been shocked were more likely to enter the compartment with which they were familiar; the nonshocked subjects were more likely to enter whichever was for them the newer compartment. We may also recall the finding of Chapman and Levy that hungry rats were less inclined than satiated ones to run to a goal box that had contained novel stimuli.

All these experiments, despite their obvious dissimilarities, have the following aspects of their design in common. Subjects were first exposed to differing degrees of one kind of arousal potential. They were then put through a task in which they encountered arousal potential of quite another kind, but this time they had some control over the amount to which they were exposed. In all cases, those who had been subjected to more arousal-inducing conditions in the first phase were more reluctant to accept arousal potential in the second phase, which is in tune with our assumption of a common pool of arousal that can receive increments from a diversity of stimulus conditions.

An experiment by Fonberg (1956) furnishes evidence of a quite different sort for the same assumption. She trained dogs to perform a certain response (R_1), the actual response varying from one subject to another, as a way of terminating stimuli that had been associated with puffs of air or electric shocks. The animals then received training in another response (R_2), which was followed by food reinforcement in the presence of a loud tone but not in the presence of a faint tone. The animals were then subjected to a Shenger-Krestovnikova (Pavlov 1927) type of conflict by exposure to tones that were intermediate in intensity between the positive and negative alimentary conditioned stimuli. They thereupon reverted to the defensive response (R_1). This finding indicates that the state produced by conflict, even when noxious stimuli have played no part in it, has enough in common with the state resulting from a noxious stimulus (fear) for stimulus generalization between the two to occur.

INTRAINDIVIDUAL AND INTERINDIVIDUAL DIFFERENCES

We can expect personality factors, cultural factors, learning, and physiological states all to play their parts in determining the level at which arousal tonus is maintained. Consequently, the rate of arousal potential that is optimal can be presumed to vary widely from individual to individual and from occasion to occasion.

The quantities of excitement, emotional intensity, motor activity, and environmental vicissitude that can be tolerated by the New York taxi driver and the Balinese farmer, the mercurial Sicilian and the dour Scot, the stunt pilot and the weekend angler, the town mouse and the country mouse will clearly differ. The Andalusian fiesta and the Pleasant Sunday Afternoon movement have, in all likelihood, few common devotees. The front-line soldier can adjust himself for months or years on end to a background of unremitting alertness that prepares him to run for cover at a moment's notice; most wild animals and many primitive human societies have had, no doubt, just such a condition as an inseparable part of living. But human beings in other circumstances may be shattered by a few minutes of mild tension.

We can picture the tonus level of arousal as creeping upward or downward if a level above or below an earlier tonus level is sustained for some time. How much arousal potential of a particular kind an individual will tolerate depends not only on the level of arousal tonus but also on how promptly and easily he has been able to assuage the arousal induced by similar conditions in the past.

Intraindividual Changes

That susceptibility to arousal may be blunted, not only by prolonged presentation of one stimulus, but also by a succession of different situations with appreciable arousal potential, is indicated by several experimental findings.

Kratin (1959) experimented with human subjects in a drowsy state, characterized by relatively slow and irregular EEG waves. It will be recalled that in such a condition a rise in arousal is marked by a brief appearance of alpha activity rather than by alpha suppression. When a tone of a particular pitch was sounded repeatedly, the alpha bursts grew gradually shorter and finally failed to appear, as one would expect. They were restored, however, when a tone of a different pitch was unexpectedly introduced. After a series of such changes in pitch, new tones could no longer evoke a rise in arousal except now and then in a weak form.

Hudson (1950) found that rats would show a mild but unmistakable tendency to avoid a novel visual pattern, even when there was no shock involved. He compared the behavior evoked by such a pattern in two groups, one of which had a succession of miscellaneous novel objects placed in their cages for twenty-four hours at a time before being introduced to the critical pattern. This treatment significantly reduced avoidance of the latter. Exposure to novel objects, even though they bear no special resemblance to one another apart from being novel, can evidently depress sensitivity to novel stimuli in general.

We may recall the experiments of Dember, Earl, and Paradise and of Williams and Kuchta, which showed how rats develop a preference for increasingly complex stimulation with continued exposure to an experimental situation (see Chapter 5).

Similar effects are familiar in human beings. Earl (1957) provides us with an illustration. Children were set the task of arranging colored wooden blocks to reproduce certain printed patterns. The patterns were subjected to an elaborate scaling procedure which associated a measure of "complexity" with each of them. The subjects were also required, at various times in the course of the experiment, to scale them for the amount of "fun" they yielded. The degree of complexity that was shown to be preferred by this technique rose as the children had more and more experience with the task, and so it looks as if a degree of complexity that would initially have produced supra-optimal arousal can become optimal as experience of a situation accumulates. An analogous experiment revealed that the distance from which the children most liked to throw darts at a target increased with practice at the task. These experiments are reminiscent of a whole host of experiments on level of aspiration. Here the goal that an individual sets himself is located near the upper limit of his ability, at a point where he has something like a 0.5 chance of attaining it, and the individual becomes more and more ambitious as practice improves ability.

These changes in level of aspiration, like the changes in preference noted by Earl, might appear amenable to a different explanation. Since human beings generally receive more reliable and more copious rewards for more difficult achievements, the level of aspiration or preferred task may be the one that maximizes the expectation of reward, i.e., the amount of reward that would result if the task were successfully completed multiplied by the subjective probability of success. Even when subjects attempt something for "fun" or for "their own satisfaction," it could be claimed that the increase in reward value with difficulty comes by generalization or association (secondary reward value) from past occasions on which social or material rewards have been won by aiming high and succeeding.

These factors will, without doubt, play their parts, and it is hard to test their adequacy as an explanation without finding, or planning to have available, persons who have never been encouraged to overcome difficulties. But the fact that rats and primates will undertake equivalents of puzzles and feats of daring when there is no correlation between success and external reward and the fact that many a human artist, scientist, thinker, and explorer has embarked on intractable enterprises with every sign of indifference to fame and fortune argue for some endogenous source of reinforcement. As Hebb (1953, 1955) has maintained, it looks as if there is a *"positive attraction of risk taking,* or mild fear, *and of problem solving,* or mild frustration." We suggest that the reinforcement for these activities comes from arousal jags, and that the tasks most challenging—which make one wonder whether they can be handled or not—are those which produce just the right amount of arousal and anticipated arousal reduction. The degree of complexity or difficulty that falls within the right range will surely mount higher and higher as the individual's sophistication grows (Dember and Earl 1957).

Personality Traits

Two traits with which specialists in personality theory have of late been concerning themselves and which certainly sound relevant to our inquiry are *intolerance of ambiguity* and *simplicity-complexity.* The former was introduced by Frenkel-Brunswik (1949), who depicted the individual with high intolerance of ambiguity as marked by "a preference for familiarity, symmetry, definiteness and regularity" and also by "a tendency toward black-white solutions, oversimplified dichotomizing." The trait is generally found to a high degree in persons who have been reared with strict, unexplained discipline and who have accordingly developed strongly ambivalent feelings toward parents. They are disturbed by any stimulus object that is apt to arouse opposite emotions or has properties that place it midway between familiar categories. They react characteristically with prejudiced, stereotyped, all-or-none evaluations or classifications, ignoring facts that do not accord with them. For example, when they are shown a series of drawings in which a cat gradually changes into a dog, they persist in perceiving a cat long after other persons would notice anomalies.

Block and Block (1951) exposed subjects to the autokinetic effect (the illusion which makes a point of light in an otherwise darkened room appear to move) and found that the subjects who were quickest at establishing norms (i.e., at imposing regularities of extent and direction on the illusory movement) were those liable to "overcontrol." They tended to "bind their tensions excessively," to keep their motivational impulses bottled up. Eysenck (1954) cites evidence that intolerance of ambiguity, measured by Frenkel-Brunswik's methods, is correlated with "tough-minded" attitudes toward social and political questions, which, he argues, are indicative of extraversion. V. Hamilton (1957) tested neurotic and normal subjects with a series of tasks that involved placing objects in either of two categories. He found that hysterics and obsessive-compulsive patients were more liable to in-

214

tolerance of ambiguity than sufferers from anxiety states or nonneurotics, as evinced by a reluctance to give responses such as, "May be either; I can't decide which." Finally, there appears to be a positive correlation between tolerance of ambiguity and self-confidence (Guilford, Christensen, Frick, and Merrifield 1957).

The simplicity-complexity dimension has been identified by factor analysis of preferences among visual forms (Eysenck 1941, Barron and Welsh 1952). Eysenck (1941, 1947) found that the aesthetic tastes of extraverts lean toward simple, regular polygons with few sides and simple, brightly colored, modern paintings; introverts tend to like complex, irregular, many-sided polygons and paintings in the academic manner with abundant detail and less vivid coloring. Barron's (1952, 1953) investigations, which combined an aesthetic-preference test with various tests of personality, represent the individual who is partial to simple, symmetrical, regularly predictable patterns as one likely to control his impulses by repression, to be subservient to authority, and to conform to established social norms. The partisan of complexity is more likely to be capable of expressing his impulses and thoughts freely, to show independence of judgment when he finds himself in a minority, and to hold "tender-minded" beliefs (which Eysenck links with introversion).

It is plain that those who have been studying these traits do not agree at all points. To what extent the various tests that have been labeled alike actually measure the same things and how best to describe what each one measures are matters which can be and have been hotly debated. Nevertheless, the data we have cited indicate that ambiguity and complexity are, in some way, associated with, or equivalent to, anxiety, and that those who have difficulty in tolerating anxiety, especially anxiety coming from their own sexual, aggressive, and other potentially antisocial impulses, will likewise have difficulty in facing ambiguity or complexity. Their failure to achieve rational, flexible control over these impulses yields them up to the drastic, exaggerated control of repression.

Ambiguity could conceivably become associated with anxiety because social disapproval or other unfortunate consequences have followed failures to classify situations promptly and accurately. Training in childhood might build up a connection between ambiguity or complexity and disorderliness, untidiness, dirt, rebellion, or lack of self-control, which would become associated with anxiety as a result of the parental disapproval that they incur. But the general picture is also compatible with our hypothesis that fear, complexity, uncertainty, and conflict all contribute to a common fund of arousal.

Ultimately, the only effective way to deal with ambiguity is to procure additional information through exploratory and epistemic behavior, but this means that the conflict must be faced and borne for a while. The conflict can be relieved more quickly by turning away from, or refusing to attend to, the troublesome stimuli, but it will then be apt to recur. The alternative is analogous to that offered by other drive states. Physiological needs can be gratified impulsively, but at the cost of baleful consequences, or gratification can be postponed in accordance with Freud's "reality principle," until it can be undertaken more safely. Fear can be assuaged rapidly by a variety of devices from alcoholic intoxication to self-deception, but the only hope of removing it permanently usually lies in eliminating or adapting to whatever caused it—and this takes time.

Physiological Measures

There are, of course, a number of distinct ways in which the functioning of arousal could differ from one individual to another (or from one period to another within an individual's lifetime). The following are the most obvious ones, coupled with physiological measures that may be supposed—in some cases very tentatively indeed—to reflect them.

1. The prevailing level of arousal: rarity and rapidity of EEG alpha waves (Saul, Davis, and Davis 1949, Gastaut 1954) or various indexes of activation of the sympathetic nervous system (Wenger 1941).

2. Lability of the level of arousal: amount of spontaneous fluctuation in EEG waves (Gastaut 1954) or palmar conductance (Mundy-Castle and McKiever 1953).

3. The intensity of changes in arousal provoked by external stimuli: rate and extent of changes in finger volume due to vasomotor reactions (Van der Merwe and Theron 1947).

4. The speed with which the organism recovers from an orientation reaction: recovery rate of GSR (Darrow and Heath 1932).

5. The speed of habituation or extinction of the orientation reaction with repeated presentation of a stimulus: rate of habituation of GSR (Mundy-Castle and McKiever 1953).

There is some evidence, varying very much in conclusiveness, for a link (positive for numbers 1, 2, and 3 and negative for 4 and 5) between each of these and emotional instability or neuroticism (see Eysenck 1953, Mundy-Castle and McKiever 1953). Several writers have connected them with the degree of control that the cortex exercises over lower centers, and so it is only natural for us to see them as reflections of how effectively the cortex dominates the RAS.

There must also be differences in the readiness with which individuals of differing temperaments will resort to various expedients for relieving or staving off high arousal. It is, for example, widely recognized that hysterics are addicted to repression. They react to anxiety- or conflict-inducing facts about the outside world or about their own make-up by failing to perceive them; in extreme cases, this may lead to symptoms like hysterical blindness, deafness, anesthesias, and amnesia. This process seems like a caricature of selective attention. In fact, Jouvet (personal communication), testing a patient with hysterical anesthesia of the foot, found that subcortical potentials corresponding to tactual stimulation of the affected foot underwent the same kind of attenuation as would be produced by distracting stimuli from another modality in a normal person (see Chapter 3). This appears to indicate that the corticifugal mechanisms that block afferent impulses in selective attention play an exaggerated role in the symptoms of hysteria.

Dysthymics (introverted neurotics) spend more time than hysterics examining a pencil maze before attacking it (Foulds 1951), which points to a propensity for resolving conflicts by exploratory behavior. The obsessive-compulsive patient is, as is well known, given to brooding, to wondering and doubting, to pettifogging distinctions and classificatory schemes—all of which amount to a morbid travesty of the epistemic behavior that we shall be taking up in Chapters 10 and 11.

EXPLORATION, AROUSAL, PERCEPTUAL CURIOSITY, AND LEARNING IN GENERAL

In this chapter and in earlier chapters, we have been considering the conditions in which exploratory responses may be learned. We must now touch on ways in which exploratory responses, and the processes that underlie them, may contribute to the learning of other, nonexploratory responses. This means raising a number of wider issues which have, as yet, scarcely been skimmed by experimenters but are likely to prove of the utmost importance for the further understanding of learning in general. These questions show better than anything else that the study of exploratory behavior is not a self-contained speciality but something intertwined with many of the most fundamental issues which are of crucial concern in psychology.

Exploratory Responses and Instrumental Learning

First, and most obviously, there are ways in which appropriate exploratory responses can facilitate, or even be a prerequisite for, the acquisition of adaptive responses. Spence (1945) has pointed out that an animal cannot be expected to solve a discrimination problem unless his receptors focus on the features distinguishing the positive from the negative cue. Ehrenfreund (1948) illustrated this point with an experiment that compared the behavior in a Lashley jumping stand of a group of rats for which the figures on the cards were at eye level with the behavior of another group for which they were not. The former group, as one would expect, learned much more quickly to jump toward the right card.

Another illustration is embodied in Ruzskaia's (1958) experiment on shape discrimination in children. The subjects were to learn to press one key on seeing a triangle and another key on seeing a quadrilateral, the correct response being reinforced by the sight of a toy car coming out of a garage. Subjects in one group were left to their own devices and showed little or no sign of mastering the task. Other groups, instructed either to look at the upper parts of the figures (which differentiated them most clearly) or to count the sides while following the contours with their fingers, performed better. Best of all was a group that was told to follow contours with both fingers and eyes while counting the sides.

Similarly, the experiments of Zaporozhets (1954, 1958) on the development of voluntary movements in children show how a child must learn to expose himself to the important stimuli in a situation, by performing the correct orienting responses, before he can learn to carry out the correct instrumental or "executive" activities. The children in these experiments were trained to press a number of keys in a succession corresponding to a series of signal lights, or to push a toy car through a maze. The children would spontaneously perform orienting responses to acquaint themselves with the principal features of the apparatus and could, in fact, only with difficulty be restrained from performing them. In the younger children, touching and feeling movements of hands and fingers were most prominent, but with increasing age, these were replaced in large measure by movements of the eyes. The more time the children spent on preliminary inspection, the fewer the trials needed subsequently to master the actions imposed by the tasks. Methods of directing them, by verbal instruction, to the most efficient forms of orientation were found to speed up the learning process considerably.

Since exploratory responses must correspond to the spatial and temporal arrangement of a set of stimuli and yet can occur in the absence of the stimuli, they are ideally suited to perform a symbolic or representative function. In this capacity, they can be used to plan or rehearse a series of actions in situations like those studied by Zaporozhets or in the course of learning a stylus maze (Zinchenko 1958). They can also supply internal stimuli to make discrimination easier (supplementing primary with secondary stimulus generalization), as in Ruzskaia's experiment.

A large number of writers have observed the phenomenon known as *vicarious trial and error* (VTE). It occurs when a human or animal subject is faced with two stimulus objects in a simultaneous-discrimination experiment, and it takes the form of turning the eyes, the head, or the whole body toward the two stimulus objects in alternation. To an observer, the subject seems to be weighing the situation, acquainting himself with the properties of the stimulus objects, and considering the alternative responses in turn. It seems reasonable to suppose that this process helps the subject to discriminate between the positive and the negative stimuli. The VTE evidently qualifies as orienting behavior, and it is evoked by a situation that can be expected to induce conflict. The evidence on whether it actually facilitates learning or is merely a by-product with no special function is, however, inconsistent and inconclusive (see Goss and Wischner 1956).

There is, however, an instructive experiment by Phillips (1957) that shows how orienting responses can improve psychophysical discrimination. Her subjects were required to compare pairs of weights. In some cases they were allowed to lift the weights one at a time as often as they wished, and in other cases the number of times each weight was lifted was prescribed by the experimenter. The proportion of correct judgments increased with the number of lifting responses, whether spontaneous or imposed.

Attention and Perceptual Learning

According to a theory that Piaget (1957, 1961) has been developing, there occur, between infancy and adulthood, a number of interrelated processes that enable perception to become progressively more objective and reliable, overcoming the distortions to which it is inherently subject. These distortions are due, Piaget maintains, to two characteristics of our perceptual equipment. The first is that the stimulus field is not homogeneous; part of it is perceived more clearly and vividly than the rest. Experiments show that stimulus objects to which we attend or, to use Piaget's term, on which we "center," have their perceived dimensions overestimated (the so-called

219

error of the standard). Secondly, the direction of centering changes from moment to moment in a more or less random fashion, so that the various elements of the stimulus field dilate and shrink in turn as we attend to one after another.

Some elements, e.g., those that are larger, will, however, attract more centerings than others, so that they will undergo a net overestimation, amounting to an illusion, in the subject's over-all impression of a figure. Nevertheless, changes in centering will alter the appearance of the figure from moment to moment and thus introduce incompatibilities between the properties that it seems to have at different times. When the child becomes capable of retaining an impression long enough to compare it with the one yielded by the next centering, there will arise a state of "disequilibrium" or, as we should call it, conflict.

The conflict, which we must regard as curiosity-inducing, will prompt the strategy of attending systematically to the various parts of the figure in turn, so as to make the distortions cancel out as far as possible and to arrive at a more stable judgment. The benefits to be gained through this strategy are an increase in the confidence that we can place in the conclusions we base on our perceptions and an increase in our ability to predict. In other words, the responses that make up the strategy are reinforced by a reduction in uncertainty or conflict and are thus learned.

Systematic changes in the focus of attention will, of course, be supplemented later by locomotor exploration. When we are thinking of buying a piece of furniture, for example, we all realize that it may be judged differently according to the angle from which it is seen. So we walk around it and look at it from a variety of angles and distances, thus cutting down our uncertainty about our future reactions to it and our chances of disagreeable surprises.

There are several pieces of experimental support for the theory. There is a whole body of experimental data to show that certain visual illusions become less pronounced with age. Especially significant from our present point of view is Noelting's (1959) discovery that adults, but not young children, will show a progressive decrease in the Müller-Lyer illusion with massed practice, even though they are given no information by the experimenter about the accuracy of their judgments, and no other obvious rewards or cues are provided. In this experiment, the subjects have no way of comparing the apparent sizes of the parts of the figure with the objective sizes, but they can compare the apparent sizes at different times. While several explanations for the result could no doubt be offered, they are compatible with the assumption that inconsistencies between the impressions received with successive centerings create a state of conflict, and that this prompts the learning of systematic changes of focus such as will minimize the inconsistencies.

Studies carried out by Vinh-Bang (Piaget and Vinh-Bang 1959) with an apparatus for filming eye movements show that the distribution of orienting responses is correlated with the direction and extent of an illusion. For example, with two vertical lines placed one above the other, about 80 per cent of his subjects concentrated most of their fixations on the upper line and tended to overestimate the length of that line. On the other hand, the minority of subjects who divided their fixations about equally between the upper and the lower line were relatively free from illusion.

It appears, however, from other experiments that the relevant centerings can be central attentive processes rather than eye movements. Fraisse, Ehrlich, and Vurpillot (1956) showed that the overestimation that constitutes the error of the standard will apply to a visual element on which attention is concentrated, even when that element is not being fixated but stimulates the peripheral retina. And Pritchard (1958) has shown that familiar visual illusions are still present when a figure is made to move about with the eyes and its appearance is thus completely unaffected by changes in fixation.

Perceptual Curiosity and Conditioning

A more general question concerns the role that the motivation underlying exploratory behavior may have in learning in general.

The question has been raised in especially challenging terms by Woodworth (1958). This writer recognizes a phenomenon that he calls "sequence learning." It occurs when a stimulus, S_1, is frequently succeeded by another stimulus, S_2, and the subject learns to execute some response in preparation for S_2 during the interval between S_1 and S_2. He does not claim that all learning conforms to this paradigm, but it seems to fit classical (Pavlovian) conditioning, instrumental (operant) conditioning, and paired-associate rote learning, among other instances.

At the beginning of the process, S_1, according to Woodworth, evokes something equivalent to a question like "What's that?" or "What's next?" or "What does S_1 portend?" It arouses a "questioning set," a "readiness for some unknown S_2," an "indefinite expectancy of something more to follow." When S_2 appears, it gives the answer to the question and transforms the indefinite into something definite, and this phase of the process provides the reinforcing factor that establishes the learning.

It is easy to identify the state that is induced by S_1 according to this theory as an increase in arousal and, in particular, of the variety that we are calling perceptual curiosity, since it is removed by the receipt of S_2. And, although we must look to the future to exploit the rich experimental potentialities of Woodworth's suggestions, there are already several facts that speak in their favor.

Many students of classical conditioning have observed that the original reaction to the conditioned stimulus usually consists of orienting behavior, which is replaced, as reinforced trials succeed one another, by conditioned orientation in the direction of the unconditioned stimulus and then by the specific conditioned response. In an instrumental-conditioning situation, e.g., when an animal has to learn to press the bar in a Skinner box, the first reaction takes the form of sniffing about and, when a few rewarded bar pressings have occurred, especially in the neighborhood of the bar. This exploratory behavior disappears as the instrumental response becomes firmly rooted. And in more complex situations, when an animal receives, and has to respond appropriately to, a chain of stimuli, the various links in the chain first elicit separate orienting responses, and then the orienting responses to all but the last link gradually drop out (Anokhin 1958).

Recently developed techniques for recording the implicit components of the orientation reaction supply more direct evidence. When a neutral sound (as conditioned stimulus) is closely followed by the application of heat, cold, or electric current to the skin or verbal instructions to press a button (as unconditioned stimulus), the first effect is a reemergence or strengthening of the orientation reaction to both conditioned and unconditioned stimuli, manifested by the vascular component (Vinogradova 1958) and by the GSR (Sokolov 1958). The orientation reaction subsequently disappears and is supplanted by the conditioned adaptive, defensive, or motor response.

Observations of the bioelectric activity of the cortex during conditioning (see Buser and Roger 1957, Fessard and Gastaut 1958) have frequently shown that the conditioned stimulus first evokes desynchronization (activation) all over the cortex, which can be recognized as part of the generalized orientation reaction, dependent on the brain-stem RAS, and which continues through the duration of the unconditioned stimulus. In later trials this is replaced by a localized desynchronization (in the area corresponding to the unconditioned stimulus) which we may identify with the localized orientation reaction dependent on the thalamic reticular system.

Facts such as these have led many writers, both Eastern (e.g., Anokhin 1958, Sokolov 1958) and Western (e.g., Jouvet 1958), to conclude that the orientation reaction is, in some way, essential to the structural changes that underlie learning. Nobody is yet in a position, of course, to state exactly how it may do so. It must be noted that the orientation reactions in question are generally short lived, although they may outlast the evoking stimuli by a few seconds. Their prompt cessation may thus, in accordance with our assumptions, have a reinforcing effect.

Some recent observations of Paramanova (1958) and Vinogradova (1958) make it necessary, however, to qualify the conclusion that conditioning cannot occur in the absence of an orientation reaction. These experimenters found that a conditioned defensive or motor response could occasionally be built up in a human subject who was drowsy and showed no signs of heightened arousal. In such exceptional instances, the conditioned response presented some peculiarities. It possessed an unusual mechanical character: it was abnormally invariable in form, had a short latent period (becoming longer in later trials), and grew up very slowly. Most interesting of all, the subject did not notice the conditioned stimulus, and the conditioned motor response seemed to him inexplicable and involuntary.

Many writers have stressed the key function of verbal responses in those forms of behavior that we call "conscious," "voluntary," or "rational." It seems that the importance of orienting responses in this connection also ought not to be overlooked. Lisina (1958) was able to train human subjects to control their normally involuntary and unconscious vascular responses with the help of orienting responses and selective attention directed to appropriate cues. They learned to dilate the blood vessels of the hand in response to shock, a reaction running counter to the natural defensive vasoconstriction response (see Chapter 4), and to produce vasoconstriction and vasodilatation at will in response to instructions from the experimenter. The former feat was accomplished by letting subjects see the recording pen of the plethysmograph, whose fluctuations, they were told, represented some aspect of the working of their bodies, and then switching off the shock as soon as vasodilatation occurred. The second was accomplished by a course of training in which subjects had vascular reactions explained to them and were taught to distinguish the sensations coming from their own vasoconstriction and vasodilatation.

We urgently need studies of the relations between arousal and aspects of other forms of learning beside classical conditioning. It has been shown in Anokhin's laboratory (Anokhin 1958) that the vasomotor components of the orientation reaction are elicited by stimuli with which an instrumental response (running to one of two food trays) is becoming associated.

In an experiment performed by Lát (1957) in Czechoslovakia, rats were trained to obtain food by pressing a lever and to escape from electric shock by jumping onto a vertical grille. There was a positive correlation between the speed of acquiring these instrumental responses and strength of the orientation reaction, judged by mobility in a novel environment and by frequency of the "rising reaction" in response to novel stimuli. EEG and GSR indexes of arousal have been recorded while subjects were exposed to lists of nonsense syllables (C. H. Brown 1937, Obrist 1950). Both indexes have higher values when subjects are set to learn than when they are not. GSR amplitudes are positively correlated with the learning rates of individual subjects, and more intense GSRs accompany the syllables coming toward the beginning and the end of a list (which are the ones learned most quickly). A syllable evokes the most pronounced alpha-wave suppression and GSR when the subject is just starting to recall it (Obrist 1950 and personal communication).

Perceptual Curiosity and Latent Learning

The learning situations that call most pressingly of all for an examination of the part that perceptual curiosity may play in them belong to a class that has been a source of trouble among learning theorists, especially for those who espouse S-R reinforcement theory. According to this type of theory, the only experiences that can promote the learned strengthening of a response are those in which (1) the response in question is performed, and (2) it is closely followed by a rewarding state of affairs, commonly taken to mean some kind of drive reduction. In the experiments to which we are referring—the so-called latent-learning experiments—at least one of these conditions seems not to be fulfilled.

Most of the relevant experiments have been concerned with latent learning in mazes (see Thistlethwaite 1951). The basic design has been put through an enormous range of variations, but it comprises a training phase and a test phase. In the training phase, the animal is given an opportunity to acquaint himself with the layout of the maze either with no extrinsic motivational and incentive conditions or with different ones from those which will be operative in the test phase. The crucial response pattern—running along a particular path—thus occurs among others in the training phase, but there is no obvious factor present to strengthen it more than the others. The test phase then shows that the crucial response has nevertheless been made more likely to occur as a result of the experiences furnished by the training phase.

There are plenty of experiments to show that latent maze learning can occur in the rat, which is embarrassing for those whose theories are not built to assimilate it. There are also plenty of experiments in which latent learning fails to occur, which militates against complacency on the part of those whose theories are all too ready to digest it. Human beings can certainly make use of information that they have absorbed in the course of casual experiences in the past, when they were differently motivated. But there are also many stimuli that they do not "notice" or do not "pay attention to" and from whose reception they are consequently unable to benefit on future occasions. This is, in fact, precisely the problem of incidental learning and attention in remembering that we examined in Chapter 3.

It is necessary to assume that, during the training phase of a latent-learning experiment, an animal is acquiring a set of implicit, symbolic habits that represent the spatiotemporal relations between the stimuli coming from the different parts of the maze. But where does the reinforcement for these responses come from? Several writers have considered the possibility that it comes from the reduction of curiosity. Unfortunately, however, although changes have been rung with quite astonishing ingenuity and fertility of imagination on the latent-learning experiment, most of the variables that influence curiosity have been strangely neglected. A fresh look at latent learning from this point of view certainly seems to be due.

There is a conclusion suggested by the literature (Spence and Lippitt 1940, Spence and Lippitt 1946, Thistlethwaite 1951) that may be worth noting. It appears that latent learning is more likely if the animal is satiated during the training phase than if he is subject to a strong drive, differing from the one that will be present during the test phase. Could this be because the drive maintains arousal at a high level and thus prevents or attenuates the arousal reduction that accompanies the inspection of the stimuli? This factor could possibly explain why stimuli that do not contribute to the completion of the task on hand are so often not remembered by human beings.

One kind of latent-learning experiment is of particular interest because it illustrates latent learning in a singularly simple and neat form, and because a response becomes associated with a stimulus without ever having previously occurred in the presence of that stimulus. The process is known as *sensory preconditioning* in the West and as "the formation of temporary connections between indifferent stimuli" in the U.S.S.R.

The experimental design requires three phases. In phase 1, two neutral stimuli, S_1 (e.g., a sound) and S_2 (e.g., a light), are presented several times in close succession. In phase 2, a response, R_x, is attached by one of the recognized conditioning procedures to S_2. In phase 3, the test phase, S_1 is presented alone and is found to evoke R_x. This kind of experiment has been successfully performed with dogs (Brogden 1939, Rokotova 1952), monkeys (Rokotova 1954), and human beings (Brogden 1947, Coppock 1958, Lebedinskaia 1958).

Various writers have proposed an explanation for the phenomenon along the following lines. It is assumed that S_2 originally evokes some kind of response, R_2, possibly implicit, which produces distinctive internal stimulation. In phase 1, R_2 would become conditioned to S_1. In phase 2, the overt response, R_x, would become conditioned not only to S_2 but also to the feedback stimuli due to R_2. When S_1 occurred in phase 3, R_x would be evoked through the intermediary of R_2 and the feedback stimuli resulting from it.

Several predictions from this kind of theory have been verified (Wickens and Briggs 1951, Coppock 1958), but the precise nature of the supposed mediating response, R_2, has been elusive. Now, the reports of Russian experimenters suggest strongly that orienting responses may perform this function. These reports generally stress that, in phase 1, S_1 invariably comes to evoke a conditioned orienting response directed toward S_2, and Lebedinskaia (1958) found, in fact, that sensory preconditioning could be obtained in young children only when conditioned orienting responses were in evidence.

Quite apart from overt orienting responses, the central correlates of orienting behavior may serve as the basis for a learned association between two stimuli. As was mentioned earlier in this chapter, a neutral stimulus, such as a sound, that regularly precedes a neutral stimulus from another modality, such as a light, acquires the power to elicit localized EEG activation patterns in the cortical area corresponding to the latter.

We are still left, however, with the more troublesome problem of whether contiguity is sufficient to establish an association between two stimuli and, if not, what supplies the reinforcement. Some of the most indomitable defenders of the S-R reinforcement position (e.g., Wolpe 1950) have argued that all stimuli must, to some extent, have drive-inducing properties. In Wolpe's view, they will all produce the "central neural excitation" that is common to all drive states. This being so, termination of a short-lasting stimulus, e.g., S_2 in phase 1 of a sensory-preconditioning experiment, will necessarily entail drive reduction and thus reward.

Such hypotheses have been dismissed as far fetched and strained by theorists of other persuasions, but they may not be so far from the truth after all. We know by now that the onset of any stimulus is likely to evoke a transient orientation reaction, and the relatively swift dying down of the increase in arousal should, if our assumptions are correct, have a rewarding effect. At any rate, this explanation yields a large supply of testable predictions concerning the stimulus properties that should be most conducive to sensory preconditioning.

Chapter 9

ART AND HUMOR

The highly variegated human activities that are classed as art form a unique testing ground for hypotheses about stimulus selection. They consist of operations through which certain stimulus patterns are made available, and so they must unhesitatingly be placed in the category of exploratory behavior. The creative artist originates these patterns, the performing artist reproduces them, and the spectator, listener, or reader secures access to them and performs the perceptual and intellectual activities that will enable him to experience their full impact. The existence of these forms of behavior and the nature of the stimulus patterns round which they center raise problems that nobody interested in exploratory behavior or in the principles governing behavior in general can afford to ignore, whether or not he has any interest in the arts as such.

Aesthetic behavior differs from the exploratory activities that we have examined in earlier chapters in its elaborateness and in the high esteem with which it is regarded. But there are also deeper differences, arising from the fact that art, unlike most exploratory behavior, has a communicative function.

The word "communication" is often used loosely for any form of information transmission. Information theory was, in fact, originally called "communication theory" (Shannon and Weaver 1949), and cybernetics has been defined as the "science of control and communication" (Wiener 1948). We may, as we have seen, speak of information being transmitted whenever events in one system have some above-chance degree of correspondence with events in another system. This covers an enormous range of phenomena, and either or both of the systems involved may be machines or other inanimate structures.

It seems best, however, to reserve the word "communication" for certain special cases of information transmission occurring between living organisms. The best characterization of them is that given by Mead (1934). One organism performs a response which gives rise to stimuli affecting the behavior of another organism. But, according to Mead's formulation, communication cannot be said to have taken

228

place unless the signal has the same meaning for the originator as for the recipient. What this amounts to is that responses that are in some measure similar to those evoked by the signal in the recipient must occur in the originator; the originator in some way shares or anticipates the effect that his communication will have. In human beings, this often takes the form of an implicit representation of the recipient's reaction.

The content of art can range over virtually the whole scope of human communication. It may be used as a source of information about the appearances of objects, the course of historical events, the workings of human nature, as a means of effecting moral improvement, as a vehicle for propagating religious, political, or philosophical ideologies. Art is, however, distinguished from other forms of communication by the importance of an element that Morris (1946) brings to our notice, namely the *communication of evaluations*. The audience of a work of art is made to regard something as important, pleasing, or beautiful, to accord it a "preferential status" as a stimulus competing for control over behavior, a concept which extends over what we have called attention and affective value. The object of these evaluations may be the work of art itself or whatever is depicted or referred to in the work. But if the word "communication" is to be justified, the creative artist and the interpretive artist must value the content and the form of their product as they intend the audience to value it. This is what is called "sincerity" or "integrity."

This element of shared evaluation helps to simplify our problem. It means that the contributions of the creator, the performer, and the audience of a work of art, despite the obvious differences between the overt actions that they comprise, must, at least in some measure, be actuated by common motivational factors and reinforced by common sources of reward value. We are therefore justified in looking for motivational factors in connection with artistic behavior in general.

While human beings may produce art and expose themselves to it for an endless variety of reasons, collative variables must play their part, as they do in all forms of exploratory behavior. They underlie, in fact, what is commonly called the "formal" or "structural" aspect of art. Art is, of course, not a phenomenon with sharp boundaries. Any communicative process or, indeed, any human activity can be carried out artistically, if the originator and the other affected individuals are similarly rewarded by its collative properties.

The study of aesthetic behavior has gone on for many centuries, but its present state can hardly inspire pride. Almost every contemporary writer on aesthetics feels entitled to make a fresh start, as if nothing had yet been settled for good and all. Nevertheless, many of them end up reformulating age-old generalizations that have a great deal of truth in them but leave a host of enigmas outstanding. There seem to be several reasons for this sorry situation:

1. Although there has been quite a sizable body of experimental work on aesthetics, some of which we shall consider in due course, it has mostly concerned itself with simple forms. Techniques of classification and measurement that would permit experimentation to be extended to more realistically complex material have been lacking. The detailed analysis of individual works to illustrate and support theories has, therefore, been a common recourse among critics and psychologists alike. But this method, while indispensable as a stopgap, suffers from all the drawbacks of the case history; there are, in particular, the dangers of biased sampling and of overlooking alternative hypotheses that might fit just as well.

2. Most students of experimental aesthetics have measured aesthetic value by questioning subjects and having them indicate verbally which stimulus patterns they prefer. It is often assumed that those are the patterns to which they would most probably expose themselves if given the choice. This is, however, a dangerous assumption and one without firm empirical support.

Berlyne (unpublished) showed subjects the patterns depicted in Fig. 4-5 in a random order, interspersed with the much more complex patterns that were used in the second experiment on orienting responses. The subjects were asked to rate each pattern for "pleasingness" and for "interestingness." There was a significant tendency to attribute more pleasingness to the less complex or incongruous members of the pairs in Fig. 4-5, and yet these were the ones that similar subjects spent less time looking at (Berlyne 1958a). Likewise, among the very complex patterns used in the other experiment, the less complex ones were rated more pleasing, although there had turned out to be no difference in eye-drawing power between these and the ones accompanying them. The more complex patterns in both series were, on the other hand, generally judged more interesting.

3. Theories of art have rarely separated scientific from normative questions. The question "What is art?" has rarely been confined to description or explanation. It has generally been confounded with the question of what constitutes good art or what is worthy of the name of art.

4. Theories have almost invariably been one-sided. They have seized on one of the numerous facets of art and treated it as crucial. The role of content and that of form have, especially, tended each to receive

230

emphasis to the exclusion of the other, often under the influence of partialities of taste.

This one-sidedness has likewise marred the two most original and valuable contributions of modern psychology to aesthetics. The Gestalt school has concentrated on formal factors, recognizing that forms that are conceded to have aesthetic value often resemble those toward which everyday perception is biased and toward which many natural phenomena are coaxed by configurations of physical forces. They have consequently tended to neglect content. The Freudians, in contrast, have pursued the analogies between art and the dream. Art, in their view, serves to "assuage unappeased wishes" (Sterba 1940) which have been frustrated and repressed, by affording them the substitute satisfaction of disguised symbolic expression. This theory has inspired many analyses of content but not accounted for the contribution of form. Formal organization in general has been related to the psychological forces that keep unruly urges within bounds. But something more detailed and quantitative than that is needed if we are to explain a domain in which everything has to be just right and a little bit more or less of this or that would turn an admired work into a failure.

5. Apart from the currents we have just mentioned, artistic behavior has been studied in too much isolation. Unique as it is, art must have points of contact with less august activities in both human beings and animals. We must consider the relations between art and the humbler phenomena (probably separated from it more completely in our culture than in most others) that are classed as "entertainment." Above all, art needs to be related to animal behavior. Much has been made of apparent rudiments of aesthetic appreciation in primates: their dance-like games, their self-adornment, and the taste of some of them for scribbling or smearing paint. Mention is also made of the use of bodily coloring to attract mates in lower vertebrates, supplemented, in the case of the bower birds, by architectural displays of twigs and flowers. The most fruitful forms of animal behavior to examine for light on aesthetics are surely, however, the very exploratory responses that have been our concern in earlier chapters.

We cannot hope here to remedy all these defects or to construct a comprehensive psychological theory of art. We shall merely consider evidence that the principles we have pieced together from facts about simple exploratory behavior are also operative in the production and appreciation of art. We shall concentrate particularly on structural factors and on ways in which collative variables contribute to them. This does not mean that we wish to belittle the importance of associative factors, conscious or unconscious.

231

Attempts to capture the essence of formal beauty have, from the philosophical writers of past centuries to the aestheticians of modern times, given prominence to two principles: the one is represented by such terms as "variety," "diversity," and "multiplicity" and the other by such terms as "unity," "uniformity," "synthesis," "order," and "organization" (see Gilbert and Kuhn 1953).

Some theories have stressed one of these principles and overlooked the other. St. Augustine, for instance, in a way which is reminiscent of some Gestalt-inspired views but does not accord too well with experimental data on aesthetic preferences, regarded the circle as the most beautiful of all geometrical figures because it possessed the most equality. Alison, in the late eighteenth century, declared that equal-sided figures are more beautiful than others because "the number of their uniform parts" is greater, a principle which placed a circle above an ellipse and a square above a rhombus, but an equilateral hexagon above a square.

At the opposite extreme, Dubos gave predominant emphasis to the expression of motion, Hogarth to the provision of variety, and Hemsterhuis to the evocation of the largest number of ideas in the shortest time.

The great majority of theories have, however, used some expression such as "unity in diversity" or "uniformity in variety," implying that aesthetic satisfaction requires the presence of both principles in some appropriate proportion. This idea is found in the writings of Descartes, Hutcheson, Baumgarten, Moses Mendelssohn, and Fechner, as well as in those of many later authors.

The principle of diversity can readily be identified with the conditions which drive arousal up to high levels. It is associated with variety and multiplicity, in which we can recognize two factors that make for complexity, namely heterogeneity and numerosity of elements. It can evidently also embrace novelty, ambiguity, and surprise. The opposing principle of order or organization seems, on the other hand, to represent the conditions that make for clear-cut cortical responses that allow arousal to be moderated.

Our interpretation is supported by the ways in which several aestheticians of recent and less recent times have described the two opposing principles and the effects that ensue when one of them predominates unduly. For example, Gilbert and Kuhn summarize Descartes's view: "That sensation or arrangement, interval or rhythm pleases which neither bores nor fatigues. The extremes to be avoided are those of

232

the confusing, intricate figure, laborious and tiring, on the one hand, and of monotony and unfulfilled desire, on the other."

The two principal variables in Birkhoff's (1933) mathematical theory of aesthetic value are complexity C and order O. C is closely related to the "effort of attention" and consequent "feeling of tension" that confrontation with an object calls forth. These are attributed to the automatic muscular adjustments in eyes, throat, etc., that are necessary for perception. We may identify them with the orienting movements and generalized muscular tensions that accompany high arousal. Birkhoff relates O to the largely unverbalized associations that result from certain properties of the object, such as symmetry, repetition, and sequence.

Graves (1951) concurs with our own conjecture that complexity or diversity excites through some form of conflict: "Conflict is the aesthetic conflict or visual tension between opposing or contrasting lines, directions, shapes, space intervals, textures, values, hues. . . . Visual conflict or tension, also called opposition, contrast or variety, is used to produce stimulus or interest." He goes on to explain how "unity demands that the conflict be resolved and integrated by dominance, the principle of synthesis. This integration is effected by subordinating the competing visual attractions to an idea or plan or orderly arrangement." Dominance is achieved when one quality—a hue, line, or shape—occupies appreciably more of the design than others.

We thus find aestheticians arriving at a view that parallels the one to which our inquiry into simpler exploratory behavior has led us: departing too far from an intermediate degree of arousal potential, upsetting the balance between the factors that raise arousal and the factors that allay arousal, results in discomfort. Since the pursuit of aesthetic enjoyment means deliberately seeking out stimulation and excitement, we must suspect that a mechanism of the arousal-jag type is in operation. This means that there must be some way of ensuring that arousal is kept within bounds and that it is speedily brought down again, a requirement fulfilled by the order or organization element.

Some patterns seem to contain just the right amount of complexity and rate of change for prolonged observation without boredom. Fire and the sea are commonplace examples. Fechner (1876) cites others, like the flapping of flags in the wind, the gyrations of flying birds, the veining of marble. The incredibly intricate, nonrepresentational patterns that cover the walls of Moorish buildings like the Alhambra in Granada seem ideally suited for a society that did not have our profusion of light reading matter, radio, and television, but had long hours of relaxed leisure to while away.

The audience's reactions to a work of art include ones determined by properties of stimulus elements, by relations between stimulus elements, and by groupings of stimulus elements. Thus, there is, first of all, plenty of scope for competition among possible targets for attention and orienting responses. Then, even when one item or aspect of the work has momentarily gained dominance over the central nervous system, we can expect clashes among alternative associations or interpretations. The mastery of the artist has to mobilize all the devices that can help to control the potential chaos.

The first requirement is to establish a hierarchy of priorities, to determine which items shall receive the major share of fixation and attention and which items (generally the same ones) shall be registered first. Virtually all the variables that have figured in our earlier discussions of attention and orienting behavior figure in the artist's traditional armory. The main theme is played louder than the accompaniment; it is higher in pitch; it changes more rapidly and less predictably. The figure of principal interest is larger than secondary figures, occupying the foreground in post-Renaissance painting, or being simply depicted on a larger scale in earlier works such as Byzantine mosaics. Once artists like Rembrandt or Caravaggio have discovered the requisite techniques, intensity of illumination coerces the gaze in the intended direction. The subject of a seventeenth-century portrait wears a vividly colored and variegated costume, while the background consists of a nebulous landscape or a drab and monotonous drapery. Secondary figures play upon deeply rooted orienting habits by looking toward, or pointing at, the area of prime importance. Locations are likewise chosen to take advantage of psychological laws, the center and, after the center, the left-hand side carrying special weight in a painting, and the beginning and end in a poem or piece of music.

Attention is preempted for one quality by introducing the quality repeatedly. A painting may be dominated by one area of the color spectrum, by one shape, by lines pointing in one direction, a musical work by one rhythmic, melodic, or harmonic motif or by one key. A hue may appear in patches of contrasting form or a form in a variety of sizes. A melody may be recognizable through alterations in key, timbre, rhythm, harmonization, through inversion, augmentation, and diminution. Instead of a quality, a relation may be repeated through varying content, getting near to the mathematical notion of an ordering. There may be harmonic or melodic progressions in which intervals between notes are retained in a succession of higher and higher or lower and lower pitches. A form may be found in an ordered series of sizes, luminous intensities, rotations, or translations. The segments of a tower may each exceed the length of the one below by a fixed proportion.

Once these ends have been achieved, the structural scheme of the work brings in other devices for keeping conflict and arousal within limits. It molds sections of the work, or the work as a whole, into grouped patterns which can be responded to as units, thus mitigating complexity. Ambiguity is diminished by enabling individual components to call out responses that are dictated by their membership of, and status within, larger wholes. Arrangement according to a familiar form means some degree of redundancy; acquaintance with part of the pattern cuts down uncertainty about what the rest will be like.

A failure to carry out these functions provokes an acute feeling of uneasiness. The juxtaposition of hues that are too close together in the spectrum, the presence of two rectangles of only slightly differing width in an architectural design, the simultaneous or successive sounding of two notes a semitone apart, may clash or jar. The resulting displeasure cannot but remind us of how the need to discriminate between stimuli that are hard to tell apart produces experimental neuroses in animals. It seems that in handling aesthetic patterns also, the nervous system requires to know whether one element is to be taken as similar to or different from another. Otherwise, there is some kind of conflict, which is, significantly enough, absent when other elements make it clear that the two are meant to be regarded as different. There need be nothing disagreeable about the juxtaposition of three neighboring hues, a series of rectangles of gradually increasing width, a chromatic scale, or many other harmonic or melodic progressions that include the interval of a minor second.

RHYTHM

One of the foremost aids to artistic organization is *rhythm*, a term that is sometimes used more or less synonymously with *meter*—the pattern of accentuations at fixed intervals that forms a framework for most music and verse. It sometimes has less definite meanings, referring to any pattern of stresses or any pattern of recurrences. There is, for example, the rhythm of prose or the "sprung rhythm," with a varying number of syllables between stresses, that has appeared in recent English poetry. In music, the word "rhythm" may denote the way in which the total duration of a bar is distributed among notes, the arrangement of notes around a stressed note, or the assembly of units into larger wholes.

The nearest equivalent to metrical rhythm in the visual arts consists of cyclical designs like the Greek-key or egg-and-dart patterns. But the word is often used by critics of painting whenever there are a number of parallel repetitions, usually approximate, of a form, line, color, or other quality. The human face, for instance, presents a rhythm of duplicated convex-upward curves from eyebrows through upper eyelids, cheekbones, and nostrils to the upper lip.

The appeal of rhythm is often attributed to periodic physiological processes inside us or to our experience of cyclical processes in external nature. But we may relate it to the problems we have been raising. First, rhythm mitigates complexity, both by grouping stimulus elements into larger perceptual units and by weaving a thread of similarity through continually changing stimulation. Secondly, it wards off conflict between alternative groupings by introducing factors that speak strongly for one of them. The deeply rooted demand for metrical grouping in the face of monotony can be seen from the way in which uniform pulses, like the ticking of a clock or metronome, are heard with stresses on every second or third pulse. But these imposed groupings are highly unstable and readily yield to one another spontaneously or through a voluntary effort.

Apart from these effects, rhythm helps to determine the location of arousal relief. In music, the accented note is actually played louder and possibly also dwelt on a little longer or heralded by a minute pause. In the case of poetry, the reader's habits give the implicit responses to certain syllables an added intensity. Thus the accented elements coincide with peaks of arousal and the intervening material with relative relaxation.

The continuation of a rhythmic pattern generates the expectation that it will persist in what is to follow. It causes the reader or listener to build up an information space relating to later material. The composer or poet is thus presented with an immense range of opportunities for controlling arousal by conforming to or deviating from these expectations, by choosing from the high-probability, low-information regions or the low-probability, high-information regions of the space. Richards (1952) attaches great importance to this aspect: "This texture of expectations, satisfactions, disappointments, surprises, which the sequence of syllables brings about, is rhythm."

A repeated rhythm will induce a set in the reader or listener to perceive stresses in the appropriate places, whether or not factors like intensity, change, novelty, or surprise also favor these stresses. In this way, a diminution in intensity or even a silence may receive accentuation. Otherwise, a disparity between the stresses induced by external

236

arousal-potential variables and those induced by internal accord with expectations can be a rich source of complexity.

The work on the experimental aesthetics of simple visual forms that began with Fechner's *Vorschule der Ästhetik* (1876) tends to confirm the view that some intermediate degree of complexity produces the most pleasing effect and that extremes of simplicity or complexity are distasteful. Witmer (1893) found ellipses (*pace* St. Augustine and Alison) to be rated above circles by the great majority of subjects. Several experimenters (see Woodworth 1938) have attempted to establish preferences of subjects among rectangles with different proportions between the lengths of longer and shorter sides. The results show considerable variability among subjects, practically every shape of rectangle tried having some adherents. But there has been a consistent tendency for preferences to cluster round the *golden section*, i.e., round the rectangle whose shorter side, A, is 0.618 as long as the longer side, B, so that $A/B = B/(A + B)$.

The golden-section ratio also turns up when preferred divisions of a straight-line segment are investigated. Angier (1903) showed his subjects a horizontal line 16 centimeters long and instructed them to move a dividing mark to whichever point, apart from the central point, sectioned the line in the most pleasing way. The mean distances along the line chosen by nine subjects were close to the golden section on either side of the center.

Pierce (1894) used a black background bearing two 10-by-5-centimeter rectangles, 60 centimeters apart, with their shorter sides horizontal. In the space between them, he placed varying numbers of similar but movable rectangles and asked the subjects to arrange them in the most pleasing way. When there was only one movable rectangle, they generally placed it in a position representing the golden section. There was a growing tendency, however, to produce symmetrical arrangements as the number of rectangles increased, yielding to asymmetry once again when there were six or more. Legowski (1908), on the other hand, who repeated the experiment with 10-by-1-centimeter rectangles, failed to confirm these last findings, as his subjects chose symmetrical patterns.

Although the golden section has evidently to compete with the relation of equality for popularity in some conditions, it has, ever since classical times, been discussed by artists and used extensively in all forms of fine and applied art (see Graves 1951). Experimenters have

237

offered a variety of explanations, supported by their subjects' introspections, for its attraction.

Pierce points out that equal spacing creates a monotonous effect when there are too few or too many vertical rectangles; in the latter case, the figure resembles a fence. Angier (1903) hypothesizes that the eye sweeps along the longer segment of the line and then, in the course of attempting a similar sweep along the shorter segment, it is checked by the end point, which brings the antagonistic oculomotor muscles into play. This process gives the shorter segment some sort of added significance which makes up for its inferiority in length. It is interesting to see Angier invoking something like frustration or surprise or conflict, which we regard as equivalents of complexity in heightening arousal value. Witmer (1893) saw the golden section as a happy medium between too much and too little variety. Külpe (1893) observed that, according to the Weber-Fechner law, the difference between A and B should appear equal to the difference between B and $(A + B)$, and he attributed the pleasingness to this fact.

It is difficult to judge between these various suggestions without more empirical analysis. But they concur in seeing the golden section as a device for avoiding the displeasing effects of excessive homogeneity and excessive heterogeneity, a function expressed by its alternative name, the *golden mean*.

MATHEMATICAL AESTHETICS

Art is sometimes felt to belong to an exalted realm beyond the degrading touch of science and mathematics. But even those with the superstitious fear that that touch may dissolve everything they prize into a "collection of formulas"—a fear that would be repudiated by many modern, Renaissance, and, no doubt, ancient artists—will concede that art is essentially a matter of proportion, intensity, space, time, and structure—all of them eminently mathematical concepts.

Birkhoff (1933) supplied formulas which allowed the values of O (order) and C (complexity) for different materials to be calculated. The complexity of a polygon is "the number of indefinitely extended straight lines that contain all the sides of the polygon." The complexity of a vase outline is the number of "characteristic points" on which the eye can rest. The complexity of a melody is the number of notes it contains. That of a line of poetry is equal to the number of elementary sounds in it plus the number of word junctures that "do not admit of liaison." The formulas for O are rather more complicated and vary with the medium. Points are given for such properties as symmetry and horizontal-vertical orientation in polygons, repetitions, cadences, and melodic or harmonic sequences in music, rhyme, alliteration, and assonance in poetry. Having devised procedures for allotting precise values to O and C within the limited types of material that he considers in detail, Birkhoff equates aesthetic measure M with the ratio O/C. He bases this equation not on experimental data but on theoretical considerations and, apparently, his own tastes.

Since Birkhoff's expression for M is one which varies directly with order, a factor that we have assumed to reduce arousal, and inversely with complexity, which we have assumed to increase arousal, it seems to represent something like a measure of simplicity or lowness of arousal value. The facts that we have considered in this and previous chapters would lead us to suspect that aesthetic reward value will actually not be an increasing function of M but rather reach a maximum at some intermediate value of M, corresponding to an optimum of arousal value. This is exactly what experimenters have generally found when they have elicited aesthetic judgments of polygons, with M values assigned to them, selected from Birkhoff's illustrations (R. C. Davis 1936, Eysenck 1941). Agreement between preferences for poetic excerpts and Birkhoff's M is somewhat better but by no means sufficient to vindicate the theory.

Eysenck (1942), after reviewing the experimental data, suggests that $O \times C$ would be a better expression for aesthetic value. This expression reflects the fact that aesthetic value can be enhanced by an increase in complexity or by an increase in order (a decrease in complexity) and the fact that extremely low C or O will make a form displeasing. Eysenck's measure could vary either directly or inversely with arousal value, according to the weightings that are given to the multiplicands C and O or, in other words, how they are scaled.

An ambitious mathematical model by Rashevski (1938) relies on the assumption that distinct cerebral units are excited by different stimulus attributes. In the case of polygons, for example, different units are brought into play by horizontal lines, vertical lines, lines of a particular tilt, and angles with a particular value. Ways are provided for working out how much excitatory and inhibitory influence each unit receives from the perception of a given figure, and such quantities can be summed to yield a measure of the total excitatory effect, which is identified with aesthetic value. Rashevski's measure sounds very much like a measure of complexity, but it actually bears a curvilinear relation to Birkhoff's M, reaching a sharply delineated maximum when M is at an intermediate value.

If we are right in surmising that complexity, order, and similar factors affect aesthetic value through their influence on arousal, we can hardly expect simple equations to provide an adequate description of the way they interact. Any quantities that we may use to represent the degree of complexity or order in a form must be related to arousal; and, as we have seen, the two are likely to work in opposite directions, making it impossible to deduce the precise intensity of arousal resulting from various complexity-order combinations without compendious research. Then, aesthetic value is, in its turn, bound to be a nonmonotonic and rather complicated function of arousal, quite apart from the contributions of other variables. These are, however, problems that are signally amenable to experimental study. The utility of information-theory measures and that of the physiological and other indexes of arousal will, no doubt, repay investigation.

VARIATIONS IN TASTE

We have already seen (in Chapter 7) that certain temperaments veer much more than others toward one or the other pole of the simplicity-complexity or arousal-repose continuum. The same holds true of certain ages and places. The art of all major civilizations shows fluctuations between the classical ideals of serenity, tranquillity, and discipline and the romantic taste for excitement, color, and drama. But the exclusive cultivation of one extreme has been rare and usually followed by a violent swing in the opposite direction. Be that as it may, preferences for certain ways of intensifying arousal or for certain ways of tempering it form essential ingredients of any way of life and are thus bound to make up a weighty part of what an artist has to communicate.

It is interesting to note how often an artistic style that breaks away from its predecessor in the direction of much higher or much lower arousal value develops some compensatory feature that tends to offset its more extreme tendencies.

For example, the movement from the early Renaissance style through high Renaissance and mannerism to baroque progressed steadily toward more movement, drama, sinuosity, light, color, and ornamentation. The baroque work intentionally amazes with its continual deviations from the obvious, the straightforward, and the plain and by the very scale of its pretensions. As his eye runs along a line, the observer is left with a high uncertainty about what he will find around the corner, and his expectations come in for some jolts.

Yet the same style has the characteristic that is sometimes referred to as its monumentality: each detail, however extravagant, is subordinated to the impression of pomp and exuberance that derives from the work as a whole. The features of a baroque painting are of less importance individually than those of a Renaissance Florentine painting. Each human figure is likely to be found in a posture that would be meaningless and displeasing if it were alone. But it fits into the unity of the over-all pattern and may very well not be noticed as a separate entity at first. The artist thus tempers the bewilderment that he stirs up by molding the components of his work into large units, to which individual identifying responses can be attached, reducing the psychological complexity. The initial effect may be one of overwhelming intricacy and confusion, but perplexity is resolved as the observer comes under the sway of the general texture and ceases to attach undue importance to its whimsied details.

At the opposite pole, contemporary painting and architecture that has come under the influence of the neoplasticist movement confines itself to straight lines, right angles, bareness, and plainness—in fact, to everything that would make for a depressing gauntness were it not for the patches of bold color that obtrude themselves between expanses of black, gray, and white. The ancient Greeks, often thought to represent the ultimate in contentment with pure abstract form, used to paint their statues and the architraves of their temples in a way that would nowadays seem garish.

The *fauve* painters and neoclassicist musicians of the early twentieth century repudiated the intricacies of texture and vagueness of shape that were cultivated, in different ways, by their late romantic and impressionist predecessors and resorted instead to relatively simple forms and lucid outlines. But while foregoing the arousal value of ambiguity and complexity, they substituted the arousal value of gaudy coloring with a preponderance of red, orange, and yellow, or of violent rhythms, harsh harmonies, and the strident sounds of wind instruments, not to mention surprise and novelty.

BALANCE

One universally recognized requirement for a satisfying aesthetic structure is balance. It is far from clear, however, that the term "balance" means the same to all who use it and, although it is surprisingly easy to decide whether or not a given work has balance, there is not much agreement on what it consists of or why it is so important.

Bilateral or reflexive symmetry, in which two halves contain the same elements with spatial relations reversed, ensures balance, but it is evident that balance can sometimes be achieved, and often more satisfyingly, by a structure that is asymmetrical; the two halves, instead of being identical, can be different but in some sense equivalent. Symmetry is, of course, usual in the architecture and the abstract design of most cultures, although modern Western buildings and abstract paintings and Japanese dwelling houses frequently possess balance without symmetry. Absolute symmetry in representational painting and sculpture is exceptional; the composition often includes what we may call quasisymmetry, the elements being similarly disposed on either side of the center but differing in details of form or color. Balance between the contents of early and late parts is also possible and held desirable in temporal artforms like music, poetry, and the novel. It is, however, mainly in connection with visual forms that balance has been most thoroughly studied and analyzed.

There have been a number of relevant experiments. One must be careful not to build too much on their outcomes, as there is always an enormous range of inter- and intraindividual variability among aesthetic judgments, even when applied to radically simplified material, and comparatively slight changes in the emphasis of the instructions and in the experimental arrangements can alter responses profoundly. The factors that subjects mention in explanation of their judgments are legion, and the early experimental psychologists who did this work usually sought subjects among their colleagues, who may well have been biased by prevailing aesthetic or psychological theories. Nevertheless, there are some recurrent findings that are illuminating.

Pierce (1894) used a number of combinations of figures on a black background. There was always a fixed vertical line in the center, other fixed lines in other parts of the display, and a variable line or figure which the experimenter moved until the subject judged that the whole pattern looked balanced. If the variable line was shorter or narrower than a corresponding fixed line on the other side, it was likely to be allotted a position further from the center. Lines and stars were placed further out than squares, empty intervals than filled intervals, and blue, green, or maroon lines than white, red, or orange lines.

Puffer (1903) objected to several features of Pierce's procedure and amended them. She did not emphasize the center of the display, as Pierce had done, by introducing a fixed central line and often other lines symmetrically disposed about the center as well. She used the psychophysical method of production, which allows the subject to adjust the variable stimulus quality, and she referred in her instructions to the attainment of a pleasing rather than a balanced effect. The tendency to locate larger forms nearer the center was generally confirmed. Turning to variables associated with interestingness, she found that outline pictures were placed nearer the center than blank rectangles, stamps that were changed for each trial nearer than unchanged stamps, and a picture favoring depth perception (an open railway tunnel) nearer than one that produced a two-dimensional impression (a railway tunnel closed off by a door). Forms that suggested movement away from the center (by tilting or bulging outwards) were placed nearer than those that suggested inward movement.

Angier (1903) added complexity to the list of operative variables with the help of the pattern illustrated in Fig. 9-1. A shorter expanse of the portion made up of squiggles balanced a longer expanse of monotonous parallel lines. When the squiggles were more densely distributed (Fig. 9-1, III), making for more material per unit area and thus still greater complexity, the preferred distribution assigned even less space to the portion that contained them.

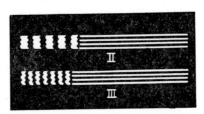

Fig. 9-1. (From Angier 1903).

The widespread exploitation of all possible means to balance in the works of well-known painters is amply expounded by Puffer (1903) and by Arnheim (1954). They are by now highly familiar to us and readily recognizable as components of what we have called arousal potential. It seems, therefore, that a work of art requires some equality in the arousal value of its two halves, which can come from symmetry or common content but can also come from subtly setting one determinant of arousal against another. However, distance from the center can apparently compensate for lack of arousal value, so that forms which are intrinsically less arousing can balance those which are more so, by being placed farther out.

Why balance is felt to be so essential can at present be answered only with hypotheses. But it is possible to state several that point to promising and largely unprospected lines of experimentation. Every instance of aesthetic judgment is, no doubt, produced by an interplay of many factors. In Puffer's experiments, for example, subjects often acted contrary to general trends if it meant leaving too much empty space somewhere in the display or having elements crowded too closely together. But the most important factors may be found listed here. More than one of them may, of course, be active.

1. The hypothesis that the need for perceptual balance depends on associations derived from experience of mechanical balance and imbalance is a tempting one, suggested by the inescapable analogies between the two sets of phenomena. But it can hardly stand being pursued too far. Many of the variables that determine perceptual balance, although they may affect the "weight" of an element in a figurative sense, bear no relation to physical weight. And even though

larger objects are by preference seen nearer the center of the display, the distances selected are generally not those which will accord with the laws of mechanical equilibrium, if weight is proportional to size.

It is, however, entirely possible that connections with physical disequilibrium in a more general sense are of importance. It may be that configurations in which there is a disproportion between the arousal value of different sections are, in practice, ones with a high probability of violent, sudden, and imminent change. As a consequence, perceptual imbalance may give rise to undifferentiated anticipatory arousal, taking the form of a vague but intense feeling that there is something wrong or that things are unstable and cannot last.

Often, the new configuration to be expected from the present state of imbalance may be clear, as, for example, when something looks top-heavy or a leaning tower seems about to topple over. Arnheim carries this idea beyond such obvious instances to abstract designs. On a plain square field, a circle just off center seems pulled toward the center, while one near a border of the square seems pulled toward the border.

We need not take a stand here on whether the phenomenon is due to some innate tendency of cerebral activities to gravitate toward "better" patterns, in accord with the Gestaltist view favored by Arnheim, or whether it is the result of learned expectations. These expectations could arise (1) because unbalanced arrangements like those just mentioned are in practice less frequently encountered than better balanced arrangements or (2) because such unbalanced arrangements are in practice frequently succeeded by the better balanced arrangements to which they perceptually tend. Either way, there will be unrelieved arousal, whether from a "tendency toward closure," from surprise or incongruity, or from expectation of change. Arnheim speaks also of the "ambiguity" of unbalanced visual figures. In our terminology, there may be some conflict between the tendency to perceive the figures as they are and a tendency to perceive them with their imbalance corrected.

2. Legowski (1908), citing introspective reports, shows that less evident relations of equality may be realized when forms are located at unequal distances from the center for the sake of balance. With the arrangement depicted in Fig. 9-2, some subjects sought to make the angles α and β equal, which would necessitate placing rectangle A farther out than B. Others wanted to make a and b equal. When the two lateral rectangles had the same height but different widths, subjects were commonly motivated to equate the areas of the imaginary rectangles stretching from the center to the outer edges of the outer figures. The net effect would thus be to introduce recondite unities

which would temper the over-all complexity. However, this explanation will not cover the variables other than size that have been found to affect balance.

3. The fact that distance from the center can compensate for deficiencies in the qualities that make for arousal value inevitably brings eye movements up for consideration. Stimuli appear to attract fixation with a strength proportionate to their arousing qualities and, it seems

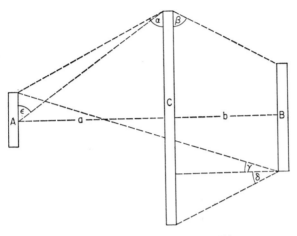

Fig. 9-2. (From Legowski 1908).

reasonable to assume, to their distance from the area of initial focus, since the more peripheral a stimulus, the greater the amplitude of any eye movement that it draws.

Explanations that lean heavily on eye movements are often criticized on at least two grounds, however. Aesthetic judgments are possible with tachistoscopic exposures which preclude the completion of eye movements, and eye movements, when they are recorded photographically, do not usually follow contours exactly or systematically but rather show an irregular pattern vaguely influenced by the shape of what is being watched.

But instead of overt eye movements one may consider the corresponding response tendencies. Implicit or incipient eye movements play key roles in several contemporary theories of form perception (Hebb 1949, Piaget 1961, Taylor 1960). The simultaneous arousal of a number of incompatible ocular orienting responses would be expected to yield highly irregular and variable patterns of overt fixation when coupled with the random processes or sources of "noise" that are characteristic of the nervous system.

In any display which demands treatment as a unit, there must be a powerful tendency to concentrate the gaze near the center, since that is the area where the mean distance from the fovea of the images of the elements of the display will be minimal, ensuring optimal receipt of information. This should be so, whether habits or innate reflexes are responsible. If there are factors which draw fixation predominantly to one side, thus creating a rival focus, the discomforts of conflict are apt to ensue.

4. There may be other reasons why an even distribution of attention between the two halves of the visual field should be preferred. Certainly, the protracted observation of an object that necessitates turning the eyes to one side will usually prompt head turning, which restores the centrality of the gaze, and ultimately causes a turning of the whole body. When somebody is compelled to watch something for more than a few seconds out of the corner of the eye because his head is encased in a cast or for some other reason, he finds the restriction highly trying. There is evidence, as we saw in Chapter 2, that perception is accompanied by generalized imitative muscular tensions, and these may well be commensurate with the arousal value of the corresponding parts of the stimulus field. If so, an unbalanced pattern which generates more tension on one side of the body than on the other could be distressing.

THE DYNAMICS OF AROUSAL

So far, we have been considering the relations between aesthetic reward value and the over-all arousal value of a work or element of a work. Much of the admiration due a creative artist is, however, earned by the mastery with which he pieces together elements of widely differing arousal value, disposing them with regard not only to their general consistency but also to the ways in which they offset, reinforce, or undo the effects of one other. This manipulation of relations between the arousal values of distinct components is most manifest in the temporal media of literature and music, where artistry means playing on the orientation reactions of the audience, switching them on and off, building them up and assuaging them, according to a plan which is intrinsically gratifying as well as fitting for the content of the work.

Although these aspects of aesthetic behavior are especially easy to discuss with reference to literature and music, just as the other aspects that we have already surveyed are most naturally referred to the visual arts, there is always some degree of analogy between the principles applicable to spatial and temporal patterns. It is possible that certain relations between stimuli affect the nervous system in the same way whether the entities between which the relations hold are presented together or in turn. Parallels between such processes as synchronous and successive association or spatial and temporal summation at synapses have long been noted. In any case, a spatial pattern of any appreciable complexity must have its parts fixated and attended to in succession, and even the elements of a simple pattern may be registered in succession according to prevalent theories that attribute form perception to scanning mechanisms. Similarly, memory makes reactions to earlier portions of a literary or musical work exist contemporaneously with reactions to the stimuli that are being received at the moment, and, once the work has been concluded, the reader or listener usually apprehends and represents to himself the total structure of the work, often in the form of a visual pattern.

In his *Song for St. Cecilia's Day*, Dryden depicts the power of music to summon up and subdue one emotion after another, but he considers emotions like martial fervor and amorous tenderness that depend on extraneous associations. We should expect, however, from our previous line of thought, that emotional states intrinsic to patterns of sound can be produced by the intensive and collative ingredients of arousal potential, and that these will underlie much of the response to absolute music. Whether auditory patterns can be satisfying in themselves in complete independence of extramusical meaning is a question that has been hotly debated.

The role of collative variables in producing intrinsic emotional arousal is recognized in Meyer's *Emotion and Meaning in Music* (1956). Meyer's highly original approach to musical aesthetics, and to the neglected problems of general psychology that are raised by music, leads him to conclusions that overlap quite remarkably with the hypotheses to which the consideration of quite different domains of behavior has led us.

Meyer starts from the thesis that "emotion or affect is aroused when a tendency to respond is arrested or inhibited." Conflict, doubt, confusion, uncertainty, and ambiguity are mentioned as apt to cause such arrest or inhibition. Emotions will, it is stated, be pleasurable if they are accompanied by the belief that there will be a resolution or that the situation is under control.

The argument goes on to point out that musical patterns can have a meaning which has nothing to do with anything extramusical that they may suggest. To have meaning, a stimulus must refer to some stimulus other than itself, in the sense that it evokes some fraction of a response corresponding to that other stimulus, e.g., an expectation of it. And patterns of sound fulfill this condition in so far as they lead

247

to expectations about other sounds following or accompanying them. In information-theory language, there is a great deal of redundancy in music since certain combinations and sequences are much more frequent than others in any musical idiom. Each musical element thus transmits information (positive or negative, i.e., reducing or increasing uncertainty) about other elements because each implies a different probability distribution, which almost inevitably means a change in uncertainty.

One proof of this is that passable samples of less variable musical styles, like those exemplified by popular songs and hymns, can be produced artificially by analyzing and reproducing conditional probabilities. There have been attempts to use machines for simulating composition from the seventeenth century to the days of modern computers. These meaningful or information-transmitting relations between musical patterns provide the composer with an infinite stock of devices for varying arousal level, because the expectations resulting from different patterns can differ enormously in clarity and definiteness (the residual uncertainty may be high or low) and because arousal can be stirred up by deviating from expectations that are firm and unequivocal. This close connection between the intellectual comprehension of structure and emotion implies, as Meyer rightly states, that "thinking and feeling need not be viewed as polar opposites but as different manifestations of a single psychological process," a lesson which, if taken to heart, would make psychologists less inclined to study perception and thinking without due attention to their intrinsic sources of motivation.

We can now take a look at some of the devices that are available to the musician for operating on arousal, basing ourselves both on Meyer's analysis and on our own previous conclusions.

First of all, the composer accepts the restrictions of a particular style and form. This means excluding most of the possible combinations of sounds and thus ensuring moderate uncertainty, which is relieved when patterns that conform with expectations are subsequently encountered. For example, a listener about to hear a scherzo expects that the piece will be in three-quarter time, that it will be lively and light, that it will consist of sections that can be represented as $A_1A_1A_2A_2B_1B_1B_2B_2A_1A_2$, that the sections denoted by the same letter will contain similar material, that A_2 and B_2 will be longer than A_1 and B_1, and that the material of the B sections will contrast with that of the A sections.

Further, virtually all music is based on some scale system, which means that only a selection of the available notes in the octave, twelve in number in traditional Western music but more or less numerous in other systems, will be used at once. There will usually also be one note, the tonic, around which the music revolves, i.e., it will occur more often than others and will be likely to end the piece or any of its major divisions.

The rules implicit in acceptance of a recognized form or scale system involve greater uncertainty at certain points than at others. Most forms include stages where new material is to be expected and stages where it is normal to recapitulate a theme that has already been heard. The use of a scale or key makes what is coming much more predictable at ends of phrases than elsewhere. There is thus room for endless exploitation of arousal and arousal relief. The composer Rossini is said to have had difficulty in getting up in the morning until he hit upon an ingenious remedy. He instructed his valet to play a dissonant chord on the piano, whereupon he was compelled to leap from his bed to play the consonant chord that resolved it.

There is also the possibility of generating especially intense arousal by employing sounds that deviate from the expected. Beethoven produces a characteristically dramatic effect by introducing, in defiance of custom, the beginning of the trio (or B sections) at the end of the scherzo of his *Seventh Symphony*. He then makes a second assault on the listener's arousal system by interrupting the theme after a few bars. Similarly, adherence to a particular key gives a unique effectiveness to chromatic notes that do not belong to the corresponding scale, whether these notes represent momentary departures or abrupt modulations into new keys.

By repeating some feature a number of times in succession, the composer can encourage the expectation that the feature will continue, enabling him to create surprise and uncertainty by rudely disappointing this expectation. This device is, however, usually a matter of repetition in some respects with variation in others: a reiterated rhythmic pattern, a harmonic sequence, or a repeated chord with changing melodic material. The repetition of exactly the same sounds over and over again may have an opposite effect and is, in fact, regularly used to build up excitement. This may be because of some primitive, physiological response to rhythmic reiteration, explaining its incantational use for the induction of mass irrational behavior or ecstatic states. But there is also the fact, stressed by Meyer, that simple, unvarying repetition is essentially structureless and ambiguous. There is a mounting expectation that the repetition cannot go on much longer, but it is not clear exactly when it will come to an end and what will replace it.

The same result can be achieved if the repetition is not exact and if it is combined with other devices to accumulate arousal. A harmonic

249

or melodic progression in which a motif goes through a series of occurrences, each higher or lower in pitch than the last one by a constant quantity, can build up a tremendous sense of impending but unspecifiable climax especially if it is an ascending progression. Wagner's *Tristan und Isolde* contains some prime examples, not uncontaminated with extramusical associations. In the last movement of Beethoven's *Ninth Symphony,* expectancy is drawn tauter and tauter as the principal theme is first stated unaccompanied on cellos and basses and then put through three repetitions, each with a more complex orchestration, harmonization, and texture than the last.

Sometimes a pattern that is inherently ambiguous generates doubt and uncertainty, which is resolved when more clearly structured material takes its place, especially when what follows invests the initially ambiguous section with a special significance. There is a famous example at the beginning of Beethoven's *Ninth Symphony* where a protracted tremolo is accompanied by an intermittent falling motif of two notes. This then turns into the signally lucid and trenchant main theme of the movement. This procedure of tossing out what are, at first hearing, independent scraps of melody and later welding them into grandiose themes became a major feature of Sibelius's distinctive style.

A pattern may have a quite definite meaning as a result of what came just before it, but what comes next is momentarily puzzling until it is seen to necessitate a reinterpretation of the pattern in question. This is a standard expedient in modulating from one key to another: a chord which can belong to either key, and thus has an ambiguous status, is used to effect the transition. At first it seems to be, say, the tonic triad of C major. However, when the next chord introduces F sharp, a note which does not occur in the scale of C major and is thus incompatible with the expectations aroused by the immediately preceding passage, the transient surprise and confusion are resolved by the listener's adjustment to a new key and his changed perception of the first chord as the subdominant triad of G major. A somewhat equivalent melodic process is common in the works of Bach and Brahms: a motif first seems to be the conclusion of one phrase but then turns out to be launching the theme on a new divagation.

Other devices do not depend on temporary ambiguity or surprise which is removed with the help of meanings supplied by later material, but seem rather to consist of simple violation of quite unequivocal expectations. We have already touched on the expectations connected with rhythm. Syncopation in music (in which an accented note occurs earlier or later than adherence to the prevailing meter would place it) makes use of these. Similar metrical deviations occur in verse, especially in such highly constricting forms as Pope's rhyming couplets, which would fall into unexpressive drabness if an iamb were not occasionally replaced by a trochee:

Hope springs eternal in the human breast.
Man never is, but always to be blest.
The soul, uneasy and confined at home,
Rests and expatiates in a life to come.

The variation on a theme, the ornament, and the grace note are all safeguards against the insipidity of exact repetition, while preserving enough resemblance to the original to keep disorientation within comfortable and controllable limits.

At other times, the expectations that are exploited concern correlations between simultaneous rather than successive stimuli. Cross rhythms, polytonality, and counterpoint excite nervous systems that are prepared, whether by repeated experience or by physiological limitations, for musical textures dominated by one rhythm, one key, or one melody at once.

We are as yet in no position to say with any confidence or precision to what all these deviations owe their savor. They may be means of keeping the influx of processed complexity in the neighborhood of an optimum. There may be a temporal division, which we cannot yet detect, between a phase of disequilibrium and an arousal-relieving phase of assimilation. The psychoanalytic suggestion that aberrations from the obvious and the regular provide satisfaction for aggressive or negativistic drives can neither be dismissed out of hand nor accepted as proven.

It is interesting how often the general plan of a literary or musical work follows the scheme of gradual heightening of arousal toward a climax, followed by progression toward alleviation, even though the scheme is invariably modulated by a multiplicity of local fluctuations of arousal. In music, it is recognizable both on the large and on the small scale. A traditional musical phrase is normally played with increasing loudness from the beginning to the climactic point in the middle and then softened as it approaches its end. It frequently rises and then falls in pitch, so that the note that receives the most pronounced accent is also the highest. It starts with the tonic, its course becomes less and less predictable as it continues, and then it concludes with high probability on a familiar cadence. Even in modern music that uses a tone row, in which each of the twelve notes of the chromatic scale occurs once, the uncertainty diminishes steadily as the row proceeds, since there are fewer and fewer notes left to be included.

The tonal system that has held sway over Western music for centuries, although many contemporary composers are partly or wholly repudiating it, enables a piece to move from the key in which it begins through more and more remote keys until it works its way back to its original key, creating a feeling of venturing far from home and then returning. Forms like the first-movement sonata form or the fugue begin with a relatively straightforward exposition of thematic material, then proceed through a development section in which the composer's ingenuity enjoys full liberty to twist out of shape, wrench apart, transpose, and remodel the themes, so that all their potentialities for novelty and expressiveness can be tapped. The development finally gives way to a recapitulation in which the themes are reintroduced in something like their initial form. Even a less ambitious work that uses simple ABA form is least arousing toward the end since the repeat of the A section is expected and its contents are no longer novel.

The expectations and sequential dependencies which the composer uses as a base line must be built up in the course of the listener's exposure to music. This has the implication, developed by Meyer, that it is necessary to learn a musical language before the significance of works composed in that language can be apprehended. It follows that a listener nurtured in a different cultural tradition cannot react to the work in accordance with the composer's intentions until he has acquired the necessary body of learned associations. In literature, on the other hand, expectedness, surprisingness, and incongruity cannot depend solely on associations between words but must be based on conventional semantic connections between words and extraverbal phenomena. Even those writers who have been eager to free literature from the constraints of ordinary descriptive or narrative discourse, e.g., those of the symbolist and surrealist schools, have used words for the sake of the imaginal and affective content that everyday usage has injected into them. They have not sought words solely as entities that occur with certain frequencies and in certain combinations. Much the same can be said of the visual media of the ballet and the film, even the abstract ballet and the avant-garde film.

A consequence is that associations, mainly learned but perhaps partly innate, have to bear the brunt of arousal value in these art forms. It is true that purely formal devices may be used as auxiliaries: harsh phonemes can alternate with smooth ones, sentence length can be varied, camera angles and distances can be normal or unusual, cutting can be speeded up or slowed down, the sequence of shots can accord with common trains of thought or be startling. James Joyce, in particular, used expressions that diverge from familiar phrases while leaving their origin clear—"Eins within a space," "And how long has he been under loch and neagh?"—obviously analogous to some of the musical techniques that we have considered. But even for Joyce, semantic evocation is primary.

The scheme of progress toward mounting arousal followed by progress toward relief has thus to work through content rather than form in literature and cognate arts, and the means that are applied to its realization are transparent and well known. The curiosity of the reader or spectator is set astir and then satisfied. In the crudest Gothic novel or mystery story, this is achieved simply by introducing extremely unlikely occurrences and then trumping up some explanation which may not be too plausible but has to be accepted because the author says that is what happened. The detective novel creates agonies of belief-disbelief conflict (suspense) by making it clear that one of the house guests must have committed the murder but supplying convincing reasons why each of them could not have done so. The subtler kind of fiction or drama endows a character with equally strong but opposed motives or personality traits, so that his future actions are uncertain, or it gives seemingly equal advantages to two characters with opposed aims so that the outcome is in the balance.

Often arousal comes not only from curiosity but also from conflict or frustration due to identification with a character. The hero faces inanimate or human obstacles to his well-defined goals, or he is rent between incompatible duties or between duty and psychological weaknesses. Finally comes the relaxation or denouement. It may consist of a happy ending. There may, on the other hand, be a highly tragic ending, which nevertheless serves to release arousal because it is inevitable or somehow appropriate, or simply because it is too late to do anything about it now and, in any case, it is "only a story."

HUMOR

Opportunities for laughter are not generally held in such awe as opportunities for aesthetic appreciation. Yet there are affinities be-between the lowliest joke and the sublimest art, quite apart from the fact that they both present general theories of behavior with challenges which, in most cases, have not been taken up. The comical, like the beautiful, can be found ready-made in nature or contrived by human talent. The value of a joke, like that of an artistic product, depends on its formal structure, with the author alternately keeping in line with our learned anticipations and sharply diverging from them. Just as we have the controversy over whether a work of art can rest entirely on its form or whether it must invariably have expressive or communicative content, there is the question of whether

253

there can be what Freud (1905a) called "harmless wit," i.e., wit that is enjoyed exclusively as an intellectual construction, or whether, as some later psychoanalysts hold (see Grotjahn 1957), there is always some latent aggressive or sexual motivation.

The joke, like the work of art, seems to have some optimal range of complexity. If it is too simple, it is dismissed as childish or flat. If it is too complicated, it is held to be labored or ponderous. But there are enormous individual variations in the degree of complexity that is preferred in humor as in art, and there is a tendency for preferred complexity to rise considerably with sophistication. Both the joke and the work of art can become tiresome if experienced too many times in close succession, but both may have to be encountered a few times before they receive maximum appreciation.

Aptness

Wit shares with art, but perhaps exhibits in a purer form, the importance of the subtle property that we call aptness or felicity. It is realized when an element is appropriate for several different reasons at once. A word in a poem may, for example, be supremely right because it not only fits the sense and accords with some sustained train of imagery but also fits the rhyme scheme, the rhythm, and the prevailing quality of sound. Empson (1930) analyzes seven types of ambiguity which, he claims, contribute to the enjoyment of poetry. They all involve multiplicity of meanings to be conveyed by the same expression or multiplicity of possible justifications for the poet's choice of that expression. A metaphor often captures the essence of whatever it stands for in a number of distinct respects. A word or statement may have several senses, embodying distinct but equally pertinent thoughts.

The trees in Shakespeare's sonnet are "bare ruined choirs" because they are "where late the sweet birds sang," because the branches resemble the vaulting of a cathedral, because the trees are made of wood like choir stalls, because the leaves and flowers are like stained-glass windows, and because the sky appears through the branches as it does through the ceiling of a ruined church. When Nash writes that "brightness falls from the air," he might be thinking of the setting sun or moon, of shooting stars, of Icarus, of swooping hawks, of a glittering ornament falling from the top of a building, or simply of light diffusing from the sky. Delilah is for Milton's Samson "that specious monster, my accomplished snare," being accomplished both in the sense of "skilled in the arts of blandishment" and that of "successful in undoing her husband."

Essentially the same phenomenon occurs in painting of various

254

styles. Perhaps the style that exploits it most obviously is cubism. In a cubist painting, a face appears alternately as a profile and as a full face; outlined areas overlap so that first one plane and then the other seems to be in front; the areas delineated by color and by outline do not coincide so that now one area, now the other, is perceived as a unit.

So, returning to wit, Dr. Samuel Johnson observes that "a woman's preaching is like a dog standing on his hinder legs. It is not done well, but you are surprised to find it done at all." Here he displays two ways in which his comparison has validity, either of which alone would have justified it and made it passable, but both of which together produce a rich gem. The pun, on the other hand, derives multiplicity of interpretation from multiplicity of meanings.

The quality of being apt or felicitous obviously relates to what Freud (1900) and Skinner (1957) discuss at length under the names of "overdetermination" and "multiple causation" respectively. In contexts where many alternative imaginal symbols or words might occur, several factors converge to determine which one will have the ascendancy. The response that comes through is one that derives strength from a variety of sources. Freud supplies plenty of examples of dream symbols and slips of the tongue, each of which is the product of up to a dozen simultaneous but separate associations.

It is not hard to see why a response that has an abundance of independent reasons for being performed should overcome its competitors. But what remains a puzzle is why it should be rewarding to come across such responses, especially in art and in wit.

Perhaps the explanation is something like this. When an element of a work of art or a joke is encountered, there is an orientation reaction, representing an effort to understand it. Arousal will sink back again to its former level when we have identified the meaning of the element, the reason for its being chosen. Normally, the discovery of one meaning or reason will be sufficient to satisfy the urge to understand and thus to annul the rise in arousal. If, however, more than one way of interpreting the element is recognized, each will produce a reduction in arousal, and the cumulative effect will be a highly rewarding momentary drop below the tonus level.

Theories of Humor

Throughout the centuries, literary men have wrestled with the riddle of laughter and contributed many a sound observation on the conditions provoking it and the functions it performs. There have, however, been comparatively few attempts at the difficult task of relating laughter to principles of general psychology and biology. Among those that have been made, the outstanding ones have been inspired either by psychoanalysis or by Gestalt psychology.

Saving. Freud (1905a) distinguished between wit, the comical, and humor. The pleasure of wit, which induces laughter through a play on words or ideas, is due to a "saving in inhibition." This may come from a temporary release of sexual or aggressive urges that are normally kept inhibited. Alternatively, in the case of "harmless" wit, there may be a delight in illogicalities and absurdities simply because they represent a temporary respite from the burden of suppressing irrelevant, frivolous, or illogical associations that a lifelong training to be rational imposes on us.

The comical forms a highly compendious category, of which various special cases are analyzed by Freud in detail. They all involve some kind of contrast between something to be taken seriously and something trivial, or between something befitting a rational adult and something worthy only of a child. The contrast may occur between our perception of ourselves and our perception of somebody else: the other man makes clumsy or unnecessarily arduous movements for some purpose that we should fulfill with ease; the naïve child says something that he would reject as absurd or improper if he knew what we know. Otherwise the contrast may occur within the same person: a dignified individual becomes comical by suffering some indignity, like slipping on a banana skin or appearing as the subject of a caricature; we brace ourselves to lift a heavy suitcase and are amused to find that it is empty.

In all these instances, there are two aspects of the situation that have to be represented by our conceptual processes; the pleasure is a consequence of the "saving in representation (*Vorstellung*)" or "cathexis (*Besetzung*)" that occurs because we find that, of the two aspects, one makes demands for less serious or arduous thought than the other.

Freud reserves the term "humor" for cases when a person is able to see a funny side in his own misfortunes. Both he and his audience then enjoy a "saving in affect," since a state of affairs that would otherwise evoke strong unpleasant emotions is taken lightly.

The word "saving" is used when one prepares or expects to spend a certain sum of money on a purchase and finds that the sum actually required is less than was anticipated. The idea underlying Freud's figurative use of the word is that the conditions that provoke laughter save "mental work." A state in which we prepare to expend a certain amount of psychological effort on some imminent stimulus situation is what we have discussed as anticipatory arousal. When it turns out that the stimulus situation can be identified, understood, and reacted to with less effort, or, in other words, has less arousal value, than we were preparing to handle, we have reward from the resultant steep drop in arousal. It may well be that Reik (1948) comes close to the core of the process when he writes that "a man who hears a witty remark laughs like someone who gets a sudden shock and realizes at once that he need not be alarmed."

The neurophysiological experiments that we mentioned in Chapter 7 allow us to conjecture that the underlying mechanism will be something of this sort. On receiving a stimulus with a high arousal value, the nervous system prepares itself for serious events demanding energetic action or, at least, for a laborious effort to make out what is going on. If the sequel is as anticipated, arousal will be maintained at the appropriate level through the interaction of, on the one hand, the arousal value of the external stimuli and the facilitating influence of the cortex on the RAS and, on the other hand, the inhibitory influence exerted on the RAS by the cortex.

But sometimes the foreshadowed emergency will fail to materialize, or it will materialize in the presence of reassuring stimuli that rob it of its menace; something heralded as strange or complex will turn out to be trivially familiar or simple, the information content of a signal will be lower than the uncertainty or expected surprisingness. Then the balance will be upset, since corticireticular inhibition, exceeding what is required, will briefly overwhelm the counteracting processes. It will be rather like a man bracing himself to withstand a blow that never comes and consequently stumbling backwards.

Perhaps such occurrences will be especially characteristic of civilized human life where sudden movements or unusual sights and sounds—which in the wild must usually denote the presence of something ominous—will more often than not come from something of no vital significance. The drop in arousal will then be quick, sudden, and steep, so that what in more primitive conditions would be a cause for alarm turns into an occasion for laughter.

Restructuring. While Freud's theory pursues the similarities that link humor with dreams, slips of the tongue, and neurotic symptoms, the theories that make use of Gestalt concepts concentrate on analogies between the appreciation of a joke and familiar phenomena from the experimental psychology of perception. Maier (1932) and Bateson (1953) dwell on the suddenness with which the point of a joke dawns on the hearer. The elements fit suddenly into a new configuration, so that we have a process resembling what happens when ambiguous figures change from one appearance to another, when figure becomes ground and vice versa, when a face is seen in the branches of a tree in the children's puzzle picture, or when an insightful solution is found for an intellectual problem. The joke may be understood all at once after a protracted and uncomfortable period of "not getting it" or after being deliberately led up the wrong path. The hearer "sees" the joke as soon as he responds to some stimulus properties or relationships within the structure of the joke which at first he missed. This is why the analogy with the figure-ground phenomenon is so tempting. Bateson cites the story of the man who incurred the suspicion of a factory guard by taking home a wheelbarrow load of excelsior every evening. It transpired that the man was interested, not in acquiring excelsior, but in acquiring wheelbarrows.

Often the ground that is transformed into figure is some alternative meaning of a work or expression, initially missed because some other meaning response is stronger. The enraged diner in a cartoon threatens to throw a dish at the headwaiter, exclaiming: "Are you the *maître d'hôtel* that this is *à la?*" His question is meaningless as long as the expression "*à la maître d'hôtel*" is taken as a standard and, therefore, unitary phrase of menu French. But it is later seen to have a literal meaning implying some responsibility for the dish on the part of the functionary it names.

Before we can understand why restructuring should give rise to pleasure, a question that these writers have not satisfactorily answered, we must consider the relations between humor and the arousal jag.

Humor and the Arousal Jag

Writers on humor often remind us that laughter occurs in response to quite a variety of conditions apart from those that produce humor. These conditions are too numerous for any one writer to have enumerated them all. But it is instructive to consider first the situations that evoke laughter in the infant. There is some controversy over how far laughter is genetically related to smiling. But during the first year of life, inexhaustible giggling and chuckling can be occasioned by stimuli that are slightly and briefly startling or frightening: tossing the infant into the air and catching him, making sudden noises or movements, and, above all, the peekaboo game of hiding and reappearing. Later comes an appreciation of incongruity, e.g., the sight of an adult with something strange on his head.

In adults, we have the laughter of relief from anxiety, the laughter of agreement, the laughter of sudden comprehension (the famous "a-ha-experience," perhaps really a "ha-ha-experience"?), the laughter of triumph, the laughter of embarrassment, and the laughter of scorn. These form a highly varied collection, yet in all of them we can see some factor that is associated with threat, discomfort, uncertainty, surprise or, in a word, arousal and some factor that signifies safety, re-adjustment, clarification, or release.

There are stories of uncontrollable laughter in people who have just survived the nearby explosion of a shell or bomb. We have all heard of the laughter that is close to tears and noticed how tragedy and comedy can often be built on the same themes. The word "funny" is also used to mean strange or perplexing.

We may thus look to the arousal jag once again to throw light on the reward value of humor. This means that we must find both factors that provoke arousal and factors that prevent arousal from rising too high or ensure speedy relief.

Whatever other factors may be present to discharge or curb arousal, there is always the influence of the playful mood or atmosphere in which humorous material is sampled. There is a whole assortment of social cues which make it possible to discriminate occasions for taking some event or remark as a joke from occasions for taking it seriously. The wag smiles or nudges his listener to set aside the repercussions that his audacity would otherwise have—and which it may still have if his efforts to have it accepted as a jest do not succeed. Not only the behavior of the jester but the whole social and physical context may bring out lighthearted rather than solemn responses to stimuli having the capacity to evoke both. The cues involved are comparable to those that enable an animal to distinguish playful fighting from a dangerous attack and inhibit him from injuring his opponent.

In the case of what Freud called "tendentious wit," arousal may be generated by the guilt and anxiety that attach to the verbalization of aggressive or sexual desires. Reassurance comes from complicity: both the raconteur and the listener are safe from punishment or social disapproval as long as both show signs of enjoying the improper anecdote. There is, of course, still the question of why society grants a dispensation for these temporary exemptions from taboo. It may be that they have some utility as a relatively harmless safety valve or, to reinterpret Freud's hypothesis, that the reinforcement value coming from the formal properties of a joke gives the inhibited response that extra measure of strength that it requires to prevail over its inhibition.

Maier and Bateson concentrate on the surprising suddenness with which the point of a joke is understood. But they do not lay much stress on the surprisingness of the configuration that precedes the final resolution, an aspect which does not receive much attention from Freud either. All types of verbal wit or humorous anecdote seem to incorporate a divergence from the expected, a change in something familiar which leaves enough resemblance to the familiar for some of its responses to be evoked and yet contains some feature that frustrates these responses and thus provokes conflict, uncertainty, and surprise. This constitutes an important source of arousal value, opening the way to the reward value of an arousal jag, and it also assimilates the formal mechanisms of humor to those of art.

Sometimes a change is simply made in a word. Freud cites the cases of the man with whom Rothschild was quite "famillionaire." There are satirical neologisms like "cocacolonization" and "sardoodledum." A favorite technique of Oscar Wilde was a slight alteration in a common catch phrase: "Nothing succeeds like excess," "Work is the curse of the drinking classes." Shaw modified not so much a common phrase as a common idea: "Do not love your neighbour as yourself. If you are on good terms with yourself, it is an impertinence; if on bad, an injury"; and "Self-sacrifice enables us to sacrifice other people without blushing." All these devices produce a moment of perplexity as responses and expectations dependent on the familiar expression or idea are thwarted. But arousal is soon alleviated when the new version is seen to have a meaning of its own and even a quota of truth.

The wit of repartee, like the humor of many anecdotes, works through deflection from a habitual train of thought. Boswell, meeting Johnson for the first time and knowing of his prejudices, says: "I do indeed come from Scotland, but I cannot help it." Both he and the reader are set for some reply about the merits or demerits of being a native of Scotland, or about whether a man should be held responsible for his birthplace. Instead the doctor answers: "That, Sir, I find is what a very great many of your countrymen cannot help." The resulting confusion is dissolved when the other meaning of "to come from" gains possession of the nervous system and evokes associations that tie everything up in full accord with the logical, if not the polite, rules of conversation. The process is closely analogous to those occasioned by musical or poetic patterns that clash with an expectation but are then invested with new meaning by a reinterpretation of what preceded them.

The phenomena that Freud subsumed under the comical embody some incongruity, as Freud acknowledges when he stresses contrast. And the incongruity or novelty is usually such as would be treated as a threat in other circumstances. The child's innocent impropriety would be embarrassing and offensive in the mouth of an adult. The sight of a man on stilts is funny at a circus. But it might well frighten a child or a member of a society with no circuses but with vivid beliefs in magic and witchcraft.

We have noted in earlier chapters how the conditions for fear and the conditions for curiosity often coincide. They are often also conditions for humor. When the writer has shown the incongruous-animal pictures in Fig. 6-1 to audiences, there has usually been a pause followed by laughter. These were, of course, merely drawings. But if the members of the audience had been confronted with a real bird with an elephant's forelegs, the first reaction might well have been terror and flight. After surveying the animal from a safe distance, they would probably have approached gingerly for a closer view and finally they might have been ready to regard the animal as funny.

Sometimes the possession of an explanation makes something ludicrous rather than fearful, as when we know how stilts work. But even without such an explanation, it is enough to know that strange phenomena arise from the fancies of professional entertainers and cartoonists and that these phenomena present us neither with a threat nor with anything that warrants arduous thought and investigation.

As Maier and others have said, humor demands objectivity. There is some condition that precludes intense and lasting states of arousal. Tragedy depends on identification. The hero suffers through some fault of character, such as we all possess, or through some ferocity of fate to which none of us is invulnerable. Any relief of arousal comes, therefore, after the drama has ended and its reverberations have faded away. The characters in a comedy can also undergo quite cruel discomfitures and disappointments, but there is some factor that exempts us from grieving over them. The figures in a cartoon film dismember and demolish one another with gruesome abandon. But, knowing that these incidents could not really have happened, we find them funny. When Cyrano de Bergerac jests about his own outsize nose, some of our sympathetic distress over his affliction can be shed through the channel of sympathetic laughter, an example of humor in Freud's restricted sense. We revel in the severe distresses that beset Malvolio or Pantaleone because they, having defects that cause them to make things unpleasant for others, are judged undeserving of commiseration. A member of a party going to witness a recent execution was reported in a newspaper to have joked about how the condemned man must be feeling. Some of his companions felt this to be in poor taste. But for the joker, the condemned man was evidently nothing but a "brutal murderer," which removed any reason for not treating his predicament as humorous.

261

Chapter 10

EPISTEMIC BEHAVIOR: KNOWLEDGE
AND THINKING *

We come finally to the motivational problems raised by behavior
that augments knowledge or, as we shall call it, *epistemic behavior*
(Greek *episteme,* knowledge). To start with, we must explain the
sense in which we are going to use the word "knowledge."

"Knowledge," no less than the word "communication," can be given
an extremely wide meaning. We can, if we choose, regard an organism
as possessing knowledge of some fact in the external world whenever that fact influences its behavior through the excitation of receptors
and sensory nerves. We can even make knowledge synonymous with
information and speak of a thermostat knowing the temperature of
a room. But these, once again, are processes for which other convenient
and recognized descriptions are in use, so that it would be a pity
to waste the word on them. It would seem more advisable to con-
fine it, in fair agreement with its everyday sense, to certain highly
specialized information-gathering and information-storing processes
dependent on symbolic processes. It would thus be applicable principally to man, though perhaps also in some minor degree to other
mammals possessed of rudimentary representational capacities.

We may proceed to narrow down step by step the sense in which we
are going to use the word "knowledge" as follows:

1. Knowledge consists of *habits.* A habit is a psychological dis-
position (Carnap 1936–1937) that is due to learning. We are willing
to say that an animal has a certain habit, or that a man has a certain
piece of knowledge, even when there is no manifestation of it in
outward behavior.

In order to tell an organism with the habit or the knowledge from
another without it, it is necessary to subject both organisms to ap-

---

* For further discussion of the relations between structural and motivational
factors in thinking, enlarging on aspects that this and the following chapter touch
on briefly, see Berlyne (1960).

propriate test conditions and to see whether or not the corresponding truth conditions are realized. A rat that has been thoroughly trained to run to the goal box of a particular maze is quite indistinguishable from a naïve rat—until placed in the maze with sufficiently intense hunger. So a man who knows a locality intimately behaves just like one who does not—until required to find his way from one point to another, to draw a map, or to describe an itinerary. To say that somebody knows something is, in other words, an abbreviation for a large, probably infinite, set of statements of the form: "Given situation A, behavior X is probable," "Given situation B, behavior Y is probable," etc.

2. The responses that are indicative of epistemic habits are endlessly varied. In general, we can say that knowledge of a particular event causes an organism to behave, in some respects, as it would behave if that event were at the moment stimulating its sense organs; it causes present behavior to be controlled by events that are past or absent. Nevertheless, although common usage is far from consistent, the word "knowledge" is not likely to be applied, unless *symbolic responses*, and especially words, are among the responses that occur in correspondence with the events in question.

A man may be consummately skilled at hitting a target with a rifle bullet. But we are not inclined to say that he knows how to hit the target unless he is able to represent to himself the processes that make possible this performance, to describe or picture to himself what it is that he has to do, and ultimately to describe or convey it to another individual in the form of hints or instructions which might guide him toward an equally good performance.

We are not deemed to know our own motives or other internal psychological processes, even those that dominate our overt behavior, unless we can symbolize them and the fact that we are responding to them (Freud 1916, Morris 1938, Dollard and Miller 1950). Otherwise, being unverbalized, they are "unconscious."

We obviously need to make more precise the notion of a symbolic response. As a first step, we must consider the definition of a *sign* that is adumbrated by Russell (1940) and Morris (1946) but most satisfactorily formulated by Osgood (1952). Osgood says

> A pattern of stimulation which is not the object is a sign of the object if it evokes in an organism a mediating reaction, this (a) being some fractional part of the total behavior elicited by the object and (b) producing distinctive self-stimulation that mediates responses which would not occur without the previous association of non-object and object patterns of stimulation.

His definition is summed up in the following scheme:

$$\boxed{S} \rightarrow r_m \dashrightarrow s_m \rightarrow R_x$$

where $\boxed{S}$ is the sign, r_m the mediating reaction (the "meaning" of the sign), s_m the self-stimulation resulting from r_m, and R_x the overt behavior evoked by s_m. Put briefly, a sign is a stimulus that evokes some but not all of the psychological effects that would be produced by the stimulus object that it stands for.

Any response that can act like Osgood's r_m, any response that can correspond to a class of objects or events but can occur when a member of the class is not present, is what we shall be calling a symbolic response. It can be overt or implicit. It can consist of a word or pattern of words, an image, a muscular twitch, or, perhaps, some other kind of response that is purely cerebral.

Thinking consists of sequences of symbolic responses, and it is through such symbolic responses that knowledge exerts its influence on overt behavior. The intervention of symbolic processes between external stimuli and overt responses and the interaction between external stimuli and symbolic processes are what give behavior guided by knowledge its special characteristics: its rationality, its flexibility, its stamp of voluntary and conscious control.

3. The symbolic responses that are repositories of knowledge will fall into Morris's (1946, 1958) *designative* and *formative* categories. The former consists of signs that correspond to discriminable kinds of stimulation and therefore to physicochemical properties; it includes images and the verbal responses that Skinner (1957) calls "tacts" (i.e., those that describe stimuli). The latter consist of signs that affect the manner in which other signs, accompanying them, are responded to; it includes words like "if" and "or," conveying logical relations (Skinner's "autoclitics").

The symbols that manifest knowledge will not belong to the appraisive category (signifying affective value and including evaluative utterances), the prescriptive category (signifying power to evoke particular overt responses, and including verbal utterances in the imperative mood, classified by Skinner as "mands"), or the expressive category (signifying power to evoke internal reactions). Epistemic symbols may, on the other hand, be influenced by symbols of these categories and influence them in their turn.

4. Epistemic symbols are *believed* symbols. The extent to which a combination of symbols is believed can be judged partly by the way in which a person utters a statement or by the formators ("I am convinced that . . ." or "That is definitely the case," etc.) with which

he accompanies the statement. But the most valid test of belief is the strength of overt behavior. This test is usually accepted as more conclusive when it conflicts with what the subject says. As Morris puts it, belief represents the degree to which an organism is disposed to respond as it is assumed it would if the signified object or event existed.

VARIETIES OF EPISTEMIC BEHAVIOR

Epistemic responses fall into three main classes. The first consists of *epistemic observation,* i.e., responses which place the subject in contact with external situations that will nourish the pertinent learning process. They include everything from the scandal seeking of the gossip, when it is rewarded not so much by the pleasure of witnessing scandalous goings on as by that of being able to recall or recount them afterwards, to the systematic observations and experiments of science. The second subclass consists of *epistemic thinking,* which is part of what psychologists have usually called "productive" or "creative" thinking. It differs from other thinking, such as "reproductive" thinking, which calls up remembered material to guide the handling of current problems, since its function is to put the individual in permanent possession of new knowledge. Lastly, there is *consultation.* This is behavior that exposes an individual to verbal stimuli issuing from other individuals. It will include asking questions, writing letters, and reading.

These three classes of epistemic behavior correspond to the principal sources of knowledge recognized by Western philosophy and accorded primacy by different schools of epistemology. Epistemic observing responses correspond to *empiricism;* epistemic thinking to *rationalism,* if the thinking is systematic and logical, and to *intuitionism,* if it is less rigorously controlled; while consultation corresponds to *authoritarianism* (see Montague 1925). It is interesting that they also correspond to the three *pramaṇas* (means of obtaining valid knowledge) of Indian philosophy, namely *pratyakṣa* (perception), *anumana* (inference), and *śabda* (verbal testimony) (see Hiriyanna 1949).

All of these responses, but especially observation, can figure in exploratory behavior. Whether or not they have an epistemic function depends on whether they leave a lasting residue of knowledge and whether their biological value and reinforcement derive from this residue as well as from the immediate sensory consequences of their performance.

As previous chapters have shown, it is possible to think of perception as a process that removes or avoids conflict. From the observer's point of view, contact between the subject and a stimulus to which a clear-cut, dominant response is attached causes information to be transmitted through the subject, which means that behavior will be relatively predictable and uncertainty about it will be relatively low. From the subject's point of view, contact with such a stimulus means avoidance of the emotional strain and inefficiency of conflict and—because it enables consequences to be foreseen and successful responses to be selected—avoidance of surprise.

The function of knowledge is to overcome the deficiencies of perception by providing internal stimuli, products of symbolic processes, to supplement the external stimuli that originate in outside objects. Perception without knowledge is at the mercy of the chance occurrences of the moment, of the various illusions to which perception is subject, and of what Piaget (1947, 1961) calls centering—the fact that the limited part of the stimulus field that is apprehended with full clarity receives disproportionate intensity, prominence, and importance in determining behavior. Knowledge allows stimuli that are not being fixated at the present instant—stimuli that belong to the past or the future, or even stimuli that will never be part of the stimulus field—to make their influence felt through their internal representatives.

Knowledge can represent past or future properties of the object that is now being perceived or hidden properties that would appear if the object were examined from another angle or from inside. *Classification* extends primary stimulus generalization and discrimination, which depend on readily perceptible physicochemical similarities and differences, by making secondary (also known as "mediated" or "acquired") generalization and discrimination possible. Objects that are superficially alike come to evoke different responses because they have different verbal labels tied to them, and objects that do not have manifest attributes in common come to be treated in the same manner through the circumstance of possessing a shared classifying label.

Besides classification, there is *ordering*. A chicken, a rat, or a monkey can learn to approach the larger or the darker of two objects when both are visible together. The human subject is capable of responding to a stimulus according to whether it bears more or less of some attribute than another object that is out of sight. Moreover, he can respond according to the position an object occupies in some ordering of a comprehensive class. He can recognize, and react fittingly to, an unusually extortionate invoice or an unusually important visitor. Spatial and temporal relations produce the most elaborate and frequently used orderings of all. We ask when or where something happened, how long it lasted, and how large it is because quite different actions may be called for according to the answers we receive, and ignorance of time and place plunges us into conflict.

Besides the knowledge that expresses a temporal or spatial relation between two events or which locates one event in a whole temporal or spatial framework, we have the knowledge that connects one event with others by way of *explanation*.

An explanation, in its most general acceptance, is a statement that answers a question beginning with "why." Children become addicted to such questions quite early after their mastery of speech (Piaget 1923, Isaacs 1930), and every society not only asks them but answers them. What will be accepted as an adequate answer to a why-question is, however, far more variable than what will pass as an answer to any other kind of question. This is, no doubt, because the why-question goes furthest beyond what can be immediately apprehended in one act of perception; it reflects fundamental attitudes to the universe and ways of organizing experience; its answer is more likely to demand elaborate epistemic procedures.

Explanations may refer the event that is to be explained to a single event, past, present, or future, or to a class of events. It may refer a property of an object to other properties of the same object or to properties of a class of objects.

But whatever type of explanation is involved, the eagerness to know why must stem ultimately from the ability of the answer to relieve conflict and guide the choice of action. Which response will be rewarded and which punished must depend not merely on the nature of an event but also on the unseen events that explain it. If a person makes a request, the consequences of complying or not complying will depend very closely on the reasons he has for making it. Likewise, we are not usually in a position to select the means that will remedy, avert, or bring about a natural occurrence unless we know what causes it.

THE DEVELOPMENT OF THINKING

As a prelude to taking up the motivational problems raised by epistemic behavior, we shall consider the stages through which the most elaborate forms of thought are likely to have developed out of simple psychological capacities (see Hull 1930, Berlyne 1954a).

Reaction

We begin by considering a series of stimulus events, S_i, in the outside world, each evoking a corresponding complex of responses, R_i, overt or implicit, in an organism. The responses are, of course, joint products of the external stimulus events and of processes inside the organism, which explains why different individuals not only perform different overt responses to identical situations but also derive different knowledge from exposure to identical events.

Predictive Redintegration

We next make two assumptions: (1) that the same series of stimulus events occurs and produces the same parallel chain of reactions repeatedly, and (2) that each of the reactions R_i produces a distinctive internal response-produced stimulus, s_i.

We can then infer, provided that reinforcing conditions are present, that R_2 (the response corresponding to the next stimulus in the series, S_2) will become associated with both S_1 and s_1 (the internal stimulus produced by R_1) as a trace conditioned response.

As a consequence, R_2, as well as being evoked by S_2, will receive added strength from the prior occurrence of S_1 and s_1. This will account for a host of cases where the response to a stimulus is made more vigorous or more probable by the receipt of a warning signal.

It will also explain phenomena usually studied as effects of set on perception. The combined influence of S_1 and s_1 may lower the threshold for recognition of S_2. In other words, R_2 will be evoked by a briefer or fainter exposure of S_2 than would otherwise be adequate. If, on the other hand, the habitual stimulus S_2 is, for once, replaced by a different stimulus, S_A, then a variety of outcomes may ensue, depending on the relative strengths of R_A and the redintegrative R_2 and on the degree of similarity between them. R_A may prevail, R_2 may prevail (causing misidentification, as when we fail to notice a misprint), a compromise between the two responses may eventuate, or, if R_2 and R_A are both strong and very dissimilar, there will be all the usual accompaniments of surprise, including raised recognition threshold, lengthened reaction time, and indexes of high arousal.

Evocative Redintegration

The next step forward is taken when some fractional component of R_2 can occur in the absence of S_2 and in response to S_1 or s_1 alone. This component r_2 can thus represent S_2 either before S_2 is due to appear (thus forming an expectation of S_2) or when S_2 is not accessible at all to the subject's receptors.

268

The outcome will be a chain of symbolic responses that can run off faster than the chain of external events that it represents and can deputize for these events in controlling behavior. So when we look out of the window and see the milkman's vehicle coming round the corner, we can turn away from the window and imagine or describe how the vehicle will stop at the first house, the milkman will get out, deposit full bottles, pick up empty bottles, return to the vehicle, etc. We can either think of each of these events at the moment it is most likely occurring or course through the whole chain before the milkman has entered the street.

Ramification

The next complications arise when an external event S_i participates in several habitual sequences, so that its corresponding internal representative, s_i, can initiate any of a number of associated responses, leading thought off in any of a multitude of directions. Some factor is thus required to decide which of many possible associations will have the upper hand at any point in thought.

In free association as used in psychotherapy, the factors that select associations may well vary from point to point, although the patient's prevailing motives seem to determine the general drift. In directed thinking aimed at solving a specific problem, control has to be much tighter, and the factors that ensure progress toward a solution must be on hand throughout the process and have a major say in selecting responses at every choice point.

A train of thought is a typical member of the class of behavior patterns for which Hull introduced the term "behavior chain." There is a goal which can only be reached by performing a sequence of responses in an appropriate order; the subject is confronted with a sequence of stimulus situations (choice points), each of which is associated with several learned responses; and at each choice point a correct response must be singled out. The kind of behavior chain that has received most study so far is that elicited from the rat by a multiple-choice maze. We might therefore expect to find some hints about the role of motivational factors in thinking from the conclusions that experiments on the behavior of rats in mazes have inspired.

Hull's account (1952) recognizes several kinds of stimuli at work in maze-running behavior, and it is not difficult to correlate them with factors that may be assumed to have a hand in thinking. They fall into two categories with rather different functions.

Cue Stimuli. This category includes the external stimuli that come from a maze and the internal stimuli that come from previous responses in the chain. In the case of autonomous thinking, only one external stimulus will normally play a part, namely, the one that initiates the train of thought. Others may, however, obtrude themselves as thinking proceeds and supply either helpful hints or troublesome distractions. Most of the cue stimuli that operate in thinking will be the internal ones produced by preceding responses.

The function of cue stimuli is to make available a restricted number of associated responses at each choice point. But precisely because of their multiple associations, cue stimuli can obviously not suffice to determine the course of a behavior chain.

Motivational Stimuli. A rat in a maze is usually acted on by a drive like hunger or thirst. Stimuli, peripheral or neural, that accompany the drive will continue through the whole running process, since they will not be removed until the goal box is reached. They will therefore become conditioned to every response in the chain. However, in accordance with the reinforcement-gradient principle, they will be most strongly conditioned to responses that come shortly before the attainment of the goal. In addition to drive stimuli, there will be stimuli produced by fractional anticipatory goal responses, i.e., representations of the specific nature of the reward that the animal expects to find in the goal box.

In thinking, there will likewise be stimuli coming from some sort of discomfort, set up by whatever situation launched the train of thought, and stimuli coming from representations of the solution. The way the solution is represented is likely, of course, to change as thinking continues.

The functions of the motivational stimuli are threefold:

1. They keep the sequence of responses going until the goal or solution is reached or else the sequence is halted by extinction (the weakening of the behavior through prolonged failure of reinforcement) or distraction (the evocation of a stronger competing behavior sequence).

2. They determine the general class of responses: running in the case of a hungry or thirsty rat, crouching and cowering in the case of a frightened rat, ideas connected with the general theme in the case of a pensive human being.

3. They determine which of the competing responses will be selected at each choice point.

Since this conceptual scheme has been derived, by analogy, from the theory of maze learning in the rat, it is encouraging to find writers who have attacked human symbolic process directly distinguishing two groups of factors with roles corresponding to those of our cue stimuli and motivational stimuli.

Why only the correct association appears, whether it be a question of a single reaction (as in the controlled-association experiment) or of a long succession of reactions (as in directed thinking), was one of the principal preoccupations of the Würzburg school. The conclusions they arrived at are typified by Ach's (1905) theory, which attributed the selection of the response to the interaction of the "idea of the stimulus" (*Reizvorstellung*) with the "idea of the aim" (*Zielvorstellung*). These two factors join to produce a "determining tendency," which steers the thought sequence toward the aim and excludes digressions.

According to Bartlett's (1932) theory of remembering, recall is the joint product of the stimulus that elicits the recall (that reminds one) and of an attitude, characterized as "very largely a matter of feeling or affect." The latter ensures that what emerges from memory is something pertinent to the present situation and not just a fortuitous association.

The way in which cue stimuli and motivational stimuli cooperate to fix upon a particular response has sometimes been pictured in accordance with the *convergence theory*, both among the early experimentalists and among recent neobehaviorists. In this view, the response selected is one that is stronger than others because it receives strength from stimuli of both classes. Suppose that the task is to supply names of capital cities, and the stimulus word is "France." The task tends to evoke words like "London," "Paris," "Rome," etc., while the word "France" evokes words like "art," "De Gaulle," "Paris." "Paris" is the word actually uttered, because it is the only member of both lists and thus has a double quota of habit strength.

The inadequacy of this theory was tellingly pointed out by Selz (1913) with examples like the following. The task is to supply opposites (strengthening responses like "small," "night," "light," each of them being the opposite of some familiar word) and the stimulus word is "day" (evoking such associations as "sun," "light," "night," etc.). If the convergence theory is correct, "light" should be as probable a response as "night," since it also draws strength from both sources.

Selz proposed instead what he called a "theory of complex completion," which may be translated into the language of modern behavior theory with the help of the principle of patterning (Hull, 1943). Positive patterning, well authenticated in the conditioned-response literature, is said to occur when a combination or succession of stimuli evokes a learned response which is either not evoked at all or evoked significantly less strongly when the component stimuli are presented separately. So, through a similar form of learning, the combination of "opposite" and "day" or some such phrase as "the opposite of day"

271

is associated with the response "night" much more strongly than with any alternative verbal response, whereas that response would not be elicited nearly so strongly by "opposite" or "night" alone.

Reorganization

An important advance is made when the elements comprising trains of thought are no longer tied to the chronological order in which the events represented by them have usually happened.

When trying to recall an event or a series of events that are related but widely dispersed in time, the human being does not have to work his way through all the intervening events that are of no interest to his present concern. He can, in the words of Bartlett (1932), "turn round on his own schemata," i.e., "go directly to that portion of the organized setting of past responses which is most relevant to the needs of the moment."

Symbolic responses that are learned at different times, but likely to be serviceable in the same situations, are grouped together into what Bartlett calls "specialized schemata" pertaining to particular "appetites, instinctive tendencies, interests and ideals." Bousfield and Cohen (1953) have shown how, when words belonging to different categories (male first names, animals, vegetables, professions) are randomly interspersed, there is a tendency for words belonging to the same category to cluster together in recall.

But the most noteworthy consequence of the ability to reorganize symbolic material into new combinations and sequences is the possibility of "the assembly of behavior segments in novel combinations suitable for problem solution" (Hull 1935, 1952). This piecing together of elements from different behavior chains into new patterns can occur with both overt and symbolic responses, allowing not only practical but also intellectual problems to be solved insightfully and forming one way in which new knowledge can be gained.

Motivational stimuli contribute to this potent new development in two ways. First, they are responsible for "short-circuiting" or "serial-segment elimination" (Hull 1952). Because they become conditioned to all the responses in the sequence but most strongly to the response nearest the goal, they cause the latter to come forward in time whenever their earlier performance is possible and conducive to reward. They are thus able to forestall and render superfluous the preliminary responses that originally led up to them. Bartlett is evidently expressing much the same idea when he writes that interest, appetite, etc., are the agents that lead a subject straight to the recollection that is required at the moment, leaping over the trivial memories that separate that moment in the past from his present situation.

Secondly, a motivational stimulus often serves as the thread on which a collection of symbols subserving a particular purpose is strung and can be collectively hauled out of storage. This is what Bartlett evidently means when he describes the schemata that are organized round an appetite or an interest. It also forms the kernel of Hull's theory of the "habit-family hierarchy." When several response sequences have led to the same goal at different times, they form a habit-family hierarchy whose members can substitute for one another or be formed into novel combinations to fit novel circumstances. The entity that integrates the hierarchy and enables it to function in this fashion is the *goal stimulus,* the stimulus produced by the fractional anticipatory goal response that acts as an expectation or representation of the final outcome.

Ratiocination

The crowning achievement of the human intellect is commonly felt to reside in the rigorous and tightly knit chains of symbolic formulas that form the substance of logic, mathematics, and the most advanced scientific theory. Here the order in which the symbolic responses appear does not have to depend on the order of the events represented by them. There may, in fact, be no such events. The order is determined rather by rules of logic or laws of thought (Piaget 1947, Inhelder and Piaget 1956, Newell, Shaw, and Simon 1958).

The relations between this brand of thinking and motivational factors have been little investigated, possibly because logic is so frequently considered to be a dispassionate activity which, to be effective, must remain aloof from the more familiar and violent sources of affect. But we are faced with the same motivational problems here as in the other stages, and perhaps even in a purer and clearer form. We may thus proceed to some general remarks summing up the problems as they relate to epistemic behavior in general.

THE MOTIVATIONAL PROBLEMS OF THINKING

Thinking is, as we have seen, one way in which new knowledge can be acquired, and it is through thinking, the manipulation of sequences of symbolic responses, that knowledge, once obtained, is utilized. Even when knowledge is sought by other means than thinking—by consulting authorities or exposing oneself to nonsymbolic stimulus events—thinking usually precedes, accompanies, and follows the process. The problem of the motivational factors that affect epistemic behavior in general can thus be considered together with those affecting thinking in particular.

273

In essence, the motivational problems that face us here are the ones that concern behavior as a whole. There is, first, the problem of the internal factors that help to determine responses. This problem is of especial acuteness in thinking (1) because the symbolic responses that may be evoked by a particular stimulus pattern are much more numerous than the overt responses and (2) because internal stimuli, whether or not they would be classified as motivational, will quite overshadow external stimuli in deciding which thought will come up at any juncture.

We have examined the unique contribution of motivational stimuli in the selection of responses from alternatives. Their special properties appear to derive simply from their lasting a long time—until the goal is reached—and their occurrence in a large variety of situations, with the result that they each become associated with a huge set of responses. Otherwise, their action follows the laws of associative learning that are applicable to all stimuli.

But apart from this question of guidance of thought, we have the connected questions of what makes a sequence of thought (or any kind of quest for knowledge) begin and what determines how long it lasts. The motivational stimuli that help to guide thought appear also to play their part in determining when thinking will start, continue, or end. But these are services that we cannot expect from any and every stimulus. They would seem to necessitate stimuli that carry weight with the arousal system. This is, therefore, where we come up most sharply against the problems of *epistemic curiosity*, the brand of arousal that motivates the quest for knowledge and is relieved when knowledge is procured. We distinguish it from the perceptual curiosity that is reduced by exposure to appropriate stimuli. It must be left to the research data of the future to clarify the exact relation that holds between them. For the present, we must adhere to the distinction.

THE ROLE OF EXTRINSIC MOTIVATION

A great deal of searching for knowledge is clearly prompted by pressing practical problems. Some extraneous drive, like hunger, thirst, pain, sex, fear, or desire for money, is aroused, and knowledge is needed to direct the subject to courses of action that conduce to the mitigation of the drive. Sometimes knowledge is welcome, not because it can help the subject to cope with a predicament of the moment, but because it might be useful when practical problems are encountered in the future. The reward value of acquiring knowledge would then be ascribed to the mechanism of secondary reward or that of fear reduction. On other occasions, stimuli, especially symbolic stimuli, may be sought purely for their secondary reward value, derived from their association with concrete satisfactions, regardless of any practical value that they might have. But the kind of free-association fantasy that forms daydreams is capable of serving this purpose without the element of belief that is one of the hallmarks of knowledge. Often the reward value of knowledge depends on some social usefulness like gaining prestige or passing an examination.

It is not surprising, therefore, that there should be theories current that interpret epistemic motivation as a derivative of such extrinsic drives.

1. *Decision theory* consists mainly of normative discussions of what methods of making decisions are most advisable. Most of its content is therefore not directly concerned with how people act in practice. But it can hardly be sealed off altogether from the empirical questions of psychology, because every statement of normative theory automatically supplies an empirical hypothesis, namely, that human beings actually behave in accord with that statement, and because human beings undoubtedly approximate the rational prescriptions of decision theory occasionally.

The process of obtaining knowledge, or, as it is commonly called in decision-theory circles, information, is central to most of the problems with which these circles are preoccupied. In one kind of situation that has been studied extensively, there are a number of possible events, some of them under the control of the subject's own actions and others which are beyond his control since they depend on the caprices of nature or the actions of human opponents. The subject has estimates of the probabilities of the events that are independent of him and of the utility of the outcome that each combination of events would have for him. He can then calculate, for each course of action or strategy that is available to him, an expected value, by multiplying the utility of each possible outcome by its probability and summing. The strategy with the maximum expected value is then the optimal strategy which he should select.

In many such situations (known as *sequential-decision situations*), the subject can choose to secure more information, postponing his definitive action. This expedient will, in accordance with information-theory definitions, reduce uncertainty, which means redistributing probabilities among the outcomes. It may change the expected values that are assigned to the various strategies and thus enable the subject, once he is in possession of the information, to identify and adopt a strategy with higher expected gain than he could detect before. If the information obtained were complete, he would, of course, know exactly which events would occur and thus be certain of the utility that would accrue from each strategy.

Gathering information in most sequential-decision situations, e.g., in industry or medicine, involves a cost, whether in money, time, effort, or discomfort. But, as Marschak (1955) shows, the decision to seek more information is justified if, and only if, the expected gain with the information exceeds the expected gain without the information by at least the cost of securing the information.

This is more or less how many persons, among those who have and those who have not studied decision theory, decide whether or not to equip themselves with specific items of knowledge. There are also many who do not act in this way when faced with problems to which the theory is applicable. We have, however, to supplement the theory with some account of the conditions in which knowledge is sought when probabilities and utilities are unknown. Most important of all, we need to consider cases where knowledge is pursued for its own intrinsic utility. For example, it is likely that an individual who is subject to a risk-taking situation—even when he knows the probabilities and utilities of the alternative outcomes and is confident that he has entrusted his fate to the best possible strategy—would be willing to pay to shorten the time that he has to wait before knowing what will happen. When people are at the mercy of future circumstances on which matters of great weight will turn, perhaps bound up with the success or failure of economic ventures, with legal proceedings, or with health, there is often no limit to the vehemence with which they will clamor for prognoses. And this clamoring is by no means restricted to times when foreknowledge enables risks to be curtailed.

2. *Psychoanalysis* (Freud 1905b, Abraham 1921) ascribes the desire to know or to explore (*der Wiss- oder Forschertrieb*) to sublimations of the various component drives of the libido or sex drive. Freud himself traced it back to a dual origin composed of scoptophilia, the desire to see sexually stimulating sights, and the urge for oral incorporation with conversion of a hunger for food into a hunger for knowledge. If knowledge is perceived as means to power or as a way of retaining residues of past sensory experiences within one, thus increasing independence and self-sufficiency, it could be construed as a substitute satisfaction for anal-aggressive or anal-retentive impulses as well.

The main trouble with these hypotheses, as with many of those that have grown out of psychoanalysis, is the failure to indicate with sufficient precision how they can be verified or falsified without the manifold biases of evidence derived from psychotherapeutic sessions. What they seem to imply in case of the desire for knowledge is that epistemic responses draw strength, through generalization, from learning processes that have occurred in early childhood. The prevalence of metaphors such as "hunger" or "thirst for knowledge," "absorbing knowledge," "retaining knowledge," etc., demonstrate that there is enough similarity between epistemic behavior on the one hand and alimentary or costive behavior on the other for verbal responses to generalize. It should therefore be quite possible for attitudes of a deeper sort to generalize also, and what happened to an individual in the critical situations of infancy may conceivably determine how ardently he seeks out certain kinds of knowledge or even knowledge in general.

But we can scarcely content ourselves with these hypotheses as the whole explanation of epistemic behavior. The obvious linkages between epistemic behavior and the various forms of exploratory behavior that are in evidence from birth on, and almost throughout the animal kingdom, point to a more autonomous biological significance. Freud maintains that the first curiosity of the child is aimed at the question "Where do babies come from?" But if this is to be taken in a literal and testable sense, it is manifestly untrue in the light of studies of children's questions (Piaget 1923, Isaacs 1930), not to mention other nonverbal and nonepistemic manifestations of curiosity. Furthermore, the psychoanalytic theory, even if it were completely vindicated, could hardly claim to answer all the questions, particularly the quantitative questions, about epistemic motivation that we should like to ask.

3. *S-R reinforcement theory,* of the kind developed by Dollard and Miller (1950) and, in so far as his behavior theory falls within this category, by Skinner (1953), sees epistemic behavior largely as an outgrowth of habits derived from the individual's previous history of extrinsic rewards. Dollard and Miller speak of drives for "being logical (eliminating contradictions)" and "being oriented (having an explanation)." They assume that being illogical or disoriented must often have had disagreeable accompaniments in the past, so that these states will have acquired drive value through learning. Skinner describes how the emission of "tacts" (verbal responses corresponding to states of affairs in the real world), first overtly and later subvocally, is encouraged through "generalized reinforcers," usually social, such as approval from parents.

While conceding that this type of explanation must contain an important measure of truth, we must raise once again the difficulty faced by all theories of stimulus selection that base themselves on generalization from past experiences. The situations that excite epistemic behavior most intensely are obviously ones that differ in some striking way from familiar situations which are already covered by an individual's store of knowledge. If the evocation of previously reinforced responses through generalization were the operative factor, we should expect that situations that are identical with those which have occasioned successful quests for knowledge in the past would be the ones to call forth epistemic behavior most intensely. But we do not conduct research into matters we feel we know all about. We may rehearse the knowledge we have about them, but we do not repeat knowledge-gathering responses aimed at them.

It may be objected that the generalization is based, not on physical similarity between a new situation about which we feel ignorant and some past situation in which we have extricated ourselves from the penalties of ignorance, but on some similarity in their relation to us, some similarity in our initial reaction to them. This is obviously a valid point, but the crux of the problem then lies in the characterization of these common reactions to situations that show our stock of knowledge to be wanting.

To sum up, we have agreed that theories that attribute epistemic behavior to extrinsic motivation have their share of validity, but they fail most seriously when they are applied to epistemic searches concerned with matters that are perplexing but trivial from a practical point of view. It is possible for a die-hard Freudian or Skinnerian to insist that even these searches must derive, in some untraceable way, from the vagaries of psychosexual development or of instrumental-learning experiences. But convincing proof of these extreme assertions has so far not been forthcoming.

We shall, however, go further and contend that even when extrinsic drives most indisputably dominate epistemic behavior, they must be supplemented by other motivational factors related to those which govern intrinsic epistemic behavior. To illustrate what we mean, we may take an example of thinking aimed at the solution of a practical problem. Let us suppose that an explorer on safari in the African jungle finds his path barred by an unfordable stream. One of the most evident advantages of thinking over blind overt trial and error in such situations is that it permits unsuccessful attempts at a solution to be identified without the wasted effort and danger of actually performing them. Often, it is true, the solution that seems workable cannot be accepted with confidence until it has been tried out. But even then, the only courses of action that are put to a practical test are ones that are judged to have a high probability of succeeding.

Many protracted spells of thinking about practical problems are concluded with the celebrated "a-ha experience," which leaves the thinker quite sure that he has found the solution and feeling that he can see exactly why it must be right. The problem is even more acute when the problem is not a matter of gaining some practical end or making an accurate prediction of a future event but a matter of finding an explanation for something that perplexes. Scientific explanations are checked by deducing and verifying some prediction about future events from them. But there are many kinds of explanation, other than the scientific, that are effective in allaying curiosity in our own and other societies, and even when an event is accounted for in terms of known scientific laws, the explanation is in most instances taken as satisfactory without being subjected to a specific empirical test. A mathematical or logical explanation can often be translated into a testable prediction, but more often than not, those with the requisite training judge its adequacy by inspecting it.

To return to the traveler whom we left on the bank of the stream, we suppose that he ponders and, after many false starts, arrives at a train of thought in which he imagines himself ordering his bearers to fell a certain tree, thinks of the tree falling athwart the stream, thinks of himself and his bearers walking along the trunk, and thinks of the whole party setting foot on the opposite bank. At this point he interrupts his thinking, evinces satisfaction, and orders his plan to be put into effect.

The prevalent behavior-theory explanation would describe how each symbolic response representing a step in the solution would evoke the next response, until eventually he came to a representation of the goal situation, namely, reaching the opposite bank of the stream. This last representation, according to this account, would terminate thinking by reducing the drive that motivated it.

But if all that is required is some pleasing symbolic response, why does the explorer not simply imagine himself on the other side of the stream without going through the preliminaries of imagining steps that would, in practice, make it possible to realize this desired state of affairs? If the explorer were an immature and maladjusted person, given to fantasy, he might well react in this way. But he would hardly have reached his present location if this were his wonted reaction to difficulties. Why is the symbolization of a rewarding stimulus situation effective in stopping directed thinking only when a realistic means to it has been discovered?

Theories that rely solely on extrinsic drive are up against a dilemma here. If relief of the drive by external agencies is necessary, such relief will not be forthcoming until thinking has stopped and given way to action. If internal stimuli from symbolic responses can relieve the drive, they should be able to do so in the form of a pipe dream.

The problem is perhaps even clearer when we consider thinking that is aimed at mathematical or logical proofs (see Newell, Shaw, and Simon 1958). A proof consists of a chain of symbolic formulas with the following characteristics:

1. The chain begins with one or more of the axioms of the system.

2. Each formula is constructed in accordance with the laws governing the use of the language of the system.

3. Each formula follows from the last in accordance with the rules of inference of the system.

4. The chain ends with the formula that is to be proved.

It is evident that writing down this last formula after an arduous spell of intellectual toil is highly gratifying and eliminates whatever drive it was that impelled the effort. It is, however, equally evident that the thinker not only can but does repeat to himself the formula that he has to prove many times before the proof has been completed. We must explain therefore why this response has a reward value when it occurs as the final stage of a valid proof that it lacks when performed in other contexts.

THE ROLE OF CONCEPTUAL CONFLICT

We shall contend that conflict among symbolic response tendencies holds the key to these difficulties, that it provides the motivation for intrinsic epistemic behavior, and that it supplements extrinsic motivation when knowledge is sought for practical or social ends. This contention will bring epistemic curiosity and perceptual curiosity close together. The two are already related through the fact that exploratory responses often serve simultaneously to expose receptors to stimuli and to deposit a permanent trace of the same stimuli in the form of knowledge. We are suggesting that the two are related also because the conditions that evoke them, while differing in many important respects, are alike in involving arousal potential.

Several writers who have concerned themselves with the question of what starts human beings thinking have given answers that come quite close to ours.

1. There are, first of all, those who describe thinking as a reaction to a gap. Gestalt psychology has inspired the idea that thinking intervenes when a conceptual configuration has something missing that is needed to give it closure and thus make it stable and "good." Bartlett (1958) speaks of gaps in information. The subject has information about some elements of the situation but lacks information about elements that come between or after them. Thinking fills in these lacunae, by interpolation or extrapolation, in accordance with the nature of the known material.

Descriptions of this kind are very apt in many ways. But they remain to some extent no more than metaphors. We still want to know exactly what constitutes a gap, how a subject recognizes one, and what determines which gaps will have precedence over others in commanding thought.

2. Other writers use terms approximating the concept of frustration. Claparède (1933), for example, says that thinking begins with a question which is the awareness of a "failure of adaptation" (*désadaptation*). He also refers to this condition as a "need" and as a "disturbance of equilibrium."

3. There are writers who have actually used the term "conflict" in senses that, while not identical with that we are adopting, are not too far from it. In Duncker's (1945) monograph on problem solving, we find the idea that conflict not only initiates thinking but guides its course as well. Thinking is said to proceed through a succession of reinterpretations of the problem situation. "Analysis of the situation," writes Duncker, "is . . . primarily analysis of a conflict," i.e., analysis of why a particular proposed solution will not work, of where the trouble arises. Successful thinking identifies and removes the various conflict elements.

Dewey (1910) expounds, with concrete examples, the way in which thinking is launched by conflict. Thinking begins with a "felt difficulty" and proceeds to its "location and definition," but these two stages, in Dewey's words, "often fuse into one conflict between conditions at hand and a desired and intended result, between an end and the means for reaching it. The object of thinking is to introduce a congruity between the two."

He supplies three enlightening examples. In the first, he tells how he was once several miles away from a place in New York where he was due for an appointment ten minutes later. After thinking about alternative means of transportation, he decided that the subway was the one most likely to convey him there in time. In such cases, "the problem is the discovery of intervening terms which, inserted between the remote end and the given means, will harmonize them with each other." In the second example, he observed something that looked like a flagpole on the bow of a boat and yet could not have that function. His thinking led him to conclude that it must be a device for helping a pilot to see the direction in which the boat was traveling. This kind of problem involves an "incompatibility of a suggested and (temporarily) accepted belief with certain other facts." Finally he cites the puzzlement with which he noticed that bubbles enter tumblers when they are being dried. It was allayed when he realized that the air inside a tumbler that has just been rinsed in hot water must be warmer than the air outside and hence have a lower pressure. In this kind of situation, "an observer trained to the idea of natural laws or uniformities finds something odd or exceptional" in the behavior of some natural phenomenon, and "the problem is to reduce the apparent anomaly to instances of well-established laws." It is a matter of finding "intermediate terms which will connect seemingly extraordinary movements with the conditions known to follow from processes supposed to be operative."

INDIVIDUAL DIFFERENCES

In conclusion, we must note some relevant findings that relate to individual differences:

Cattell's (1957) factor analyses of human motives have repeatedly turned up an "erg" or drive, varying in prevailing strength from one individual to another, that he calls *exploration* (*curiosity*). It is represented in desires to read books, newspapers, and magazines, to listen to music, to know more about science, to satisfy curiosity about everything going on in one's neighborhood, to see more paintings and sculpture, to learn more about mechanical and electrical gadgets, to see a good film or play, all of which are measured by a variety of indirect, objective techniques. It also has significant positive correlations with the personality traits of premsia (protected emotional sensitivity, unrealistic tender-mindedness) and radicalism (Cattell and Baggaley 1958). The factor seems clearly to be concerned with epistemic behavior in particular, but its composition points to a motivational affinity, in keeping with our suppositions, between epistemic behavior, aesthetic behavior, and diversive exploratory behavior.

In pursuing the factors that underlie ability to think creatively, Guilford (1956) and his collaborators have identified a dimension of *sensitivity to problems*. An individual's endowment with this factor can be measured by means of the Seeing Problems test (in which he is asked to list problems raised by a common object such as a candle) and the Seeing Deficiencies test (in which he is introduced to a series of general plans for solving particular problems and has to state what new problems are raised by each plan). The dependence of epistemic behavior on responsiveness to discrepancies and lacunae seems here to be borne out, especially by the role of the latter test.

Chapter 11

TOWARD A THEORY OF EPISTEMIC
BEHAVIOR: CONCEPTUAL CONFLICT
AND EPISTEMIC CURIOSITY

Experimental studies of conflict between overt responses are difficult enough to conduct and have been scanty, considering the importance of the topic. To extend the notion of conflict to implicit responses thus amounts to quite a bold scouting expedition. It is not
unreasonable, however, to suppose that there can be incompatibilities
between symbolic responses and that the conflict engendered by them,
which we shall call *conceptual conflict*, may affect the central nervous
system in much the same way as other forms of conflict.

Among a number of recent writers who have recognized something
like our conceptual conflict (e.g., Heider 1946, Osgood and Tannenbaum 1955, Cartwright and Harary 1956), Festinger (1957) and Abelson (Abelson and Rosenberg 1958, Abelson 1958) have come closest
to our concept, while concentrating on different aspects of the phenomenon.

Festinger's "dissonance" is a relation that can obtain between two
"cognitive elements" (beliefs, evaluations, perceptions) or between a
cognitive element and an overt action that the subject either is con-
templating or has already executed. He actually subsumes the second
case under the first by referring to the cognitive element corresponding
to the action (i.e., the memory or the thought of performing it). Most
of his discussion is, however, devoted to the second case. He also deals
preponderantly with dissonances between evaluations rather than between factual beliefs. Dissonance is defined in terms of logical contradiction ("p implies not-q"), but, taken strictly, this definition does not
fit many of the instances that are analyzed. The statement "Car A is
superior to car B," and the statement "I have bought car B," are certainly not contradictory in the usual sense that they cannot both be
true. It seems better to invoke the more general notion of conflict.

When dissonance is present, there is held to be a drive toward its
reduction, with a strength depending on the importance of the areas

between which the clash occurs and the proportion (suitably weighted) of all relations between these areas that happen to be dissonant.

Dissonance can be reduced in a variety of ways, e.g., by changing evaluations of conflicting elements, by reducing the importance attached to them, by propagating rumors to justify hard-pressed beliefs or evaluations, or by seeking social support from other persons who share them. Most interesting of all, in view of our current interest in stimulus selection, is Festinger's prediction that dissonance will help to determine what stimuli are sought out, favoring pursuit of those which are likely to moderate dissonance and avoidance of those which are apt to aggravate it. In harmony with this prediction, it was found that motorists tend to expose themselves to advertisements that commend the make of car that they have bought rather than to advertisements extolling the virtues of other makes that they might have chosen. There are, however, other hypotheses that might explain such phenomena differently.

Abelson's theory of "cognitive imbalance" is even more frankly focused on discrepancies among evaluations rather than factual beliefs. Cognitive elements can be valued positively, negatively, or neutrally, and between any two of these elements there can be an associative relation (expressed by words like "is," "has," "includes," "likes," "helps," "produces," "implies") or a dissociative relation (expressed by words like "avoids," "hates," "hinders," "defeats," "destroys," "is incompatible with"). Imbalance is said to exist when two positively or two negatively valued elements are dissociatively linked or when a positively valued and a negatively valued element are associatively linked, and there is assumed to be a "pressure toward the attainment of cognitive balance."

Imbalance can be reduced by reorganizing attitudes and belief in any of the following four ways:

1. *Denial.* The evaluation of one of the elements involved is changed. For example, a man who would like both to be slim and to eat rich foods, but realizes that it is impossible to satisfy both likes, professes that he never liked rich foods anyway.

2. *Bolstering.* One of the elements is linked with other ideas that are associated with strong attitudes and with whose assistance the opposing belief or evaluation can be outweighed. For example, the smoker who is worried about lung cancer decides that smoking is a bad habit and costs too much money.

3. *Differentiation.* A distinction is made within one of the conflicting elements, such that some aspect of it is valued positively and the other negatively. For example, a tendency to believe in the truth of the Bible and a tendency to believe in the theory of evolution are

284

reconciled by differentiating literal truth and figurative truth and attributing only the latter to the Bible.

4. *Transcendence.* The conflicting elements are combined into some larger unit which is collectively viewed with favor or disfavor. For example, a partiality for both science and religion, perceived as leading in opposing directions, may give rise to the feeling that a well-rounded life requires the cultivation of both.

Our own concern with conceptual conflict leads us in different directions from those pursued by Festinger and Abelson. We are interested primarily in conflicts arising out of the denotative content rather than the affective tone of beliefs or thoughts and also in the relations between such conflicts and the pursuit of knowledge.

Nevertheless, there is much in common between these conceptions, despite their divergent emphases. The ways in which dissonance or imbalance can be removed, according to these other authors, parallel the ways in which the acquisition of knowledge can relieve conflict, as we shall see. Furthermore, all these theories are alike in recognizing that the beliefs, attitudes, and other symbolic processes of an individual do not exist in isolation but interact, that there can be discrepancies between them that the individual is motivated to remedy.

This is one respect in which the human nervous system differs from the electronic computer, with which it is so often compared. The computer is apt to come to a halt as soon as any obstacle is placed in the way of its functioning, e.g., when it is given some instruction that it cannot execute or when the information that is necessary for a particular operation is lacking. The human nervous system does not accept such situations passively. On the other hand, computers may one day be programed to react constructively to conflicts between instructions or deficiencies in information. They will then be able to raise and solve problems of their own formulation and exercise control over the information that they take in.

VARIETIES OF CONCEPTUAL CONFLICT

Conceptual conflict can presumably result, like other forms of conflict, from innate antagonism, learned antagonism, or occlusion. In so far as symbolic representations embody evaluations—characterizations of things as good or bad, pleasant or unpleasant—they may well involve autonomic processes, glandular processes, or processes in the limbic system of the lower brain. If an individual is subjected simultaneously to conditions that lead him to evaluate the same entity both favorably and unfavorably, physiological processes that are innately antagonistic may be aroused at once.

285

When muscular activities are represented in thought, weak action currents are detectable in the muscles that these activities would bring into play. It is thus possible, here again, that there would be some physiological incompatibility when activities that would mean contraction and relaxation of the same muscles are called to mind at once.

The possibilities for occlusion that arise from the ramification of associations are impossible to overlook. Whether it is practicable to think two thoughts at once is a question that is inherently difficult to settle. But let us suppose that each thought is, on the average, associated with n other thoughts, and let us even suppose that n thoughts could be entertained simultaneously. Each of these n thoughts would then arouse n other thoughts in the next unit of time, producing a total of n^2, then n^3, and so on. The limits of channel capacity, however capacious, must rapidly be overstepped.

Most conceptual conflict will, however, fall clearly into the learned-antagonism class. Training in the use of language, in the facts of external nature, and in the techniques of thinking will have made the subject averse to, or incapable of, fusing certain elements into one symbolic unit. He will have learned that the various stimulus properties that populate the universe and form the substance of his own thoughts are not independent of one another. Some occur together more often and some less often. Some are invariably found in juxtaposition and some never. There may thus arise an acquired mutual inhibitory relation between the concepts, or their combination may become drive inducing. Some of the major types of conceptual conflict that can come about in this way may be enumerated as follows, without maintaining that the list is complete or that the boundaries between them are sharp.

Doubt. There is, first of all, the conflict between tendencies to believe and to disbelieve the same statement. Doubt will presumably create maximum conflict when the tendencies to believe and to disbelieve are equal in strength, and when maximally strong but incompatible overt responses are associated with them. The agonies of Othello illustrate the point admirably.

We class doubt provisionally as learned antagonism. It is, however, entirely possible that it involves some kind of excitatory and inhibitory neural processes with an innate physiological opposition between them.

Perplexity. When there are factors inclining the subject toward each of a number of mutually exclusive beliefs, e.g., when there is some evidence favoring each of them but no way of knowing for certain which is true, we have the second type of conceptual conflict. This is the kind of situation for which the information-theory measure of uncertainty was originally designed and to which it can be most naturally applied. Perplexity must encompass doubt, since there will be factors simultaneously supporting and inhibiting each of the alternative beliefs when it is contemplated separately.

Contradiction. It was long believed among philosophers that the ability to recognize logical contradictions is inborn and one of the peculiar glories of the human mind. This view is now much less prevalent for several reasons: the demonstration by logicians and mathematicians that what is and is not a contradiction varies with the axiom system that is under consideration, the studies of developmental psychologists like Piaget who show that the logical capacities necessary for avoidance of contradiction are acquired gradually, and, finally, a mass of experimental and anecdotal evidence that few adults are infallibly immune to illogicality. It seems reasonable, therefore, to suppose that human beings eschew fallacious thinking, in so far as they do so, as a result of learning, because the overt expression of thinking that violates the laws of thought leads to disapproval and ridicule from parents, teachers, and peers, or otherwise that illicit deduction comes to be associated with sad disappointments in the course of attempts to predict and control events. Either way, symbolic sequences that make for contradiction will come to arouse a drive, provided that the contradiction is recognized as such.

Conceptual Incongruity. The fourth type of conceptual conflict occurs when a subject has learned to believe that property A is unlikely to be found together with property B, and yet sources of knowledge indicate that a certain object or event has both A and B. Earlier chapters have dealt with perceptual incongruity, which occurs when properties regarded as incompatible are perceived together. In that case, the conflict is between the perceptual responses evoked through stimulation of receptors and those evoked centrally through redintegration. Conceptual incongruity, on the other hand, arises out of learned conflict between symbolic responses. Perceptual incongruity would occur when a person who expects all swans to be white first sees a black swan. Conceptual incongruity would occur when a person who has hitherto believed that all swans are white hears, reads, or deduces that black swans exist.

Confusion. Stimulus patterns that are ambiguous or can be confused with one another may give rise to conflicting symbolic responses in much the same way as they arouse conflicting identifying or overt responses. When we first see a hybrid animal like the tigon, the stimulus pattern is sufficiently similar to those produced by a lion and a tiger to evoke responses corresponding to both and yet not so much nearer the one than the other that one set of responses will predominate.

An experience of this kind might leave one wondering which the animal could have been. But conceptual and perceptual ambiguity or confusion is probably most frequently a product of symbolic stimuli—drawings, letters of the alphabet, verbal descriptions—either because the person creating them has not succeeded in conveying his intent unequivocally or because the symbolic pattern undergoes distortion between leaving him and impinging on the recipient's receptors. In information-theory language, there is apt to be noise at several points along the channel.

Irrelevance. This is by far the hardest kind of learned conceptual conflict to define, let alone to explain. But there is no doubt about the strength of the learned aversive quality that it can have. In any form of psychotherapy that uses free association, the patient invariably takes a few days to accustom himself to flitting inconsequentially from topic to topic and, in fact, rarely succeeds in doing so to more than a minor extent. His previous training to speak and think coherently provokes resistance long before his free association has led him to touch on anything delicate or anxiety-laden.

The learning process involved may be partly the same as that responsible for the clustering of words belonging to a common category in recall: we learn to connect thoughts with certain supraordinate concepts or topics, and there is a disinclination to entertain ideas on a different topic until all available ideas pertaining to the topic of the moment have been exhausted. It may be partly a matter of learning to distinguish the ways in which thoughts conducive to successful thinking are related to the problem on hand. Finally, we are all so thoroughly taught to follow threads in other people's conversation that severe frustration and arousal are apt to result when efforts to connect one utterance with the last meet with difficulty. Generalization or punishment will explain why similar discomfort supervenes when our own utterances or thoughts are not linked together perspicuously.

In information-theory terms, doubt and ambiguity are states of high uncertainty, since the subject is faced with a number of alternative states of affairs leading to different expectations with regard to future events, and he must treat them as more or less equally probable. Conceptual incongruity means a state of affairs with a low initial probability and thus a high information content, while contradiction means a state with a probability of zero and bearing an infinite amount of information (see Bar Hillel and Carnap 1953). Irrelevant thoughts correspond to signals that are statistically independent of important events and consequently bear no information about them, leaving high uncertainty undiminished. So in all cases, we have the makings of intense arousal.

We have noted how both cue stimuli and motivational or drive-inducing stimuli are required both to propel a quest for knowledge and to control its course. It is plain that some pattern including stimuli of both sorts will be needed to set the quest in motion in the first place.

The clearest example of such a pattern is a question. Some quests for knowledge start out with an explicit question, either put to the subject by another person or formulated to himself as a consequence of his own thoughts or observations. But this does not always seem to be the case. There are even instances of diversive epistemic curiosity, when somebody is eager to learn something new without much caring what. All specific epistemic behavior must, however, be launched by the equivalent of a question.

In the grammatical structure of a question, the cue and motivational components are fairly distinct. The yes-or-no question, e.g., "Has the train for London left yet?" contains a reference to an event which serves as a cue, confining associations to a narrowly restricted section of the individual's repertoire. The interrogative word order supplies the motivation, indicating that conflict between expectations of affirmation and denial exists in the questioner. In the kind of question that begins with an interrogative adverb, e.g., "When does the next train for London leave?" there is a similar cue element, but the interrogative adverb provides a motivating perplexity conflict; it implies an information space, with some attendant uncertainty in the questioner. He must know the kinds of answers that are given to questions beginning with "when," especially to questions about the times of trains. He may even be able to assign probabilities to the various times that the train might depart, making it possible to work out a measure of his uncertainty.

There is ample testimony in everyday life to the power with which questions can impel the delivery of an answer if known, or a search for an answer otherwise. The gruffest and surliest of crosspatches finds it hard to ignore a direct question to the point of saying nothing at all. Persistent interrogation, even without accompanying physical and psychological pressures, has led many a criminal to make revelations very much opposed to his interests. The skillful lecturer or writer excites curiosity and an eagerness to remain with him by putting questions which have never occurred to his listeners or readers. Celebrated thinkers have not infrequently been stimulated to a lifetime's inquiry through thinking of questions about matters that ordinary men take for granted.

Once the quest for an answer has begun, the uncertainty and conflict implicit in the question will inevitably be augmented by conceptual conflicts of other kinds:

1. The question itself may embody conceptual incongruity. For example, "What crops do some ants cultivate in underground farms?" is especially likely to stimulate curiosity in a person who has never heard of fungus-growing ant colonies, since it embodies the assertion, contrary to his prior beliefs, that insects can engage in agriculture.

2. In a subject who is versed in entomology, any utterance that juxtaposes "ants" with "farms" will, through patterning, evoke associations peculiar to fungus-growing ants. In one who is not, there will be no associations peculiar to the combination. But, knowing how difficult it is to keep the mind blank, we shall expect some thoughts to emerge. The thoughts that are most likely to come up are those which are associated with the separate elements. The word "ants" will give rise to thoughts about small, black, busy insects and the word "farming" to thoughts of life in human rural communities. The two trains of thought will not fit in with each other, and the resultant associations will not help in the discovery of an answer to the question, so that irrelevance conflict will grow. We may, in fact, advance the hypothesis that the arousal value of situations where a subject is completely baffled by a problem comes partly from frustration and partly from the fact that, in default of others, irrelevant thoughts obtrude themselves.

3. After a period of thought or other epistemic behavior, the subject may light upon a number of possible answers. But as long as they all seem worth considering and there is no cause for preferring one to the others, there will be perplexity conflict.

4. Finally, one answer may be singled out as the most plausible one. But if the subject has no way of being sure that it is correct, there will be doubt conflict.

Thus conflict from a variety of sources will be present to keep epistemic curiosity alive, to keep the epistemic process moving, and to determine in what direction it will turn at each choice point.

THE REDUCTION OF CONFLICT BY THE
ACQUISITION OF KNOWLEDGE

Incompatible beliefs, like incompatible habits generally, can lie dormant in the nervous system without generating any disturbance or impelling any change in the network of knowledge. Conceptual conflict and its attendant disequilibrium will not emerge until some external stimulus pattern, verbal or nonverbal, or some thought process causes incompatible symbolic responses to be aroused in combination.

There are, of course, plenty of learned responses that are capable of alleviating conceptual conflict besides those that augment knowledge. Stimulus patterns that may not square with the subject's established beliefs, or thoughts that may detonate their latent inconsistencies, can often simply be avoided. Psychoanalytic writers (e.g., Freud 1913, Abraham 1921) have vividly described the sort of person who goes about in terror of knowing and understanding, who enjoys mysteries and decries anything that might possibly foist clarity or certainty onto him.

How likely an individual is to behave in these ways will depend on his personality and on how unsuccessful he has previously been in disposing of puzzles by facing them. The policy of safeguarding beliefs by shielding them from possible jolts is, however, apt to postpone trouble rather than eliminate it, which must militate against recourse to it.

Beliefs may likewise change passively, especially in their evaluative aspects, under the pressure of conceptual conflict, in much the same way as they can be tugged out of shape by the forces that make for rationalization and wishful thinking. Changes of this sort are among the processes discussed by Festinger and Abelson. But the forms that beliefs assume in this manner will reflect the interplay of internal stresses and strains more than they will correspond to external reality. The replacement of one belief by another that is less troublesome will aggravate rather than lessen conflict in a person of adequate psychological health, intelligence, and intellectual training, unless it is sanctioned by logical thinking or new external evidence.

A new belief that assuages conflict may be fostered by external stimuli that impinge on the subject through no effort of his own. As many social-psychological studies (e.g., Cantril 1941, Allport and Postman 1947) have graphically depicted, periods of political and social upheaval are apt to bring with them a barrage of unprecedented experiences that unseat established expectations and beliefs. In such circumstances, human beings are extraordinarily suggestible and liable to be taken in by propaganda, to espouse any fanatical social movement that forces itself on their attention, or to accept and spread rumors, provided only that they can derive from these sources the explanations and predictions that their prior beliefs are at a loss to supply.

The conception of knowledge that we have outlined obliges us to consider all these processes as ways in which knowledge can be modified. Some would refuse to regard any but a true belief as an item of knowledge. But this is essentially an extrapsychological criterion; to use the subdivisions of *semiotic* (the science of signs and symbols) proposed by Morris (1938, 1946), this is a matter of *semantics* (the study of the relations between signs and what they stand for), whereas the psychology of symbolic processes is directly concerned only with *pragmatics* (the study of the relations between signs and the organisms that use them). Whether a belief is true or not may well affect the domain of psychology in the long run, since it determines the likelihood that a subject will encounter stimulus situations that run counter to his beliefs. Apart from this consideration, however, and with regard to events outside the present stimulus field, a false belief must affect behavior in exactly the same way as a valid one.

But even if they are classifiable as changes in knowledge, the mechanisms that we have just been reviewing do not count as epistemic behavior as long as the stimuli that generate the new belief are independent of what the subject himself does. Epistemic responses bring about knowledge-furnishing stimulus patterns that would not have been available without them.

Whatever the means by which conceptual conflict is reduced—whether it be through knowledge accruing as a consequence of epistemic behavior, through knowledge acquired independently of epistemic behavior, or through any other of the mechanisms that we have mentioned—there would seem to be only three ways in which the reduction in conflict can be effected, namely, by making the competing response tendencies less incompatible, by introducing a new response tendency that is stronger than those which are in competition, or by strengthening or weakening one or more of the competing response tendencies and thus rendering the conflict unequal. We shall refer to these three ways as *conciliation, swamping,* and *disequalization.*

Conciliation

Since the incompatibilities that make for acquired-antagonism conflict are products of learning, other learning should be able to undo them. Inhibitory bonds can be disinhibited, and acquired drive-inducing power can be removed.

To make the incompatible compatible is evidently the principal function of knowledge of the strange and wonderful, whether of the useless kind found in the odd-facts features of magazines or of the kind that can herald undreamed-of practical gains. It is discovered that, after all, black swans exist, that there are ants that cultivate crops, that

292

somebody once wrote a full-length novel without using the letter *e* even once, that there is a mule receiving a pension from the Italian government, or that yaws can be cured by the injections that the white man administers.

Such knowledge is welcomed with eagerness, presumably because high arousal is induced when anything suggestive of a bizarre or astonishing fact is first encountered, and the arousal is diminished by exposure to evidence that convinces of its truth. The process thus follows the pattern of the arousal jag.

Swamping

In the second case, the subject acquires a new response tendency that is much stronger than the conflicting tendencies and is thus able to dominate them. In this way uncertainty $\left(-\sum_i p_i \log_2 p_i\right)$ will be cut down to a subthreshold quantity, since we end up with one very strong, and two or more very weak, response tendencies, and conflict will be eliminated.

This process is especially likely when a subject is faced with novel combinations of concepts or with irrelevances. Irrelevant responses are almost bound to be fairly feeble. So when a new response that is associated with the combination as such or that is otherwise relevant to the problem is hit upon, it will readily preponderate over them.

It may be best to take a specific example. If a person with no special knowledge of marine biology is asked, or asks himself, "How does the starfish eat?" he will have no associations available that are peculiar to the thought of a starfish eating. The most likely responses are thus going to be those associated with eating, and those associated with the starfish. "Eating" will predominantly evoke thoughts about vertebrates inserting edible objects into holes in their faces, and this will be recognized as inapplicable to the starfish, which does not appear to have a face. "Starfish" will evoke thoughts derived from memories of pictures of starfishes, which are usually of the dorsal surface and so include no feature that seems pertinent to eating. The subject may even find himself completely at a loss and allow his fancy to wander farther and farther from any line of thought that could lead to a solution. When, however, he has ascertained that the starfish has an aperture on its ventral surface and that its stomach emerges through this aperture to envelop prey, he has some strong associations that will in future be called up by the unified concept of an eating starfish and will exclude the less apposite thoughts that would have occurred earlier in the same context.

The emergence of a new prepotent line of association may

293

mitigate not only conflicts due to irrelevance but also conflicts due to contradiction or occlusion. Swamping by a new response sequence will, of course, be most easily established when the other, conflicting responses have yielded to some degree of extinction through failure to bring a solution nearer.

Disequalization

Conceptual conflicts, like other conflicts, can be reduced by increasing the difference in strength between competing response tendencies, i.e., strengthening one, weakening the other, or both. In other words, one of the contestants is made to win the competition or, at least, to have the upper hand. Situations where perplexity conflicts are attenuated by eliminating some of the alternatives are cases in point. Disequalization is, no doubt, the commonest way in which conceptual conflicts are allayed by the absorption of new knowledge. There is usually some measure of perplexity commingled with conflicts of the other types.

More often than not, a fact of which one becomes newly aware is one that could have been specified as a possibility beforehand. A sophisticated human adult probably meets few problems in his everyday life for which he cannot supply guesses at a solution. To acquire knowledge and to feel the lack of knowledge, one must generally have some knowledge to begin with. Only the expert in a field can tell where information is lacking and use observations or verbal formulas which would mean nothing to the uninitiated to fill in the gaps.

Information, in the technical sense, cannot be received without having an information space already set up; the signal that appears must belong to one of a number of alternative classes that might have appeared, and it must have a probability allotted to it. But one must already be in possession of information before one can establish an information space, since the space must itself be selected from a set of alternative information spaces.

So knowledge relieves uncertainty by strengthening one expectation at the expense of the others and relieves doubt by confirming or discounting the belief in question.

Herein may lie the answer to the problem about the explorer that we raised in the last chapter. It is true that the explorer can immediately picture himself on the other side of the stream, as the logician or mathematician can, from the start, repeat to himself the expression that is to be proved. But these thoughts cannot be entertained with conviction, i.e., the corresponding symbolic responses are overlaid with conflict-inducing inhibition, unless they can be preceded by the discovery of a valid solution. Only when the explorer has conceived of a chain of events that would in fact place him and his party beyond the stream, or the logician has worked out a valid proof, can the representation of the desired result be released from inhibition and conflict eliminated.

Confusion may be resolved similarly. Knowledge about hidden properties of an object may make clear to which class it should be assigned and which symbolic label should be attached to it to govern secondary generalization and discrimination. Knowledge of measurements that cannot be estimated at a glance may show where an entity should be placed in an ordering (Berlyne 1960).

Disequalization can plainly be achieved by other means than the acquisition of knowledge, some of which are analyzed by Abelson and by Festinger, e.g., denial, bolstering, obtaining social support for beliefs that are held with some misgiving, seeking out stimulus situations that are likely to reinforce such beliefs and keeping away from those that might implant doubt.

EXPERIMENTAL EVIDENCE

Conceptual Conflict and Indexes of Arousal

As we saw in Chapter 7, there is evidence that indexes of arousal, like alpha-wave blocking and the GSR, are especially marked when subjects meet with experiences that are surprising or hard to understand. It is usually impossible to say how far conflict between symbolic responses may be behind this reaction and how far it is due to the interplay of other, more immediate and primitive, responses.

Conflict among symbolic responses can be identified with more confidence as the responsible agent when manifestations of high arousal accompany intellectual effort. Setting subjects intellectual tasks, such as problems in mental arithmetic, produces GSR (Sears 1933), the breakup of alpha activity (Berger 1930), and increased muscular tension (Courts 1942). Wechsler (1925) said that the GSR is most prominent when an arithmetical problem is first attacked and subsides during later stages of calculation. Toman (1943) likewise claimed that alpha blocking marks only the presentation of a problem and not the actual problem-solving work. Other workers have not corroborated this claim (see Ellingson 1956), but it would fit in with our hypotheses, since conflict should be most acute when the initial impact of a problem arouses perplexities and divergent lines of attack. It should be quite mild when a clear-cut computing procedure has been selected and is being put into effect.

There have been two experiments in which the degree of conceptual

295

conflict has been manipulated. In one of them, Cooper and Siegel (1956) asked students to indicate their attitudes to each of twenty social groups with the help of a rating scale ranging from "like intensely" to "dislike intensely." Each of them then heard three statements expressing favorable evaluations of groups that fell near the middle of his order of preference and a fourth statement praising the group that ranked lowest in his esteem. This fourth statement, which will, of course, have been most incompatible with the subject's own beliefs, produced significantly greater GSRs than the other three.

The second of these experiments was performed by Berlyne (unpublished). Thirty-two adjective-noun pairs were selected from a list, kindly supplied by Dr. J. T. Jenkins, in such a way that half of the pairs (e.g., "devilish butter," "beautiful abortion") had components that were far apart in Osgood's "semantic space," i.e., they produced highly divergent responses on the semantic-differential test of meaning (Osgood, Suci, and Tannenbaum 1957). The other half (e.g., "green butter," "beautiful lady") had components that were close together, i.e., they produced highly similar semantic-differential responses. Each subject was given eight high-distance and eight low-distance pairs in a random order. He was instructed to treat each pair as a unified concept and carry out the semantic-differential test on it.

It was found that subjects took slightly but significantly longer to complete the ratings for the high-distance pairs. We can presume that the adjective and the noun in high-distance pairs induced conflict by inclining each rating response in discrepant directions, and, as we have noted before, a lengthening of reaction time is known to result from other types of conflict. At the end of the experiment, each pair was presented to a subject who had not had it in his list during the earlier phase, and he was asked to estimate how likely it was that the adjective would apply to the noun, e.g., how likely, in some sense, butter is to be green or an abortion to be beautiful. The likelihoods were rated significantly lower for high-distance pairs, verifying that their components were related in a way that should make for conceptual conflict of the incongruity type.

Conceptual Conflict and Intrinsic Epistemic Curiosity

An endeavor to explore some relations between conceptual conflict and epistemic curiosity was made in another experimental project by Berlyne (1953, 1954b, 1954c). The first objective was to verify that curiosity can be intensified simply by putting questions to subjects. There was an experimental group that received (1) a prequestionnaire of forty-eight questions about invertebrate animals, each followed by two alternative answers between which a choice had to be made, (2) a list of seventy-two statements about invertebrate animals, including answers to all the questions in the prequestionnaire, and (3) a postquestionnaire consisting of the questions of the prequestionnaire in a re-randomized order but without the answers, so that answers had to be supplied by the subjects. A control group underwent exactly the same procedure except that the prequestionnaire was omitted.

The outcome was that the experimental group supplied a mean of 32.4 correct answers in the postquestionnaire, as compared with 27.2 for the control group. The difference was significant and was taken as evidence that questions heighten epistemic curiosity, facilitating the retention of facts that answer the questions when they are subsequently encountered.

The exact mechanism by which this takes place is impossible to specify with present knowledge. The recognition of the answer may cause the question to be recalled, rearousing the curiosity, the curiosity may be revived in some other manner, or it may persist in some form between the putting of the question and the receipt of the answer. Be that as it may, the rehearsal of the answer by the subject will reduce the curiosity to a subthreshold value, furnishing reinforcement for the learning process. The higher the initial level of curiosity, the greater the curiosity reduction and thus the more effective the learning is likely to be.

There was evidence that questions intensify, not only specific curiosity directed at their answers, but more general curiosity about their topic. At the end of the experiment, subjects were asked to indicate which of the twelve animals that had figured in the questions they would like to know more about. The experimental group, which, it will be remembered, differed only in having had the prequestionnaire, marked off significantly more animals than the control group (a mean of 5.4 as compared with 3.4).

The next objective was to ascertain which classes of questions aroused more curiosity than others. This was done in two ways. The proportions of correct answers retained by the experimental group were compared for different classes, and the subjects were also required to mark the three questions out of each consecutive set of twelve in the prequestionnaire whose answers they would most like to know. These two measures of curiosity, which we shall call the *retention test* and the *marking test* respectively, turned out to have a highly significant measure of agreement.

The disturbing effects of previous knowledge were controlled for by two expedients. First, subjects in the experimental group were told to indicate which questions they felt they could answer with certainty;

these questions were then omitted from consideration. The data for the control group were likewise adjusted on the assumption that they would, on the average, have known the same numbers of answers. Secondly, half of the answers provided in the list of statements were untrue, the subjects being dehoaxed afterwards, so that previous knowledge would hinder retention as often as it would help.

Predictions concerning the effects on curiosity of two of the determinants of degree of conflict (C), namely the number of competing response tendencies and their degree of incompatibility, were supported.

Number. If questions give rise to divergent and conflicting trains of thought, the concepts figuring in the question must have associations already attached to them, i.e., they must be familiar to the subject. Starting from this assumption, it was hypothesized that questions about animals that subjects had heard of would arouse more curiosity than those about unfamiliar animals. This hypothesis was examined by presenting subjects of both groups with a list of the twelve animals that would figure in the experiment, before it began, and having them rate them for familiarity. Questions about more familiar animals aroused significantly more curiosity according to both tests. The control group showed a tendency to recall statements about more familiar animals more readily, but statistical analysis confirmed that there was a curiosity-increasing effect of questions about more familiar animals over and above this tendency.

The number-of-competing-response-tendencies variable received a more direct test in an earlier experiment that used the same general procedure. There the retention test showed multiple-choice questions with four alternatives to arouse more curiosity than ones with two alternatives.

Degree of Incompatibility. During the prequestionnaire, experimental-group subjects were instructed to indicate which questions surprised them, and the marking test showed subjects to be more desirous of knowing the answers to these than to other questions.

A further test was made by calling on a group of thirty judges, taken from the same population as the subjects. They received a list of eight of the animals figuring in the experiment (two fictitious and two highly unfamiliar animals were omitted). Opposite the name of each animal were four phrases, representing the predicates implied by the four questions about each animal in the questionnaire. The judges had to mark off the two phrases that seemed least likely of the four to fit the animal concerned. The marking test revealed that the two questions per animal incorporating the predicates that the

298

judges deemed least applicable were more curiosity-arousing than the others.

Conceptual Conflict and Extrinsic Epistemic Curiosity

An experiment by Irwin and Smith (1957) is highly instructive with respect to the part that conceptual conflict plays when knowledge is sought for the sake of some extraneous reward. They used packs of cards, each bearing a positive or a negative number. Subjects were allowed to see as many cards as they wished, but a small charge ($\frac{1}{2}$ cent in some cases and 1 cent in others) was made for each card that they saw. After seeing as many or as few cards as they chose, they were to conclude the session by guessing whether the mean of the numbers in the whole pack was positive or negative. A prize, amounting to 50 cents for some and $1 for others, was received if the guess was correct.

At each point in the experiment, therefore, subjects had to decide between seeing one more card, which meant a gain in information but a slight monetary loss, or venturing a guess about the mean and thus securing or forfeiting the prize. The motivation to see a card can be classified as epistemic curiosity, since the resulting stimulus pattern was clearly sought neither for its own sake nor, in most cases, for the guidance of some immediate response. The information the card bore was generally stored in the form of a modification of internal symbolic representations which determined overt behavior, i.e., a guess, after quite a lapse of time.

The response of looking at a card was obviously actuated by the perplexity conflict between guessing "positive" and guessing "negative." When a guess had been formulated, there was also conflict between the tendency to voice it, motivated by hope of winning the prize, and the tendency to withhold it, motivated by fear of losing. The additional conflict, between asking for another card and stating a guess, was not one that could be resolved by acquiring more knowledge.

The only way to reduce the first two conflicts would be to see all the cards, and subjects would undoubtedly have waited to see them all, were it not for the cost imposed. It is only to be expected, therefore, that more cards would be looked at when the cost was $\frac{1}{2}$ cent than when it was 1 cent, and this was indeed found.

But, if the cost is held constant, the number of cards looked at tells us how much information it took to reduce epistemic curiosity to the point where it could no longer outweigh the reluctance to pay. Since degree of conflict depends on the absolute strength of compet-

299

ing response tendencies, the prospect of a $1 prize should induce a more intense desire to win and a more intense fear of losing than a 50-cent prize, which means a higher level of initial conflict and curiosity. It is not surprising, therefore, that the higher prize led subjects to look at significantly more cards.

The rate at which perplexity is relieved by disequalization would vary inversely with the absolute value of the mean (its distance from zero) and the standard deviation of the numbers on the cards. And more cards were, in fact, seen when the mean was (plus or minus) 0.5 than when it was (plus or minus) 1.5 and when the standard deviation was 7.5 than when it was 2.0.

Irwin and Smith also arranged for their subjects to rate the confidence with which they made their guesses. This is of particular interest to us because of the likelihood that a rating of confidence reflects the degree of doubt conflict. Subjects who paid $\frac{1}{2}$ cent per card recorded more confidence than those who paid 1 cent; they could afford to pay for enough information to reduce their doubt and curiosity to a lower level before committing themselves to a guess. It is even more instructive that confidence was greater when the mean was farther from zero and when the standard deviation had the lower value, which means when the numbers borne by the cards were able to diminish uncertainty more effectively.

Other pertinent data are yielded by a somewhat similar experiment carried out by Becker (1958). The epistemic response consisted of pressing a switch, which caused one or the other of two counters to advance a unit. Subjects were provided with descriptions of two to five populations, from one of which, they were told, the items of information (i.e., the movements of the counters) were selected. The populations differed in the proportions of left-counter and right-counter items that they contained.

After pressing the switch as many times as they wished, the subjects were to guess which population the items actually came from. They were put through a series of such problems and were given to understand that their chances of winning a monetary bonus depended on the ratio that the excess of correct over incorrect guesses bore to the number of items of information drawn.

More epistemic responses were performed when the problem was a hard one, requiring discrimination between a population with 3,000 left-counter items and 3,000 right-counter items and a 4,000/ 2,000 population, than with an easy problem, involving discrimination between a 3,000/3,000 and a 1,000/5,000 population. Furthermore, the number of epistemic responses increased with the number of alternative populations to be considered. These are conditions in which, respectively, the opposing guessing responses would be more nearly equal in strength and more numerous, and thus conflict would be more intense.

Both experiments thus corroborate our supposition that collative variables will not only govern intrinsic epistemic behavior but even contribute to the motivation of extrinsic epistemic behavior.

CONCLUSIONS

The study of exploratory behavior, as we have already seen, forces on our consideration a whole spate of basic theoretical questions relating to motivation and learning in general. Epistemic behavior, forming an even more uncharted region, must likewise raise wider issues and, in particular, make us conscious of the deplorable neglect from which the motivational aspects of intellectual activity have suffered.

Some reconsideration of the motivations and reinforcements affecting symbolic learning is demanded, to cite an illustrative experiment, by Porter's (1957) finding that the learning of a verbal response is not facilitated when it is immediately followed by cessation of an electric shock. Pain reduction is, of course, known to be quite a powerful reinforcing agent for nonverbal responses in human beings and animals. And many motivational conditions, e.g., monetary rewards and social approval, are capable of affecting verbal learning (see Young 1936). But the corresponding motivational states must work through symbolic representations, which means that such factors as uncertainty and conceptual conflict might play their part.

In case we may seem to be hankering unnecessarily after new problems, we may cite some recent conclusions of Piaget (1957), inspired by long investigation of intellectual development in children. Intellectual development embraces a number of attainments, amounting to new ways of organizing responses, symbolic and nonsymbolic. The child arrives at more and more roundabout techniques for solving practical problems, at perceptual constancies (e.g., of shape, size, and brightness), and at conceptual constancies (e.g., of the object, of quantity, of space, of time). He acquires the practice of systematically varying his fixations so as to counteract the illusions and distortions to which the nonhomogeneity of the perceptual field is apt to lead. Most important and striking of all, he gradually builds up more and more powerful and coherent logical structures, permitting him to conduct his thought processes with maximum flexibility, combined with consistency of outcome. It is noteworthy that, once a child is in possession of a logical structure, he does not usually justify a con-

301

clusion by mentioning experiences of external events that show that it happens to be true; he appeals to inference from general principles and evinces a conviction that what he says has to be true.

Piaget contends that the nature of these phenomena compels the conclusion that the course of development is governed not only by maturation and by pressure of environmental events but by a further class of factors that he calls "equilibrium." Equilibrium can exist in varying degrees, but there is an inexorable, autonomous movement toward better and better equilibrium as the child matures. He gives up his earlier and cruder ways of perceiving and thinking because he finds that they lead to surprises and frustrations, since the expectations which they generate often turn out to be erroneous and frequently leave him unable to anticipate what is going to happen next. As his nervous system develops, he is able to adopt more advanced ways of perceiving and thinking which permit him to have greater confidence in his judgments and to make predictions in more and more contexts.

We may reinterpret Piaget's view by regarding what he calls equilibrium as a class of hitherto overlooked sources of drive and reward propelling the learning processes that give rise to generalized habits of perception and thought. The drive states that are fomented by disequilibrium arise not out of visceral disturbances or aversive external stimuli, but out of unsatisfactory relations between the subject's own responses. Changes in behavior that remove disequilibrium are ones that avert surprise and uncertainty. Ability to recognize and respond to invariants amid the shifting appearances of objects must diminish complexity and moderate the impact of change. So, once more, we find testimony to the importance of conceptual conflict.

Work on simulation of intellectual processes with computers furnishes another view of the matter. Pursuit of the analogies between computers and brains has helped to obscure the necessity of considering motivational aspects of thinking, since current computers, like human subjects in psychological laboratories, have the experimenter's motives artificially instilled in them. But the recent movement toward a more flexible use of the computer, approaching the more creative forms of human thought, must unavoidably bring up the problem.

For example, Shaw, Newell, Simon, and Ellis (1958) have discussed how a machine should be constructed to function as a general problem solver, a device that would simulate a wide range of intellectual feats from proving theorems to playing chess. The machine, as conceived by them, and the programs with which they have successfully converted existing computers to such uses, involve the following elements: (1) a representation of the essential properties of a solution, (2) a representation of the data that are initially given, (3) a means of selecting some of these initial data and performing specifiable operations on them to yield new data, and (4) a device for comparing the products of these operations with the representation of the solution, and noting wherein they fail to match.

Element 4 is what corresponds to the mechanism of epistemic curiosity. It works through the equivalent of conceptual conflict, and its function is an eminently motivational one; its recognition of match or mismatch determines whether the search for a solution ends or continues, and its characterization of the mismatch determines the direction in which the search for a solution is pursued. Future research may well be aimed at devising a problem-solving machine that will improve its technique in the light of its experience. The reduction of mismatch or conflict would then have to be the reinforcing agent, causing the immediately preceding operations to move up in the machine's order of precedence.

It is, after all, fairly obvious that conceptual conflict must underlie the notions of truth and falsity. Modern philosophers have emphasized that truth and falsity are properties not of facts but of sentences, i.e., of representations of facts. They have also distinguished two senses in which a sentence can be true (e.g., Carnap 1936–1937). It is *synthetically* true or *P-valid* if, like the truths of science, it agrees with external reality. It is *analytically* true or *L-valid* if, like the truths of mathematics or logic, it cannot be denied without contradicting rules that govern the use of language. Neither of these notions could have arisen, nor could have any value, if discrepancies between symbolic processes—between the response to an empirical statement and the response to an observation of nature, or between the response to a logicomathematical formula and the response to an axiom or rule of inference—did not produce special psychological discomforts and impel a quest for other, less dissatisfying representational patterns.

The doubts that several writers (e.g., Pap 1953, Apostel, Mays, Morf, and Piaget 1957) have, on both logical and psychological grounds, expressed about the sharpness of the analytic-synthetic dichotomy can only lend further weight to our contention that the two criteria of truth have roots in related motivational processes

BIBLIOGRAPHY

Abelson, R. (1958). Modes of resolution of belief dilemmas. Paper read to Western Psychological Association, Monterey, Calif.

Abelson, R., and M. Rosenberg (1958). Symbolic psychologic: a model of attitudinal recognition. *Behav. Sci.*, 3, 1–13.

Aborn, M., and H. Rubinstein (1952). Information theory and immediate recall. *J. Exp. Psychol.*, 44, 260–266.

Abraham, K. (1921). Über Einschränkungen und Umwandlungen der Schaulust bei den Psychoneurotikern nebst Bermerkungen über analoge Erscheinungen in der Völkerpsychologie. In "Klinische Beiträge zur Psychoanalyse aus den Jahren 1907–1920." Internationaler Psycho-analytischer Verlag, Leipzig, Vienna, and Zürich. [Restrictions and transformations of scoptophilia in neuroses, with remarks on analogous phenomena in folk psychology, in "Selected Papers," Hogarth, London, 1927].

Ach, N. (1905). "Über die Willenstätigkeit und das Denken." Vandenhoeck & Ruprecht, Göttingen.

Adlerstein, A., and E. Fehrer (1955). The effect of food deprivation on exploratory behavior in a complex maze. *J. Comp. Physiol. Psychol.*, 48, 250–253.

Alekseeva, A. (1956). [Conditioned reflexes to multi-component chained stimuli in conditions of free motor activity]. *Zh. Vys. Nerv. Deiat.*, 6, 568–578.

Allport, F. H. (1955). "Theories of Perception and the Concept of Structure." Wiley, New York.

Allport, G. W., and L. J. Postman (1947). "The Psychology of Rumor." Holt, New York.

Alpert, R. (1953). Perceptual determinants of affect. Unpublished M.A. thesis, Wesleyan University, Middletown, Conn.

Angier, R. P. (1903). The aesthetics of unequal division. *Psychol. Rev. Monogr. Suppl.*, 4, 541–561.

Anokhin, P. K. (1949). [Key questions in the study of higher nervous activity]. In P. K. Anokhin (ed.). "Problemy Vysshei Nervnoi Deiatel'-nosti." Acad. Med. Sci., Moscow. ["Problems of Higher Nervous Activity"].

Anokhin, P. K. (1958). [The role of the orienting-investigatory reaction in the formation of the conditioned reflex]. In L. G. Voronin et al. (eds.).

"Orientirovochny refleks i orientirovochno-issledovatel'skaia deiatelnost'." Acad. Pedag. Sci., Moscow. ["The Orienting Reflex and Exploratory Behavior"].

Apostel, L., W. Mays, A. Morf, and J. Piaget (1957). "Les Liaisons analytiques et synthétiques dans le comportement du sujet." *Etudes d'Epistémologie Génétique,* vol. IV. Presses Universitaires de France, Paris.

Armington, J. C., and L. L. Mitnick (1959). Electroencephalogram and sleep deprivation. *J. Appl. Physiol.,* 14, 247–250.

Arnheim, R. (1954). "Art and Visual Perception." University of California Press, Berkeley, Calif.

Arrow, K. J. (1951). Alternative approaches to the theory of choice in risk-taking situations. *Econometrica,* 19, 404–437.

Attneave, F. (1954). Some informational aspects of visual perception. *Psychol. Rev.,* 61, 183–193.

Attneave, F. (1955). Symmetry, information and memory for patterns. *Amer. J. Psychol.,* 68, 209–222.

Attneave, F. (1957). Physical determinants of the judged complexity of shapes. *J. Exp. Psychol.,* 53, 221–227.

Baerends, G. P. (1955). Egg recognition in the herring gull. *Acta Psychol.,* 11, 93–94.

Bagby, J. W. (1957). A cross-cultural study of perceptual predominance in binocular rivalry. *J. Abn. Soc. Psychol.,* 54, 331–334.

Bahrick, H. P. (1954). Incidental learning under two incentive conditions. *J. Exp. Psychol.,* 47, 170–172.

Baldwin, J. M. (1895). "Mental Development in the Child and in the Race." Macmillan, New York.

Bar Hillel, Y., and R. Carnap (1953). Semantic information. *Brit. J. Phil. Sci.,* 4, 147–157.

Barnes, G. W., and G. B. Kish (1957). Reinforcing properties of intense auditory stimulation. *J. Comp. Physiol. Psychol.,* 50, 40–43.

Barnes, G. W., and G. B. Kish (1958). On some properties of visual reinforcement. *Amer. Psychologist,* 13, 417.

Barnett, S. A. (1958). Experiments on "neophobia" in wild and laboratory rats. *Brit. J. Psychol.,* 49, 195–201.

Barron, F. (1952). Personality style and perceptual choice. *J. Pers.,* 20, 385–401.

Barron, F. (1953). Complexity-simplicity as a personality dimension. *J. Abn. Soc. Psychol.,* 48, 163–172.

Barron, F., and G. S. Welsh (1952). Perception as a possible factor in personality style: its measurement by a figure preference test. *J. Psychol.,* 33, 199–207.

Bartlett, F. C. (1932). "Remembering." Cambridge University Press, London.

Bartlett, F. C. (1958). "Thinking." Methuen, London.

Bartoshuk, A. K. (1956). EMG gradients and EEG amplitude during motivated listening. *Canad. J. Psychol.,* 10, 156–164.

Bateson, G. (1953). The role of humor in human communication. In H. von Foerster (ed.). "Transactions of the Ninth Conference on Cybernetics." Josiah Macy, Jr. Foundation, New York.

Beach, H. D. (1957). Effect of morphine on the exploratory drive. *Canad. J. Psychol.*, 11, 237–244.

Becker, G. M. (1958). Sequential decision-making: Wald's model and estimates of parameters. *J. Exp. Psychol.*, 55, 628–636.

Beebe-Center, J. E., P. Black, A. C. Hoffman, and M. Wade (1948). Relative per diem consumption as a measure of preference in the rat. *J. Comp. Physiol. Psychol.*, 41, 239–251.

Bekhterev, V. M. (1928). "Obshchie Osnovy Refleksologii." 4th ed. State Publishing House, Moscow. ["General Principles of Human Reflexology." International Publishers, New York, 1933].

Berger, H. (1930). Über das Elektrenkephalogramm des Menschen. II. *J. Psychol. Neurol.*, 40, 160–179.

Beritov (Beritashvili), I. S. (1956). [Morphological and physiological bases of temporary connections in the cerebral cortex]. *Trudy Inst. Fiziol. Beritashvili*, 10, 3–72.

Berkun, M. M., M. L. Kessen, and N. E. Miller (1952). Hunger reducing effects of food by stomach fistula versus food by mouth measured by a consummatory response. *J. Comp. Physiol. Psychol.*, 45, 550–554.

Berlyne, D. E. (1950a). Novelty and curiosity as determinants of exploratory behaviour. *Brit. J. Psychol.*, 41, 68–80.

Berlyne, D. E. (1950b). Stimulus intensity and attention in relation to learning theory. *Quart. J. Exp. Psychol.*, 2, 71–75.

Berlyne, D. E. (1951). Attention to change. *Brit. J. Psychol.*, 42, 269–278.

Berlyne, D. E. (1953). Some aspects of human curiosity. Unpublished Ph.D. thesis, Yale University, New Haven, Conn.

Berlyne, D. E. (1954a). Knowledge and stimulus-response psychology. *Psychol. Rev.*, 61, 245–254.

Berlyne, D. E. (1954b). A theory of human curiosity. *Brit. J. Psychol.*, 45, 180–191.

Berlyne, D. E. (1954c). An experimental study of human curiosity. *Brit. J. Psychol.*, 45, 256–265.

Berlyne, D. E. (1955). The arousal and satiation of perceptual curiosity in the rat. *J. Comp. Physiol. Psychol.*, 48, 238–246.

Berlyne, D. E. (1957a). Attention to change, conditioned inhibition ($_sI_R$) and stimulus satiation. *Brit. J. Psychol.*, 48, 138–140.

Berlyne, D. E. (1957b). Conflict and choice time. *Brit. J. Psychol.*, 48, 106–118.

Berlyne, D. E. (1957c). Conflict and information-theory variables as determinants of human perceptual curiosity. *J. Exp. Psychol.*, 53, 399–404.

Berlyne, D. E. (1957d). Uncertainty and conflict: a point of contact between information-theory and behavior-theory concepts. *Psychol. Rev.*, 64, 329–339.

Berlyne, D. E. (1958a). The influence of complexity and novelty in visual figures on orienting responses. *J. Exp. Psychol.*, 55, 289–296.

Berlyne, D. E. (1958b). The influence of the albedo and complexity of stimuli on visual fixation in the human infant. *Brit. J. Psychol.*, 49, 315–318.

Berlyne, D. E. (1958c). Supplementary report: complexity and orienting responses with longer exposures. *J. Exp. Psychol.*, 56, 183.

Berlyne, D. E. (1958d). Exploration of stimuli associated with pain. Paper read to Western Psychological Association, Monterey, Calif.

Berlyne, D. E. (1960). Les équivalences psychologiques et les notions quantitatives. In *Etudes d'Epistémologie Génétique*, vol. XII. Presses Universitaires de France, Paris.

Berlyne, D. E., and J. Slater (1957). Perceptual curiosity, exploratory behavior and maze learning. *J. Comp. Physiol. Psychol.*, 50, 228–232.

Bernhaut, M., E. Gellhorn, and A. T. Rasmussen (1953). Experimental contributions to the problem of consciousness. *J. Neurophysiol.*, 16, 21–36.

Bexton, W. A., W. Heron, and T. H. Scott (1954). Effects of decreased variation in the sensory environment. *Canad. J. Psychol.*, 8, 70–76.

Bindra, D., and N. Spinner (1958). Response to varying degrees of novelty: the incidence of various activities. *J. Exp. Anal. Behav.*, 1, 341–350.

Birch, H. G. (1945). The relation of previous experience to insightful problem-solving. *J. Comp. Psychol.*, 38, 367–382.

Birkhoff, G. (1933). "Aesthetic Measure." Harvard University Press, Cambridge, Mass.

Block, J., and J. Block (1951). An investigation of the relationship between intolerance of ambiguity and ethnocentrism. *J. Pers.*, 19, 303–311.

Bonvallet, M., P. Dell, and G. Hiebel (1954). Tonus sympathique et activité électrique corticale. *EEG Clin. Neurophysiol.*, 6, 119–144.

Bousfield, W. A., and B. H. Cohen (1953). The effects of reinforcement on the occurrence of clustering in the recall of randomly arranged associates. *J. Psychol.*, 36, 67–81.

Brady, J. V., and D. G. Conrad (1956). Intracranial self-stimulation in primates as a function of electrode location and prior self-stimulation. *Amer. Psychologist*, 11, 438.

Brandt, H. F. (1944). "The Science of Seeing." Philosophical Library, New York.

Breese, B. B. (1899). On inhibition. *Psychol. Monogr.*, 3, no. 1.

Bremer, F. (1954). The neurophysiological problem of sleep. In J. F. Delafresnaye (ed.). "Brain Mechanisms and Consciousness." Blackwell, Oxford.

Brim, O. G., and D. B. Hoff (1957). Individual and situational differences in desire for certainty. *J. Abn. Soc. Psychol.*, 54, 225–233.

Briullova, S. V. (1958). [On some peculiarities of the orientation reflex in persons who have undergone closed traumata of the cerebral cortex and persons suffering from neuroses]. In L. G. Voronin et al. (eds.). "Orientirovochny refleks i orientirovochno-issledovatel'skaia deiatelnost'."

Acad. Pedag. Sci., Moscow. ["The Orienting Reflex and Exploratory Behavior"].

Broadbent, D. E. (1952a). Listening to one of two synchronous messages. *J. Exp. Psychol.*, 44, 51–55.

Broadbent, D. E. (1952b). Speaking and listening simultaneously. *J. Exp. Psychol.*, 43, 267–273.

Broadbent, D. E. (1958). "Perception and Communication." Pergamon, London and New York.

Brodal, A. (1957). "The Reticular Formation of the Brain-stem: Anatomical Aspects and Functional Correlations." Oliver & Boyd, Edinburgh and London.

Brogden, W. J. (1939). Sensory pre-conditioning. *J. Exp. Psychol.*, 25, 323–332.

Brogden, W. J. (1947). Sensory pre-conditioning of human subjects. *J. Exp. Psychol.*, 37, 527–539.

Bronshtein, A. I., N. A. Itina, A. G. Kamenetskaia, and V. A. Sytova (1958). [The orientation reactions of newborn infants]. In L. G. Voronin et al. (eds.). "Orientirovochny refleks i orientirovochno-issledovatel'-skaia deiatelnost'." Acad. Pedag. Sci., Moscow. ["The Orienting Reflex and Exploratory Behavior"].

Brown, C. H. (1937). The relation of magnitude of galvanic skin responses and resistance levels to the rate of learning. *J. Exp. Psychol.*, 20, 262–378.

Brown, J. (1954). The nature of set-to-learn and of intra-material interference in immediate memory. *Quart. J. Exp. Psychol.*, 10, 12–21.

Brown, J. S., and I. E. Farber (1951). Emotions conceptualized as intervening variables with suggestions toward a theory of frustration. *Psychol. Bull.*, 38, 465–495.

Brown, J. S., and A. Jacobs (1949). The role of fear in the motivation and acquisition of responses. *J. Exp. Psychol.*, 39, 747–759.

Bruce, R. H. (1938). The effect of lessening the drive upon performance by white rats in a maze. *J. Comp. Psychol.*, 25, 225–248.

Bruner, J. S., J. Matter, and M. L. Papanek (1955). Breadth of learning as a function of drive level and mechanization. *Psychol. Rev.*, 62, 1–10.

Bühler, C. (1928). Zwei Grundtypen von Lebensprozessen. *Z. Psychol.*, Abt. 1, 108, 222–239.

Bühler, C. (1931). "Kindheit und Jugend." Hirzel, Leipzig.

Bühler, C., H. Hetzer, and F. Mabel (1928). Die Affektwirksamkeit von Fremdheitseindrücken im ersten Lebensjahr. *Z. Psychol.*, Abt. 1, 107, 30–49.

Buser, P., and A. Roger (1957). Interprétation du conditionnement sur la base des données électroencéphalographiques. *Rep. Fourth Int. Cong. EEG Clin. Neurophysiol.* 417–444.

Bush, R. R., and F. Mosteller (1955). "Stochastic Models for Learning." Wiley, New York.

Butler, R. A. (1953). Discrimination learning by rhesus monkeys to visual-exploration motivation. *J. Comp. Physiol. Psychol.*, 46, 95–98.

Butler, R. A. (1954). Incentive conditions which influence visual exploration. *J. Exp. Psychol.*, 48, 19–23.
Butler, R. A. (1958). The differential effect of visual and auditory incentives
on the performance of monkeys. *Amer. J. Psychol.*, 71, 591–593.
Butler, R. A., and H. M. Alexander (1955). Daily patterns of visual exploration behavior in the monkey. *J. Comp. Physiol. Psychol.*, 48,
247–249.
Butler, R. A., and H. F. Harlow (1954). Persistence of visual exploration
in monkeys. *J. Comp. Physiol. Psychol.*, 47, 258–263.
Bykov, V. D. (1958). [On the dynamics of the orienting-investigatory re-
action in the formation of positive and inhibitory conditioned reflexes
and their modification]. In L. G. Voronin et al. (eds.). "Orientirovochny
refleks i orientirovochno-issledovatel'skaia deiatelnost'." Acad. Pedag.
Sci., Moscow. ["The Orienting Reflex and Exploratory Behavior"].
Campbell, B. A., and F. D. Sheffield (1953). Relation of random activity
to food deprivation. *J. Comp. Physiol. Psychol.*, 46, 320–322.
Cantril, H. (1941). "The Psychology of Social Movements." Wiley, New
York.
Cantril, H. (1957). Perception and interpersonal relations. *Amer. J.
Psychiat.*, 114, 119–126.
Carnap, R. (1936–1937). Testability and meaning. *Phil. Sci.*, 3, 419–471;
4, 1–40.
Carr, R. M., and C. D. Williams (1957). Exploratory behavior of three
strains of rats. *J. Comp. Physiol. Psychol.*, 50, 621–623.
Cartwright, D., and F. Harary (1956). Structural balance: a generalization
of Heider's theory. *Psychol. Rev.*, 63, 277–293.
Cattell, R. B. (1957). "Personality and motivation structure and measurement." World, Yonkers, N.Y.
Cattell, R. B., and A. R. Baggaley (1958). A confirmation of ergic and
engram structures in attitudes objectively measured. *Austral. J. Psychol.*,
10, 287–318.
Chance, M. R. A., and A. P. Mead (1955). Competition between feeding
and investigation in the rat. *Behaviour*, 8, 174–182.
Chapman, D. W. (1932). Relative effects of determinate and indeterminate
aufgaben. *Amer. J. Psychol.*, 44, 163–174.
Chapman, R. M., and N. Levy (1957). Hunger drive and reinforcing
effect of novel stimuli. *J. Comp. Physiol. Psychol.*, 50, 233–238.
Charlesworth, W. R., and W. R. Thompson (1957). Effect of lack of visual
stimulus variation on exploratory behavior in the adult white rat.
Psychol. Rep., 3, 509–512.
Chechulin, S. I. (1923). [New material on the physiology of the extinction
of the orienting-investigatory reflex]. *Arkh. Biol. Nauk*, 23, 148–
154.
Chisholm, R. M. (1946). The contrary-to-fact conditional. *Mind*, 55, 289–
307.
Claparède, E. (1933). La genèse de l'hypothèse. *Arch. de Psychol.*, 24,
1–154.

Clare, R. H., and C. H. Bishop (1955). Dendritic circuits: the properties of cortical paths involving dendrites. *Amer. J. Psychiat.*, 111, 818–825.

Cohn, R. (1946). The influence of emotion on the human electroencephalogram. *J. Nerv. Ment. Dis.*, 104, 351–357.

Cooper, J. B., and H. E. Siegel (1956). The galvanic skin response as a measure of emotion in prejudice. *J. Psychol.*, 42, 149–155.

Coppock, W. S. (1958). Pre-extinction in sensory pre-conditioning. *J. Exp. Psychol.*, 55, 213–219.

Courts, F. A. (1942). Relations between muscular tension and performance. *Psychol. Bull.*, 39, 347–367.

Danziger, K., and M. Mainland (1954). The habituation of exploratory behaviour. *Austral. J. Psychol.*, 6, 39–51.

Darchen, R. (1952). Sur l'activité exploratrice de *Blatella germanica*. *Z. Tierpsychol.*, 9, 362–372.

Darchen, R. (1954). Stimuli nouveaux et tendance exploratrice chez *Blatella germanica*. *Z. Tierpsychol.*, 11, 1–11.

Darchen, R. (1957). Sur le comportement d'exploration de *Blatella germanica*. Exploration d'un plan. *J. Psychol. Norm. Path.*, 54, 190–205.

Darrow, C. W. (1935). Emotion as functional decortication: the role of conflict. *Psychol. Rev.*, 42, 566–578.

Darrow, C. W. (1936). The galvanic skin reflex (sweating) and blood-pressure as preparatory and facilitative functions. *Psychol. Bull.*, 33, 73–94.

Darrow, C. W., and L. L. Heath (1932). Reaction tendencies relating to personality. In K. S. Lashley (ed.). "Studies in the Dynamics of Behavior." University of Chicago Press, Chicago.

Darrow, C. W., H. Jost, A. P. Solomon, and J. C. Mergener (1942). Autonomic indications of excitatory and homeostatic effects in the electroencephalogram. *J. Psychol.*, 14, 115–130.

Darrow, C. W., J. Pathman, and G. Kronenberg (1946). Level of autonomic activity and electroencephalogram. *J. Exp. Psychol.*, 36, 355–365.

Darwin, C. (1874). "The Descent of Man." Macmurray, London.

Dashiell, J. F. (1925). A quantitative demonstration of animal drive. *J. Comp. Psychol.*, 5, 205–208.

Dashiell, J. F. (1930). Direction orientation in maze running by the white rat. *Comp. Psychol. Monogr.*, no. 7 (2).

Davis, J. D. (1958). The reinforcing effect of weak light onset as a function of the amount of food deprivation. *J. Comp. Physiol. Psychol.*, 51, 496–498.

Davis, R. C. (1930). Factors affecting the galvanic reflex. *Arch. Psychol.*, no. 115.

Davis, R. C. (1936). An evaluation and test of Birkhoff's aesthetic measure and formula. *J. Gen. Psychol.*, 15, 231–240.

Davis, R. C., A. M. Buchwald, and R. W. Frankmann (1955). Autonomic and muscular responses and their relation to simple stimuli. *Psychol. Monogr.*, no. 405.

Davis, R. T., P. H. Settlage, and H. F. Harlow (1950). Performance of normal and brain-operated monkeys on mechanical puzzles with and without food incentive. *J. Genet. Psychol.*, 77, 305–311.

Dell, P. C. (1956). Les systèmes réticulaires du tronc cérébral et l'adrénaline circulante. In "Progress in Neurobiology." *Proc. First Int. Meet. Neurobiol.*

Dell, P. C. (1958). Some basic mechanisms of the translation of bodily needs into behaviour. In G. E. W. Wolstenholm and C. M. O'Connor (eds.). "Ciba Foundation Symposium on the Neurological Basis of Behaviour." Little, Brown, Boston.

Dell, P. C., M. Bonvallet, and A. Hugelin (1954). Tonus sympathique et contrôle réticulaire de la motricité spinale. *EEG Clin. Neurophysiol.*, 6, 599–618.

Dember, W. N. (1956). Response by the rat to environmental change. *J. Comp. Physiol. Psychol.*, 49, 93–95.

Dember, W. N., and R. W. Earl (1957). Analysis of exploratory, manipulatory, and curiosity behaviors. *Psychol. Rev.*, 64, 91–96.

Dember, W. N., R. W. Earl, and N. Paradise (1957). Response by rats to differential stimulus complexity. *J. Comp. Physiol. Psychol.*, 50, 514–518.

Dember, W. N., and H. Fowler (1958). Spontaneous alternation behavior. *Psychol. Bull.*, 55, 412–428.

Dember, W. N., and B. A. Millbrook (1956). Free choice by the rat of the greater of two brightness changes. *Psychol. Rep.*, 2, 465–467.

Denny, M. R. (1957). Learning through stimulus satiation. *J. Exp. Psychol.*, 54, 62–64.

Desai, M. M. (1939). Surprise. *Brit. J. Psychol. Monogr. Suppl.*, no. 22.

Desmedt, J. E., and K. Mechelse (1958). Suppression of acoustic input by thalamic stimulation. *Proc. Soc. Exp. Biol. Med.*, 99, 772–775.

Desmedt, J. E., and K. Mechelse (1959). Corticofugal projections from temporal lobe in cat and their possible role in acoustic discrimination. *Proc. Physiol. Soc. Ann. Meet.*, London.

De Valois, R. C. (1954). The relation of different levels and kinds of motivation to variability of behavior. *J. Exp. Psychol.*, 47, 392–398.

Dewey, J. (1895). The theory of emotion. II. The significance of emotions. *Psychol. Rev.*, 2, 13–32.

Dewey, J. (1910). "How We Think." Heath, Boston.

Dolin, A. O., I. I. Zborovskaia, and S. K. Zamakhover (1958). [On the characteristics of the role of the orienting-investigatory reflex in conditioned-reflex activity]. In L. G. Voronin et al. (eds.). "Orientirovochny refleks i orientirovochno-issledovatel'skaia deiatelnost'." Acad. Pedag. Sci., Moscow. ["The Orienting Reflex and Exploratory Behavior"].

Dollard, J., and N. E. Miller (1950). "Personality and Psychotherapy." McGraw-Hill, New York.

Duffy, E. (1957). The psychological significance of the concept of "arousal" or "activation." *Psychol. Rev.*, 64, 265–275.

Dulany, E. E. (1957). Avoidance learning of perceptual defense and vigilance. *J. Abn. Soc. Psychol.*, 55, 333–338.

Duncker, K. (1945). On problem solving. *Psychol. Monogr.*, no. 270.

Dykman, R. A., W. G. Reese, C. R. Galbrecht, and P. J. Thomasson (1959). Psychophysiological reactions to novel stimuli: measurement, adaptation and relationship of psychological variables in the normal human. *Ann. N.Y. Acad. Sci.*, 79, 43–107.

Dzhavrishvili, T. D. (1956). [Concerning two-way temporary connections]. *Trudy Inst. Fiziol. Beritashvili*, 10, 163–187.

Earl, R. W. (1957). Problem solving and motor skill behaviors under conditions of free choice. Unpublished Ph.D. thesis, University of Michigan, Ann Arbor, Mich.

Edwards, W. (1953). Probability-preferences in gambling. *Amer. J. Psychol.*, 66, 349–364.

Edwards, W. (1955). The prediction of decisions among bets. *J. Exp. Psychol.*, 50, 201–214.

Ehrenfreund, D. (1948). An experimental test of the continuity theory of discrimination learning with pattern vision. *J. Comp. Physiol. Psychol.*, 41, 408–422.

Ellingson, R. R. (1956). Brain waves and problems of psychology. *Psychol. Bull.*, 53, 1–34.

Elliott, M. H. (1928). The effect of change of reward on the maze performance of rats. *U. Calif. Publ. Psychol.*, 4, 19–30.

Empson, W. (1930). "Seven Types of Ambiguity." New Directions, London.

Engel, E. (1956). The role of content in binocular resolution. *Amer. J. Psychol.*, 69, 87–91.

Engel, R. (1928). Experimentelle Untersuchungen über die Abhängigkeit der Lust und Unlust von der Reizstärke beim Geschmacksinn. *Arch. ges. Psychol.*, 64, 1–36.

Estes, W. K. (1950). Toward a statistical theory of learning. *Psychol. Rev.*, 57, 94–107.

Estes, W. K., and M. S. Schoeffler (1955). Analysis of variables influencing alternation after forced trials. *J. Comp. Physiol. Psychol.*, 48, 357–362.

Eysenck, H. J. (1941). The empirical determination of an aesthetic formula. *Psychol. Rev.*, 48, 83–92.

Eysenck, H. J. (1942). The experimental study of the "good gestalt": a new approach. *Psychol. Rev.*, 49, 344–364.

Eysenck, H. J. (1947). "Dimensions of Personality." Routledge, London.

Eysenck, H. J. (1953). "The Structure of Human Personality." Methuen, London.

Eysenck, H. J. (1954). "Psychology of Politics." Routledge, London.

Fantz, R. L. (1957). Form preference in newly hatched chicks. *J. Comp. Physiol. Psychol.*, 50, 412–438.

Fantz, R. L. (1958a). Pattern vision in young infants. *Psychol. Rec.*, 8, 43–48.

Fantz, R. L. (1958b). Visual discrimination in a neonate chimpanzee. *Perc. Mot. Skills*, 8, 59–66.

Farber, I. E. (1948). Response fixation under anxiety and non-anxiety conditions. *J. Exp. Psychol.*, 38, 111–131.

Farber, M. L. (1944). Suffering and the time perspective of the prisoner. *U. Iowa Studies in Child Welfare*, 20, 155–227.

Fechner, G. T. (1876). "Vorschule der Ästhetik." Breitkopf & Härtel, Leipzig.

Fehrer, E. (1956). The effects of hunger and familiarity of locale on exploration. *J. Comp. Physiol. Psychol.*, 49, 549–552.

Fenichel, O. (1945). "The Psychoanalytic Theory of Neurosis." Norton, New York.

Fessard, M. A., and H. Gastaut (1958). Corrélations physiologiques de la formation des réflexes conditionnés. In M. A. Fessard et al. "Le Conditionnement et l'apprentissage." Presses Universitaires de France, Paris.

Festinger, L. (1957). "Theory of Cognitive Dissonance." Row, Peterson, Evanston, Ill.

Flugel, J. C. (1948). L'appétit vient en mangeant: some reflexions on the self-sustaining tendencies. *Brit. J. Psychol.*, 38, 171–190.

Flynn, J. P., and E. A. Jerome (1952). Learning in an automatic multiple-choice box with light as incentive. *J. Comp. Physiol. Psychol.*, 45, 336–340.

Fonberg, E. (1956). On the manifestation of conditioned defensive reactions in stress. *Bull. Soc. Sci. et Lett. de Łódz*, 7, 7–8.

Forgays, D. G., and H. Levin (1958). Learning as a function of change of sensory stimulation: I. Food-deprived vs. food-satiated animals. *J. Comp. Physiol. Psychol.*, 51, 50–54.

Forgus, R. H. (1958). The effect of different kinds of form pre-exposure on form discrimination learning. *J. Comp. Physiol. Psychol.*, 51, 75–78.

Foulds, G. A. (1951). Temperamental differences in maze performance: I. Characteristic differences among psychoneurotics. *Brit. J. Psychol.*, 42, 209–217.

Fraisse, P., S. Ehrlich, and E. Vurpillot (1956). Etudes de la centration perceptive par la méthode tachistoscopique. *Arch. de Psychol.*, 35, 193–214.

Freeman, G. L. (1940). The relationship between performance level and bodily activity level. *J. Exp. Psychol.*, 26, 602–608.

Freeman, G. L. (1948). "The Energetics of Human Behavior." Cornell University Press, Ithaca, N.Y.

Frenkel-Brunswik, E. (1949). Intolerance of ambiguity as an emotional and perceptual personality variable. *J. Pers.*, 18, 108–143.

Freud, S. (1900). "Die Traumdeutung." Deuticke, Leipzig and Vienna. [The interpretation of dreams, in A. A. Brill (ed.), "Selected Works of Sigmund Freud," Modern Library, New York, 1938].

Freud, S. (1905a). "Der Witz und seine Beziehung zum Unbewussten."

Deuticke, Leipzig and Vienna. [Wit and its relation to the unconscious, in A. A. Brill (ed.), "Selected Works of Sigmund Freud," Modern Library, New York, 1938].

Freud, S. (1905*b*). "Drei Abhandlungen zur Sexualtheorie." Deuticke, Leipzig and Vienna. [Three contributions to the theory of sex, in A. A. Brill (ed.), "The Basic Writings of Sigmund Freud," Modern Library, New York, 1938].

Freud, S. (1913). Bemerkungen über einen Fall von Zwangsneurose. In "Sammlung kleiner Schriften zur Neurosenlehre," 3. Folge. Deuticke, Leipzig and Vienna. [Notes upon a case of obsessional neurosis, in S. Freud, "Collected Papers," vol. III, Hogarth, London, 1924].

Freud, S. (1915). Triebe und Triebschicksale. *Inter. Z. f. ärztl. Psychoanal.,* 3, 84–100. [Instincts and their vicissitudes, in S. Freud, "Collected Papers," vol. IV, Hogarth, London, 1925].

Freud, S. (1916). Das Unbewusste. In "Sammlung kleiner Schriften zur Neurosenlehre." 4. Folge. Deuticke, Leipzig, and Vienna. [The Unconscious, in S. Freud, "Collected Papers," vol. IV, Hogarth, London, 1925].

Friedman, M., and L. J. Savage (1948). The utility analysis of choices involving risk. *J. Polit. Econ.,* 56, 279–304.

Fry, G. A., and S. H. Bartley (1935). The effect of one border in the visual field upon the threshold of another. *Amer. J. Physiol.,* 112, 414–421.

Funkenstein, D. H. (1956). Norepinephrine-like and epinephrine-like substances in relation to human behavior. *J. Nerv. Ment. Dis.,* 124, 58–68.

Fuster, J. M. (1957). Tachistoscopic perception in monkeys. *Fed. Proc.,* 16, 43.

Galambos, R. (1956). Suppression of auditory nerve activity by stimulation of efferent fibres to cochlea. *J. Neurophysiol.,* 19, 424–437.

Galambos, R., G. Sheatz, and V. G. Vernier (1956). Electrophysiological correlates of a conditioned response in cats. *Science,* 123, 376–377.

Gastaut, H. (1954). The brain stem and cerebral electrogenesis in relation to consciousness. In J. F. Delafresnaye (ed.). "Brain Mechanisms and Consciousness." Blackwell, Oxford.

Gibson, E. J. (1940). A systematic application of the concepts of generalization and differentiation to verbal learning. *Psychol. Rev.,* 47, 196–229.

Gibson, E. J., and R. R. Walk (1956). The effect of prolonged exposure to visually presented patterns on learning to discriminate them. *J. Comp. Physiol. Psychol.,* 49, 239–242.

Gilbert, K. E., and H. Kuhn (1953). "A History of Esthetics." Indiana University Press, Bloomington, Ind.

Girdner, J. B. (1953). An experimental analysis of the behavioral effects of a perceptual consequence unrelated to organic drive states. *Amer. Psychologist,* 8, 354–355.

Glanzer, M. (1953*a*). Stimulus satiation: an explanation of spontaneous alternation and related phenomena. *Psychol. Rev.,* 60, 257–268.
315

Glanzer, M. (1953*b*). The role of stimulus satiation in spontaneous alternation. *J. Exp. Psychol.*, 45, 387–393.

Glanzer, M. (1958*a*). Curiosity, exploratory drive, and stimulus satiation. *Psychol. Bull.*, 55, 302–315.

Glanzer, M. (1958*b*). Stimulus satiation in situations without choice. *J. Comp. Physiol. Psychol.*, 51, 332–335.

Glickman, S. E. (1958). Effects of peripheral blindness on exploratory behaviour in the hooded rat. *Canad. J. Psychol.*, 12, 45–51.

Goodman, N. (1947). The problem of counter-factual conditionals. *J. Philos.*, 44, 113–128.

Goss, A. E., and G. J. Wischner (1956). Vicarious trial and error and related behavior. *Psychol. Bull.*, 53, 35–54.

Gottschaldt, K. (1926). Über den Einfluss der Erfahrung auf die Wahrnehmung von Figuren. *Psychol. Forsch.*, 8, 261–317.

Granit, R. (1955). Brain control of the sense organs. *Acta Psychol.*, 11, 117–118.

Grastyán, E., K. Lissák, and F. Kékesi (1956). Facilitation and inhibition of conditioned alimentary and defensive reflexes by stimulation of the hypothalamus and reticular formation. *Acta Physiol. Hung.*, 9, 133–151.

Grastyán, E., K. Lissák, I. Madarász, and H. Dunhoffer (1959). Hippocampal electrical activity during the development of conditioned reflexes. *EEG Clin. Neurophysiol.*, 11, 409–430.

Graves, M. E. (1951). "The Art of Color and Design." McGraw-Hill, New York.

Green, R. T. (1956). Surprise as a factor in the von Restorff effect. *J. Exp. Psychol.*, 52, 340–344.

Green, R. T. (1958*a*). Surprise, isolation and structural change as factors affecting recall in a temporal series. *Brit. J. Psychol.*, 49, 21–30.

Green, R. T. (1958*b*). The attention-getting value of structural change. *Brit. J. Psychol.*, 49, 311–314.

Grice, G. R. (1948). The acquisition of a visual discrimination habit following response to a single stimulus. *J. Exp. Psychol.*, 38, 633–642.

Grindley, G. C. (1929). Experiments on the influence of the amount of reward on learning in young chickens. *Brit. J. Psychol.*, 20, 173–180.

Grotjahn, M. (1957). "Beyond Laughter." McGraw-Hill, New York.

Guernsey, M. (1928). Eine genetische Studie über Nachahmung. *Z. Psychol.*, Abt. 1, 107, 105–178.

Guilford, J. P. (1956). The structure of intellect. *Psychol. Bull.*, 53, 267–293.

Guilford, J. P., P. R. Christensen, J. W. Frick, and P. R. Merrifield (1957). The relations of creative-thinking aptitudes to non-aptitude personality traits. Report no. 20. Psychology Laboratory, University of Southern California, Los Angeles.

Gwinn, G. T. (1949). The effects of punishment on acts motivated by fear. *J. Exp. Psychol.*, 39, 260–269.

Haber, R. N. (1958). Discrepancy from adaptation level as a source of affect. *J. Exp. Psychol.*, 56, 370–375.

Hadley, J. M. (1941). Some relationships between electrical signs of central and peripheral activity. II. During "mental work." *J. Exp. Psychol.*, 28, 53–62.

Hall, J. F. (1956). The relationship between external stimulation, food deprivation, and activity. *J. Comp. Physiol. Psychol.*, 49, 339–341.

Hamilton, J. A., and I. Krechevski (1933). Studies on the effect of shock upon behavior plasticity in the rat. *J. Comp. Psychol.*, 16, 237–253.

Hamilton, V. (1957). Perceptual and personality dynamics in reactions to ambiguity. *Brit. J. Psychol.*, 48, 200–215.

Hamilton, W. (1859). "Lectures on Metaphysics and Logic." Blackwood, Edinburgh.

Harlow, H. F. (1950). Learning and satiation of response in intrinsically motivated complex puzzle performance by monkeys. *J. Comp. Physiol. Psychol.*, 43, 289–294.

Harlow, H. F., N. C. Blazek, and G. E. McClearn (1956). Manipulatory motivation in the infant rhesus monkey. *J. Comp. Physiol. Psychol.*, 49, 444–448.

Harlow, H. F., M. K. Harlow, and D. R. Meyer (1950). Learning motivated by a manipulation drive. *J. Exp. Psychol.*, 40, 228–234.

Harlow, H. F., and G. E. McClearn (1954). Object discrimination learned by monkeys on the basis of manipulation motives. *J. Comp. Physiol. Psychol.*, 47, 73–76.

Harlow, H. F., and R. R. Zimmermann (1958). The development of affectional responses in infant monkeys. *Proc. Amer. Phil. Soc.*, 102, 501–509.

Haslerud, G. M. (1938). The effect of movement of stimulus objects upon avoidance reactions in chimpanzees. *J. Comp. Psychol.*, 25, 507–528.

Havelka, J. (1956). Problem-seeking behaviour in rats. *Canad. J. Psychol.*, 10, 91–97.

Hayes, K. J. (1960). Exploration and fear. *Psychol. Rep.*, 6, 91–93.

Hebb, D. O. (1946). On the nature of fear. *Psychol. Rev.*, 53, 259–276.

Hebb, D. O. (1949). "The Organization of Behavior." Wiley, New York.

Hebb, D. O. (1953). On human thought. *Canad. J. Psychol.*, 1953, 7, 99–110.

Hebb, D. O. (1955). Drives and the C.N.S. (conceptual nervous system). *Psychol. Rev.*, 62, 243–254.

Hebb, D. O., and H. Mahut (1955). Motivation et recherche du changement perceptif chez le rat et chez l'homme. *J. Psychol. Norm. Path.*, 52, 209–221.

Hefferline, R. F. (1950). An experimental study of avoidance. *Genet. Psychol. Monogr.*, 42, 231–334.

Heider, F. (1946). Attitudes and cognitive organization. *J. Psychol.*, 21, 107–112.

Helmholtz, H. (1869). Exposé élémentaire de la transformation des forces naturelles. In "Mémoire sur la conservation de la force." Masson et Cie, Paris.

Helson, H. (1948). Adaptation-level as a basis for a quantitative theory of frames of reference. *Psychol. Rev.*, 55, 297–313.

Henderson, R. L. (1953). Stimulus intensity dynamism and secondary reinforcement. Unpublished Ph.D. thesis, University of Missouri, Columbia, Mo.

Hernández-Peón, R. (1957). Discussion of Buser and Roger (1957).

Hernández-Peón, R., C. Guzmán-Flores, M. Álvarez, and A. Fernández-Guardiola (1956). Photic potentials in the visual pathway during "attention" and photic "habituation." *Fed. Proc.*, 15, 91–92.

Hernández-Peón, R., and K. E. Hagbarth (1955). Interaction between afferent and cortically induced reticular responses. *J. Neurophysiol.*, 18, 44–55.

Hernández-Peón, R., and H. Scherrer (1955). Habituation to acoustic stimuli in cochlear nucleus. *Fed. Proc.*, 14, 71.

Hernández-Peón, R., H. Scherrer, and M. Jouvet (1956). Modification of electrical activity in cochlear nucleus during "attention" in unanaesthetized cats. *Science*, 123, 331–332.

Hess, E. H., and W. C. Gogel (1954). Natural preferences of the chick for objects of different colors. *J. Psychol.*, 38, 483–493.

Hick, W. E. (1952). On the rate of gain of information. *Quart. J. Exp. Psychol.*, 4, 11–26.

Hinde, R. A. (1954). Factors governing the changes in strength of a partially inborn response as shown by the mobbing behaviour of the chaffinch (*Fringilla coelebs*). I and II. *Proc. Roy. Soc. B.*, 142, 306–331, 331–358.

Hiriyanna, M. (1949). "Essentials of Indian Philosophy." Macmillan, New York.

Hochberg, J., and E. McAlister (1953). A quantitative approach to figural "goodness." *J. Exp. Psychol.*, 46, 361–364.

Holland, J. G. (1957). Techniques for behavioral analysis of human observing. *Science*, 125, 348–350.

Holland, J. G. (1958). Human vigilance. *Science*, 128, 61–67.

Honig, W. K. (1958). Prediction of preference transposition and transposition-reversal from the generalization gradient. Unpublished Ph.D. thesis, Duke University, Durham, N.C.

Hovland, C. I., and A. H. Riesen (1940). Magnitude of galvanic and vasomotor responses as a function of stimulus intensity. *J. Gen. Psychol.*, 23, 103–121.

Hudson, B. B. (1950). One-trial learning in the domestic rat. *Genet. Psychol. Monogr.*, 41, 99–145.

Hugelin, A. (1955a). Analyse de l'inhibition d'un réflexe nociceptif (réflexe linguo-maxillaire) lors de l'activation du système réticulo-spinal dit "facilitateur." *C. R. Soc. Biol.*, 149, 1893–1894.

Hugelin, A. (1955b). Les bases physiologiques de la vigilance. *Encéphale*, 3, 267–292.

Hugelin, A., and M. Bonvallet (1957a). Tonus cortical et contrôle de la facilitation motrice d'origine réticulaire. *J. Physiol. Path. Gén.*, 49, 1171–1200.

Hugelin, A., and M. Bonvallet (1957b). Etudes expérimentales des interrelations réticulo-corticales—proposition d'une théorie de l'asservissement réticulaire à un système diffus cortical. *J. Physiol. Path. Gén.*, 49, 1201–1223.

Hugelin, A., and M. Bonvallet (1957c). Analyse des post-décharges réticulaires et corticales engendrées par des stimulations électriques réticulaires. *J. Physiol. Path. Gén.*, 49, 1225–1234.

Hugelin, A., and M. Bonvallet (1958). Effets moteurs et corticaux d'origine réticulaire au cours des stimulations somesthésiques—rôle des interactions cortico-réticulaires dans le déterminisme du sommeil. *J. Physiol. Path. Gén.*, 50, 951–977.

Hull, C. L. (1930). Knowledge and purpose as habit mechanisms. *Psychol. Rev.*, 37, 511–525.

Hull, C. L. (1935). The mechanism of the assembly of behavior segments in novel combinations suitable for problem solution. *Psychol. Rev.*, 42, 219–245.

Hull, C. L. (1943). "Principles of Behavior." Appleton-Century-Crofts, New York.

Hull, C. L. (1952). "A Behavior System." Yale University Press, New Haven, Conn.

Hurwitz, H. M. B. (1956). Conditioned responses in rats reinforced by light. *Brit. J. Anim. Behav.*, 4, 31–33.

Hurwitz, H. M. B., and De, S. C. (1958). Studies in light-reinforced behavior. II. Effect of food deprivation and stress. *Psychol. Rep.*, 4, 71-77.

Inhelder, B., and J. Piaget (1956). "De la logique de l'enfant à la logique de l'adolescent." Presses Universitaires de France, Paris. ["The Growth of Logical Thinking from Childhood to Adolescence," Basic Books, New York, 1958].

Inhelder, E. (1955). Zur Psychologie einiger Verhaltensweisen—besonders des Spiels—von Zootieren. *Z. Tierpsychol.*, 12, 88–144.

Irwin, F., and W. A. S. Smith (1957). Value, cost and information as determiners of decision. *J. Exp. Psychol.*, 54, 229–232.

Isaacs, N. (1930). Children's "why" questions. In S. Isaacs. "Intellectual Growth in Young Children." Routledge, London.

Ivanov-Smolenski, A. G., M. O. Gurevich, V. N. Skosyrev, and Z. A. Soloveva (1933). "Eksperimental'noe issledovanie vysshei nervnoi deiatel'nosti rebenka." State Medical Publishing House, Moscow. ["The Experimental Investigation of the Higher Nervous Activity of the Child"].

Jacobson, E. (1929). Electrical measurements of neuromuscular states during mental activities. I. Imagination of movement involving skeletal muscle. *Amer. J. Physiol.*, 91, 567–605.

Jasper, H. H. (1954). Functional properties of the thalamic reticular system. In J. F. Delafresnaye (ed.). "Brain Mechanisms and Consciousness." Blackwell, Oxford.
319

Jouvet, M. (1957). Etude neurophysiologique chez l'homme de quelques mécanismes sous-corticaux de l'attention. *Psychol. Française*, 2, 254–260.

Jouvet, M. (1958). Discussion of Fessard and Gastaut (1958). In M. A. Fessard et al. "Le conditionnement et l'apprentissage." Presses Universitaires de France, Paris.

Jouvet, M., O. Benoit, and J. Courjon (1956). Action de l'épilepsie expérimentale par stimulation corticale sur les réponses des formations spécifiques et non spécifiques à des signaux acoustiques. *Rev. Neurol.*, 94, 871.

Jouvet, M., and J. E. Desmedt (1956). Contrôle central des messages acoustiques afférents. *C. R. Acad. Sci.*, 243, 1916–1977.

Jouvet, M., and C. Lapras (1959). Variations des réponses électriques somesthésiques au niveau du thalamus chez l'homme au cours de l'attention. *C. R. Soc. Biol.*, 153, 98–101.

Jouvet, M., and F. Michel (1958). Recherches sur l'activité électrique cérébrale au cours du sommeil. *C. R. Soc. Biol.*, 152, 1167–1170.

Kappauf, W. E., and H. Schlosberg (1937). Conditioned responses in the white rat. III. Conditioning as a function of the length of the period of delay. *J. Genet. Psychol.*, 50, 27–45.

Karsten, A. (1928). Psychische Sättigung. *Psychol. Forsch.*, 10, 142–254.

Kasatkin, N. I., N. S. Mirzoiants, and A. P. Khokhitva (1953). [On orienting conditioned reflexes in infants in the first year of life]. *Zh. Vys. Nerv. Deiat.*, 3, 192–202.

Keehn, J. D. (1959). The effect of a warning signal on unrestricted avoidance behaviour. *Brit. J. Psychol.*, 50, 125–135.

Kelleher, R. T. (1958). Stimulus-producing responses in chimpanzees. *J. Exp. Anal. Behav.*, 1, 87–102.

Keller, J. S. (1941). Light aversion in the white rat. *Psychol. Rec.*, 4, 235–250.

Kennedy, J. L. (1959). A possible artifact in electroencephalography. *Psychol. Rev.*, 66, 347–352.

Kish, G. B. (1955). Learning when the onset of illumination is used as reinforcing stimulus. *J. Comp. Physiol. Psychol.*, 48, 261–264.

Kish, G. B., and J. J. Antonitis (1956). Unconditioned operant behavior in two homozygous strains of mice. *J. Genet. Psychol.*, 88, 121–124.

Kittel, C. (1958). "Elementary Statistical Physics." Wiley, New York.

Kivy, P. N., R. W. Earl, and E. L. Walker (1956). Stimulus context and satiation. *J. Comp. Physiol. Psychol.*, 49, 90–92.

Kling, J. W., L. Horowitz, and J. E. Delhagen (1956). Light as a positive reinforcer for rat responding. *Psychol. Rep.*, 2, 337–340.

Koffka, K. (1935). "Principles of Gestalt Psychology." Routledge, London; Harcourt, Brace, New York.

Köhler, W. (1917). "Intelligenzprüfungen an Menschenaffen." Springer, Berlin. ["The Mentality of Apes," Kegan Paul, Trench, Trubner & Co., London; Harcourt, Brace, New York, 1925].

Köhler, W. (1921). "Die physischen Gestalten in Ruhe und im stationären Zustand." Philosophische Akademie, Erlangen, Germany.

Konorski, J. (1948). "Conditioned Reflexes and Neuron Organization." Cambridge University Press, London.

Konorski, J., and E. Szwejkowska (1952). Chronic extinction and restoration of conditioned reflexes. IV. The dependence of the course of extinction and restoration of conditioned reflexes on the "history" of the conditioned stimulus. (The principle of the primacy of first training.) *Acta Biol. Exp.*, 16, 95–113.

Kostenetskaia, N. A. (1949). [The formation of inhibitory conditioned reflexes to indifferent stimuli]. *Trudy Fiziol. Lab. Pavlova*, 15, 124–137.

Kratin, G. (1959). [Analysis of "indifferent" stimuli from the encephalogram in man]. *Fiziol. Zh. SSSR*, 45(1), 16–23.

Krechevsky, I. (1932). "Hypotheses" in rats. *Psychol. Rev.*, 39, 516–532.

Krechevsky, I. (1937a). Brain mechanisms and variability: variability within a means-end readiness. *J. Comp. Psychol.*, 23, 121–138.

Krechevsky, I. (1937b). Brain mechanisms and variability: variability where no learning is involved. *J. Comp. Psychol.*, 23, 139–164.

Krechevsky, I. (1937c). Brain mechanisms and variability: limitations of the effect of cortical injury upon variability. *J. Comp. Psychol.*, 23, 351–364.

Kreuger, W. C. F. (1932). Learning during directed attention. *J. Exp. Psychol.*, 15, 517–527.

Külpe, O. (1893). "Grundriss der Psychologie." Engelmann, Leipzig.

Külpe, O. (1904). Versuche über Abstraktion. *Ber. I. Kong. exp. Psychol.*, 56–58.

Kupalov, P. S., and W. H. Gantt (1928). [On the relation between the strength of a conditioned stimulus and the magnitude of a conditioned reflex]. *Trudy Fiziol. Lab. Pavlova*, 2, 3–12.

Kvasov, D. G. (1958). [The reflex organization of reception and the proprio-muscular apparatus (of the sense-organs)]. In L. G. Voronin et al. (eds.). "Orientirovochny refleks i orientirovochno-issledovatel'skaia deiatelnost'." Acad. Pedag. Sci., Moscow. ["The Orienting Reflex and Exploratory Behavior"].

Ladygina-Kots, N. N. (1935). "Ditia shimpanze i ditia cheloveka v ikh instinktakh, emotsiiakh, igrakh, privychnikh i vyrazitel'nykh dvizheniiakh." Darwin Museum, Moscow. ["The Young of the Chimpanzee and the Children of Man in Their Instincts, Emotions, Games, Habitual and Expressive Movements"].

Lagutina, N. I. (1955). [An investigation of the central mechanisms of alimentary, defensive, orientation and other reflexes under conditions of electrical stimulation of various points of the cerebral cortex]. *Vsesoyuzn. S'ezd Fiziol., Biokhim. i Farm.*

Lagutina, N. I. (1958). [Concerning the structure of the orientation reflex]. In L. G. Voronin et al. (eds.). "Orientirovochny refleks i orientirovochno-issledovatel'skaia deiatelnost'." Acad. Pedag. Sci., Moscow. ["The Orienting Reflex and Exploratory Behavior"].

Lanier, L. H. (1941a). An experimental study of "affective conflict." *J. Psychol.*, 11, 199–217.

Lanier, L. H. (1941b). Incidental memory for words differing in affective value. *J. Psychol.*, 11, 219–228.

Lashley, K. S. (1942). An examination of the "continuity theory" as applied to discriminative learning. *J. Gen. Psychol.*, 26, 241–265.

Lát, J. (1957). [The problematics of the study of the higher nervous activity of freely moving animals and research into so-called spontaneous reactions]. *Česk. Psychol.*, 1, 25–38.

Lawrence, D. H. (1950). Acquired distinctiveness of cues. II. Selective association in a constant stimulus situation. *J. Exp. Psychol.*, 40, 175–188.

Lawrence, D. H., and G. R. Coles (1954). Accuracy of recognition with alternatives before and after the stimulus. *J. Exp. Psychol.*, 47, 208–214.

Lawrence, D. H., and D. L. La Berge (1956). Relationship between recognition accuracy and order of reporting stimulus dimensions. *J. Exp. Psychol.*, 51, 12–18.

Lebedinskaia, E. I. (1958). [On the interrelation of conditioned orientation and conditioned motor reflexes in the formation of a temporary connection between two indifferent stimuli]. In L. G. Voronin et al. (eds.). "Orientirovochny refleks i orientirovochno-issledovatel'skaia deiatelnost'." Acad. Pedag. Sci., Moscow. ["The Orienting Reflex and Exploratory Behavior"].

Legowski, L. W. (1908). Beiträge zur experimentellen Ästhetik. *Arch. f. d. ges. Psychol.*, 12, 236–311.

Lehmann, A. (1892). "Hauptgesetze des menschlichen Gefühlslebens." Reisland, Leipzig.

Leontiev, A. N., and T. V. Rozonava (1951). [The formation of associative connections: an experimental investigation]. *Sovetsk. Pedag.*, 10, 60–77.

Leuba, C. (1955). Toward some integration of learning theories: the concept of optimal stimulation. *Psychol. Rep.*, 1, 27–33.

Levin, H., and D. G. Forgays (1959). Learning as a function of sensory stimulation of various intensities. *J. Comp. Physiol. Psychol.*, 52, 195–201.

Lewin, K. (1935). "A Dynamic Theory of Personality." McGraw-Hill, New York.

Lewis, D. J., and J. W. Cotton (1957). Learning and reinforcement as a function of drive strength during acquisition and extinction. *J. Comp. Physiol. Psychol.*, 50, 184–194.

Li, C-L., C. Cullen, and H. H. Jasper (1956). Laminar microelectrode analysis of cortical unspecific recruiting responses and spontaneous rhythms. *J. Neurophysiol.*, 19, 131–143.

Liberman, A. E. (1958). [Some new data on the pupillary component of the orientation reflex in man]. In L. G. Voronin et al. (eds.). "Orientirovochny refleks i orientirovochno-issledovatel'skaia deiatelnost'." Acad. Pedag. Sci., Moscow. ["The Orienting Reflex and Exploratory Behavior"].

Lindsley, D. B. (1951). Emotion. In S. S. Stevens (ed.). "Handbook of Experimental Psychology." Wiley, New York.

Lindsley, D. B. (1957a). Psychophysiology and motivation. In M. R. Jones (ed.). "Nebraska Symposium on Motivation 1957." University of Nebraska Press, Lincoln, Neb.

Lindsley, D. B. (1957b). Psychophysiology and perception. In "The Description and Analysis of Behavior." University of Pittsburgh Press, Pittsburgh, Pa.

Lindsley, O. R. (1956). Operant conditioning methods applied to research on chronic schizophrenics. *Psychiatr. Res. Rep.*, 5, 118–139.

Lipps, T. (1903–1906). "Ästhetik." Franz, Hamburg and Leipzig.

Lisina, M. I. (1958). [The role of orientation in the conversion of involuntary into voluntary reactions]. In L. G. Voronin et al. (eds.). "Orientirovochny refleks i orientirovochno-issledovatel'skaia deiatelnost'." Acad. Pedag. Sci., Moscow. ["The Orienting Reflex and Exploratory Behavior"].

Lissák, K. (1955). [New experimental aspects in the investigation of diencephalic mechanisms and processes of higher nervous activity]. *Zh. Vys. Nerv. Deiat.*, 5, 636–643.

Logan, F. A. (1954). A note on stimulus intensity dynamism (V). *Psychol. Rev.*, 61, 77–80.

Loomis, A. L., E. N. Harvey, and G. Hobart (1936). Electrical potentials of the human brain. *J. Exp. Psychol.*, 21, 127–144.

Lorenz, K. (1956). Plays and vacuum activities. In "L'Instinct dans le comportement de l'animal et de l'homme." Masson et Cie, Paris.

Lowell, E. L. (1952). The effect of conflict on motivation. Unpublished Ph.D. thesis, Harvard University, Cambridge, Mass.

Löwenfeld, B. (1927). Systematisches Studium der Reaktionen der Säuglinge auf Klänge und Geräusche. *Z. Psychol.*, Abt. 1, 104, 62–96.

Lubow, R. L., and J. J. Tighe (1957). A test of the discrepancy hypothesis of motivation using intensity of visual stimulation. *J. Comp. Physiol. Psychol.*, 50, 592–595.

Luce, D. R. (1956). "A Survey of the Theory of Selective Information and Some of Its Behavioral Applications." Revision of Technical Report no. 8. Bureau of Applied Social Research, New York.

Luria, A. R. (1932). "The Nature of Human Conflicts." Liveright, New York.

MacCorquodale, K., and P. E. Meehl (1951). On the elimination of cue entries without obvious reinforcement. *J. Comp. Physiol. Psychol.*, 48, 73–76.

Maier, N. R. F. (1932). A Gestalt theory of humour. *Brit. J. Psychol.*, 23, 69–74.

Maier, N. R. F., and T. C. Schneirla (1937). "Principles of Animal Psychology." McGraw-Hill, New York.

Majorana, A. (1950). Ricerche sull'apprendimento dei ratti in labirinto—sul comportamento investigativo dei ratti. *Riv. Psicol.*, 46 (4), 1–19.

Makarov, P. O. (1952). "Neirodinamika zritel'noi sistemy cheloveka." University of Leningrad Press. ["Neurodynamics of the visual system in man"].

Malmo, R. B. (1957). Anxiety and behavioral arousal. *Psychol. Rev.*, 64, 276–287.

Malmo, R. B. (1958). Measurement of drive: an unsolved problem in psychology. In M. R. Jones (ed.). "Nebraska Symposium on Motivation 1958." University of Nebraska Press, Lincoln, Neb.

Malmo, R. B. (1959). Activation: a neurophysiological dimension. *Psychol. Rev.*, 66, 367–386.

Marler, P. (1956). "Behavior of the Chaffinch, *Fringilla coelebs*." Brill, Leiden, Netherlands.

Marschak, J. (1954). Towards an economic theory of organization and information. In R. M. Thrall et al. (eds.). "Decision Processes." Wiley, New York.

Maruszewski, M. (1957). [On the interaction of the two signal systems in orientation reactions]. *Voprosy Psikhol.*, 3 (1), 78–87.

Marx, M. H., R. L. Henderson, and C. L. Roberts (1955). Positive reinforcement of the bar-pressing response by a light stimulus following dark operant pretests with no aftereffect. *J. Comp. Physiol. Psychol.*, 48, 73–76.

Masserman, J. H. (1946). "Principles of Dynamic Psychiatry." Saunders, Philadelphia.

McClearn, G. E. (1959). The genetics of mouse behavior in novel situations. *J. Comp. Physiol. Psychol.*, 52, 62–67.

McClelland, D. C., J. W. Atkinson, R. A. Clark, and E. L. Lowell (1953). "The Achievement Motive." Appleton-Century-Crofts, New York.

McDougall, W. (1908). "An Introduction to Social Psychology." Methuen, London; Luce, Boston.

McGeoch, J. A., and A. L. Irion (1952). "The Psychology of Human Learning." Longmans, New York.

McReynolds, P. (1956). A restricted conceptualization of human anxiety and motivation. *Psychol. Rep.*, 2, 293–312.

McReynolds, P., and J. Byran (1956). Tendency to obtain new percepts as a function of the level of unassimilated percepts. *Perc. Mot. Skills*, 6, 183–186.

Mead, G. H. (1934). "Mind, Self and Society." University of Chicago Press, Chicago.

Meehl, P. E. (1950). On the circularity of the law of effect. *Psychol. Bull.*, 47, 52–75.

Melzack, R. (1952). Irrational fear in the dog. *Canad. J. Psychol.*, 6, 141–147.

Merkel, J. (1885). Die zeitlichen Verhältnisse der Willensthätigkeit. *Phil. Studien*, 2, 73–127.

Meyer, L. B. (1956). "Emotion and Meaning in Music." University of Chicago Press, Chicago.

Mikhalevskaia, L. I. (1957). [Peculiarities of the relation between orientation and conditioned motor reactions in the determination of thresholds of visual sensitivity]. Paper read to conference on problems of the orientation reflex, Moscow.

Milerian, E. A. (1955). [Electrical activity of the cerebral cortex during attention to auditory stimuli]. *Voprosy Psikhol.*, 6 (2), 101–112.

Miles, R. C. (1958). Learning in kittens with manipulatory, exploratory and food incentives. *J. Comp. Physiol. Psychol.*, 51, 39–42.

Miller, G. A. (1956). The magical number seven, plus or minus two: some limits on our capacity for processing information. *Psychol. Rev.*, 63, 81–97.

Miller, G. A., and F. C. Frick (1949). Statistical behavioristics and sequences of responses. *Psychol. Rev.*, 56, 311–324.

Miller, G. A., and J. A. Selfridge (1950). Verbal context and the recall of meaningful material. *Amer. J. Psychol.*, 63, 176–185.

Miller, N. E. (1944). Experimental studies in conflict. In J. McV. Hunt (ed.). "Personality and the Behavior Disorders." Ronald, New York.

Miller, N. E. (1955). Shortcomings of food consumption as a measure of hunger; results from other behavioral techniques. *Ann. N.Y. Acad. Sci.*, 63, 141–143.

Miller, N. E. (1956). Effects of drugs on motivation: the value of using a variety of measures. *Ann. N.Y. Acad. Sci.*, 65, 318–333.

Miller, N. E. (1958). Central stimulation and other new approaches to motivation and reward. *Amer. Psychologist*, 13, 100–108.

Miller, N. E., and J. Dollard (1941). "Social Learning and Imitation." Yale University Press, New Haven, Conn.

Miller, N. E., and M. L. Kessen (1952). Reward effects of food via stomach fistula compared with those of food by mouth. *J. Comp. Physiol. Psychol.*, 45, 555–564.

Milner, P. M. (1957). The cell assembly: mark II. *Psychol. Rev.*, 64, 242–252.

Montague, W. P. (1925). "The Ways of Knowing." Macmillan, New York.

Montgomery, K. C. (1952). A test of two explanations of spontaneous alternation. *J. Comp Physiol. Psychol.*, 45, 287–293.

Montgomery, K. C. (1953a). Exploratory behavior as a function of "similarity" of stimulus situations. *J. Comp. Physiol. Psychol.*, 46, 129–133.

Montgomery, K. C. (1953b). The effect of activity deprivation upon exploratory behavior. *J. Comp. Physiol. Psychol.*, 46, 438–441.

Montgomery, K. C. (1953c). The effect of the hunger and thirst drives upon exploratory behavior. *J. Comp. Physiol. Psychol.*, 46, 315–319.

Montgomery, K. C. (1954). The role of the exploratory drive in learning. *J. Comp. Physiol. Psychol.*, 47, 60–64.

Montgomery, K. C. (1955). The relation between fear induced by novel stimulation and exploratory behavior. *J. Comp. Physiol. Psychol.*, 48, 254–260.

Montgomery, K. C., and J. A. Monkman (1955). The relation between fear and exploratory behavior. *J. Comp. Physiol. Psychol.*, 48, 132–136.

Montgomery, K. C., and M. Segall (1955). Discrimination learning based upon the exploratory drive. *J. Comp. Physiol. Psychol.*, 48, 225–228.

Montgomery, K. C., and P. G. Zimbardo (1957). Effect of sensory and behavioral deprivation upon exploratory behavior in the rat. *Perc. Mot. Skills*, 7, 223–229.

Moon, L. E., and T. M. Lodahl (1956). The reinforcing effect of changes in illumination on lever pressing in the monkey. *Amer. J. Psychol.*, 69, 288–290.

Morgan, C. T. (1957). Physiological mechanisms of motivation. In M. R. Jones (ed.). "Nebraska Symposium on Motivation 1957." University of Nebraska Press, Lincoln, Neb.

Morris, C. R. (1938). Foundations of the theory of signs. *Int. Encycl. Unified Sci.*, vol. I, no. 2.

Morris, C. R. (1946). "Signs, Language and Behavior." Prentice-Hall, Englewood Cliffs, N.J.

Morris, C. R. (1958). Prospects for a new synthesis: science and the humanities as complementary activities. *Daedalus*, 87, 94–101.

Moruzzi, G., and H. W. Magoun (1949). Brain stem reticular formation and the activation of the EEG. *EEG Clin. Neurophysiol.*, 1, 455–473.

Mote, F. A., and F. W. Finger (1942). Exploratory drive and secondary reinforcement in the acquisition and extinction of a simple running response. *J. Exp. Psychol.*, 31, 57–68.

Mowbray, G. H. (1952). Simultaneous vision and audition: the detection of elements missing from overlearned sequences. *J. Exp. Psychol.*, 44, 292–300.

Mowrer, O. H. (1950). "Learning Theory and Personality Dynamics." Ronald, New York.

Mowrer, O. H., and P. Viek (1948). An experimental analogue of fear from a sense of helplessness. *J. Abn. Soc. Psychol.*, 43, 193–200.

Muenzinger, K. F. (1934). Motivation in learning. I. Electric shock for correct response in the visual discrimination habit. *J. Comp. Psychol.*, 17, 267–277.

Mundy-Castle, A. C., and B. L. McKiever (1953). The psycho-physiological significance of the galvanic skin response. *J. Exp. Psychol.*, 46, 15–24.

Myers, A. K., and N. E. Miller (1954). Failure to find a learned drive based on hunger: evidence for learning motivated by "exploration." *J. Comp. Physiol. Psychol.*, 47, 428–436.

Narbutovich, I. O. (1938). [The modification of the higher nervous activity of a sanguine dog under the influence of a change in an established stereotype of conditioned stimuli]. *Trudy Fiziol. Lab. Pavlova*, 8, 337–348.

Narbutovich, I. O., and N. A. Podkopaev (1936). [The conditioned reflex as an association]. *Trudy Fiziol. Lab. Pavlova*, 6, 5–25.

Newell, A., J. C. Shaw, and H. A. Simon (1958). Elements of a theory of human problem solving. *Psychol. Rev.*, 65, 151–166.

Nikitina, G. M., and E. G. Novikova (1958). [On peculiarities of the ontogenetic development of the orientation reaction in animals]. In L. G. Voronin et al. (eds.). "Orientirovochny refleks i orientirovochno-

issledovatel'skaia deiatelnost'." Acad. Pedag. Sci., Moscow. ["The Orienting Reflex and Exploratory Behavior"].

Nissen, H. W. (1930). A study of exploratory behavior in the white rat by
means of the obstruction method. *J. Genet. Psychol.*, 37, 361–376.

Noelting, G. (1959). L'apprentissage perceptif de l'illusion Müller-Lyer
chez l'enfant et l'adulte. *Arch. de Psychol.*

Obrist, W. D. (1950). Skin resistance and electroencephalographic changes
associated with learning. Unpublished Ph.D. thesis, Northwestern University, Evanston, Ill.

Olds, J. (1956). A preliminary mapping of electrical reinforcing effects in
the rat brain. *J. Comp. Physiol. Psychol.*, 49, 281–285.

Olds, J., and P. Milner (1954). Positive reinforcement produced by electrical stimulation of septal area and other regions of rat brain. *J. Comp.
Physiol. Psychol.*, 47, 419–427.

Osgood, C. E. (1952). The nature and measurement of meaning. *Psychol.
Bull.*, 49, 197–237.

Osgood, C. E. (1957). A behavioristic analysis of perception and language
as cognitive phenomena. In "Contemporary Approaches to Cognition."
Harvard University Press, Cambridge, Mass.

Osgood, C. E., G. J. Suci, and P. H. Tannenbaum (1957). "The Measurement of Meaning." University of Illinois Press, Urbana, Ill.

Osgood, C. E., and P. H. Tannenbaum (1955). The principle of congruity
in the prediction of attitude change. *Psychol. Rev.*, 62, 42–55.

Pap, A. (1953). Reduction-sentences and open concepts. *Methodos*, 5,
3–30.

Paramanova, I. P. (1958). [The influence of the extinction and the recovery
of the orientation reflex on the formation of conditioned connections].
In L. G. Voronin et al. (eds.). "Orientirovochny refleks i orientirovochno-issledovatel'skaia deiatelnost'." Acad. Pedag. Sci., Moscow.
["The Orienting Reflex and Exploratory Behavior"].

Pavlov, I. P. (1927). "Conditioned Reflexes." Clarendon Press, Oxford.

Peckham, G. W., and E. G. Peckham (1887). Some observations on the
mental powers of spiders. *J. Morph.*, 1, 383–419.

Petelina, V. V. (1958). [The vegetative component of the orientation reaction of the vestibular, visual and auditory analyzers]. In L. G.
Voronin et al. (eds.). "Orientirovochny refleks i orientirovochno-issledovatel'skaia deiatelnost'." Acad. Pedag, Sci., Moscow. ["The Orienting Reflex and Exploratory Behavior"].

Petrinovich, L., and R. Bolles (1954). Deprivation states and behavioral
attributes. *J. Comp. Physiol. Psychol.*, 47, 450–453.

Phillips, L. W. (1957). Vicarious trial-and-error and psychophysical judgment. Unpublished Ph.D. thesis, University of California, Berkeley,
Calif.

Piaget, J. (1923). "Le Langage et la pensée chez l'enfant." Delachaux &
Niestlé, Neuchâtel & Paris. ["The Language and Thought of the Child,"
Routledge, London, 1926].

Piaget, J. (1936). "La Naissance de l'intelligence chez l'enfant." Delachaux & Niestlé, Neuchâtel & Paris. ["The Origins of Intelligence in Children," International Universities Press, New York, 1952].

Piaget, J. (1945). "La Formation du symbole chez l'enfant," Delachaux & Niestlé, Neuchâtel & Paris. ["Play, Dreams and Imitation in Childhood," Norton, New York, 1951].

Piaget, J. (1947). "La Psychologie de l'intelligence." Colin, Paris. ["The Psychology of Intelligence," Routledge, London, 1950].

Piaget, J. (1957). Logique et équilibre dans les comportements du sujet. In L. Apostel, B. Mandelbrot, and J. Piaget. "Logique et équilibre." *Etudes d'Epistémologie Génétique,* vol. II. Presses Universitaires de France, Paris.

Piaget, J. (1961). "Les Mécanismes perceptifs." Presses Universitaires de France, Paris.

Piaget, J., and Vinh-Bang (1959). Mouvements oculaires dans la perception des horizontales, verticales et obliques. *Arch. de Psychol.*

Pierce, E. (1894). Aesthetics of simple forms. I. Symmetry. *Psychol. Rev.,* 1, 483–495.

Polezhaev, E. F. (1958). [The role of the orientation reflex in the co-ordination of the cerebral cortex]. In L. G. Voronin et al. (eds.). "Orientirovochny refleks i orientirovochno-issledovatel'skaia deiatelnost'." Acad. Pedag. Sci., Moscow. ["The Orienting Reflex and Exploratory Behavior"].

Polezhaev, E. F. (1959a). [Characteristics of cortical coordination with external inhibition]. *Doklady Akad. Nauk SSSR,* 126, 909–912.

Polezhaev, E. F. (1959b). [Novelty as a stimulus for special reactions]. *Byull. Eksptl. Biol. i Med.,* 2, 9–14.

Popov, A. K. (1958). [On the relation between the GSR and rating responses with frequent presentation of electrocutaneous stimuli in man]. In L. G. Voronin et al. (eds.). "Orientirovochny refleks i orientirovochno-issledovatel'skaia deiatelnost'." Acad. Pedag. Sci., Moscow. ["The Orienting Reflex and Exploratory Behavior"].

Popov, N. A. (1921). [Extinction of the orientation reflex]. *Russk. Fiziol. Zh.,* 3, 1–5.

Popov, N. A. (1953). Observations électroencéphalographiques sur les réactions corticales chez l'homme. *L'Année Psychol.,* 53, 415–429.

Porter, L. W. (1957). Effect of shock-cessation as an incidental reward in verbal learning. *Amer. J. Psychol.,* 70, 421–426.

Postman, L., P. A. Adams, and L. W. Phillips (1955). Studies in incidental learning: II. The effects of association value and of the method of testing. *J. Exp. Psychol.,* 49, 1–10.

Poulton, E. C. (1956). Listening to overlapping calls. *J. Exp. Psychol.,* 52, 334–339.

Premack, D., G. Collier, and C. L. Roberts (1957). Frequency of light-contingent bar pressing as a function of the amount of deprivation for light. *Amer. Psychologist,* 12, 411.

Pritchard, R. M. (1958). Visual illusions viewed as stabilized retinal images. *Quart. J. Exp. Psychol.,* 10, 77–81.

Prokasy, W. F. (1956). The acquisition of observing responses in the absence of differential external reinforcement. *J. Comp. Physiol. Psychol.*, 49, 131–134.

Puffer, E. D. (1903). Studies in symmetry. *Psychol. Rev. Monogr. Suppl.*, 4, 467–539.

Rashevski, N. (1938). Contribution to the mathematical biophysics of visual perception with special reference to the theory of aesthetic values of geometrical patterns. *Psychometrika*, 3, 253–271.

Razran, G. H. S. (1939a). Studies in configural conditioning: I. Historical and preliminary experimentation. *J. Gen. Psychol.*, 21, 307–330.

Razran, G. H. S. (1939b). Studies in configural conditioning. III. The factors of similarity, proximity, and continuity in configural conditioning. *J. Exp. Psychol.*, 24, 202–210.

Razran, G. H. S. (1957). The dominance-contiguity theory of the acquisition of classical conditioning. *Psychol. Bull.*, 54, 1–46.

Reid, R. L. (1958). The role of the reinforcer as a stimulus. *Brit. J. Psychol.*, 49, 202–209.

Reik, T. (1948). "Listening with the Third Ear." 3d ed. Farrar, Straus & Young, New York.

Rensch, B. (1957). Ästhetische Faktoren bei Farb- und Formbevorzugungen von Affen. *Z. Tierpsychol.*, 14, 71–99.

Restorff, H. von (1933). Über die Wirkung von Bereichsbildungen im Spurenfeld. (Analyse von Vorgängen im Spurenfeld.) *Psychol. Forsch.*, 18, 299–342.

Ricci, G., B. Doane, and H. Jasper (1957). Microelectrode studies of conditioning: technique and preliminary results. Paper read to First International Congress of Neurological Sciences, Brussels.

Richards, I. A. (1952). "Principles of Literary Criticism." Routledge, London; Harcourt, Brace, New York.

Richter, C. P. (1922). A behavioristic study of the activity of the rat. *Comp. Psychol. Monogr.*, 1, no. 2.

Rikman, V. V. (1928). [Concerning the strength of conditioned reflexes]. *Trudy Fiziol. Lab. Pavlova*, 2, 13–24.

Roberts, C. L., M. H. Marx, and G. Collier (1958). Light-onset and light-offset as reinforcers for the albino rat. *J. Comp. Physiol. Psychol.*, 51, 575–579.

Roberts, W. W. (1958). Both rewarding and punishing effects from stimulation of posterior hypothalamus with same electrode at same intensity. *J. Comp. Physiol. Psychol.*, 51, 400–407.

Robinson, J., and W.H. Gantt (1947). The orienting reflex (questioning reaction): cardiac, respiratory, salivary and motor components. *Johns Hopkins Hospital Bull.*, 80, 321–253.

Rochester, N., J. H. Holland, L. H. Haibt, and W. C. Duda (1956). Tests of a cell assembly theory of the action of the brain using a large digital computer. *IRE Trans. Info. Theory*, IT.2, *Symposium on Information Theory*, 80–93.

Roger, A., L. G. Voronin, and E. N. Sokolov (1958). [An EEG investigation

of temporal connections with extinction of the orientation reflex in man].
Zh. Vys. Nerv. Deiat., 8, 8–16.

Roitbak, A. I. (1958). [Electrical phenomena in the focus of a conditioned
stimulus]. *Trudy Inst. Fiziol. Beritashvili*, 11, 121–154.

Rokotova, N. A. (1952). [The formation of temporary connections in the
cerebral cortex under the action of several indifferent stimuli]. *Zh.
Vys. Nerv. Deiat.*, 2, 753–759.

Rokotova, N. A. (1953). [Conditioned investigatory reflexes in the chim-
panzee]. *Trudy Inst. Fiziol. Pavlova*, 2, 295–305.

Rokotova, N. A. (1954). [Concerning the physiological mechanisms of
temporary connections with indifferent stimuli]. *Zh. Vys. Nerv. Deiat.*,
4, 516–525.

Rosenzweig, S. (1944). An outline of frustration theory. In J. McV. Hunt
(ed.). "Personality and the Behavior Disorders," Ronald, New York.

Rossi, G. F., and A. Zanchetti (1957). The brain-stem reticular formation.
Arch. Ital. Biol., 95, 199–435.

Rubin, E. (1915). "Synsoplevede Figurer." Gyldendal, Copenhagen.
["Visuell wahrgenommene Figuren," Gyldendal, Copenhagen, 1921].

Russell, B. (1940). "An Inquiry into Meaning and Truth." Norton, New
York.

Ruzskaia, A. G. (1958). [Orienting-investigatory activity in the formation
of elementary generalizations in the child]. In L. G. Voronin et al.
(eds.). "Orientirovochny refleks i orientirovochno-issledovatel'skaia
deiatelnost'." Acad. Pedag. Sci., Moscow. ["The Orienting Reflex and
Exploratory Behavior"].

Samson, E. W. (1951). "Fundamental Natural Concepts of Information
Theory." Air Force Cambridge Research Center, Cambridge, Mass.

Saul, L., H. Davis, and P. Davis (1949). Psychological correlations with
the EEG. *Psychosom. Med.*, 11, 361–376.

Schafer, R., and G. Murphy (1943). The role of autism in a visual figure-
ground relationship. *J. Exp. Psychol.*, 32, 335–343.

Schiller, P. H. (1951). Figural preferences in the drawings of a chimpanzee.
J. Comp. Physiol. Psychol., 44, 101–111.

Schlosberg, H. (1954). Three dimensions of emotion. *Psychol. Rev.*, 61,
81–88.

Schoenfeld, W. N., J. J. Antonitis, and P. J. Bersh (1950). Unconditioned
response rate of the white rat in a bar-pressing apparatus. *J. Comp.
Physiol. Psychol.*, 43, 41–48.

Schrödinger, E. (1945). "What is Life?" Macmillan, New York.

Sears, R. (1933). Psychogalvanic responses in arithmetical work. *Arch.
Psychol.*, no. 155.

Selye, H. (1946). The general adaptation syndrome and the diseases of
adaptation. *J. Clin. Endocrinol.*, 6, 117–230.

Selz, O. (1913). "Über die Gesetze des geordneten Denkverlaufs." Spemann,
Stuttgart.

Seward, J. P., and G. H. Seward (1934). The effect of repetition on reaction
to electric shock. *Arch. Psychol.*, no. 168.

Shakhnovich, A. R. (1958). [On the pupillary component of the orientation reflex under the action of stimuli that are specific for vision and non-specific (subsidiary) stimuli]. In L. G. Voronin et al. (eds.). "Orienti-rovochny refleks i orientirovochno-issledovatel'skaia deiatelnost'." Acad. Pedag. Sci., Moscow. ["The Orienting Reflex and Exploratory Behavior"].

Shannon, C. E., and W. Weaver (1949). "Mathematical Theory of Communication." University of Illinois Press, Urbana, Ill.

Sharpless, S., and H. Jasper (1956). Habituation of the arousal reaction. *Brain*, 79, 655–680.

Shaw, J. C., A. Newell, H. A. Simon, and T. O. Ellis (1958). A command structure for complex information processing. Paper read at Western Joint Computer Conference, Los Angeles, Calif.

Sheffield, F. D. (1948). Avoidance training and the contiguity principle. *J. Comp. Physiol. Psychol.*, 41, 165-177.

Sheffield, F. D., J. J. Wulff, and R. Backer (1951). Reward value of copulation without sex drive reduction. *J. Comp. Physiol. Psychol.*, 44, 3–8.

Sherrington, C. S. (1906). "Integrative Action of the Nervous System." Cambridge University Press, London; Yale University Press, New Haven, Conn.

Shkol'nik-Iarros, E. G. (1958). [Efferent paths from the visual cortex]. *Zh. Vys. Nerv. Deiat.*, 8, 123–136.

Siegel, P. S., and F. J. Pilgrim (1958). The effect of monotony on the acceptance of food. *Amer. J. Psychol.*, 71, 756–759.

Skinner, B. F. (1938). "The Behavior of Organisms." Appleton-Century-Crofts, New York.

Skinner, B. F. (1951). How to teach animals. *Sci. Amer.*, 191, Dec. 1951, 26–29.

Skinner, B. F. (1953). "Science and Human Behavior." Macmillan, New York.

Skinner, B. F. (1957). "Verbal Behavior." Appleton-Century-Crofts, New York.

Smith, A. A., R. B. Malmo, and C. Shagass (1954). An electromyographic study of listening and talking. *Canad. J. Psychol.*, 8, 219–227.

Smith, D. E., and J. E. Hochberg (1954). The effect of "punishment" (electric shock) on figure ground perception. *J. Psychol.*, 38, 83–87.

Smock, C. D. (1955a). The influence of psychological stress on the "intolerance of ambiguity." *J. Abn. Soc. Psychol.*, 50, 177–182.

Smock, C. D. (1955b). The influence of stress on the perception of incongruity. *J. Abn. Soc. Psychol.*, 50, 354–356.

Sokolov, E. N. (1954). Higher nervous activity and the problem of perception. Paper read to Fourteenth International Congress of Psychology, Montreal.

Sokolov, E. N. (1957a). [On the reflex mechanisms of sense-reception]. In "Materiali soveshchaniia po psikhologii." Acad. Pedag. Sci., Moscow.

Sokolov, E. N. (1957b). [Perception and reflex activity]. *Voprosy Psikhol.*, 3(6), 20–39.

Sokolov, E. N. (1958). "Vospriiate i uslovny refleks." University of Moscow Press. ["Perception and the Conditioned Reflex"].

Sokolov, E. N., and N. P. Paramanova (1956). [Concerning the role of the orientation reflex in the formation of motor conditioned reactions in man]. *Zh. Vys. Nerv. Deiat.*, 6, 702–709.

Solomon, R. L., and L. C. Wynne (1954). Traumatic avoidance learning: the principles of anxiety conservation and partial irreversibility. *Psychol. Rev.*, 61, 353–385.

Soloveichik, D. I. (1928). [The modification of the normal activity of the cerebral cortex with a change in the usual conditions of the experiment]. *Trudy Fiziol. Lab. Pavlova*, 2, 61–80.

Spence, K. W. (1936). The nature of discrimination learning in animals. *Psychol. Rev.*, 43, 427–449.

Spence, K. W. (1945). An experimental test of the continuity and non-continuity theories of discrimination learning. *J. Exp. Psychol.*, 35, 253–266.

Spence, K. W., and R. Lippitt (1940). "Latent" learning of a simple maze problem with relevant needs satiated. *Psychol. Bull.*, 37, 429.

Spence, K. W., and R. Lippitt (1946). An experimental test of the sign-gestalt theory of trial and error learning. *J. Exp. Psychol.*, 36, 491–502.

Staples, R. (1932). The response of infants to colors. *J. Exp. Psychol.*, 15, 119–141.

Starzl, T. E., C. W. Taylor, and H. W. Magoun (1951). Collateral afferent excitation of reticular formation of brain stem. *J. Neurophysiol.*, 14, 479–496.

Stennett, R. G. (1957a). The relationship of alpha amplitude to the level of palmar conductance. *EEG Clin. Neurophysiol.*, 9, 131–138.

Stennett, R. G. (1957b). The relationship of performance level to level of arousal. *J. Exp. Psychol.*, 54, 54–61.

Sterba, R. (1940). The problem of art in Freud's writings. *Psychoanal. Quart.*, 9, 256–268.

Sutherland, N. S. (1957). Spontaneous alternation and stimulus avoidance. *J. Comp. Physiol. Psychol.*, 50, 358–362.

Taylor, J. G. (1960). "The Behavioural Basis of Perception." Yale University Press, New Haven, Conn. (In press.)

Thiessen, D. D., and J. L. McGaugh (1958). Conflict and curiosity in the rat. Paper read to Western Psychological Association, Monterey, Calif.

Thistlethwaite, D. (1951). A critical review of latent learning and related experiments. *Psychol. Bull.*, 48, 97–129.

Thompson, W. R. (1953a). Exploratory behavior as a function of hunger in the "bright" and "dull" rats. *J. Comp. Physiol. Psychol.*, 46, 323–326.

Thompson, W. R. (1953b). The inheritance of behaviour: behavioural differences in fifteen mouse strains. *Canad. J. Psychol.*, 7, 145–155.

Thompson, W. R., and W. Heron (1954a). The effect of early restriction on activity in dogs. *J. Comp. Physiol. Psychol.*, 47, 77–82.

Thompson, W. R., and W. Heron (1954b). The effects of restricting early experience on the problem-solving capacity of dogs. *Canad. J. Psychol.*, 8, 17–31.

Thompson, W. R., and W. H. Higgins (1958). Emotion and organized behavior: experimental data bearing on the Leeper-Young controversy. *Canad. J. Psychol.*, 12, 61–68.

Thompson, W. R., and Kahn, A. (1955). Retroaction effects in the exploratory activity of "bright" and "dull" rats. *Canad. J. Psychol.*, 9, 173–182.

Thompson, W. R., and L. M. Solomon (1954). Spontaneous pattern discrimination in the rat. *J. Comp. Physiol. Psychol.*, 47, 104–107.

Thomson, R. (1955). The reward-value of changes in illumination for the rat. Unpublished M.A. (Hons.) thesis, University of Aberdeen, Scotland.

Thorpe, W. H. (1956). "Learning and Instinct in Animals." Methuen, London; Harvard University Press, Cambridge, Mass.

Thrall, K. W., C. H. Coombs, and R. L. Davis (eds.) (1954). "Decision Processes." Wiley, New York.

Tinbergen, N. (1951). "The Study of Instinct." Clarendon Press, Oxford.

Tinklepaugh, O. L. (1928). An experimental study of representative factors in monkeys. *J. Comp. Psychol.*, 8, 197–236.

Toman, J. E. P. (1943). The electroencephalogram during mental effort. *Fed. Proc.*, 2, 49.

Traugott, N. N., L. Y. Balonov, D. A. Kaufman, and A. E. Lichko (1958). [On the dynamics of the disturbance of orientation reflexes in some psychotic syndromes]. In L. G. Voronin et al. (eds.). "Orientirovochny refleks i orientirovochno-issledovatel-skaia deiatelnost'." Acad. Pedag. Sci., Moscow. ["The Orienting Reflex and Exploratory Behavior"].

Ullman, A. D. (1951). The experimental production and analysis of a "compulsive eating symptom" in rats. *J. Comp. Physiol. Psychol.*, 44, 575–581.

Valentine, C. W. (1914). The colour perception and colour preferences of an infant during its fourth and eighth months. *Brit. J. Psychol.*, 6, 363–386.

Van der Merwe, A. B., and P. A. Theron (1947). A new method of measuring emotional stability. *J. Gen. Psychol.*, 37, 109–123.

Vatsuro, E. G. (1957). [Secretory and motor components of a conditioned alimentary reflex as indices of some cortical processes]. *Zh. Vys. Nerv. Deiat.*, 7, 83–91.

Vedaev, R. P., and I. G. Karmanova (1958). [On the comparative physiology of the orientation reflex]. In L. G. Voronin et al. (eds.). "Orientirovochny refleks i orientirovochno-issledovatel'skaia deiatelnost'." Acad. Pedag. Sci., Moscow. ["The Orienting Reflex and Exploratory Behavior"].

Vernon, M. D. (1952). "A Further Study of Visual Perception." Cambridge University Press, London.

Vinogradova, O. S. (1958). [On the dynamics of the orientation reflex in the process of closing conditioned connections]. In L. G. Voronin et al.

(eds.). "Orientirovochny refleks i orieɪ.tirovochno-issledovatel'skaia deiatelnost'." Acad. Pedag. Sci., Moscow. ["The Orienting Reflex and Exploratory Behavior"].

Vinogradova, O. S., and E. N. Sokolov (1955). Concerning the extinction of the vascular component of the orientation reflex]. *Zhur. Vys. Nerv. Deyat.*, 5, 344–350.

Voitonis, N. I (1949). "Predistoriia intellekta." Acad. Sci., Moscow and Leningrad. ["The Prehistory of the Intellect"].

Wada, T. (1922). An experimental study of hunger in its relation to activity. *Arch. Psychol.*, no. 57.

Walker, A. E., and T. A. Weaver (1940). Ocular movements from the occipital lobe in the monkey. *J. Neurophysiol.*, 3, 353–357.

Walker, E. L. (1956). The duration and course of the reaction decrement and the influence of reward. *J. Comp. Physiol. Psychol.*, 49, 167–176.

Walker, E. L. (1958). Action decrement and its relation to learning. *Psychol. Rev.*, 65, 129–142.

Walker, E. L., W. N. Dember, R. W. Earl, C. L. Fawl, and A. J. Karoly (1955). Choice alternation: III. Response intensity vs. response discriminability. *J. Comp. Physiol. Psychol.*, 48, 80–85.

Wallerstein, H. (1954). An electromyographic study of attentive listening. *Canad. J. Psychol.*, 8, 228–238.

Watson, J. B. (1919). "Psychology from the Standpoint of a Behaviorist." Lippincott, Philadelphia.

Watson, R. H. J. (1954). The effects of age and experience on the performance of the white rat in a test of emotionality. Paper read to British Psychological Society, Nottingham, England.

Weaver, W. (1948). Probability, rarity, interest and surprise. *Sci. Mon.*, 67, 390–392.

Wechsler, D. (1925). Measurement of emotional reactions. *Arch. Psychol.*, no. 76.

Weiner, I. H., and E. Stellar (1951). Salt preference of the rat determined by a single-stimulus method. *J. Comp. Physiol. Psychol.*, 44, 394–401.

Welker, W. I. (1956a). Some determinants of play and exploration in chimpanzees. *J. Comp. Physiol. Psychol.*, 49, 84–89.

Welker, W. I. (1956b). Variability of play and exploratory behavior in chimpanzees. *J. Comp. Physiol. Psychol.*, 49, 181–185.

Welker, W. I. (1956c). Effects of age and experience on play and exploration of young chimpanzees. *J. Comp. Physiol. Psychol.*, 49, 223–226.

Welker, W. I. (1957). "Free" versus "forced" exploration of a novel situation by rats. *Psychol. Rep.*, 3, 95–108.

Welker, W. I. (1959). Escape, exploratory and food-seeking responses of rats in a novel situation. *J. Comp. Physiol. Psychol.*, 52, 106–111.

Wenger, M. A. (1941). The measurement of individual differences in autonomic balance. *Psychosom. Med.*, 3, 427–434.

Werner, H., and S. Wapner (1952). Toward a general theory of perception. *Psychol. Rev.*, 59, 324–338.

334

Wertheimer, M. (1923). Untersuchungen zur Lehre von der Gestalt. *Psychol. Forsch.*, 4, 301–350.

Wickens, D. D., and G. E. Briggs (1951). Mediated stimulus generalization as a factor in sensory preconditioning. *J. Exp. Psychol.*, 42, 197–200.

Wickens, D. D., R. S. Gehman, and S. N. Sullivan (1959). The effect of differential onset time on the conditioned response strength to elements of a stimulus complex. *J. Exp. Psychol.*, 58, 85–93.

Wiener, N. (1948). "Cybernetics." Technology Press, Cambridge, Mass.

Wiener, N. (1950). "The Human Use of Human Beings." Houghton Mifflin, Boston.

Wilcocks, R. W. (1928). The effect of an unexpected heterogeneity on attention. *J. Gen. Psychol.*, 1, 266–319.

Williams, C. D., and J. C. Kuchta (1957). Exploratory behavior in two mazes with dissimilar alternatives. *J. Comp. Physiol. Psychol.*, 50, 509–513.

Wilson, N. J., and W. P. Wilson (1959). The duration of human electroencephelographic arousal responses elicited by photic stimulation. *EEG Clin. Neurophysiol.*, 11, 85–91.

Witmer, L. (1893). Zur experimentellen Ästhetik einfacher räumlicher Formverhältnisse. *Phil. Studien*, 9, 96–144, 209–263.

Wolpe, J. (1950). Need-reduction, drive-reduction, and reinforcement: a neurophysiological view. *Psychol. Rev.*, 57, 19–26.

Wolpe, J. (1958). "Psychotherapy by Reciprocal Inhibition." Stanford University Press, Stanford, Calif.

Woodworth, R. S. (1938). "Experimental Psychology." Holt, New York.

Woodworth, R. S. (1958). "Dynamics of Behavior." Holt, New York.

Wundt, W. (1874). "Grundzüge der physiologischen Psychologie." Engelmann, Leipzig.

Wundt, W. (1896). "Grundriss der Psychologie." Engelmann, Leipzig.

Wyckoff, L. B. (1952). The role of observing responses in discrimination learning. Part I. *Psychol. Rev.*, 59, 431–442.

Yerkes, R. M., and A. W. Yerkes (1929). "The Great Apes." Yale University Press, New Haven, Conn.

Yoshii, N., and K. Tsukiyama (1952). EEG studies on conditioned behavior of the white rat. *Jap. J. Physiol.*, 2, 186–193.

Yoshii, N. K. Tsukiyama, and K. Horiuchi (1953). EEG studies on fatigue induced by enforced swimming in the rat. *Jap. J. Physiol.*, 3, 102–106.

Young, P. T. (1936). "Motivation of Behavior." Wiley, New York.

Zachiniaeva, I. A. (1950). [Summation of two conditioned stimuli reinforced by two different alimentary unconditioned stimuli]. In P. K. Anokhin (ed.). "Problemy vysshei nervnoi deiatel'nosti." Acad. Med. Sci., Moscow. ["Problems of Higher Nervous Activity"].

Zagorul'ko, T. M., and T. N. Sollertinskaia (1958). [On the comparative analysis of the mechanisms of the orientation reflex]. In L. G. Voronin et al. (eds.). "Orientirovochny refleks i orientirovochno-issledovatel'skaia deiatelnost'." Acad. Pedag. Sci., Moscow. ["The Orienting Reflex and Exploratory Behavior"].

Zaporozhets, A. V. (1954). Development of voluntary movements. Paper read to Fourteenth International Congress of Psychology, Montreal.

Zaporozhets, A. V. (1958). [The role of orienting activity and form in the formation and persistence of voluntary movements]. In L. G. Voronin et al. (eds.). "Orientirovochny refleks i orientirovochno-issledovatel'skaia deiatelnost'." Acad. Pedag. Sci., Moscow. ["The Orienting Reflex and Exploratory Behavior"].

Zimbardo, P. G., and N. E. Miller (1958). Facilitation of exploration by hunger in rats. *J. Comp. Physiol. Psychol.*, 51, 43–46.

Zimbardo, P. G., and K. C. Montgomery (1957a). Effects of "free-environment" rearing upon exploratory behavior. *Psychol. Rep.*, 3, 589–594.

Zimbardo, P. G., and K. C. Montgomery (1957b). The relative strengths of consummatory responses in hunger, thirst, and exploratory drive. *J. Comp. Physiol. Psychol.*, 50, 504–508.

Zinchenko, V. P. (1958). [Concerning the formation of an orienting form]. In L. G. Voronin et al. (eds.). "Orientirovochny refleks i orientirovochno-issledovatel'skaia deiatelnost'." Acad. Pedag. Sci., Moscow. ["The Orienting Reflex and Exploratory Behavior"].

NAME INDEX

Abelson, R., 283–285, 291, 295
Aborn, M., 73
Abraham, K., 276, 291
Ach, N., 271
Adams, P. A., 74
Adlerstein, A., 120
Alekseeva, A., 97
Alexander, H. M., 153
Alison, A., 232, 237
Allport, F. H., 63
Allport, G. W., 62, 291
Alpert, R., 202, 203, 205
Álvarez, N., 53
Angier, R. P., 237, 238, 243
Anokhin, P. K., 60, 99, 222, 223
Antonitis, J. J., 143, 145, 147
Apostel, L., 303
Aristotle, 23, 196
Armington, J. C., 166
Arnheim, R., 243
Arrow, K. J., 25
Atkinson, J. W., 194, 201–203
Attneave, F., 39, 40, 161
Augustine, Saint, 232, 237

Bach, J. S., 250
Backer, R., 169
Baerends, G. P., 58
Bagby, J. W., 65
Baggaley, A. R., 282
Bahrick, H. P., 73
Baldwin, J. M., 155
Balonov, L. Y., 180
Bar Hillel, Y., 288
Barnes, G. W., 141, 142, 144
Barnett, S. A., 127
Barron, F., 215
Bartlett, F. C., 20, 73, 271–273, 280
Bartley, S. H., 56
Bartoshuk, A. K., 179
Bateson, G., 257, 259
Baumgarten, A. G., 232
Beach, H. D., 118

Becker, G. M., 300
Beebe-Center, J. E., 201
Beethoven, L. van, 249, 250
Bekhterev, V. M., 81
Bélanger, D., 166
Benoît, O., 53, 182
Berger, M., 295
Beritov (Beritashvili), I. S., 56
Berkun, M. M., 169
Berlyne, D. E., 16, 21, 31, 32, 57, 59,
    60, 64, 65, 76, 96–100, 102, 105,
    107–111, 113, 115, 133, 135, 160,
    161, 188, 230, 262n., 267, 295, 296
Bernhaut, M., 173
Bersh, P. J., 145
Bexton, W. A., 187, 190
Bindra, D., 125, 126
Birch, H. G., 152
Birkhoff, G., 42, 233, 238, 239
Bishop, C. H., 51
Black, P., 201
Blazek, N. C., 152
Block, Jack, 214
Block, Jeanne, 214
Bolles, R., 121
Bonvallet, M., 49, 180
Boswell, J., 260
Bousfield, W. A., 272
Brady, J. V., 199
Brahms, J., 250
Brandt, H. F., 97
Breese, B. B., 60, 64, 66
Bremer, F., 179
Briggs, G. E., 226
Brim, O. G., 210
Briullova, S. J., 179
Broadbent, D. E., 13, 14, 26, 64, 72, 75
Brodal, A., 46
Brogden, W. J., 226
Bronshtein, A. I., 86, 173, 180
Brown, C. H., 224
Brown, J., 74
Brown, J. S., 31, 32, 166
Bruce, R. H., 169

337

Freeman, G. L., 50
Frenkel-Brunswik, E., 214
Freud, S., 10, 31, 164, 167, 172, 196, 216, 254–257, 259–261, 263, 276, 277, 291
Frick, F. C., 37
Frick, J. W., 215
Friedman, M., 208
Fry, G. A., 56
Funkenstin, D. H., 166
Fuster, J. M., 48

Galambos, R., 53, 88
Galbrecht, C. R., 81, 82
Gantt, W. H., 68, 81, 87
Gastaut, H., 27, 51, 83, 94, 216, 222
Gehman, R. S., 70
Gellhorn, E., 173
Gibson, E. J., 31, 68
Gilbert, K. E., 232
Girdner, J. B., 140, 145, 146
Glanzer, M., 129–131, 194
Glickman, S. E., 118
Gogel, W. C., 58
Goodman, N., 27
Goss, A. E., 219
Gottschaldt, K., 210
Granit, R., 48
Grastyán, E., 83, 88
Graves, M. E., 233, 237
Green, R. T., 76
Grice, G. R., 62
Grindley, G. C., 114
Grossberg, J., 122
Grotjahn, M., 254
Guernsey, N., 196
Guilford, J. P., 215, 282
Gurevich, M. O., 159
Guzmán-Flores, C., 53
Gwinn, G. T., 198

Haber, R. N., 203
Hadley, J. M., 49
Hagbarth, K. E., 179
Haibt, L. H., 55
Hall, J. F., 165
Hamilton, J. A., 198
Hamilton, V., 214
Hamilton, W., 23
Harary, F., 283
Harlow, H. F., 96, 124, 150–154, 205
Harlow, M. K., 150
Harvey, E. N., 173
Haslerud, G. M., 176
Havelka, J., 128

Hayes, K. J., 127
Heath, L. L., 216
Hebb, D. O., 31, 42, 55, 56, 75, 131, 132, 166, 169, 176, 189, 191, 194, 196, 198, 214, 245
Hefferline, R. F., 141, 142
Heider, F., 283
Heisenberg, W., 25
Helmholtz, H., 37
Helson, H., 202
Hemsterhuis, F., 232
Henderson, R. L., 140, 143, 146
Hernández-Peón, R., 53, 85, 89, 179
Heron, W., 116–118, 187, 190
Hess, E. H., 56
Hetzer, H., 176, 204
Hick, W. E., 33
Hiebel, G., 49
Higgins, W. H., 210
Hinde, R. A., 122
Hiriyanna, M., 265
Hobart, G., 173
Hochberg, J. E., 40, 62
Hoff, D. B., 210
Hoffman, A. C., 201
Hogarth, W., 232
Holland, J. G., 140
Holland, J. H., 55
Honig, W. K., 57
Horiuchi, K., 192
Horowitz, L., 141, 145–147
Hovland, C. I., 171
Hudson, B. B., 115, 212
Hugelin, A., 48, 49, 54, 92, 180
Hull, C. L., 8, 10, 34, 66, 69, 165, 167, 168, 267, 269, 272, 273
Hurwitz, H. M. B., 140, 142, 145–147
Hutcheson, F., 232

Inhelder, B., 273
Inhelder, E., 149
Irion, A. L., 31, 73
Irwin, F., 299, 300
Isaacs, N., 27, 277
Itina, N. A., 86, 173, 180
Ivanov-Smolenski, A. G., 69, 159, 160

Jacobs, A., 166
Jacobson, E., 27
Jasper, H. H., 47, 51, 56, 94n., 174, 175
Jenkins, J. T., 296
Jerome, E. A., 141, 142
Johnson, S., 255, 260
Jost, M., 49
Jouvet, M., 53, 54, 85, 181, 182, 217, 222

339

SUBJECT INDEX

345

Change, 22–23
  and arousal, 175
  and attention in performance, 66
  and investigatory responses, 141–146, 158
  and locomotor exploration, 111
  and optimal arousal potential, 203
Circular reaction, primary, 155
  secondary, 155–157
  tertiary, 157–158
Classification, 266
Cognitive imbalance, 285–286
Collative variables, 44
  and aesthetic behavior, 229–253
  and arousal, 174–179
  and optimal arousal potential, 202–209
Color, and arousal, 172
  and attention in performance, 60
  and orienting responses, 97
Communication, 228–229
  of evaluations, 229
Complex completion theory, 271–272
Complexity, 38–44
  and arousal, 178
  and attention, in learning, 71
    in performance, 66
  and conflict, 41–43
  determinants of, 38–39
  and inquisitive locomotor exploration, 133
  and inspective locomotor exploration, 111–112
  and investigatory responses, 149, 160–162
  and novelty, 43–46
  and optimal arousal potential, 202–204
  and orienting responses, 99–100
  and uncertainty, 40–41
Compression reaction, 82
Conceptual conflict, 280–303
  and arousal, 295–296
  and epistemic curiosity, 296–298
    extrinsic, 299–301
    intrinsic, 296–298
  varieties of, 285–288
Conceptual incongruity, 287
Conciliation, 292–293
Conditioned inhibition, mutual, 11–12
Configural conditioning, 8
Conflict, 9–16
  and aesthetic organization, 234–235
  and arousal, 177–178
  and attention in remembering, 76–77
  biological significance, 14–16
  and complexity, 41–43

Conflict, conceptual (see Conceptual conflict)
  degree of, 31–37
    determinants, 32–34
    and uncertainty, 34–37
  and optimal arousal potential, 205–209
  and orienting responses, 102–103
  and perceptual learning, 219–220
  sources of, 10–14
Conflict hypothesis of effects of novelty, 21–22
Confusion, 287–288
Consultation, 265
Contradiction, 287
Contrast and locomotor exploration, 112–113
Convergence theory, 271
Cortex (see Cerebral cortex)
Cortical activation and arousal, 50–51
Counterfactual conditionals, problem of, 27
Cue stimuli, 269–270
Curiosity, epistemic, 283–303
  perceptual (see Perceptual curiosity)

Decision theory, and epistemic responses, 275–276
  and uncertainty, 25
Defensive reactions, 90–92
Degree, of conflict (see Conflict)
  of incompatibility between responses, 33–34
Designative symbolic responses, 264
Desynchronization, 47
Disequalization, 292, 294–295
Dissonance, 283–284
Diversity, principle of, 222–223
Diversive exploration, and arousal potential, 194
  definition, 80
Doubt, 286
Drawing in apes, 150
Drinking and locomotor exploration, 119
Drive, identification with arousal, 166–170
  three concepts of, 165–171
Drive reduction and reward, 167–168

Eating and locomotor exploration, 119
EEG (electroencephalograph) and boredom, 190
  and imagined bodily movement, 27
  and orientation reaction, 82, 85–86
Efficiency and arousal, 50

Intellectual activities, 6
Intelligence and locomotor exploration, 117–118
Intensity of stimulus, and arousal, 171
  and attention, in learning, 67–68
    in performance, 59–60
  and investigatory responses, 143–144
  and locomotor exploration, 112–113
  and optimal arousal potential, 200–201
  and orienting responses, 97
Intensive variables, and arousal, 171–173
  and optimal arousal potential, 200–202
Interindividual differences, in defenses against arousal, 217
  in epistemic behavior, 282
  in physiological measures, 216
  relating to exploratory behavior, 211–212, 214–217
Intolerance of ambiguity, 214–216
Intraindividual variation, 211–214
Intrinsic exploration, definition, 79
Investigatory responses, 136–162
  definition, 79
  extrinsic, 138–140
  intrinsic, in human adults and older children, 159–162
    in human infants, 154–159
    in mice and rats, 140–148
    in monkeys and apes, 148–154
Irrelevance, 288

Knowledge, 262–295
  functioning of, 266–267
  and reduction of conflict, 290–295

Latent learning, 224–227
Learned antagonism, 11–13
Learning and relief of perceptual curiosity, 196–197
Locomotor exploration, 104–135
  definition, 79
  determinants of, 106–134
  and learning, 134–135
Ludic behavior, 4–7

Method of active choice, 60–61
Mobbing, 122–123
Morphine and locomotor exploration, 118
Motivation, problems of, 2–4
Motivational dispositions, 2–3

Motivational problems of thinking, 273–303
Motivational states and attention, in performance, 63
  in remembering, 73–74
Motivational stimuli, 270
Mutual conditioned inhibition, 11–12

Nonspecific thalamic system (thalamic reticular system), 46–48, 51
Novelty, 18–25
  absolute, 19–20
  and arousal, 174–175
  and attention, in learning, 68–70
    in performance, 64–66
    in remembering, 75
  complete, 19
  and complexity, 43–44
  degree of, 22
  and inquisitive locomotor exploration, 131–133
  and inspective locomotor exploration, 106–110
  and investigatory responses, 144–146, 148–149, 151
  long-term, 19
  and optimal arousal potential, 203–205
  and orienting responses, 98
  problem of, 20–23
  relative, 19–20
  short-term, 19
  variables supplementary to, 22–25
  varieties of, 19–22

Observing responses (extrinsic exploration), 79, 138–140
Occlusion, 13–14
  and complexity, 43
Oddity and attention in remembering, 75–76
Ordering, 266–267
Orientation reaction, 80–96
  and arousal, 92–96
  components, 81–83
  dynamics of, 86–88
  extinction of, 87
  functions of, 83–86
  generalized, 94
  localized, 94
  and orienting responses, 95–96
  phasic, 93–94
  and signal value, 87–88
  tonic, 93–94